D1066094

HUMAN RIGHTS AFTER HITLER

HUMAN RIGHTS AFTER HITLER

THE LOST HISTORY OF PROSECUTING AXIS WAR CRIMES

DAN PLESCH

Georgetown University Press
Washington, DC

Library of Congress Cataloging-in-Publication Data

Names: Plesch, Dan, author.
Title: Human Rights after Hitler : The Lost History of Prosecuting Axis War Crimes / Dan Plesch.
Description: Washington, DC : Georgetown University Press, 2017. | Includes bibliographical references and index.
Identifiers: LCCN 2016031003 (print) | LCCN 2016040144 (ebook) | ISBN 9781626164314 (hc : alk. paper) | ISBN 9781626164338 (eb)
Subjects: LCSH: United Nations War Crimes Commission—History. | War crime trials—History—20th century. | World War, 1939–1945—Atrocities. | Holocaust, Jewish (1939–1945)—Historiography.
Classification: LCC KZ1174.5 .P58 2017 (print) | LCC KZ1174.5 (ebook) | DDC 341.6/9—dc23
LC record available at https://lccn.loc.gov/2016031003

♾ This book is printed on acid-free paper meeting the requirements of the American National Standard for Permanence in Paper for Printed Library Materials.

18 17 9 8 7 6 5 4 3 2 First printing

Printed in the United States of America

Cover design by Charles Brock, Faceout Studio.
Cover image by Anastasiya Piatrova / Alamy (Auschwitz-Birkenau concentration and extermination camp).

CONTENTS

List of Illustrations ix
Foreword by Benjamin B. Ferencz xi
Acknowledgments xv
Abbreviations xix
Introduction 1

1 **Prosecuting Rape: The Modern Relevance of World War II Legal Practices** **11**
Key Issues of Prosecuting SGBV Crimes Today 13
Conclusion 29

2 **A New Paradigm for Providing Justice for International Human Rights Violations** **46**
Legal and Political Amnesia 48
Creation of the United Nations War Crimes Commission 48
Official Resistance to Prosecuting War Crimes 50
Chinese and Indian Leadership 51
A Global System of Complementary Justice 53
The Development of Key International Legal Principles 59
Conclusion 62

3 **When the Allies Condemned the Holocaust** **69**
Early Allied Condemnations of the Holocaust and Nazi Atrocities 70
The Declaration 75

Abandonment of the Jews Nonetheless 82
Conclusion 83

4 Pursuing War Criminals All Over the World 87

A Global Achievement 90
Commission Members and Court Structures 92
Conclusion 104

5 The Holocaust Indictments: Prosecuting the "Foot Soldiers of Atrocity" 112

Belgium 114
Czechoslovakia 117
Denmark 118
France 118
Greece 119
Luxembourg 120
The Netherlands 120
Norway 122
Poland 122
Yugoslavia 128
United Kingdom 128
United States 129
Conclusion 129

6 Fair Trials and Collective Responsibility for Criminal Acts 138

The Fundamentals of Fair Trials 141
"It Wasn't Illegal When the Action Was Taken" 143
Hearsay 145
The Rights of the Accused 145
Command Responsibility 146
Superior Orders 147
Group Responsibility 148
Conspiracy and Common Design 149
Reprisals and the Execution of Hostages 150
Securing the Rights of the Accused 151
Conclusion 152

7 Crimes against Humanity: The "Freedom to Lynch" and the Indictments of Adolf Hitler 158

Crimes against Humanity 160
The Crimes of Aggression and Genocide 171

Universal Jurisdiction 173
Conclusion 174

8 Liberating the Nazis 178
Forgetting the Nazi Past to Build a West German Future 178
Early Protests against Prisoner Release 180
Hostility to the Commission 180
Opposition to the Commission's Closure 182
Ongoing Prosecution of War Crimes 185
Prisoner Release 185
Conclusion 189

9 The Legacy Unleashed 192
The People's Human Rights 192
The UNWCC as an International Human Rights Agreement 195
Complementarity and the UNWCC 198
Toward a "UNWCC 2.0"? 202
Conclusion 205

Appendixes
A. *Timeline of the Allies' Principal Political Responses to Axis Atrocities* 211
B. *A Note on the UNWCC's Archives and Related Material* 214
C. *The Role of the UNWCC in Obtaining ICTY Verdicts* 218
D. *An Early UNWCC Charge File against a Group of Germans Involved in the Treblinka Death Camp* 222
E. *An Early Polish Charge File against a Group of Germans Involved in the Concentration Camp System* 231
Index 241
About the Author 251

ILLUSTRATIONS

Figures

1.1 Rape Cases Documented in the UNWCC Archive 16
2.1 Number of Trials Carried Out by International Military Tribunals, by UNWCC Supported Tribunals, and by UN-Supported Judicial Bodies 49
2.2 The Structure of the UNWCC 57
6.1 The "Versailles List" of War Crimes Used by the UNWCC 144
7.1 UNWCC Indictment of Adolf Hitler, Rudolf Hess, Heinrich Himmler, and Other Nazis 159

Tables

4.1 Total Number of Persons Charged by the Governments and Listed by the UNWCC 90
4.2 Number of German Persons Charged by the Governments and Listed by the UNWCC 91
4.3 Number of Italian Persons Charged by the Governments and Listed by the UNWCC 92
4.4 Number of Japanese Persons Charged by the Governments and Listed by the UNWCC 100
4.5 Far East Sub Commission Lists of Japanese War Criminals 103
4.6 Joint Trials Conducted in East Asia by British and Indian Judges 105
5.1 Charges Brought for Anti-Jewish Persecution Submitted by UNWCC Member States 115
6.1 Progress Report of War Crimes Trials from Data Available as of March 1, 1948 140
8.1 Individuals and Units Charged by National Offices, by Year 179

FOREWORD

The work of the United Nations War Crimes Commission (UNWCC) started before the United Nations charter had been adopted. The commission is an illustration of human determination to seek justice under law in order to deter enormous crimes against humanity similar to those that were committed during the twelve-year reign of what Adolf Hitler had hoped would be the "Thousand Year Reich." In 1939, with the invasion of Poland, Hitler started his march of conquest against all of Germany's peace-loving neighbors. This crime of aggression was accompanied by incredible crimes against humanity on a scale never conceived by human imagination. Beginning in 1935 Nazi racial laws divested Jews of all the normal rights of citizenship. The victims were not marked for total annihilation until 1941.

I was a student at Harvard Law School from 1941 to 1943. I served as a researcher for Professor Sheldon Glueck, who wrote extensively about war crimes and tribunals established to try the malefactors. He was a member of the International War Crimes Commission that had been created in London and their reports crossed my desk. Those reports provide an unusual insight into the courage and determination of refugees from the lands occupied by Germany who believed that recording the atrocities would one day lead to justice against the perpetrators.

Much of the material thus assembled was based on evidence which, though truthful and alarming, would hardly be admissible in a court of law today. But the material sounded an alarm. In July 1941 German extermination squads were given their marching instructions: eliminate every man, woman, and child with traces of Jewish ancestry. The same applied to the Gypsies and any other suspected or potential enemies of the reich. Their brutality of cold-blooded slaughter, which included shooting children one at a time, is nearly incomprehensible to a rational human mind. Then, on January 20, 1942, Nazi leaders assembled in a villa on the Wannsee in Berlin and discussed in considerable detail how they planned to murder about twelve million people. Their report was called "The Final Solution of the Jewish Question."

After I graduated in 1943, I joined a US Army anti-aircraft artillery battalion that was preparing for the invasion of France. As an enlisted man under General Patton, I fought in every campaign in Europe. As Nazi atrocities were being uncovered, I was transferred to the newly created War Crimes Branch of the Army to gather evidence of Nazi brutality and apprehend the criminals. On the day after Christmas 1945 I was honorably discharged with the rank of sergeant of infantry. I returned to New York and prepared to practice law. Shortly thereafter, I was recruited to serve with the Nuremberg war crimes trials.

The International Military Tribunal prosecution against Herman Goering and other leading Nazis was already in progress under the leadership of the American prosecutor, Robert H. Jackson, who was on leave from his seat on the US Supreme Court. The United States decided to conduct a dozen additional trials in Nuremberg in order to hold accountable a broad segment of leaders responsible for crimes against humanity. I was put in charge of a group of researchers scouring the German archives for evidence, such as daily reports from the Eastern Front and minutes of the Wannsee Conference. Those contemporaneous, top-secret documents alone would have been adequate to prove beyond any reasonable doubt the veracity of Nazi crimes.

Brig. Gen. Telford Taylor, the successor to Justice Jackson, was designated chief of counsel for the dozen subsequent proceedings. When confronted with the evidence my team had collected in Berlin, Taylor appointed me to be chief prosecutor in the case of *US v. Otto Ohlendorf et al.*—often called the "Einsatzgruppen Trial." We accused twenty-two high-ranking SS officers, many of whom had doctoral degrees, of murdering in cold blood over a million men, women, and children because they did not share the race, religion, or ideology of their executioners. The prosecution rested its case after a mere two days. It was a plea of humanity to law. I was then twenty-seven years old and it was my first case. I have never stopped trying to substitute law for war.

My army duties during the war led me to enter several concentration camps as their prisoners were being liberated. I had peered into hell. Yet I have never forgotten one particular incident, when an inmate who had been assigned as a clerk in one of the concentration camps approached me. His duty was to issue new identity cards for incoming SS officers. Of course he was expected to destroy the old cards. Instead he had saved them and buried them in a box near the electrified fence. When I entered the camp he asked me to accompany him as he dug up the box and revealed the vital information about all the SS officers who were accomplices to the mass murder that was carried on in that camp every day. Every time he failed to destroy a card he took his life into his own hands. Nevertheless, he risked his life believing that one day there would be a day of reckoning. The day had come when he handed me the box.

So it was with the United Nations War Crimes Commission: a seventeen-nation multilateral body initiated by refugee governments from the German-occupied territories, which met in London to assemble evidence of the atrocities being committed by German officers and ordinary soldiers. Their eyewitness reports provided evidence to substantiate *prima facie* cases for the accused to answer, often describing horrors in language that was inadequate to express the reality. These reports had limited evidentiary value but they were a clear reflection of human determination to seek justice. They laid the foundations for thousands of trials.

The UNWCC members were some of the most distinguished lawyers from all of Europe. Their formal charges, reports, and pleas for help were used by their governments. When the war was over, the greater drama of the Nuremberg courts obscured a great deal of the material that had been painstakingly assembled; the onset of McCarthyism resulted in the suppression of its files as well as the early release of many of those I myself had prosecuted. The legal arguments justifying war crimes trials were studied and became the subject of extended debate by other committees of the British government. Unfortunately, nations were not yet ready to consider law as a substitute for war.

Dan Plesch's book is an eye-opener. It demonstrates the human determination to protect society against crimes against humanity, which unfortunately continue to deface the human landscape, and they supply a wealth of precedent and practice to reinforce our efforts today.

Benjamin B. Ferencz
Former US chief prosecutor of the Nazi Einsatzgruppen extermination units at the Nuremberg Trials
July 2016

ACKNOWLEDGMENTS

There are many people I would like to thank for contributing to the research resulting in this book. Most important are the staff, members, and officials of the national governments who were part of the UNWCC, along with those who gave sworn evidence as witnesses and victims of alleged crimes; all deserve deep appreciation. If this book does something to infuse into our own time their sense of justice and legal wisdom then it will have done its job. Some of their published work, the fifteen volumes of law reports, the official history, and various articles by Egon Schwelb, Lord Wright, and others, opened the door into the UNWCC for those who wished to look. Back in the 1980s my friend and mentor John Stanleigh was the first to make me aware that the story of war crimes was far larger than what happened at Nuremberg. John served as a war crimes investigator in Norway at the end of the war while serving in the British Army. Born John Schwartz, he had escaped Nazi Germany and the death that awaited the rest of his Jewish family and fought with the British special forces.

A generation ago a number of scholars began to work on the UNWCC, notably Arieh Kochavi and Chris Simpson. Without them I would have found it hard to find my way. Iradj Berhadji and Jo Godfrey at I.B. Tauris publishers encouraged me to explore the UNWCC and the declaration on the persecution of the Jews when I began writing my book *America, Hitler, and the UN* in 2009. The current book germinated in a foundational chapter that began to explore the UNWCC. In the same period I benefited from conversations with many members of the SOAS (School of Oriental and African Studies), which as an institution has been most supportive of my work

I also have benefited greatly from my research partnership with Shanti Sattler, which resulted in several joint publications. I will always recall her quick understanding of the value of the commission. The vicissitudes of our struggle to obtain, analyze, publish, and proselytize on the work of the commission from 2011 through 2014 is a tale all its own.

Around 2009 I became aware of the existence of the commission's archive held at the United Nations in New York and of the rules governing its access. Individuals were required to have the endorsement of their national governments and of the UN secretary-general as well. Only then were they permitted to read but not make any written note or copy of the material in the archive. As a dual national I had no luck in getting an endorsement from the US mission in New York, but the United Kingdom promptly provided authorization and then the UN did as well. Armed with this support I set off for New York accompanied by two assistants, Shanti Sattler and Greg Chaffin. We encountered the second hurdle: the staff at the archives provided microfilm to read but forbade me from walking across the room to dictate to Shanti and Greg what I could remember reading or from leaving the building to do the same in a neighboring café every twenty minutes or so. At this point I was able to consult with Bridget Sisk, the head of the archives, and her staff. After a brief interlude they concluded that they had been overzealous and that the prohibition should only apply to individual case files. With the archive partly opened we were able to make much progress.

Radu Ioanid and Paul Shapiro of the United States Holocaust Memorial Museum determined that as a US federal agency, the USHMM should seek a copy of the still-restricted commission archive. Samantha Power, US ambassador to the United Nations, determined that the museum should have access, followed by the UK government (after representations from myself and the Wiener Library), thus bringing the archive of the commission into public use as originally envisaged by its members and attracting some media attention. This in turn encouraged EU ambassador Thomas Mayr Harting to donate to me the archive of his father, Herbert Mayr Harting, the Czechoslovak representative on the commission, which contained that government's draft 1944 indictment of Adolf Hitler and Harting's handwritten amendments.

At the International Criminal Court, Hans Bevers and especially researcher Morten Bergsmo acted to make the section of the archive released in 2001 also available digitally.

The British Academy and then the Oak Foundation, through its program officer, James Logan, provided early and essential support for the project when we first accessed the commission's minutes and papers, while support from the Carnegie Corporation helped the project reach fruition. Justice Richard Goldstone reacted with intellectual warmth and generosity to *America, Hitler, and the UN* and provided important endorsement to the project. Mark Ellis and the International Bar Association provided both institutional and financial support for the research. They joined Shanti and me in organizing a public conference on the UNWCC in 2013. Then, with the help of a range of writers—William Schabas, Carsten Stahn, Joseph Powderly, Kerstin von Lingen, Graham Cox, Wen-Wei Lai,

Christopher Simpson, Harry M. Rhea, Mark S. Ellis, Kip Hale, Donna Cline, Lutz Oette, Wolfgang Form, Susana SáCouto, and Chante Lasco—we produced a special issue of the *Criminal Law Forum* examining this topic. Chapter 1 in this book is a modified version of Dan Plesch, Susana SáCouto, and Chante Lasco, "The Relevance of the United Nations War Crimes Commission to the Prosecution of Sexual- and Gender-Based Crimes Today," *Criminal Law Forum* 25, no. 1–2 (2014): 349–81, © Springer Science+Business Media Dordrecht 2014, used by permission.

I am indebted to Leah Owen, who helped make the archive, especially the charge files, searchable and worked as research assistant on the project through 2015. Her range of skills has been a boon. Martin Burke provided prompt and excellent editing. Martin Brown, Peter Svik, and Leyla Tiglay helped with translations. Christelle Meta worked on the French cases and trial reports. The book also forms part of the broader project that Thomas G. Weiss and I direct on the wartime history and the future UN, supported by the Carnegie Corporation of New York. I am very grateful, too, to the care and interest in this project shown by Don Jacobs and his colleagues at Georgetown University Press, and the hard work of my agent Darryl Samaraweera. The British Library is a wonderful place to research and write.

Finally, it is worth mentioning that, given my family history, this is the last book I imagined writing. My father was a refugee from the Nazis and I gained from him a commitment to remember but move on. Once I encountered the facts, they imposed a duty to not let them be neglected any longer. It is my wife and children, though, whom I thank, for providing a context of domestic sanity while I explored the horrors and inhumanity documented in this book.

ABBREVIATIONS

BBC	British Broadcasting Corporation
CHN	charge number
CN	case number
CROWCASS	Central Register of War Criminals and Security Suspects
DN	document number
ECCC	Extraordinary Chambers in the Courts of Cambodia
ECOSOC	United Nations Economic and Social Council
FESC	Far Eastern Sub-Commission in Chunking
FN	file number
ICC	International Criminal Court
ICTR	International Criminal Tribunal for Rwanda
ICTY	International Criminal Tribunal for (the Former) Yugoslavia
IMT	International Military Tribunal (usually refers to Nuremberg Tribunal)
IMTFE	International Military Tribunal for the Far East (the Tokyo Trials)
ITAO	International Technical Assistance Office
JAG	Judge Advocate General
LIA	London International Assembly
NATO	North Atlantic Treaty Organization
NMT	Nuremberg Military Tribunal
NOC	National Offices Conference of UNWCC
POW	prisoner of war
R2P	"Responsibility to Protect" doctrine
RGN	reference guide number (UK Archives)
RN	registered number (UNWCC records)
RP	record page

SCSL	Special Court for Sierra Leone
SD	Sicherheitsdienst ("Security Service")
SGBV	Sexual and Gender-Based Violence
SPET	Special Panels for Serious Crimes in East Timor
SS	Schutzstaffel ("Protection Squad")
UDHR	Universal Declaration of Human Rights
UN	United Nations
UN ARMS	United Nations Archives and Records Management Section
UNDP	United Nations Development Program
UNIO	United Nations Information Organization
UNWCC	United Nations War Crimes Commission

INTRODUCTION

Adolf Hitler and tens of thousands of Nazis and their allies were indicted as war criminals by the international community during and after the end of World War II, resulting in over two thousand internationally supported criminal trials by courts across Europe and Asia. Despite this large number of prosecutions, the world's historical memory is limited to the trials of the few dozen top officials who were tried before the international tribunals in Nuremberg and Tokyo.

These thousands of indictments were considered by a commission of seventeen Allied nations—including the United States—each of which brought its national cases to the commission, which acted as a pretrial examining magistrate. Member states adopted this method to give international legitimacy to their efforts and rebut accusations of victors' justice. The commission worked in secret because of the immediate pressures of the war, and it could not therefore include neutral states, let alone the enemy; nevertheless, it sought to apply the highest international standards of law and had diplomatic status as an international organization.

The commission, officially named the United Nations War Crimes Commission, was set up after much political wrangling at the end of 1943 to gather evidence against suspected war criminals.[1] Its task was to implement the Great Powers declaration signed in Moscow in November 1943 and similar earlier statements, which warned the Nazis that they would face prosecution for war crimes.[2] In the declaration, American, British, and Soviet leaders stated their intent to determine how to dispose of the Nazi leadership and that many other Nazis who were accused of crimes would face justice in the territories where the offenses had occurred. Within five years the commission brought proceedings against war criminals, including thousands of exterminators of the Jews, while the war still raged through 1944 and 1945, and it pioneered international criminal justice practices concerning sexual violence, head of state immunity, conspiracy, and many other issues of relevance in the twenty-first century.

The United Nations (UN) alliance of the Second World War has only recently been given attention by scholars.[3] However, the UN Charter of 1945 is explicit: the first members of the United Nations were those that signed the declaration by United Nations of 1942 and all charter signatories in 1945 were required to have adhered to this declaration. By 1944, when the commission began its work, there were forty-four signatories, with the commission members forming a subgroup within the overall membership.

The 1944 Oscar-nominated movie *None Shall Escape* demonstrates the idea that during the war the United Nations was a wartime alliance preparing for the postwar world in which it would try Nazis for war crimes. The movie is structured around flashbacks from a war crimes court to the criminal actions of the accused during the war. Popular culture at the time echoed the countless official statements that the United Nations were fighting the war and preparing the peace.

This book tells the story of the rise and fall of the UN War Crimes Commission and the moral and practical lessons we can learn from the heroes of this unsung political movement for international justice. For those involved with the commission, international justice was an aim of the war and a defining moral distinction between the Allied and Axis powers (as the Nazis and their allies styled themselves). We can see this distinction in an excerpt of a 1947 report that the UNWCC wrote for the new United Nations Economic and Social Council (ECOSOC):

One side, that of the Axis, asserted the absolute responsibility of belligerents, who, it was asserted, were under no obligation to respect human rights, but were entitled to trample them underfoot wherever the military forces found them inconvenient for the waging of war. This is the totalitarian war as envisaged by the Axis powers. This doctrine was repudiated as contrary not only to morality but to recognized international law which prescribed metes and bounds for the violation even in war of human rights.[4]

This commission paper on the implications of war crimes trials for human rights had been requested by the UN committee responsible for drawing up what we now know as the Universal Declaration of Human Rights (UDHR).

The UDHR was a culmination of the political effort to counter Nazi ideology. To counter Axis victories early in the war, the Allies rallied their people with ideas as well as weapons. Nazi ideals espoused the notion that only "Aryans" were truly human; the rest were subspecies. This racist attitude demanded a response on behalf of humanity generally. In formulating this response to such attitudes and to the racist and extremist policies fomented in Europe, the British and French Empires undermined their own claims to superiority over the peoples they had colonized.[5]

The first multinational expression of these values was made on New Year's Day 1942, three weeks after the bombing of Pearl Harbor and five years before the Universal Declaration of Human Rights. In the "Declaration by United Nations," twenty-six Allied states called for the "preservation of human rights and justice in their own lands as well as in other lands" under a new banner—the United

Nations.[6] The Declaration by United Nations incorporated the Atlantic Charter, which was issued by British prime minister Winston S. Churchill and US president Franklin D. Roosevelt (FDR) the previous August, which itself developed into FDR's "Four Freedoms" speech at the beginning of 1941.[7]

The unprecedented crimes of the Axis required new international law to provide a legal as well as a military response, as declared by the exiled European governments and China in January 1942, perhaps emboldened by Hitler's defeat at the gates of Moscow.[8] Churchill and FDR made repeated statements that the Nazis would face legal accountability after the war.[9] Nearly four years before the opening of the Nuremberg trials the Allies were setting out the objective of pursuing justice as well as victory.

The decision to pursue justice did not appear out of thin air. Soon after the Nazis overran Europe, exiled politicians, jurists, and diplomats living in London organized networks with colleagues at Harvard University and from elsewhere in the United States to develop a common view of the legal and political response that would accompany the military reaction to aggression, even as the cities they met in were being bombed nightly by enemy war planes. Political and public pressure produced a public multinational condemnation of the ongoing Nazi extermination of the Jews as early as 1942.[10] It is puzzling that this recorded history is overlooked in most scholarship concerning the Holocaust, Nazi crimes in general, and the history and law of war crimes. There are a number of possible explanations. In much of the West the post-1945 priority was to rebuild Germany against the communist threat, and in so doing bury the past. Although the UN War Crimes Commission was desperate to make sure that its work become a repository for future public research, the exigencies of the Cold War led the United States to ensure that the entire archive was made secret in 1949. UN legal advisor Ivan Kerno, a Czech national with documented links to US diplomatic and intelligence organizations, unilaterally declared the archive closed even to government prosecutors despite the opposition of the commission's chair, Lord Wright, and representatives of some member states.[11]

This policy remained in place until the Waldheim affair in the 1980s, one inadvertent result of which was to create a theoretical opening of some part of the archives. Kurt Waldheim, UN secretary-general in the 1970s, faced substantial allegations that he had committed war crimes while serving as an intelligence officer for the German army in the brutal war with the resistance in Yugoslavia in the 1940s, including a UNWCC-supported indictment against him by the Yugoslav government. The "change in access" rule benefited only a few because the rule stated that researchers could not make notes during their reading of any part of the archive—even when personally authorized to read the papers by their own governments and the UN secretary-general. I opened a dialogue over the matter with UN authorities, with the US and other governments, and with the International Criminal Court (ICC) in the winter of 2011. As a result, more and more material became available, until, in 2014, the US government made a full copy of the UNWCC record open and available to all at the US Holocaust Memorial Museum.[12] In parallel, declassification processes by member states and the digitization of archives has made more material available. Nevertheless, the lack of scholarly attention to the commission's work is a concern, not least since it published a short but comprehensive official history in 1948 that resides in many law libraries. It also sought to establish international criminal law through the publication of fifteen volumes of law reports covering a portion of UNWCC cases. These law reports are cited as authority today. For example, many of the judgments of the tribunal set up to try war criminals in the former Yugoslavia in the 1990s cite UNWCC law report cases.

Today, disillusionment with the baroque practices of the ICC and the winding down of the ad hoc tribunals that were created to address events in the Great Lakes region of Africa and the Balkans of eastern Europe has led to renewed interest in the role of national courts in applying international criminal legal standards. As Carsten Stahn has explored in detail, the UNWCC provides such a powerful example for national courts that he urges the creation of a "UNWCC 2.0" for the modern era. Stahn argues that the UNWCC offers "an alternative to the centralized and situation-specific enforcement model under the umbrella of United Nations peace maintenance. The Commission represents a cooperative approach to justice and sovereignty . . . in terms of cooperation between major powers and use of international expertise and advice in criminal proceedings, international criminal justice is still in search of a modern UNWCC 2.0."

Some initial moves have been made toward this. An important initiative for holding war criminals accountable came from William Hague when he served as foreign minister of the United Kingdom. In 2012 he sent officials to the Middle East to help collect evidence for criminal prosecutions for war crimes in Syria. This is the type of initiative that could greatly benefit from a wider understanding of the role of the UNWCC in the past.

This book presents findings from study of the UNWCC's archive and associated political activity. It begins by demonstrating the twenty-first-century relevance of the UNWCC, with the example of the prosecution of sexual violence as a war crime. Chapter 2 provides an explanation of why the commission's work provides a new paradigm for enforcing legal retribution for major human rights violations. Chapter 3 demonstrates that, contrary to conventional understanding, the Allies did in fact repeatedly and in detail condemn what we now call the Holocaust, as well as other crimes committed by the Nazis. Chapter 4 lays out the global reach of this coalition of states working for international criminal justice. Chapter 5 spotlights in gruesome detail the Europe-wide indictments for the extermination of the Jews, which began long before the Nazi surrender. Chapter 6 examines how far these legal processes can be regarded as delivering a fair legal process. Chapter 7 looks at the highest level of politics, the indictments against

Hitler and other leaders, and the development of the key concepts of the legal responsibility of heads of state, crimes against humanity, the crime of aggressive war, and genocide. Chapter 8 revisits the halt to prosecutions, the early release of convicted war criminals, and the end of the commission. Finally, chapter 9 looks at lessons learned and how the UNWCC's restored legacy can help in policy and practice today. The following discussion introduces the key ideas in these chapters.

The Soviet Union began its own war crimes processes, and, for a variety of reasons, never joined the commission. Clearly, the Soviet Union and Stalin in particular were responsible for many crimes, not least the execution of thousands of Poles during the Katyn massacre and the mass rapes by Red Army troops in Germany. This book does not consider the Soviet trials, nor indeed trials of collaborators in European countries or controversial actions by the Western Allies. The analysis herein follows the commission's practice in drawing on both of the world's two main legal systems: Anglo-Saxon common law and continental European civil law.

Support by the UNWCC for national prosecutions of rape demonstrates that rediscovering World War II legal practices can be valuable to those advocating major international prosecutions today. Why should scholars and activists concerned about protecting human rights today spend time examining work of a bygone age? Rape and other gender-based crimes against humanity are controversial topics today. It had been thought that the first-ever prosecutions for rape as a war crime occurred during the tribunal in the former Yugoslavia. Since then, international tribunals and the International Criminal Court have had a mixed record on the issue even in the face of intensifying advocacy that "gender-based" crimes be taken seriously.

However, scores of cases were prosecuted against the Nazis and their allies for crimes of rape and forced prostitution before courts and tribunals in a range of locations, from Guam to Greece, Poland, France, the Philippines, Hong Kong, and Yugoslavia. Convictions were obtained in the 1940s for individual criminal acts against individual women, for mass rape and forced prostitution, and for group responsibility and the responsibility of commanders for crimes of sexual violence committed by subordinates.

The trials that did take place addressed only a tiny fraction of all the actual crimes that had happened and did not address sexual crimes committed by Allied soldiers. Taken together, however, this material provides a far greater foundation for action today than has previously been known. Nations that are ambivalent about the issue today can be asked to at least live up to their established legal practice in the 1940s.

By the time of its closure in 1948, more than thirty-six thousand individuals and units had been indicted as war criminals by the commission; these resulted in some two thousand reported trials that were conducted in a score of national jurisdictions from Oslo to Singapore. This sheer quantity of cases in itself provides the basis for a very different understanding of international law than the one that is based on the less than fifty cases held at Nuremberg and Tokyo. In addition, the quality of the legal debates and advisory opinions and the attention to fair trial processes adds a qualitative change of perspective that is at least as important as the sheer number of cases. A comparison of the UNWCC's work to its twentieth- and twenty-first-century equivalents also highlights the comprehensive nature of the work itself. The number of successful trials easily outnumber the work of the International Military Tribunals at Nuremberg and Tokyo plus the International Criminal Tribunals in the former Yugoslavia and Rwanda, the hybrid tribunals in Cambodia, Timor Leste, Sierra Leone, and Lebanon, and the entire caseload to date of the International Criminal Court.

The infamous and secret Wannsee Conference where Nazi officials planned the extermination of Europe's Jews in the Final Solution took place in January 1942; by the end of that year their secret was out, and the extermination of the Jews was condemned publicly by the Americans, the British, the Soviets, and their allies in detailed descriptions of the exterminations related to the UNWCC's trials. The records overturn one of the most important accepted truths concerning the Holocaust: that, despite the heroic efforts of escapees from Nazi-occupied Europe, the Allies never officially accepted the reality of the Holocaust and therefore never condemned it until the camps were liberated at the end of the war.

The book documents not only that the extermination of the Jews was condemned officially and publicly by the Allies but that specific features of the extermination were publicized, including a favored method—lethal gas—and the central place of execution—Poland. As early as the summer of 1942, months before Stalingrad and two years before D-Day, the Polish government in London accused the Nazis of mass killings with gas and were supported by the British, who sought publicity for their claims. This early documented condemnation of the extermination of the Jews of Europe opens new questions about the failure of the Allies to help the Jews, who were publicly stated to be at risk of murder, and provides additional material to contradict Holocaust denial.

The military defeat of the perpetrators of the war of aggression, and their massive crimes against humanity, were not merely accompanied by a public condemnation of their most extreme actions. They also faced the prospect of legal rather than summary justice from the Allied states. By 1947 the commission was supporting more than twenty war crimes courts and tribunals organized by its member states. It provided legal and practical advice to national jurisdictions and international legitimacy to national processes. In 1944 a nation would submit charges to the commission, which would determine whether there was a case to answer—that is, a *prima facie* case—and, when so endorsed, that nation would proceed to trial. This process was used across Europe and the Far East, with over thirty thousand cases being considered, many against multiple defendants. These included, by way of example, an affidavit from one British soldier, Harry Ogden, supporting charges concerning his maltreatment by his captors at the prisoner of war camp alongside the death camp at Auschwitz.

It is notable that states large and small, from the United States to Luxembourg, considered it necessary and important to obtain international support for their national actions. Even the US military courts in Guam—thousands of miles from the commission's offices and in the heart of US national military operations in the Pacific—tried Japanese troops as part of this international process.

Ultimately thousands of soldiers were tried for war crimes after World War II. Yet the model used in trials today, such as those conducted by the International Criminal Court and ones held in Africa, seem to concentrate solely on the leadership, echoing the model of Nuremberg.

Many European states initiated prosecutions against Nazis for the extermination of the Jews while they were still under occupation, and continued to do so through the commission until 1948. This contrasts with the general assumption that the main Nuremberg and subsequent Einsatzgruppen trials stand alone as attempts to bring justice for the Holocaust. A survey of the commission's records shows without doubt that in all the occupied states where the Holocaust occurred, many Nazis were indicted for these exterminations.

Torture was prosecuted in every jurisdiction and in thousands of cases. It attracted no attention from legal scholars, as there was a surprising consensus on what constituted torture, and included "water treatment"—partial drowning—now known as water boarding. The United States, for example, routinely pursued this type of torture as a crime in prosecutions against the Japanese. Notwithstanding this prior practice, the US government redefined water treatment as not torture in the aftermath of 9/11. Studies of the commission's work by both Lutz Oette and Wolfgang Form have demonstrated this. The records of numerous convictions of Germans for their treatment of US prisoners for assault also sits ill with post-9/11 tolerance of prisoner abuse.

A study of the system established by the UNWCC and the information that is available on national trials shows a consistent pattern of fair trials. For example, prosecuting people for being part of a conspiracy to commit crimes against humanity is nowadays regarded by specialists as largely a creation of the International Criminal Tribunal for the former Yugoslavia and the narrow example of Nuremberg.

However, in 1944 the commission wrestled with the idea that entire organizations—such as the Gestapo or whole units of troops—could be charged and found guilty of crimes as collective units, regardless of who pulled the trigger. The result was that, in trial after trial, prosecutions were made and convictions obtained of whole groups of perpetrators for crimes such as murder and torture. These examples should be used to serve notice on members of today's murderous organizations as well as their national leaders. They also could set precedents for some other offenses that are much debated today.

Some US leaders in World War II adamantly believed that international courts should no more have authority over the Nazis' crimes against fellow Germans than it would over Americans who had lynched their fellow citizens. In light of this fact, one of the greatest achievements of the Nuremberg tribunal was the prosecution of Germans for crimes against their own citizens—for crimes against humanity and for launching an aggressive war. These achievements came about in part as a result of the political battles within the UNWCC from 1943 to 1945, which were then implemented more widely than is usually acknowledged.

The idea that some acts are so heinous as to be beyond humanity is perhaps as old as civilization. This idea first took legal form, however, in the preamble to the Hague Convention of 1899 and in sporadic form during and in the aftermath of World War I. The joint declaration of France, Great Britain, and Russia, issued in response to the Armenian Genocide on May 29, 1915, for example, declared:

> In view of those new crimes of Turkey against humanity and civilization [changed from "Christianity and civilization"], the Allied governments announce publicly to the Sublime-Porte that they will hold personally responsible [for] these crimes all members of the Ottoman government and those of their agents who are implicated in such massacres.

The Hague Convention provided a legal basis for prosecutions of crimes committed by Axis forces against the Allies. For example, several Japanese soldiers were convicted of war crimes for forcing a British Sikh soldier to cut his hair and smoke tobacco, in violation of his religion. Nevertheless, interference in the internal affairs of another state, even an enemy state, was highly controversial at the time. Knowing the strength of this conservative tradition, Franklin Roosevelt sent Herbert Pell to the commission as his ambassador. In March 1944 Pell proposed that the Nazi crimes against German Jews be prosecuted as "crimes against humanity"; in various forms, his fellow commissioners joined him. They faced a brick wall of legal and political resistance within the British and American foreign ministries, however, and the US secretary of state went so far as to engineer the dismissal of Pell in December 1945. As a wealthy and now indignant former congressman, Pell took his case to the American press, forcing the State Department to support the idea of prosecutions for crimes against humanity. The publicity given to the scale of the horrors in Germany in the summer of 1945 forced the US government into action—and resulted in the charter establishing the Nuremberg tribunal and later the Tokyo tribunal, both of which encompassed crimes against humanity.

The great achievement of Nuremberg in finally giving crimes against humanity the power of international law did not stand alone. Building on the achievement at Nuremberg, the commission and some of its members used crimes against humanity in a variety of jurisdictions around the world. Together these give a more solid foundation to trials for crimes against humanity today.

Among the reasons given by US and British policymakers for curtailing prosecutions of Nazis was the understanding that at least some of them would be needed to rebuild Germany and confront communism, which at the time was seen as the greater danger that required a strong Germany. President Truman made anticommunism the priority over holding the Nazis to account for their crimes. Internally, his administration was determined to close down the UN War Crimes Commission as fast as possible and curtail trials in Germany. The spirit of the times was against them for a while, but soon huge groups of Schutzstaffel (SS) men were released without charge. Even action against the perpetrators of the massacre of British RAF officers attempting to escape from prison camp Stalag Luft III—a flight made iconic by the film *The Great Escape*—was curtailed.

The commission's files contain indictments against thousands of Nazis who were then allowed to go free. US intelligence officials, who had been at the forefront of prioritizing anticommunism over anti-Nazism, classified its archive in 1949, ignoring the commission's own pleas that more research and public debate was needed. Examination of the material is now beginning to revolutionize legal and political responses to international crimes. A huge improvement in the prevention of human rights abuses in our own time through the more effective and just punishment of violations can be achieved by drawing on the vast treasure trove of lost practices from the 1940s explored in this book.

Notes

1. UNWCC, *Complete History of the United Nations War Crimes Commission and the Development of the Laws of War* (London: Her Majesty's Stationery Office, 1948).
2. Moscow Statement on Atrocities signed by Franklin D. Roosevelt, Winston S. Churchill, and Joseph Stalin, October 1943; http://avalon.law.yale.edu/wwii/moscow.asp, accessed September 2016.
3. Michael Howard, "The United Nations: From War Fighting to Peace Planning," in *The Dumbarton Oaks Conversations and the United Nations 1944–1994*, ed. Ernest R. May and Angeliki E. Laiou, 1–7 (Cambridge, MA: Harvard University Press, 1998); Dan Plesch, *America, Hitler, and the UN* (London: I. B. Tauris, 2011); William Schabas, Carsten Stahn, Joseph Powderly, Dan Plesch, and Shanti Sattler, eds., "Symposium: The United Nations War Crimes Commission and the Origins of International Criminal Justice," *Criminal Law Forum* 1–2 (2014); Dan Plesch and Thomas G. Weiss, eds., *Wartime Origins and the Future United Nations* (London: Routledge, 2015); Thomas G. Weiss, "The United Nations Before and After 1945," *International Affairs* 91, no. 66 (2015) 1221–35; Thomas G. Weiss and Pallavi Roy, eds., "The UN and the Global South, 1945 and 2015: Past as Prelude?" *Third World Quarterly* 37, no. 7 (2016). See also https://www.soas.ac.uk/cisd/research/.
4. UNWCC, "Information Concerning Human Rights Arising from Trials of War Criminals," report to the UN Human Rights Division, Report No. DN E/CN.14-AM9, 1948, available at http://www.unwcc.org/documents/.

5. See, for example, https://www.nelsonmandela.org/omalley/index.php/site/q/03lv02167/04lv02264/05lv02303/06lv02304/07lv02305/08lv02309.htm.
6. United Nations, "A Joint Declaration by the United States, the United Kingdom, the Union of Soviet Socialist Republics, China, Australia, Belgium, Canada, Costa Rica, Cuba, Czechoslovakia, Dominican Republic, El Salvador, Greece, Guatemala, Haiti, Honduras, India, Luxembourg, Netherlands, New Zealand, Nicaragua, Norway, Panama, Poland, South Africa, and Yugoslavia," Washington, DC, January 1, 1942, available at http://avalon.law.yale.edu/20th_century/decade03.asp, accessed September 2016.
7. Franklin D. Roosevelt and Winston S. Churchill, "The Atlantic Charter," August 14, 1941, available at http://avalon.law.yale.edu/wwii/atlantic.asp, accessed September 2016; speech by Franklin D. Roosevelt, "The Four Freedoms," January 6, 1941, available at http://avalon.law.yale.edu/20th_century/decade01.asp, accessed September 2016.
8. Inter-Allied Information Committee, "Punishment for War Crimes: The Inter-Allied Declaration," signed at St. James's Palace London, January 13, 1942, 16.
9. M. E. Bathurst, "The United Nations War Crimes Commission," *American Journal of International Law* 39, no. 3 (1945): 565–68; US Department of State, "Punishment for War Crimes," in Foreign Relations of the United States: Diplomatic Papers, 1942, General: British Commonwealth and Far East, vol. 1 (1942), 45, at https://history.state.gov/historicaldocuments/pre-truman; US Department of State Bulletin, August 22, 1942, 710, and October 10, 1942, 797.
10. House of Commons Official Report, London, December 17, 1942.
11. Christopher Simpson, *The Splendid Blond Beast: Money, Law, and Genocide in the Twentieth Century* (Monroe, ME: Common Courage, 1993); and Christopher Simpson, "Shutting Down the United Nations War Crimes Commission," *Criminal Law Forum* 25, no. 1–2 (2014): 133–46.
12. At https://www.ushmm.org/information/press/press-releases/museum-makes-united-nations-war-crimes-archive-public, accessed September 2016.

1

PROSECUTING RAPE

THE MODERN RELEVANCE OF WORLD WAR II LEGAL PRACTICES

In the twenty-first century there is a concerted international campaign to end sexual violence in war. Sometimes this is falsely characterized as an invention of the late twentieth century. In fact, these types of acts were prosecuted as crimes all over the world in the 1940s, sometimes by states that are reluctant to do so today. This chapter is based largely on earlier work written with Susana SáCouto and Chante Lasco of the War Crimes Project at American University, to whom I am indebted. If there was ever a tendency to dismiss as irrelevant the attempt to draw on musty, generations-old legal papers for use in the world of the Internet, then these World War II examples of prosecutions for crimes of rape and forced prostitution provide the necessary shock needed to show the importance of recovering all the lost wisdom. Recorded at the time with the plain language of "rape" and "forced prostitution," today the terminology has changed to include these crimes within the overarching description of sexual and gender-based violence.

Sexual and gender-based violence (SGBV) is not limited to rape and forced prostitution; it also includes a wider range of violence, persecution, and poor treatment directed against people (usually women) because of their gender. Gender-based violence was widespread throughout the Second World War, and many UNWCC cases covered violence that specifically targeted women or that disproportionately affected them. Both crimes were prosecuted in the UNWCC-supported trial of Auschwitz commandant Rudolf Hoess, for example, which addressed the forced sterilization of Jewish men and women (which, from distressing medical reports, seems to have been particularly injurious for female victims) as well as forced insemination and other medical experimentation targeting women.[1] While sex-selective violence often targeted adult men (who were singled out to be killed), there are also a number of cases in which Nazi officials were charged with targeting women to be rounded up and sent to camps; this, too, can be considered gender-based violence.[2] While the UNWCC did address a wide range of what would now be identified as SGBV, this chapter will focus on the particular issue of rape and other forms of sexual violence, because it is through these cases that one can see how the commission was most dramatically ahead of its time and where its work is particularly relevant to contemporary debates.

Important legal precedents and practices can be found in the legal processes of the 1940s and the actions of nations to criminalize sexual violence in war. This evidence effectively rebuts the idea being proposed by defendants in the twenty-first century that these acts are not crimes at all—the so-called *nullum crimen sine lege* challenge to bringing SGBV cases to court at all. The definitions of SGBV offenses in the domestic and military codes of the 1940s—and especially how prosecutors approached issues of consent and coercion—can guide present-day tribunals dealing with these issues. These offenses were included in the list of war crimes agreed upon by UNWCC member states. Charges for these crimes were brought by prosecutors in a wide range of jurisdictions across Europe and Asia, resulting in many successful convictions and providing an important precedent.

It is not just the types of crime but also the types of responsibility for crimes in UNWCC-supported cases where the roots of the current concepts of criminal culpability are much stronger than previously supposed. Today there is a tendency to require higher standards of evidence for SGBV crimes than for other offenses, but the practices at work during the 1940s support requiring the same and not higher standards. UNWCC-supported cases also indicate that the tradition of protecting witnesses from degrading questions was being followed as early as the post–World War II era, which reinforces rulings issued by modern tribunals and offers some important examples to tribunals that have not yet codified such rules.

The importance of having UNWCC-supported cases to refer to during the prosecution of SGBV cases before contemporary tribunals cannot be overstated. For centuries, acts of sexual violence were viewed as "a detour, a deviation, or the acts of renegade soldiers . . . pegged to private wrongs and . . . [thus] not really the subject of international humanitarian law."[3] Indeed, such crimes were often perceived as "incidental" or "opportunistic" in relation to a war zone's "core" crimes.[4] Even when recognized as criminal, SGBV offenses committed in the context of conflict or mass violence are often tacitly encouraged or tolerated, which makes it challenging for prosecutors to link the perpetrator with the crime. Not surprisingly, commentators have noted that while significant improvements have been made in the prosecution of SGBV crimes by contemporary tribunals, particularly in the last fifteen years,[5] these cases continue to be plagued by prosecutorial omissions and errors as well as a tendency on the part of judges to require higher evidentiary standards.[6] That UNWCC member states investigated and prosecuted similar crimes nearly seventy years ago—holding both the direct and the indirect perpetrators responsible for such crimes and offering some level of protection to witnesses participating in these cases—is incredibly significant.

In addition to the value the UNWCC archives afford for tribunals prosecuting conflict-related SGBV cases today, the jurisprudence that emerged from UNWCC cases is of great importance to contemporary policy debates. Indeed, the active role states took in pursuing crimes of sexual violence in the 1940s provides a strong foundation for pursuing such crimes today, likely more than prosecutors may realize. Four permanent members of the UN Security Council—China, France, the United Kingdom, and the United States—were members of the UNWCC, and, along with Russia, were party to the Hague Conventions, which were relied upon by many states to prosecute rape and forced prostitution during and after the war. Similarly, a number of European Union member states—including Belgium, France, Greece, Italy, and Poland—endorsed the identification of rape and forced prostitution as war crimes as early as the 1940s. Since the issue of sexual violence committed in the context of conflict or mass violence continues to be the subject of debate within UN and European Union forums, the valuable work carried out in the 1940s should be applied in detail to these debates.[7]

The documented work of the UNWCC revolutionize our understanding of the legal precedents and practices that can be used in the prosecution of sexual violence. However, the data presented here are incomplete, as the commission records, though extensive, have gaps, especially in the reports of national prosecutions.

Key Issues of Prosecuting SGBV Crimes Today

Several issues still obstruct more effective prosecutions today. Among them are:

1. Whether acts of sexual and gender-based violence committed as part of a conflict are in fact crimes under national or international law;
2. The definition of SGBV crimes, including how they incorporate the idea of physical or mental force, that is, coercion;
3. What theories of criminal responsibility can be used to identify perpetrators—particularly top leaders—who are accountable for SGBV crimes;
4. The treatment of victims and witnesses involved in these crimes.

An examination of archives from the United Nations War Crimes Commission and the many associated tribunals overturn conventional wisdom on all these topics.

The UNWCC's Recognition of Sexual Violence Offenses as War Crimes

The UNWCC was the first multinational criminal law organization to endorse treatment of SGBV crimes as international crimes.[8] It recommended to member states a working list of offenses to use in their military or domestic penal codes.[9]

According to the commission's official minutes, it considered three lists late in 1943, at a time when the Nazis were still firmly in control of continental Europe and committing crimes with impunity.[10] Notably, rape was explicitly included as a war crime in all three draft lists of offenses considered by the commission;[11] forced prostitution was included in two of the three.[12] Both were included in the final list sent to UNWCC member states and used by the organization to coordinate its review of cases.[13] Of the thirty-two crimes listed by the UNWCC, rape appears as number five and forced prostitution as number six.[14] Hence, there was consensus among the Allied powers that an act of sexual violence committed against one of their nationals by enemy forces constituted an international crime.[15] The minutes echo this consensus: the index contains neither a reference to rape nor to prostitution, indicating that no state's representative considered the issue controversial.

World War II Case Files Involving Sexual Violence

Rape, attempted rape, and forced prostitution were all subject to internationally supported legal proceedings, as seen in UNWCC-supported charges being brought and in the national trials conducted across Europe and South and East Asia. Furthermore, France, Poland, and the United States charged individuals with forced prostitution.[16]

Countries that prosecuted cases of sexual and gender-based crimes before national tribunals or military tribunals (or both) include Australia, Belgium, China, Denmark, France, Greece, Italy, Poland, and the United States, as well as the UNWCC itself.[17] Australia, China, Denmark, France, Greece, Italy, Poland, the United States, and Yugoslavia all prosecuted individuals for rape.[18] Reports of some of these prosecutions were submitted to the UNWCC by the national jurisdictions that carried them out, while many trial records survive in countries' individual national archives (a small portion of which have been reviewed for this book; many are yet to be retrieved from these archives).[19]

Figure 1.1 summarizes the number of rape and forced prostitution cases based on an analysis of the UNWCC charge files. Charge files are the dossiers of evidence prepared by national governments and submitted by them to the commission for its judgment as to whether the commission supported the indictment. Not all cases that were brought to trial or reported to the commission appear to have been processed as charge files, particularly those conducted in the Pacific region. The sheer volume of material in the UNWCC archive can give the impression of completeness. However, it is important to realize that the circumstances of war and the immediate postwar period placed huge obstacles in the way of keeping complete and accurate records.

"Rape Is Not a War Crime": Nullum Crimen Challenges to Prosecution of SGBV Crimes

The legal basis for prosecution of crimes of sexual violence as serious international crimes is well established. The statutes of both the International Criminal Tribunal for the former Yugoslavia (ICTY) and the International Criminal Tribunal for Rwanda (ICTR), for instance, explicitly recognize rape as a crime against humanity.[20] Similarly, the law establishing the Extraordinary Chambers in the Courts of Cambodia (ECCC) includes rape as a crime against humanity.[21] Article 7(1)(g) of the Rome Statute, which established the International Criminal Court, goes further and lists additional acts of sexual violence as crimes against humanity, including: "rape, sexual slavery, enforced prostitution, forced pregnancy, enforced sterilization, or any other form of sexual violence of comparative gravity."[22] So-called hybrid courts, which combine national and UN authority—such as the Special Court for Sierra Leone (SCSL) and the Special Panels for Serious Crimes in East Timor (SPET)—have followed the ICC's example by explicitly recognizing several sexual and gender-based crimes as crimes against humanity, including rape, sexual slavery, enforced prostitution, forced pregnancy, and any other form of sexual violence.[23] Moreover, the ICTY, ICTR, SCSL, and SPET have all convicted individuals of rape and sexual violence as crimes against humanity, among other SGBV crimes.[24]

While these developments demonstrate a strong precedent for the prosecution of SGBV crimes as serious international crimes, challenges to such prosecutions continue to arise. One such challenge is based on the legal principle of *nullum crimen sine lege*, which holds that persons cannot be held criminally accountable for conduct that did not constitute an offense at the time it took place.[25] A contemporary example of such a challenge occurred relatively recently at the ECCC. As indicated earlier, the law establishing the ECCC provides it with jurisdiction over, *inter alia*, the crime against humanity of rape.[26] The closing order in Case 002, a prosecution of several of the surviving senior leaders of the Khmer Rouge government, charged each of the accused with rape based on a finding that, "by imposing the consummation of forced marriages, the perpetrators committed a physical invasion of a sexual nature against a victim in coercive circumstances in which the consent of the victim was absent."[27]

On appeal, however, the pretrial chamber replaced the charge of rape as a crime against humanity with the "crime against humanity of other inhumane acts (sexual violence)" based on the same facts, after finding that "rape did not exist as a crime against humanity in its own right in 1975–1979."[28] In other words, the chamber determined that the prosecution of rape as a crime against humanity was barred before the ECCC by the principle of *nullum crimen sine lege*.[29] The chamber acknowledged that rape existed as a *war crime* during the relevant time period and

	Number of charges involving sexual violence
Australia vs. Japanese national	1
Belgium vs. German nationals	6
Czechoslovakia vs. German national	1
Denmark vs. German national	1
France vs. German nationals	66
Greece vs. Bulgarian nationals	12
Greece vs. German nationals	4
Greece vs. Italian nationals	5
Netherlands vs. German nationals	2
Norway vs. German national	1
Poland vs. German nationals	14
United States vs. Japanese national	1
Yugoslavia vs. Albanian national	1
Yugoslavia vs. Bulgarian nationals	3
Yugoslavia vs. German nationals	15
Yugoslavia vs. Hungarian nationals	2
Yugoslavia vs. Italian nationals	16
Total	151

FIGURE 1.1. Rape Cases Documented in the UNWCC Archive

based its finding on the inclusion of this offense in several instruments that predate the work of the UNWCC, including the US Army's Lieber Code of 1863 and the Hague Conventions of 1899 and 1907.[30] However, the chamber was not convinced that rape constituted a *crime against humanity* during the same period. In support of its conclusion, the chamber stressed the inconsistency between the law issued by the occupying Allies in Germany, Control Council Law No.10—which explicitly recognized rape as a crime against humanity—and the charters of the International Military Tribunal (IMT) and the International Military Tribunal for the Far East (IMTFE)—the Nuremberg and Tokyo tribunals, respectively—which did not.[31] The chamber also stressed that there was scant evidence of prosecution of rape as a crime against humanity in the post–World War II period.[32]

Had the ECCC been aware of the UNWCC-supported cases, it might have come to a different conclusion by the time the Khmer Rouge came to power in 1975. Many of the post–World War II tribunals focused on rape as a war crime—which arguably has a stronger basis under customary international law (since aspects of international law derive from state practice, custom, tradition, and the unwritten rules by which states usually behave). Other post–World War II tribunals, including the IMTFE, treated crimes against humanity as essentially subsumed within war crimes.[33] The distinction between the two centers primarily on the nationality of the perpetrator vis-à-vis the victim.[34] Significantly, in at least one UNWCC-supported case brought by the Chinese War Crimes Military Tribunal, against Japanese officer Takashi Sakai, the tribunal referred to the offenses at issue as both "war crimes" and "crimes against humanity."[35] In the trial record submitted by the tribunal to the UNWCC it noted:

> In inciting or permitting his subordinates to murder prisoners of war, wound soldiers, nurses and doctors of the Red Cross and other non-combatants, and to commit acts of rape, plunder, deportation, torture and destruction of property, [Sakai] had violated the Hague Convention concerning the Laws and Customs of War on Land and the Geneva Convention of 1929. These offences are war crimes and *crimes against humanity* (emphasis added).[36]

As will be discussed in more detail later, rape was charged in UNWCC-supported cases, including ones prosecuted in Australia, China, Italy, the United States, Yugoslavia, Denmark, France, Greece, and Poland. Although the records reviewed to date are unclear regarding whether the tribunals adjudicating these cases similarly considered rape to constitute both a war crime and a crime against humanity, records from UNWCC-supported trials that have yet to become public might well reveal this to be the case. Moreover, the fact that rape that occurred in the context of a conflict or mass violence was prosecuted widely, albeit infrequently, lends support to the argument that rape was clearly recognized as a serious crime in the post–World War II era.

In addition, even if prosecuted as a war crime rather than as a crime against humanity, the notion that rape that occurred in the context of a conflict or mass violence was widely understood to trigger individual criminal responsibility—regardless of the nationality of the victim—may have provided the judges at the ECCC with a better sense of the seriousness with which such offenses were taken in the immediate postwar period, most notably the nearly thirty years prior to the period of time during which Khmer Rouge leaders were accused of having committed the crimes at issue. Indeed, had the ECCC been aware of how extensively rape was prosecuted in the 1940s—and the approach taken by post–World War II tribunals with respect to this and other such crimes—it might have come to a different conclusion.

The UNWCC cases may also have relevance to the crimes against the so-called comfort women who were abused by Japanese forces in Korea and raped by Japanese troops in China. Part of the political response in both cases is that these were not considered crimes at the time, even though many Japanese were prosecuted for these crimes in other parts of Asia. At the time, following a series of treaties in the late nineteenth and early twentieth centuries, both Taiwan and Korea were considered to be part of Japanese territory, meaning that criminal acts committed by Japanese in both places could not be prosecuted as war crimes (which, by definition, take place between two countries; it was for this reason that German crimes against German Jews, for example, were not prosecuted as war crimes). This highlights the fact that the forced prostitution and widespread rape of the comfort women were legally recognized for what they were but it also explains the failure to address those crimes due to the question of whether state sovereignty and established law trump human rights.

Data on Rape Cases

In light of the potential impact of these cases on contemporary debates about when rape was recognized as a serious international crime, it is useful to briefly explore a few of the UNWCC-supported rape cases available for review thus far. Full trial records of these cases are still being uncovered from the archives of the United Nations and the national archives of UNWCC member states, but several reports that individual countries have submitted to the UNWCC clearly indicate that cases involving sexual and gender-based violence were often investigated and prosecuted.

For example, charges of rape were brought by an Australian military court against Tanaka Chuichi and two others on July 12, 1946, and by the Chinese War Crimes Military Tribunal of the Ministry of National Defense against Takashi Sakai on August 29 of that same year.[37] The Greek government tried Italian lieutenant Giovanni Ravalli and Bulgarian lieutenant Anton Kaltcheff for rape on February 15, 1946, before the Special War Crimes Court of Athens.[38] A Polish case from 1947 also included rape among a range of charges against some 150 individuals.[39] Moreover, the UNWCC cited in its 1948 human rights report to the United Nations the case of Hans Muller, who was tried for rape before a French tribunal in November 1945.[40]

It is important to note that in several of these instances, rape or rape-related charges were brought in the absence of any other alleged crimes, which underscores the fact that prosecutors believed crimes of sexual violence alone were sufficient to warrant prosecution. For example, the Australians prosecuted Yoshio Yaki for the rape and related torture of a woman named Betty Woo, though there were no other charges.[41] Other cases in which only rape was charged can be found across a wide range of member states. In one Greek case against Bulgarian national Boris Tsernosemski, "president of the Community of Siderohorion Kavalla," the defendant was charged with raping two women.[42] One Belgian case from 1944 charged a group of soldiers, led by one Obersturmbannführer Burkhaus, for the gang rape of a woman whose house they were occupying; the court identified them as a unit through Burkhaus's signature on a requisition paper they had inadvertently left at the scene.[43] Another court indicted a group of soldiers (again, as a unit, led by Willy Jobst) for mass rape, attempted rape of a minor, and forced prostitution. A Danish case was made against a German policeman for rape as a violation of the Danish penal code.[44] France—the most active country in drawing up rape prosecutions more broadly—indicted German soldiers for rape as a lone charge (that is, on its own) in twelve cases, spanning the whole country across the course of the war, as well as one case for rape and forced prostitution.[45] Just as important, the records also indicate that prosecutors charged and in many instances won convictions for rape. Yoshio Yaki was convicted of rape and torture and sentenced to death.[46] Takashi Sakai, who was prosecuted by the Chinese for—among other offenses—inciting or permitting his subordinates to rape civilians, was also convicted of rape and torture and sentenced to death.[47] Other successful prosecutions include the cases of the Greek government against Ravalli and Kaltcheff for rape and other charges, as well as a Greek case against defendants Friedrich Wilhelm Mueller and Bruno Oswald for rape and additional crimes.[48]

The United States reported a large number of prosecutions to the commission, and these include rape charges, largely for Japanese perpetrators of sexual violence and forced prostitution against Philippine victims. A review of the US trial reports finds fifteen such cases, which addressed both senior officials under "command responsibility" charges and individuals accused of committing rape themselves.[49]

In several cases rape was not listed as a specific charge but it does seem to have been charged or prosecuted under broader charges of "inhumanity" or "ill-treatment." The Polish government included details of rapes committed by German personnel for cases taking place in the cities of Warsaw and Slonim and at the Auschwitz-Birkenau death camp, but the specific charges leveled against perpetrators did not include rape. Rather, there was a list of broader charges including "systematic terrorism," "inhuman conditions," and torture.[50] Other countries, such as Greece and France, likewise included rape under accounts of "particulars of alleged crime[s]," but sometimes did not specifically list it as a charge or subsumed it into broader charges of "inhumanity," "torture," or "ill-treatment."[51] US reports of prosecutions also include a case where rape was extensively discussed in the trial record but ultimately seems to have been subsumed into broader charges of "torture" and "ill-treatment."[52]

The interpretation of these is unclear; each of these countries also charged rape as an offense in its own right, meaning that the courts certainly did see rape as a chargeable crime. But they do not seem to have done so in every case. It may be an issue of specific cases receiving different treatment by different officials or changing policies toward the handling of cases, but in any case it does reflect the range of different responses to sexual violence under international law. While subsuming rape under "torture" or "ill-treatment" charges may not be desirable by modern standards—Justice Richard Goldstone, for example, has publicly regretted that he and other ICTY officials were often limited to charging rape as a form of torture or ill-treatment in the absence of knowledge about the UNWCC precedent—it still underlines the fact that sexual violence was taken seriously by postwar prosecutors and seen as part of a broader pattern of "inhumanity."[53]

In sum, the record of UNWCC-supported trials in Asia and Europe suggests that rape committed in the context of conflict or mass violence was punishable as a serious crime nearly seventy years ago.[54] Indeed, the frequent indictment and conviction for rape offenses following World War II strengthen the argument that rape was recognized as a crime against humanity under customary international law during the war, or at least by the time of the war's conclusion. This brief review highlights how critical past court records are for contemporary courts and tribunals tasked with deciding the merits of *nullum crimen* challenges in rape cases occurring in the context of a conflict or mass violence.[55]

How Can We Define Sexual and Gender-Based Crimes?

It is important to note that the UNWCC did not define any of the offenses in the list of war crimes it provided to member states. The definitions and elements of these offenses came from domestic and military penal codes applied by each country's tribunal or military commission that tried UNWCC-supported cases.[56] A preliminary review of these cases reveals that member states prosecuting SGBV crimes dealt with the same issues that contemporary tribunals continue to wrestle with, including how to analyze issues of consent and coercion in situations of conflict or mass violence.

Lack of Agreement by the Victim as a Necessary Element of Rape

Many, if not most, domestic jurisdictions today define rape as including a lack of consent to sexual acts on the part of the victim.[57] There are, however, a wide range of approaches in national systems regarding whether this requires that the defendant use physical force, whether the victim must attempt to physically resist the defendant, and to what extent threats against the victim or others render the victim unable to genuinely consent.[58] Some jurisdictions also take into account the circumstances surrounding the incident to determine if the victim is particularly vulnerable or the circumstance negates an ability to genuinely consent.[59] When addressing rape as a war crime or as a crime against humanity, the analysis is complicated by the ways in which consent or lack thereof is affected by situations of armed conflict or mass violence.

Different courts have taken different positions on this question.[60] For instance, although the first ad hoc tribunal case that addressed the legal elements of rape defined the crime without reference to non-consent—requiring only that the prosecution show "a physical invasion of a sexual nature, committed on a person under circumstances which are coercive"[61]—later ICTY and ICTR cases introduced non-consent as an element of the crime by requiring proof that the sexual act was committed without the consent of the victim and that the perpetrator knew such consent was absent.[62] While the tribunals concede in these later cases that lack of consent can be established through the "existence of coercive circumstances under which meaningful consent is not possible,"[63] the absence of consent remains central to the definition of rape.[64] Indeed, in its first case involving allegations of rape, the Special Court for Sierra Leone defined the elements of rape as including "nonconsensual penetration" of the victim,[65] although, like the ad hoc tribunals, the court acknowledged that "consent of the victim must be given voluntarily, as a result of the victim's free will, assessed in the context of the surroundings," and that "in situations of armed conflict, coercion is almost always universal."[66] Finally, while the ICC's Elements of Crimes does not explicitly require that the prosecution establish lack of consent,[67] it does require a showing that the perpetrator committed a physical invasion of a sexual nature against the victim "by force, or by threat of force or coercion, such as that caused by fear of violence, duress, detention, psychological oppression or abuse of power, against such person or another person, or by taking advantage of a coercive environment, or the invasion was committed against a person incapable of giving genuine consent."[68] Notably, the court has yet to interpret this phrase, and, as one commentator has noted, there is a risk that "judges of the ICC will deviate from the more principled focus on coercion . . . and will [instead] attempt to embrace, in a single test, concepts [of non-consent and coercion]" that have marked the jurisprudence of the *ad hoc* tribunals.[69]

The archival records suggest that the way in which post–World War II courts approached issues of consent could be of interest to contemporary tribunals struggling with this issue in conflict-related rape cases. UNWCC-supported cases dealt with situations ranging from forcible rapes committed with the use of physical force or firearms,[70] to cases alleging the use of alcohol or drugs to render the victim unable to consent,[71] to cases in which threats to family members were used to compel victims into sexual intercourse.[72]

An example of the latter type was the Australian case (mentioned earlier) against Yoshio Yaki, who was tried in Rabaul in Papua, New Guinea.[73] Yaki was a Japanese sergeant who admitted to having had sexual intercourse with the victim, Betty Woo, but he argued it was with her consent. The brief record of the trial provided to the UNWCC states that Betty Woo provided evidence to the court that Yaki had forced her to have sexual intercourse with him by threatening to behead her husband if she refused. Woo stated that she refused and Yaki tied her to a tree for three hours and put ants on her face and body. She then returned to where she had previously lived and was told that her husband had been beheaded. She subsequently went to Yaki's place, where she said Yaki forced her to drink, dance, and then have sexual intercourse with him. Yaki denied having tied Woo to a tree and denied knowledge that her husband had been beheaded. Although the trial record is brief and does not describe the court's reasoning in great detail, Yaki was convicted and executed by hanging on March 12, 1946, suggesting that as early as 1946 the courts recognized threats and harm to one's family members as relevant to an analysis of the issue of consent in rape cases.

The relationship between force and consent was a central issue in another UNWCC-supported case, the US case against Guam national Nicolas Sablan, who was charged with assault with intent to rape. In that case, victim Dolores Santos Cruz testified that Sablan, who worked for the local police, came to her house, accused her of theft, and threatened to take her to jail.[74] She testified that when she did not admit to the alleged theft, Sablan removed some of his clothing and threatened her, saying, "If you don't consent to do something with me, I will kill you." When asked what Sablan's exact words were, the victim replied, "He wanted to have sexual intercourse with me." The victim also testified that Sablan grabbed her, hit her, threw her down stairs, and threatened her with a dagger he had on his side.[75] Defense counsel argued lack of force, stating:

> Gentlemen, what does assault with intend [*sic*] to commit rape mean? It means that at the time of the assault the accused must have the intention to ravish or to have sexual intercourse with the woman by violence and against her will. Mere intent to have sexual intercourse is not enough—it must be intent to rape. . . . All that the girl said was that [Sablan] took her by the hand and asked her to have sexual intercourse. She said she did not want to do it—her words were "No, because I promised my mother I would not do that." He then released her hand and insisted no more. Gentlemen, if that is an assault with intent to commit rape, then ninety-nine out of every hundred men walking down the streets today are guilty of assault with intent to commit rape.[76]

The judge advocate responded by recounting the victim's testimony regarding Sablan holding both of her hands, slapping her, and threatening to kill her with the dagger he had on his side.[77] Sablan was found guilty of, among other crimes, two counts of assault with intent to commit rape for this incident, which suggests that the judge advocate gave significant weight to the circumstances surrounding the incident when analyzing whether the accused intended to have sexual intercourse with the victim without her consent.[78] In other words, it appears that the judge advocate understood the surrounding circumstances as rendering genuine consent implausible, thus leading to a finding of intent to rape on the part of the perpetrator. The very brief details about this case and the Yaki case suggest that domestic tribunals recognized that threats to the victim or others, or taking advantage of surrounding circumstances, renders victims unable to refuse sexual acts. For instance, in at least one case emerging from Yugoslavia, the limited records indicate that the accused was convicted of rape in situations when he controlled wartime rations and the victim came to him for food. The accused "seized the opportunity to rape [the] 13-year-old girl."[79] This suggests that the court took into account the coercive environment in determining whether rape had occurred. Of course, more complete records of UNWCC-supported trials would help provide more information to contemporary tribunals that are contending with issues of consent and coercive circumstances.

Attempted Rape

In the context of world war, it is extraordinary from a twenty-first-century perspective that "attempted rape" was listed as an offense in the 1940s by a wide range of countries. Belgium, France, Greece, Poland, and Yugoslavia all—at one point or another—charged German, Italian, and Bulgarian alleged war criminals—with attempted rape,[80] while the United States—in the Yamashita trial and elsewhere—achieved convictions for it.[81]

The legal basis under international law was, according to Nuremberg prosecutor Brig.-Gen. Telford Taylor (quoted in a UNWCC report on human rights to the UN Economic and Social Council), "most unsettled." Taylor was, however, a firm supporter of its inclusion, suggesting that, just because external circumstances prevented the completion of a criminal act did not mean that an attempted murderer (or, by extension, attempted rapist) should be seen as innocent of any crime.[82] Regardless of the precise international status of the definition, however, the widespread prosecution of attempted rape in a range of jurisdictions shows that courts were well aware of the trauma and severity associated with even the threat or attempt of rape.

Coercion as an Element of Forced Prostitution

Forced prostitution is included in the statutes of several contemporary international tribunals.[83] Although no prosecutions of this crime have taken place before these tribunals, the ICC Elements of Crimes defines the crime against humanity of enforced prostitution as requiring, among other elements, that the perpetrator has caused "one or more persons to engage in one or more acts of a sexual nature by force, threat of force or coercion."[84] Thus, the prosecution of forced prostitution in UNWCC-supported cases—and the way in which the issue of coercion was addressed in those cases—adds to the historical and legal foundations for potential future cases involving this charge.

As noted previously, several cases of forced prostitution were charged in domestic jurisdictions as part of the UNWCC effort.[85] Additionally, the commission itself brought charges in ten cases; in one of the cases, forced prostitution was included.[86] Coercion was a central issue in a forced prostitution case that was prosecuted by the US Navy JAG Military Commission in July 1945 and reported to the UNWCC.[87] Samuel Shinohara, a Japanese national and a resident of Guam at the time of the alleged offenses, was charged with treason, theft, assault and battery, desecration of a flag, and two counts—or "specifications"—of "taking a female for the purpose of prostitution."[88] The victim, with regard to "Specification 1," was a seventeen-year-old girl named Alfonsina Flores, who testified that Shinohara and Sakai—an aide to Governor Hayashi—went to her family's ranch, where they told her mother, in her presence, that they were looking for her seventeen-year-old daughter.[89] Flores stated that her mother told her she had to go with the men because if she did not, Flores and her whole family would be killed.[90] Flores testified that Shinohara told her mother that she would clean and serve in the house of the Japanese governor and would receive the best care.[91] Flores's mother accompanied Shinohara, Sakai, their driver, and the girl back to a house referred to as the Kerner House, where Sakai and Hayashi resided when on the island, at which point Flores realized that she "was being turned over to a man."[92] According to Flores's evidence, Shinohara told her then she must listen or she would be beheaded.[93] The commission asked Flores at what point she understood that she might be required to "serve the sexual appetite of the Japs," to which she responded she knew as soon as she heard Shinohara was looking for a seventeen-year-old girl.[94]

The commission then questioned Flores regarding the sexual intercourse that she said took place between her and one of the Japanese men, asking, "Did you consent to the wishes of the Jap in this occasion?," to which she responded, "I cried and he started to hold me. I didn't want to yield."[95] The defense questioned Flores regarding her ability to come and go from the Kerner House, to visit her family and to have her family visit her.[96] Flores maintained that Shinohara had threatened to punish her if she left the Kerner House and that she feared she or her family would be killed if she did not obey Shinohara.[97] Defense counsel questioned Flores about the money she was given in exchange for housework she did at the Kerner House and Flores acknowledged she was paid small amounts on occasion but not what she and her family had been promised.[98] She remained at the Kerner House for six months, until Shinohara stopped coming there, at which point she left and did not return.[99]

Under the Guam Penal Code applied in this case, Shinohara was charged under Section 266(b), which prohibited taking a female for the purpose of prostitution with her consent procured by misrepresentation.[100] Shinohara was found guilty of two counts of "taking a female for the purpose of prostitution," but regarding the count involving Flores, the commission recategorized the offense, from taking a female for the purpose of prostitution with her consent procured by misrepresentation, a violation of Section 266(b) to instead be taking a female for the purpose of prostitution against her will and without her consent, which is a violation of Section 266(a).[101] The commission changed the charge from being one of misrepresentation to one of non-consent at the same time that it pronounced its finding of guilt on the latter charge.[102] On October 13, 1945, the commission's findings, of guilt for the two counts of taking a female for the purpose of prostitution as well as treason and assault and battery, were approved by the island commander.[103] On January 30 of the following year, however, the commander in chief of the US Navy Pacific Fleet "disapproved" the conviction on the first count of taking a female for the purpose of prostitution, stating that, due to the recategorization of the crime from "misrepresentation" to non-consent, the defendant had been found guilty of a crime for which he had not been charged, thus depriving him of the opportunity to prepare a defense.[104]

On August 24, 1948, Shinohara's sentence of death by hanging was commuted to fifteen years of imprisonment.[105] While issues of fairness and the rights of the accused were the primary focus of the commander's review of the case, it highlights interesting factors that may emerge in contemporary cases involving enforced prostitution, including: the extent to which a broader situation of armed conflict or wartime occupation affects the ability of a victim to leave a situation of forced prostitution;[106] the ways in which individuals in positions of power may leverage coercive circumstances to compel a victim into forced prostitution; and the different ways in which forced prostitution can occur—that is, not only in formal brothels but, as in this case, at a residence. It is important to note that the analysis of these issues may also be relevant to cases being heard in contemporary tribunals involving charges that share aspects of forced prostitution, such as enslavement and sexual slavery.[107] As such, more information regarding UNWCC-supported forced prostitution cases could offer important guidance to contemporary tribunals dealing with these issues.[108]

Theories of Criminal Responsibility for SGBV Crimes

The jurisprudence of contemporary international tribunals has recognized that an accused need not have physically perpetrated a crime in order to be found directly liable (responsible) for that crime. Thus, in addition to convicting the accused for physically perpetrating crimes of sexual violence, the tribunals have held many of those accused criminally responsible for instigating, ordering, or aiding and abetting them.[109] In addition, under the statutes of various international criminal bodies, superior responsibility for the acts of a subordinate can be established when there is a military commander or other superior who has effective control over the subordinate, when the superior knew or should have known that the subordinate had committed or was about to commit a crime, or when the superior failed to take necessary and reasonable measures to either prevent the crimes from being committed or to punish their commission.[110] This has had significant consequences for the prosecution of crimes of sexual violence committed in the context of conflict, mass violence, or repression, as such crimes are often tacitly encouraged or tolerated even if not directly perpetrated or officially sanctioned by the accused in positions of authority.

Considerable challenges remain, however, in the effort to hold perpetrators—particularly senior military and civilian officials—accountable for SGBV crimes. For instance, defendants charged with superior responsibility for rape or other acts of sexual violence often argue they were unaware that their subordinates were committing such acts and thus should not be held criminally liable for such crimes.[111] Although the tribunals have recognized that the knowledge element of the superior responsibility test can be established through circumstantial evidence, recent jurisprudence suggests that contemporary tribunals sometimes require direct evidence of such knowledge in cases involving sexual and gender-based violence.[112] In the *Kajelijeli* case the ICTR refused to find that the accused knew or had reason to know of numerous acts of sexual violence committed by his subordinates despite significant evidence tendered in support of his knowledge of the crimes. For instance, the chamber heard testimony placing him at the scene or in the immediate vicinity of the rapes,[113] indicating that he had been present when his subordinates had told victims that they would be sexually assaulted.[114] Other evidence was presented that he was "informed of all the acts perpetrated by his [subordinates]," was in "permanent contact" with them, and received reports from them on what they had done.[115] Thus, although the tribunals have recognized that circumstantial evidence can be used to prove that a superior had reason to know crimes had been or were about to be committed by his subordinates, here the tribunal appeared to reject that standard and required direct evidence of a superior's knowledge of his subordinates' actions.[116]

Notably, many of the theories of liability used by contemporary tribunals today were used in the UNWCC-supported cases. Indeed, reports from national jurisdictions to the UNWCC concerning rape charges suggest these cases encompassed a broad spectrum of modes of liability, including direct perpetrators charged with committing the crime, commanders charged under superior responsibility, and other characterizations of participation that constitute precursors to a joint criminal enterprise such as "common design."[117] The brief facts given in some of the reports from the member states to the UNWCC refer to many prosecutions for direct perpetration of rape, such as in the US prosecution of Guam national Nicholas Sablan,[118] cases in France,[119] more than one case in Poland,[120] and a case in Denmark against a German officer.[121] In addition, several cases in Greece were brought against Bulgarian nationals for individually perpetrating rape.[122] In addition to these prosecutions for direct perpetration, several UNWCC-supported prosecutions were brought against commanders accused of superior responsibility for rape by their subordinates. In France, Alois Brunner "et tous son sous-ordres" ("and all of his subordinates" in the Drancy and other concentration camps) were charged with a range of crimes involving the "enslavement of young girls and women for forced prostitution." Though Brunner had not engaged in any of these acts himself, his prominent command role in the concentration camp system in France meant that he and his command staff were charged with their commission.[123]

Just as in many contemporary cases in which rape is treated as an international crime, superiors in those UNWCC-supported cases denied knowledge of acts of sexual violence committed by their subordinates.[124] For instance, in the case mentioned above brought by the Chinese War Crimes Military Tribunal against Japanese officer Takashi Sakai, the accused pled not guilty to rape and other crimes on the grounds that he was not responsible for the acts of his subordinates, as he had no knowledge of them.[125] This plea was rejected and Sakai was found guilty of "inciting or permitting his subordinates to . . . rape, plunder and deport civilians." The report on Sakai's trial submitted by the tribunal to the commission concludes that:

> In inciting or permitting his subordinates to murder prisoners of war, wounded soldiers, nurses and doctors of the Red Cross and other noncombatants, and to commit acts of rape, plunder, deportation, torture and destruction of property, [Sakai] had violated the Hague Convention concerning the Laws and Customs of War on Land and the Geneva Convention of 1929. These offences are war crimes and crimes against humanity. . . . That a field Commander must hold himself responsible for the discipline of his subordinates, is an accepted principle. It is inconceivable that he should not have been aware of the acts of atrocities committed by his subordinates. . . . All the evidence goes to show that the defendant knew of the atrocities committed by his subordinates and deliberately let loose savagery upon civilians and prisoners of war.[126]

Thus, for the purpose of establishing the responsibility of the superior, the tribunal in this case applied a mode of liability to the offense of rape in the same way it applied liability to the other charged offenses. The tribunal seems to be acknowledging that once the defendant gave his subordinates carte blanche to commit unlawful killings and other atrocities, he should have known that rapes and other violations would occur and that he would be held responsible for these offenses as a result. As contemporary courts continue to address cases involving superior responsibility for rape and other acts of sexual violence, this example lends support to the notion that as early as the 1940s courts recognized that superiors should be held criminally accountable for failing to prevent or punish such offenses and that the same standards of evidence should be used.

This is particularly apparent in many of the cases pursued by the United States in the Pacific theater. In the US case against Gen. Tomoyuki Yamashita, for example, the prosecution stated that Japanese servicemen under his command were "permitted" to carry out acts, including "torture, rape, murder and mass execution of very large numbers of residents of the Philippines, including women and children." The commission dismissed the defense position that he could not be held accountable for acts his subordinates committed 150 miles away, finding instead that,

> where murder and rape and vicious, revengeful actions are widespread offences, and there is no effective attempt by a commander to discover and control the criminal acts, such a commander may be held responsible, even criminally liable, for the lawless acts of his troops, depending upon their nature and the circumstances surrounding them.[127]

The *Yamashita* trial, while one of the more well-known prosecutions for command responsibility rape, was not an aberration. Other cases dealt with officials who, though lower in rank, were still implicated in cases of rape wrought by their subordinates, such as the trial of Sgt.-Maj. Naoki Hamasaki, who on February 24, 1947, was convicted of "unlawfully permit[ting] members of the Imperial Japanese Army then under his command to rape a number of Philippine women."[128] As in the Yamashita case, the court appears to have rejected defense claims that it was unreasonable to prosecute Hamasaki for the actions of his subordinates in order to convict him of permitting rape—tellingly phrased as "boys will be boys" types of analogies and that the subordinates were like a "wild tiger" that could not reasonably be expected to be controlled.[129] Notably, Hamasaki was not convicted of several other command-responsibility charges (e.g., for killings committed by his subordinates), which suggests that the doctrine of command responsibility did not automatically lead to convictions but was the subject of genuine judicial deliberation and also applied to rape.

Treatment of SGBV Victims as Witnesses

The evolution of protections for SGBV victims as witnesses in both domestic and international tribunals has included a wide range of support services, privacy mechanisms, and the promulgation of rules with regard to the questioning of witnesses.[130] A rule common to many domestic jurisdictions and incorporated into the rules in force at the ad hoc tribunals and at the ICC prohibits questions regarding the victim's prior sexual history.[131] The UNWCC cases reveal how some of the national courts handled the questioning of SGBV victims prior to the creation of such codified protections. While some instances illustrate the gender stereotypes of the times, others demonstrate that, even as early as the 1940s, courts understood that invasive questions violated victims' dignity and rights.

In the *Shinohara* case discussed above, there were two counts, or specifications, of "taking of a female for the purpose of prostitution."[132] While the first involved the aforementioned victim Alfonsina Flores, the second involved a victim named Nicholasa Mendiola, a woman whose reputation was thoroughly examined during the course of the trial and again on appeal.[133] During cross-examination the defense counsel asked the victim: "Prior to the Japanese occupation, have you ever received any physical examination at the hospital here in Agana?"[134] The victim responded: "What kind of physical examination? There were many physical examinations."[135] The defense counsel asked: "For venereal disease?" To which the victim responded: "I do not want to answer that question. It lowers my reputation but if I must answer it then I will."[136] The record then states that "the commission announced that the witness did not have to answer the question."[137] While contemporary courts in many jurisdictions would have disallowed the question to begin with, the fact that the commission ruled that the victim did not have to answer the question suggests that the commission understood that respect for victims' dignity required it to impose some limitations on the questioning by defense counsel.

In another US case in Guam, Guam national Nicolas Sablan was charged with two counts of assault with intent to rape under the Guam penal code.[138] Count 2 involved a victim named Agueda Duenas Diego.[139] During cross-examination the defense counsel asked Duenas Diego if the accused had previously spent the night with her, prior to the night of the alleged assault.[140] The judge advocate objected to the question, stating it was irrelevant and improper, but the military commission overruled the objection,[141] although it then advised the victim that "she could claim her constitutional rights and refuse to answer any question that might tend to degrade or incriminate her."[142] The victim then answered that the accused had slept there once.[143] She was asked if he slept there more than once, to which she responded "no."[144] She was then asked if she had been having sexual relations with another man named Shimada, which she refused to answer "on the ground that it might tend to degrade her."[145] The question was not pressed further. Although the commission allowed a number of intrusive questions, it made clear that the victim had the right to not answer questions that "might tend to degrade . . . her." Contemporary cases demonstrate that defense counsels continue to press victims on their prior sexual histories and to object to rules prohibiting such lines of questioning.[146] The UNWCC-supported cases indicate that, although only recently codified in the rules of some contemporary tribunals, the practice of protecting witnesses from degrading questions dates back to the post–World War II era. As such, they reinforce rulings issued by tribunals that follow this practice and offer important precedents to tribunals that have not yet codified such rules when dealing with this issue.

Conclusion

Prosecution of international crimes of sexual violence will be greatly helped by the rediscovery of the work conducted by the Allies during World War II. That these legal rules and precedents are valuable in the most politically charged type of crimes opens up the discussion of the wider value today of this wartime effort.

There are also smaller research questions that would make valuable research projects beyond the scope of the current study. A good part of feminist writing on SGBV needs revision so that the efforts of activists in the 1990s and after are understood within the proper context and knowledge that these crimes were pursued as "normal" war crimes generations beforehand.

Susan Brownmiller, for example, correctly notes that "no international tribunals were called to expose and condemn Allied atrocity, no war-crimes depositions were taken from 'enemy' women, no incriminating top-secret documents from our side of the war were held up to merciless light," and regrets that "a theorist of rape must admit that the evidence has been unfairly weighted."[147] In this sense the discovery of more documents from the dominant perspective is unlikely to help this unfair weighting, but the widespread prosecution of rape by the Allies that went unquestioned at the time and was for its time highly progressive (or even somewhat progressive by today's standards) is nonetheless indispensable. How did this careful and fairly enlightened attitude toward prosecution of sexual violence exist alongside one-sided prosecutions, and how did it wither away to the point that leading jurists in the 1990s were unaware of it and the precedents it established?

Such scholarship might also look at the role of female commissioners in the UNWCC. While generally male dominated, in the 1945–1947 period the commission in London included female representatives of Denmark, France, and the Netherlands. To what extent did they have an impact on the formation of policy and cause it to address gender-specific concerns (as with female representatives in other foundational UN settings, such as Bertha Lutz and Wu Yi-fang in the drafting of the UN Charter)?[148] It is important to establish how rape and forced prostitution became war crimes at the end of the First World War. In the original postwar "Versailles List" of war crimes used by the commission and originally developed after the war, these two crimes were items five and six in a list of thirty-two items (following only "murder and massacre/systematic terrorism," "putting hostages to death," "torture of civilians," and "deliberate starvation of civilians"). While the specific order of the list may not be meaningful, it does nonetheless suggest that it was given a high priority by postwar planners and it thus merits further attention.

Notes

This chapter is based on "The Relevance of the United Nations War Crimes Commission Trials to the Prosecution of Sexual and Gender-Based Crimes Today," *Criminal Law Forum* 25, no. 1–2 (2014): 349–81, © Springer Science+Business Media (Dordrecht, Netherlands, 2014,), coauthored with Susana SáCouto and Chante Lasco of the War Crimes Research Office at American University's Washington College of Law. Used by permission.

1. UNWCC, *Law Reports of Trials of War Criminals,* vol. 7 (London: Her Majesty's Stationery Office, 1948), 14–16. Available at www.unwcc.org/wp-content/uploads/2013/03/Law-Reports-Volume-7.pdf.
2. UNWCC, "Czechoslovak Cases against German War Criminals," RN 116/Cz/G/5, CN 5–48, notes on the case 16.
3. See Patricia Viseur Sellers, "Individual(s') Liability for Collective Sexual Violence," in *Gender and Human Rights*, ed. Karen Knop, 153–94 (Oxford: Oxford University Press, 2004), 153, 190. See also Rhonda Copelon, "Gender Crimes as War Crimes: Integrating Crimes Against Women into International Criminal Law," *McGill Law Journal* 46 (2000): 223. Copelon notes that only after rape began being discussed as a "weapon of war" in the former Yugoslavia was it transformed "from private, off-duty, collateral, and inevitable excess to something that is public or 'political' in the traditional sense." See the press release from Human Rights Watch, "Human Rights Watch Applauds Rwanda Rape Verdict," September 1, 1998, available at www.hrw.org/press98/sept/rrape902.htm, which notes that, "despite these legal precedents, rape has long been mischaracterized and dismissed by military and political leaders as a private crime, the ignoble act of the occasional soldier. Worse still, it has been accepted precisely because it is so commonplace. Longstanding discriminatory attitudes have viewed crimes against women as incidental or less serious violations."
4. See Patricia Viseur Sellers and Kaoru Okuizumi, "International Prosecution of Sexual Assaults," *Transnational Law and Contemporary Problems* 7 (1997): 61–62, which notes that, "sexual assaults committed during armed conflict are often rationalized as the result of a perpetrator's lust, libidinal needs, or stress"; Chile Eboe-Osuji, "Rape and Superior Responsibility: International Criminal Law in Need of Adjustment," ICC, Guest Lecture Series of the Office of the Prosecutor, June 20, 2005, 6, which argues that "the theory of individualistic opportunism proceeds . . . from the . . . modest premise that rape is a crime of opportunity which, during conflict, is frequently committed by arms-bearing men, indulging their libidos, under cover of the chaotic circumstances of armed conflict."
5. See Cate Steains, "Gender Issues," in *The International Criminal Court: The Making of the Rome Statute*, ed. Roy S. Lee, 357–90 (The Hague: Kluwer Law International, 1999), 361–64. Steains concludes that because earlier international law failed to do so, the Rome Statute's inclusion of "a range of sexual violence crimes, in addition to rape, under crimes against humanity creates an important new precedent."
6. See, e.g., Susana SáCouto and Katherine Cleary, "The Importance of Effective Investigation of Sexual Violence and Gender-Based Crimes at the International Criminal Court," *American University Journal of Gender, Social Policy, and the Law* 17 (2009): 337–59. Indeed, despite evidence of the widespread use of rape in the Balkans conflict and during the Rwandan genocide, the record is quite mixed with respect to the ability of the ad hoc ICTY and ICTR tribunals to successfully prosecute sexual violence. For example, despite the widely acknowledged use of rape and sexual violence as an integral part of the genocide in Rwanda, ten years into the Rwanda tribunal's history only 10 percent of completed cases resulted in a sentence

containing a rape conviction and "no rape charges were even brought by the Prosecutor's office in 70 per cent of . . . adjudicated cases." Binaifer Nowrojee, "'Your Justice Is Too Slow': Will the ICTR Fail Rwanda's Rape Victims?" UN Research Institute for Social Development paper, November 2005, 3.

7. Richard Goldstone, foreword to "The United Nations War Crimes Commission Symposium," *Criminal Law Forum* 25, no. 1–2 (2014): 1.
8. The author recognizes the research contributions of his colleagues Susana SáCouto, director, and Chante Lasco, gender jurisprudence collections coordinator, at the War Crimes Research Office at American University's Washington College of Law (WCL); and Shanti Sattler at the University of London's School of Oriental and African Studies (SOAS). The International Military Tribunal at Nuremberg and the International Military Tribunal in the Far East heard evidence of sexual and gender-based violence and considered such evidence in support of charges of other inhumane acts as crimes against humanity, but neither explicitly included rape or enforced prostitution in their foundational charters or judgments. See Dianne Luping, "Investigation and Prosecution of Sexual and Gender-based Crimes Before the International Criminal Court," *American University Journal of Gender, Social Policy, and the Law* 17, no. 2 (2009): 436–43.
9. UNWCC, "War Crimes Committee: Report of the Subcommittee," 8, enclosed as part of "United Nations War Crimes Commission: Notes of a Second Unofficial Meeting Held on 2nd December 1943, at 3:00 p.m. at the Royal Courts of Justice, London." The list of offenses is included as annex 1. Available at https://www.legal-tools.org/doc/3e7e05/.
10. Two lists were discussed in UNWCC, "United Nations Commission for the Investigation of War Crimes: Notes of Unofficial Meeting held at 2:30 p.m. on 26th October 1943, at the Royal Courts of Justice, London," available at https://www.legal-tools.org/doc/ad8990. See also "Second Unofficial Meeting 2nd December 1943," note 3. The third list of offenses was discussed in UNWCC, "War Crimes Committee: Report of the Subcommittee," 9, enclosed as part of "Second Unofficial Meeting 2nd December 1943," the list is included as annex 1. The first three meetings are often described as "unofficial," although at the fifth meeting the commission retroactively approved the actions of the earlier meetings upon the arrival of the US commissioner. See UNWCC, "Minutes of Fifth Meeting held on 18th January 1944," 1.
11. UNWCC, "Unofficial Meeting 26th October 1943," note 5. The first draft list of offenses shows rape under item no. 1 in the category "Grave crimes against person and property committed without any pretence of legal authority or order." The second draft list of offenses includes rape under "A" in the "second category," described as "Acts not directly connected with warfare and which have caused death, illness, bodily harm, or loss of liberty to those to whom they were applied." See also "Second Unofficial Meeting 2nd December 1943," note 3; the final list of war crimes is enclosed as annex 1, and rape appears as item 5.
12. Forced prostitution was not included in the first draft of offenses given in the notes of the October 26, 1943, meeting. In the second draft of offenses, within the second

category item no. 8 is "Abduction of women with the object of prostitution." In "Second Unofficial Meeting 2nd December 1943," item no. 6 is "Abduction of girls and women for the purpose of enforced prostitution."

13. UNWCC, "War Crimes Committee: Report of Subcommittee," 9.
14. UNWCC, "Second Unofficial Meeting 2nd December 1943." Rape appears as item 5 and "Abduction of girls and women for the purpose of enforced prostitution" as item 6.
15. The list of offenses adopted and disseminated by the UNWCC was based on the list that was agreed to at the 1919 Paris Peace Conference by the Commission on Responsibilities, a commission of experts tasked with making recommendations regarding the prosecution of war crimes committed during World War I. Notably, the list included both crimes. UNWCC, "Second Unofficial Meeting 2nd December 1943," 9. For a more detailed explanation of the Paris Peace Conference, see Harry Rhea's discussion of the International Criminal Court in "The Commission on the Responsibility of the Authors of the War and on Enforcement of Penalties and Its Contribution to International Criminal Justice After World War II," *Criminal Law Forum* 25, no. 1–2 (2014): 147–69.
16. UNWCC, "Polish Charges against German War Criminals," RN 6974/P/G/1233, CN 1233 (previously submitted as CN 5897/p/g/643, adjourned on July 25, 1947); Case of Samuel T. Shinohara, *Record of Proceedings of a Military Commission Convened at Agana, Guam, by Order of the Island Commander*, July 28, 1945, WW2 JAG case files, Pacific-Navy, available at www.fold3.com. Also: "French Charges against German War Criminals," RN 50/Fr/G/22, CN 24; RN 51/Fr/G/23, CN 25; and RN 54/Fr/G/26, CN 28, all March 7, 1944. Note that all "[country] Charges against" documents are housed at the UNWCC archives.
17. Case against Yoshio Yaki, *Australian Military Forces: Record of Military Court* (Japanese War Criminals), FN 21376, available at https://www.legal-tools.org/doc/a2a2d7/; "Belgian Charges against German War Criminals," RN 3174/B/G/297, CN D.540, May 23, 1946; "Belgian Charges against German War Criminals," RN 3811/B/G/316, CN 313-821-830, December 23, 1946; "Belgian Charges against German War Criminals," RN 3811/B/G/316, CN 313, August 6, 1946, 43; "Belgian Charges against German War Criminals," RN 5084/B/G/354, CN 1557 (May 1, 1947); *Chinese Cases against Japanese Nationals*, Trial and Law Reports Series 27, "Summary Translation of the Proceedings of the Military Tribunal, Nanking, on the Trial of Takashi Sakai," August 27, 1946, available at https://www.legal-tools.org/doc/3789a0/; "Danish Charges against German War Criminals," RN 5287/D/G/104 (Case against Hans Harry Foul Kruger), June 12, 1947; "Italian Charges against German War Criminals," RN 778/9/G/6, CHN 6, April 13, 1945; "French Charges against German War Criminals," RN 54/Fr/G/26, CHN 28, March 7, 1944; "Greek Charges against Bulgarian War Criminals," RN 3758/Gr/B/89, CN B/63 and CN 285/24, August 1, 1946; "Polish Charges against German War Criminals," RN 5438/P/G/372, CN 372, June 2, 1947; Case of Nicholas T. Sablan, Record of Proceedings of a Military Commission Convened at Agana, Guam, by Order of the Island Commander, March 30, 1945, WW2 JAG case files, Pacific-Navy, available

at www.fold3.com. All registration numbers cited here and throughout appear are as they are cited in the still-restricted archives of the UNWCC held in UN ARMS in New York. The charge files are organized alphabetically by the state undertaking the prosecution and then chronologically using the codes of each state's own system. The numbers refer to the commission's own overall lists.

18. Case against Yoshio Yaki, *Chinese Cases against Japanese Nationals*, Trial and Law Reports Series 27, "Summary Translation on the Trial of Takashi Sakai,"; Italian Charges against German War Criminals, CHN 6, RN 778/9/G/6, April 13, 1945; "Danish Charges against German War Criminals," RN 5287/D/G/104 (Case against Hans Harry Foul Kruger); "French Charges against German War Criminals," RN 54/Fr/G/26, CN 28, March 7, 1944; "Greek Charges against Bulgarian War Criminals," RN 3758/Gr/B/89, CN B/63 and CN 285/24, August 1, 1946; "Polish Charges against German War Criminals," RN 5438/P/G/372, CN 372, June 2, 1947.
19. See, for example, the UNWCC's index of reports received, www.legal-tools.org /uploads/tx_ltpdb/File%2020632.pdf.
20. See Article 5(g) of "Statute of the International Tribunal for the Prosecution of Persons Responsible for Serious Violations of International Humanitarian Law Committed in the Territory of the Former Yugoslavia since 1991," UN Security Council (UNSC) Resolution 827 (1993), UN doc. S/25704, 36 (1993), and UN doc. S/25704/Add.1 (1993), adopted by the Security Council on May 25, 1993, UN doc. S/RES/827 (1993); and Article 3(g) of "Statute of the International Tribunal for Rwanda," UNSC Res. 955 (1994), UN doc. S/RES/955. Note that the statute of the ICTR also provides for jurisdiction over rape as a war crime. See Article 4(e), which enumerates war crimes, including "outrages upon personal dignity, in particular humiliating and degrading treatment, rape, enforced prostitution and any form of indecent assault."
21. See Article 5 of "The Law on the Establishment of the Extraordinary Chambers in the Courts of Cambodia for the Prosecution of Crimes Committed during the Period of Democratic Kampuchea (Establishment Law)," as amended October 27, 2004, in NS/RKM/1004/006.
22. See Article 7(1)(g) of "Rome Statute of the International Criminal Court" (opened for signature July 17, 1998, entered into force July 1, 2002), United Nations Treaty Series 2187, 3. Under article 8(2)(b)(xxii) the ICC claims jurisdiction over crimes of sexual violence that are categorized as war crimes in international conflicts, including "rape, sexual slavery, enforced prostitution, forced pregnancy . . . enforced sterilization, or any other form of sexual violence also constituting a grave breach of the Geneva Conventions"; under Article 8(e)(vi) it claims jurisdiction over crimes of sexual violence in non-international conflicts, including "rape, sexual slavery, enforced prostitution, forced pregnancy (as defined in article 7 paragraph 2(f)), enforced sterilization, and any other form of sexual violence also constituting a serious violation of article 3 common to the four Geneva Conventions." Additionally, Article 6(b) of "Elements of Crimes of the International Criminal Court" (adopted

September 9, 2002) specifies that acts that can constitute genocide committed by causing serious bodily injury include "acts of torture, rape, sexual violence or inhuman or degrading treatment."

23. See Section 5, Article 2 of Statute of the Special Court for Sierra Leone, and United Nations Transitional Authority in East Timor (UNTAET) Regulation No. 2000/15, "On the Establishment of Panels with Exclusive Jurisdiction Over Serious Criminal Offences," Section 5.1(g). See also Ciara Damgaard, "The Special Court for Sierra Leone: Challenging the Tradition of Impunity for Gender-Based Crimes?" *Nordic Journal of International Law* 73 (2004): 488.
24. See, e.g., Prosecutor v. Kunarac et al., ICTY Judgment, CN IT-96-23 and CN IT-96-23/1-T February 22, 2001. For SGBV convictions by other tribunals see, e.g., Prosecutor v. Jean-Paul Akayesu, ICTR Judgment, CN ICTR-96-4-T, September 2, 1998; Prosecutor v. Brima et. al., SCSL Judgment, CN SCSL-04-16, June 20, 2007; Prosecutor v. Sesay et al., SCSL Judgment, CN SCSL-04-15-T, March 2, 2009; Prosecutor v. Taylor, SCSL Judgment, CN SCSL-03-01, May 18, 2012; Prosecutor v. Soares, SPET Judgment, CN DI-58-99-SC, September 20, 2002; Prosecutor v. Fereira, SPET Judgment, CN BO-06.1-99-SC, April 5, 2003. Notably, the jurisprudence from these tribunals makes clear that rape and other acts of sexual violence can also constitute other international crimes, such as the war crime of torture or an act of genocide. See, e.g., Prosecutor v. Furundzija, ICTY Judgment, CN IT-95-17/1-T, December 10, 1998; and Prosecutor v. Delalic et al., ICTY Judgment, CN IT-96-21, November 16, 1998, 496. For other examples see "Crimes of Sexual Violence" at the ICTY website, www.icty.org/sid/10312.
25. See, e.g., Article 22(1) of the Rome Statute: "A person shall not be criminally responsible under this Statute unless the conduct in question constitutes, at the time it takes place, a crime within the jurisdiction of the Court."
26. The Law on the Establishment of the Extraordinary Chambers in the Courts of Cambodia, for the Prosecution of Crimes Committed during the Period of Democratic Kampuchea (Establishment Law), as amended on October 27, 2004, DN NS/RKM/1004/006.
27. Case 002/01 (Closing Order), ECCC CN 002/19-09-2007-ECCC-OCIJ, September 15, 2010, 1431 (see also 1427).
28. Case 002/01, Pre-Trial Chamber Decision on Appeals by Nuon Chea and Ieng Thirith against the Closing Order, CN 002/19-09-2007-ECCC/OCIJ, February 15, 2011, 7.
29. Ibid.
30. Ibid., 151.
31. Control Council Law No. 10 was issued by the Allied Control Council on December 20, 1945. The law authorized the four nations occupying Germany after World War II—France, the Union of Soviet Socialist Republics, the United Kingdom, and the United States—to establish tribunals in their respective zones in order to try individuals accused of war crimes, crimes against peace, and crimes against humanity. See *Trials of War Criminals Before the Nuernberg Military Tribunals under Control*

Council Law 10, vol. 1: "The Medical Case," October 1946–April 1949 (Washington, DC: US Government Printing Office, 1949), 16.

32. Case 002/01, Nuon Chea and Ieng Thirith, 152.
33. See Neil Boster and Robert Cryer, *The Tokyo International Tribunal: A Reappraisal* (Oxford: Oxford University Press, 2008).
34. UNWCC, *Complete History of the United Nations War Crimes Commission and the Development of the Laws of War* (London: HM Stationery Office, 1948), 188–89, available at www.cisd.soas.ac.uk/documents/un-war-crimes-project-history-of-the-unwcc.52439517.
35. "Summary Translation on the Trial of Takashi Sakai."
36. Ibid., 6. For more on trials held in China and China's role in the UNWCC, see Wen-Wei Lai, "China, the Chinese Representative, and the Use of International Law to Counter Japanese Acts of Aggression: China's Standpoint on the Period Covered by UNWCC Jurisdiction," *Criminal Law Forum* 25, no. 1–2 (2014): 111–32.
37. "Report of Trial by the Chinese War Crimes Military Tribunal of the Ministry of National Defence of Takashi Sakai," August 27, 1946, available at https://www.legal-tools.org/uploads/tx_ltpdb/File%2013729-13756.pdf.
38. "Synopsis of Miscellaneous Trials (Canadian, Czechoslovak, Polish, Greek, Chinese, Dutch, and Norwegian)," 7, available at https://www.legal-tools.org/uploads/tx_ltpdb/File%2021077-21089.pdf.
39. "Polish Charges against German War Criminals," RN 7069/P/G/1280, CN 1280, December 3, 1947. See also UNWCC DN C.I mtg., December 10, 1947.
40. UNWCC, "Information Concerning Human Rights Arising from Trials of War Criminals: Report Prepared by the UN War Crimes Commission in Accordance with the Request Received from the United Nations," DN E/CN.4/W.19, May 15, 1948, 147. See also "United Nations War Crimes Commission First Supplement to the Synopsis of Trial Reports," DN C.204, June 27, 1946, 11, which states that Hans Muller was tried by the military tribunal at Angers on November 20, 1945, and was found "guilty but with extenuating circumstances" of rape committed against a French civilian and was sentenced to two years of prison. Available at https://www.legal-tools.org/doc/8f39f8.
41. Case against Yoshio Yaki. Yaki was convicted and the sentence of execution by hanging was carried out on December 13, 1945. See media reports of the crime and the sentence in *Morning Bulletin* (Rockhampton, Australia), "Death Sentences for Japs," December 14, 1945, available at http://trove.nla.gov.au/ndp/del/article/56440467.
42. "Greek Charges against Bulgarian War Criminals," RN 3758/Gr/B/89, CN B/63 and CN 285/24, August 1, 1946.
43. "Belgian Charges against German War Criminals," RN 1574/B/G/128, CN 378, September 2, 1945.
44. "Danish Charges against German War Criminals," (Case against Hans Harry Foul Kruger).
45. "French Charges against German War Criminals," RN 648/Fr/G/274 and RN 653/Fr/G/279, CN 322, March 8, 1945; RN 665/Fr/G/291, CN 335, March 26,

1945; RN 681/Fr/G/307, CN 378, March 26, 1945; RN 1527/Fr/G/663, CN 799, September 14, 1945; RN 1530/Fr/G/666, CN 808 (corrected version), July 9, 1946; RN 1684/Fr/G/712, CN 887 December 18, 1945; RN 1716/Fr/G/744, CN 989 (plus additions), March 27 1946; RN 2161/Fr/G/923, CN 1132 (corrected version), February 21, 1946; RN 3242/Fr/G/1365, CN 1573, June 3, 1946; RN 3433/Fr/G/1465, CN 1605, June 24, 1946; RN 5981/Fr/G/2099, CN 2321, July 22, 1947.

46. Case against Yoshio Yaki.
47. "Synopsis of Miscellaneous Trials (Canadian, Czechoslovak, Polish, Greek, Chinese, Dutch, and Norwegian)," 8.
48. Ibid., 7.
49. Case of Nicolas T. Sablan; United States of America v. Takuma Higashiji, UNWCC CN 166J, September 24, 1945; United States of America v. [unknown] Toshimitsu, UNWCC CN 171J, January 16, 1946; United States of America v. Masaharu Homma, UNWCC CN 184J, January 3, 1946; United States of America v. Tadashi Yoshida, Isamu Mori, Toshio Nozaki, et al., UNWCC CN 203J, June 17, 1946; United States of America v. Takeshi Kono, UNWCC CN 205J, June 12, 1946; United States of America v. Masanori Sugimoto, Masayoshi Murata, Masashi Masuyama, et al., UNWCC CN 206J, June 14, 1946; United States of America v. Mikio Taneichi, Yuzo Sakata, Taichi Yamada, et al., UNWCC CN 215J, May 27, 1946; United States of America v. Noriyuki Otsuka and Tadaktaa Kuwano, UNWCC FN P-119, CN 227J and CN 228J, July 1, 1946; United States of America v. Masakazu Yamaguchi, UNWCC CN 229J, August 19, 1946; United States of America v. Naoki Hamasaki, UNWCC CN 249J, January 27, 1947; United States of America v. Yasuo Hirose and Masaru Takata, UNWCC CN 250J, February 10, 1947; United States of America v. Hisamatsu Imamura, Toshiro Uchida, Mitsumasu Yano, et al., UNWCC CN 267J, March 20, 1947; United States of America v. Jiro Mizoguchi, Kiichi Kinoshita, Shigamosa Hirata, et al., UNWCC CN 371J, March 8 1946.
50. "Polish Charges against German War Criminals, RN 304/P/G/30, CN 30, September 20, 1944; RN 785/P/G/37, CN 38 (annex), April 23, 1945; RN 4947/P/G/173, CN 173, April 9, 1947; RN 7807/P/G/1504, CN 150, February 19, 1948.
51. See, for example, "Greek Charges against Italian War Criminals," RN 7275/Gr/It/95, CN 208/45, January 6, 1948; and "French Charges against German War Criminals," RN 4747/Fr/G/1950, CN 2210, February 27, 1947.
52. United States of America v. Noriyuki Otsuka and Tadataka Kuwano, January 25, 1947.
53. Goldstone, "Symposium," 13–14.
54. It is notable that the UNWCC chose the list of offenses created at the 1919 Paris Peace Conference because Axis powers Italy and Japan "had taken part in drawing [up the list] in its present form and Germany had not objected to it." See "Unofficial Meeting 2nd December 1943," 2. The UNWCC believed this historical underpinning would help guard against future criticism that it was creating new law. See also UNWCC, *Complete History of the United Nations War Crimes Commission*, 478.

55. It should be noted that the ICTY has dismissed *nullem crimen* challenges raised in cases involving charges of rape as a war crime or crime against humanity where the acts in question were committed after 1991. See Prosecutor v. Kunarac et al., 436–60; and Prosecutor v. Furundzija, 165–86. The precedent provided by the UNWCC-supported trials are most beneficial in the context of *nullem crimen* challenges involving acts committed prior to 1991, such as allegations involving the Khmer Rouge from 1975 to 1979.
56. UNWCC, "Unofficial Meeting 2nd December 1943, 3. Note that the domestic tribunals and commissions often cited international instruments such as the Hague Convention of 1907 as the legal basis for bringing charges against an accused. For instance, Article 46, which provides that "family honour and rights, the lives of persons, and private property, as well as religious convictions and practice, must be respected," was cited by national jurisdictions prosecuting rape in the documents they submitted to the UNWCC.
57. The ICTY trial chamber reviewed a number of approaches to this element taken by jurisdictions in Prosecutor v. Kunarac et al., 453–56; the chamber cited the following jurisdictions as ones that define rape as intercourse without consent: the United Kingdom, Canada, New Zealand, India, South Africa, Zambia, and Belgium.
58. Ibid., 443–45. The ICTY trial chamber cited jurisdictions that incorporate the use of force in their definitions, including Bosnia and Herzegovina, Germany, South Korea, China, Norway, Austria, Spain, and Brazil. The trial chamber also noted that Germany and Bosnia and Herzegovina's criminal codes recognize threats to the victim or to a third party as constituting force, for the purpose of defining rape. The cited portion of the Bosnia and Herzegovina code provides: "Whoever coerces a female not his wife into sexual intercourse by force or threat of imminent attack upon her life or body or the life *or body of a person close to her*, shall be sentenced to a prison term of one to ten years" (emphasis added).
59. Ibid., 442, 447–49. The judgment cites jurisdictions that incorporate this concept into the definition of rape, including Switzerland, Denmark, Sweden, Finland, Estonia, and Japan.
60. Scholars have taken differing views on this issue. See, e.g., Janet Halley, "Rape in Berlin: Reconsidering the Criminalisation of Rape in the International Law of Armed Conflict," *Melbourne Journal of International Law* 9 (2008): 78. Halley explores the jurisprudence regarding the issue of consent in conflict-related rape and the relationship of consent to coercive circumstances, suggesting that the presumption that such circumstances vitiate consent is problematic.
61. Prosecutor v. Jean-Paul Akayesu, 598.
62. Prosecutor v. Kunarac et al., 460; Prosecutor v. Gacumbitsi, ICTR Appeals Judgment, CN ICTR-2001-64-A, July 7, 2005, 153.
63. Prosecutor v. Kunarac et al., 460; Prosecutor v. Gacumbitsi, 155.
64. For a general discussion of non-consent in the jurisprudence of international tribunals, see Katie O'Byrne, "Beyond Consent: Conceptualising Sexual Assault in International Criminal Law," *International Criminal Law Review* 11 (2011): 500–502, 504–8.
65. Prosecutor v. Brima et al., 693.

66. Ibid., 694.
67. Elements of Crimes of the ICC, Articles 7(1)(g)-(1), 8(2)(b)(xxii)-1, and 8(2)(e)(vi)-1.
68. Ibid.
69. O'Byrne, "Beyond Consent," 513.
70. "Polish Cases against German War Criminals," RN 5438/P/G/372, CN 372, June 12, 1947; "Greek Cases against Bulgarian War Criminals," RN 6756/Gr/B/130, CN 451/36, and CN Gr/B/13, October 24, 1947; "Danish Charges against German War Criminals" (Case against Hans Harry Foul Kruger).
71. "Polish Cases against German War Criminals," RN 5996/P/G/702, CN 702 (July 24, 1947); "Greek Cases against Italian War Criminals," RN 47, 4553/Gr/It/37, CHN 206, CN Gr/1/37 (alleging that Italian national Marjoe Di Prima from Plermo, commanding officer of a disarming unit, gave underage girls cocaine before raping them), January 4, 1947.
72. Case against Yoshio Yaki.
73. Ibid.
74. Case of Nicholas T. Sablan, 29–30. The JAG record assigns its own page numbering system to the documents, henceforth cited as "JAG RP." This note is to JAG RP 40–41.
75. Ibid.
76. Ibid., JAG RP 63. No page number on document.
77. Ibid., JAG RP 65. No page number on document.
78. Ibid., 39, JAG RP 50.
79. "Yugoslav Charges against Italian War Criminals," RN 235/Y/It/8, CHN R/I/8 (September 25, 1944).
80. "Belgian Charges against German War Criminals," RN 1805/B/G/159, CN 150, November 14, 1945; "Greek Charges against Italian War Criminals," RN 6945/Gr/It/84, CN 109/45, November 14, 1947; "Yugoslav Charges against German War Criminals," RN 4021/Y/G/200, CN R/M/200, November 14, 1947.
81. Trial transcript of United States of America v. Masaharu Homma, December 19, 1945; trial transcript of United States of America v. Tomoyuki Yamashita, UNWCC RN 50J, December 7, 1945.
82. UNWCC, "Information Concerning Human Rights Arising from Trials of War Criminals," 216.
83. Rome Statute, Article 7(1)(g); ICTR Statute, Article 4(e); SCSL Statute, Article 2(g).
84. "Elements of Crimes of the International Criminal Court," Article 7(1)(g)-3.
85. "Polish Cases against German Nationals," RN 6974/P/G/1233, CN 1233 (previously submitted as no. 5897/P/G/643, adjourned on July 25, 1947, for further information); "French Charges against German War Criminals," RN 50/Fr/G/22; RN 51/Fr/G/23, CHN 25, and RN 54/Fr/G/26, CHN 28, all March 7, 1944.
86. "UNWCC Charges against German War Criminals," RN 10/Com/G/10, May 10, 1945. The crimes concerned events at Riga at the end of 1941; charges were brought against Nazi official Altemeyer based upon statements from German officers who

were prisoners of the American army in Germany. The commission brought the matter to the attention of Soviet authorities. More research is needed into the evidence given to US authorities in Germany and into the Soviet trials in Latvia on this case. The atrocities in and around Riga in December 1941 were notorious as an early example of mass executions. The commission took up the case in this unusual circumstance in which member states sought to draw the attention of a nonmember but allied state, the USSR, to a crime. The file contains relevant correspondence.

87. Case of Samuel T. Shinohara.
88. Ibid., 2, JAG RP 16.
89. Ibid., 57 [8], JAG RP 78.
90. Ibid., 57 [8], JAG RP 78.
91. Ibid., 58 [17–18], JAG RP 79.
92. Ibid., [22].
93. Ibid.
94. Ibid., 62 [77–80], JAG RP 83. Flores testified: "I knew they were not going to make a good girl out of me."
95. Ibid., [83].
96. Ibid., 59–64, JAG RP 80–85.
97. Ibid., 61–62, JAG RP 82–83.
98. Ibid., 63, JAG RP 84.
99. Ibid., 63, JAG RP 84.
100. Ibid., JAG RP 396. No page number on document.
101. Ibid.
102. Ibid.
103. Ibid., JAG RP 287. No page number on document.
104. Ibid., JAG RP 287 and RP 396. No page number on document.
105. Ibid. JAG RP 289. No page number on document.
106. Another UNWCC case suggests the court's possible consideration of a situation involving coercive circumstances. In a Polish case against a German national, forced prostitution charges were brought, alleging that the accused—Dr. H. Wilhelm, "while administrating" the Botanic Garden in Krakow—forced the women working at the Botanic Garden into prostitution by threatening to send them to forced labor camps or denounce them to the Gestapo if they refused. This threat and the broader context of intimidation may have played a role in the case, although complete trial records are needed in order to draw any conclusions. For further information see "Polish Cases against German War Criminals," RN 6974/P/G/1233, CN 1233 (previously submitted as CN 5897/p/g/643), adjourned on July 25, 1947.
107. For instance, imposing on victims a "deprivation of liberty"—an element of enslavement and sexual slavery under Articles 7(1)(c) and 7(1)(g)-2 of the "Elements of Crimes of the ICC"—often requires evidence similar to that used to prove that victims were "forced" into prostitution. See "Elements of Crimes of the ICC" Article 7(1)(g)-3, which requires proof that the "perpetrator caused one or more persons to engage in one or more acts of a sexual nature by force, or by threat of force or

coercion, such as that caused by fear of violence, duress, detention, psychological oppression or abuse of power, against such person or persons or another person, or by taking advantage of a coercive environment or such person's or persons' incapacity to give genuine consent"). See, e.g., Prosecutor vs. Kunarac et al., 108. Here the accused argued on appeal that he should not have been convicted of enslavement because "the victims testified that they had freedom of movement within and outside the apartment and could therefore have escaped or attempted to change their situation."

108. For further information see "Polish Cases against German War Criminals," RN 6974/P/G/1233, CN 1233 (previously submitted as CN 5897/P/G/643), adjourned on July 25, 1947; "French Charges against German War Criminals," RN 50/Fr/G/22; RN 51/Fr/G/23, CHN 25, and RN 54/Fr/G/26, CHN 28, all March 7, 1944.
109. Prosecutor v. Gacumbitsi, ICTR Judgment, CN ICTR-2001-64-T (June 17, 2004), 292; Prosecutor v. Jean-Paul Akayesu, 692; Prosecutor v. Gacumbitsi, ICTR Appeals Judgment, 185–87; Prosecutor v. Nikolic, ICTY Sentencing Judgment, Case No. IT-94-2-S (December 18, 2003), 119.
110. See Rome Statute, Article 28; ICTY Statute, Article 7(3): "The fact that any of the acts referred to in articles 2 to 5 of the present Statute was committed by a subordinate does not relieve his superior of criminal responsibility if he knew or had reason to know that the subordinate was about to commit such acts or had done so and the superior failed to take the necessary and reasonable measures to prevent such acts or to punish the perpetrators thereof." ICTR Statute, Article 6(3) contains the same language as ICTY Statute Article (7)(3).
111. See, e.g., Prosecutor v. Jean-Paul Akayesu, 451–60; Prosecutor v. Delalic et al., February 20, 2001, 383–93. See also Chile Eboe-Osuji, *International Law and Sexual Violence in Armed Conflicts* (Leiden: Martinus Nijhoff, 2012).
112. See, e.g., Prosecutor v. Galic, ICTY Appeals Judgment, CN IT-98-29-A, November 30, 2006, 117 and 182n518, which affirm, at least in principle, that a conviction of superior responsibility may be made on the basis of circumstantial evidence alone.
113. Prosecutor v. Kajelijeli, ICTR Judgment, Dissenting Opinion of J. Ramaroson, CN ICTR-98-44A-T, December 1, 2003, 17, 19, 37, 42, 73.
114. Ibid., 19, 33, 38.
115. Ibid., 17, 39.
116. Prosecutor v. Kajelijeli, ICTR Judgment, CN ICTR-98-44A-T, December 1, 2003, 683, 924.
117. "Polish Cases against German War Criminals," RN 5229/P/G/308, CN 308, May 21, 1947, and RN 5523/P/G/433, CN 433, June 19, 1947: "The phrase 'Common Design,' where used in connection with the perpetrators, means that the said perpetrators are charged with violation of the laws and usages of war in that they, acting in pursuance of a common design to commit the acts hereinafter alleged and as members of the Gestapo Staff and Command in Cracow did, between November 1939 and about February 1945, willfully, deliberately and wrongfully encourage, aid, abet and participate in the subjection of civilian nationals of nations then at war

with the German Reich, to cruelties and mistreatment, including killings, death by execution, beatings, tortures, starvation, abuses and indignities." The language suggests this mode of liability overlaps with current categories of criminal participation including aiding and abetting as a form of individual criminal responsibility and joint criminal enterprise. See, e.g., Rome Statute, Article 25; ICTY Article 7(1); ICTR Article 6(1), comparing jurisprudence regarding joint criminal enterprise. Also Prosecutor v. Simic et al., ICTY Judgment, CN IT-95-9-T, October 17, 2003, 149, with the finding that terminology such as "common purpose" or "acting in concert together and with others" connotes joint criminal enterprise liability. For more on the development of this mode of liability at the UNWCC, see Kip Hale and Donna Cline, "Holding Collectives Accountable: The UNWCC's Undervalued Role in Developing Collective Responsibility, Yesterday and Today," *Criminal Law Forum* 25, no. 102 (2014): 261–90.

118. Case of Nicolas T. Sablan.
119. Such as "French Charges against German War Criminals," RN 5981/Fr/G/2099, CN 2321, July 22, 1947, in which a German national was accused of raping a twenty-year-old woman.
120. "Polish Cases against German War Criminals," RN 5514/P/G/424, CN 424, June 19, 1947.
121. "Danish Charges against German War Criminals" (Case against Hans Harry Foul Kruger). The report states that on April 26, 1945, "the accused dressed in the uniform of the German police accosted in 2 cases women which he happened to come across in the street and threatening to use his pistol he forced them to sexual intercourse."
122. "Greek Cases against Bulgarian War Criminals," RN 3733/Gr/B/64, CN B/63 and 285/24, brought against a Bulgarian mayor of Orphanos and a corporal of the gendarmerie for raping four women in Orphanos, August 1, 1946; RN 3758/Gr/B/89, CN B/63 and CN 285/24, brought against Boris Tsernosemski, "president of the Community of Siderohorion Kavalla" for raping two women, August 1, 1946; RN 4065/Gr/B/105, CN B/63 and CN 285/24, against Lt. Gregory Solef for raping two women and castrating a priest, among other offenses, September 19, 1946; RN 277, 5025/Gr/B/118, CN I4/46 and CN Gr/B/118, against a sergeant-major of the gendarmerie, Stephan Slatef, for raping an eighteen-year-old girl, April 25, 1947; RN 398, 7063/Gr/B/156, CN 491/46, CN Gr/B/157, against Ivan Georgi Katsarov in Stavroupoli, who was accused of raping several Greek women, including one who was under age at the time (some Greek cases involving direct perpetration allege that the rapes resulted in the deaths of the victims) November 18, 1947; RN 359, 6756/Gr/B/130, CN 451/36 and CN Gr/B/13, October 24, 1947, a case brought against Nicola Yantzev, a rural guard in Nea Santa, who was accused of going to the house of Constantia Bika in July 1942, where he raped and assaulted her, resulting in her death some days later from hemorrhage. See also RN 323, 6957/Gr/B/151, CHN 360/46, CN Gr/B/152, a case against Kosta Mitsev, a gendarme in Doxato, who was accused of entering by force the house of Nicolaos Pispas in December 1942, where he allegedly raped Pispas's daughter Polyxeni several times, resulting in her death

"some hours later," November 18, 1947; RN 323, 6961/Gr/B/155, CHN 360/46, CN Gr/B/156, a case against gendarme Petko Stefan Netev for the alleged rape, in February 1943, of Eftymia Lazaridis, who afterward committed suicide, November 27, 1947. It should be noted that the record does not indicate any murder charges for the resulting deaths in any of these cases.

123. "French Charges against German War Criminals," RN 4/F/G/4, CN 8, February 1, 1944; RN 7/F/G/7, CN 35, March 7, 1944; RN 8/F/G/8, CN 10, March 7, 1944; RN 13/F/G/13, CN 7, February 1, 1944.
124. This specifically occurred in the Yamashita case, detailed later in the text. See UNWCC, *Law Reports*, 4–35.
125. "Summary Translation on the Trial of Takashi Sakai."
126. Ibid., 5.
127. UNWCC, *Law Reports*, 4–35.
128. United States of America v. Naoki Hamasaki, 13, 382.
129. Ibid., 21–22.
130. Domestic protections include "rape shield laws" in place in many jurisdictions of the United States, which limit the nature of the questions that victims of sexual assault or rape can be asked. For an overview of these laws, see "Rape Shield Statutes," available at www.ndaa.org/pdf/NCPCA%20Rape%20Shield%202011.pdf. The United Kingdom has similar protections under Section 41 of the Youth Justice and Criminal Evidence Act 1999, available at www.justice.gov.uk/courts/procedure-rules/criminal/docs/2012/crim-proc-rules-2013-part-36.pdf. For an overview of European Union laws on this issue, see "The Legal Process and Victims of Rape: A Comparative Analysis of the Laws and Legal Procedures Relating to Rape, and Their Impact upon Victims of Rape, in the Fifteen Member States of the European Union." Available at www.drcc.ie/wp-content/uploads/2011/03/rapevic.pdf. For protections in international tribunals, see International Criminal Court Rules of Procedure and Evidence, UN Doc. PCNICC/2000/1/Add.1 (2000), Rule 16(2), which obligates the registrar to "take gender-sensitive measures to facilitate the participation of victims of sexual violence at all stages of the proceedings." See also Rule 87, which provides that the chamber may order protective measures, such as expunging a victim's or witness's identifying information, allowing use of a pseudonym, nondisclosure orders, admitting testimony obtained via closed-circuit television, videoconferencing, or *in camera*. Rule 88(1) provides further: the chamber "may, taking into account the views of the victim or witness, order special measures such as, but not limited to, measures to facilitate the testimony of a traumatized victim or witness, a child, an elderly person or a victim of sexual violence." See also Rule 75 of the ICTY Rules of Procedure and Evidence, DN IT/32/Rev. 49, May 22, 2013, which provides for general protections for all victims and witnesses, stating that a chamber may order protective measures, including the use of a pseudonym, the redaction of identifying information from public records, or the giving of testimony through image- or voice-altering devices or closed-circuit television. See also Rule 75 of the Rules of Procedure and Evidence of the ICTR (adopted June 29, 1995, as amended April 10, 2013), DN ITR/3/REV.1, which uses the same language as ICTY Rule 75; Rule 34(A)(ii) of the ICTY Rules of

Procedure and Evidence, which provides that the Victim Witness Support Unit shall "provide counselling and support for [victims and witnesses], in particular in cases of rape and sexual assault." See also ICTR Rule 34 (A)(ii), which provides for the Victim Witness Support Unit to provide "physical and psychological rehabilitation, especially counselling in cases of rape and sexual assault."

131. Ibid. See ICTY Rules of Procedure and Evidence, Rule 96(iv): "Prior sexual conduct of the victim shall not be admitted in evidence or as defence"; ICTR Rules of Procedure and Evidence, Rule 96(iv) contains the same language. Also see ICC Rules of Procedure and Evidence, Rule 70(d): "Credibility, character or predisposition to sexual availability of a victim or witness cannot be inferred by reason of the sexual nature of the prior or subsequent conduct of a victim or witness."
132. Case of Samuel T. Shinohara.
133. Ibid., 2, JAG RP 16 (charging document); ibid., 74–80, JAG RP 95–101 (trial record); ibid., 43, JAG RP 372 (appeals record). In Shinohara's appeal, defense counsel cited the argument put forth by his counsel at trial, who asserted the following: "Gentlemen, a woman who has been convicted of vagrancy before the war, is unmarried at the time but the mother of a 12 year old child, had a venereal examination before the war, and who went to Piti to look over a whorehouse, and two weeks later went to stay there and stayed two days and nights without working, is not a person who entered a life of prostitution under duress. . . . This unfortunate woman knew what work she was to do and entered it voluntarily. As to her credibility, I call your attention to the fact that upon cross examination, in answer to the question: 'Have you ever been convicted of a crime?' she said, 'No.' Recall the testimony of Sgambelluri, who said she had been convicted of vagrancy before the war."
134. Ibid., 78, JAG RP 99.
135. Ibid.
136. Ibid.
137. Ibid.
138. Case of Nicholas T. Sablan, 2.
139. Ibid., 34, JAG RP 45. The charges identify this victim as Ida Duenas Diego but she gives her name as Agueda Duenas Diego during her testimony. See 2, JAG RP 11.
140. Ibid., 34–35, JAG RP 45–46.
141. Ibid.
142. Ibid.
143. Ibid., 35 [26–27], JAG RP 46.
144. Ibid., [27].
145. Ibid., [37].
146. Prosecutor's Office of Bosnia and Herzegovina v. Zrinco Pincic, Court of Bosnia and Herzegovina Appellate Verdict, CN KRZ-08-502, November 28, 2008, 10, detailing defense argument on appeal that the trial panel erred in limiting the defense's cross-examination's of Witness A regarding her prior sexual history. The appellate panel cited Article 264 of the Criminal Procedure Code (CPC) of Bosnia and Herzegovina (BiH), which states, in relevant part, that the defense is not permitted to

ask the complaining witness about "any sexual experiences prior to the commission of the criminal offense in question. No evidence offered to show the injured party's involvement in any previous sexual experience, behavior, or sexual orientation shall be admissible." The appellate panel found that the trial panel did not err by limiting cross-examination to exclude questioning about previous sexual acts and that it properly prevented defense counsel from questioning the expert witness on prior rapes suffered by Witness A, pursuant to Article 264 of the CPC of BiH.

147. Susan Brownmiller, *Against Our Will: Men, Women, and Rape* (New York: Fawcett-Columbine, 1975).

148. Torild Skard, "Getting Our History Right: How Were the Equal Rights of Women and Men Included in the Charter of the United Nations?" *Forum for Development Studies* 35, no. 1 (2008): 37–60.

2

A NEW PARADIGM FOR PROVIDING JUSTICE FOR INTERNATIONAL HUMAN RIGHTS VIOLATIONS

A renaissance in international criminal justice that is drawn from the lost lessons of World War II can empower the international community today, and not just on issues of sexual violence. Ongoing and apparently unstoppable war crimes in Africa and the Middle East as well as the turgid performance of the International Criminal Court together invite us to give up on international criminal justice altogether.

One hoped-for lesson of this book is to learn that the United Nations at war achieved far more effective prosecution of war crimes than is remembered. But more important is the fact that even at a time when a Nazi victory seemed almost certain, the Allies put legal justice among their primary war aims, created a mechanism while the war was still in progress, and convicted thousands of war criminals after the war. Faced with comparatively minor adversaries today, those who advocate abandoning international criminal justice risk encouraging simple defeatism.

The four-country Nuremberg International Military Tribunal considered twenty-four cases. By contrast, between 1944 and 1948 over eight thousand cases involving thirty-six thousand individuals and units were approved for prosecution at scores of civil and military tribunals supported by the seventeen-member-nation UNWCC. Member nations of the commission presented cases to it for consideration in the form of dossiers—charge files—summarizing the case. If the cases were approved, the individuals and units were listed as accused war criminals and the nations concerned sought to apprehend them and bring them to trial in national courts.

This body of legal and political action by nation-states changes the paradigm—the framework of thinking—for international criminal justice today.[1] The

UNWCC should be considered as a major platform on which to build international criminal justice to add to those foundations of the International Military Tribunal at Nuremberg. The commission worked under enemy fire—including the bombardment of London by V-1 and V-2 rockets—and deserves respect for this if for no other reason. Faced with enemy bombardment, some of the world's finest lawyers went about the business of organizing justice. Nuremberg took place amid that city's rubble after the fighting was over, but in 1944 and 1945 the commissioners went to work not knowing if they would survive the day.

German bombers restarted night attacks on London in February 1944, and followed with bombings by V-1 cruise missiles—the "doodlebugs"—in June and V-2 ballistic missiles in September. The last V-2 exploded in London late in March 1945. In the final paragraph of the final meeting minutes of the commission record, Lord Wright reminded Professor André Gros of France of "their first meeting in the cellar of the Law Courts when the 'doodle bombs' were falling."[2]

By the standards of the twenty-first century, the commissioners would be regarded as combat veterans deserving of hero status and medals. In their day they were just getting on with the job. Several friends of US commissioner and former congressman Ambassador Herbert Pell were killed.[3] The UN officers club in St. James's Square, where Pell was wont to entertain, was bombed out.[4]

The UNWCC's Far Eastern Sub-Commission in Chungking, China, also operated in a combat zone, and conditions in China were extremely harsh. When the commission worked in hazardous conditions, then they did so knowing both that the victims of the Nazis were subjected to revolting treatment and that the resistance was taking the time to send out evidence of these crimes to be used in legal proceedings.

The popular understanding and support for international criminal justice as demonstrated by the preliberation indictments of war criminals revolutionizes our understanding of resistance movements and international justice. If there has been any connection between the two it has been to focus on rough justice meted out to alleged collaborators. The record shows that long before the appearance of the Nuremberg trials, a great many internationally supported war crimes cases had been developed by states working through the commission.

This chapter presents an overview of the central organizational achievements of the commission and its associated courts and tribunals and emphasizes their potential to contribute to international criminal justice in the twenty-first century. International criminal justice should not be seen as a Western creation. This account highlights Chinese, Ethiopian, and Indian actions taken to bring justice to war criminals in the 1940s and details the system set up in the mid-1940s to provide a legal response to human rights violations as well as the actions of some key individuals involved in the effort. Several specific issues discussed later are previewed (such as the crime of aggression, the defense of only following orders, and the collective responsibility for crimes committed by a group).

Legal and Political Amnesia

Before launching into this analysis, we need to answer the obvious question: If the UNWCC is so important, why was its work neglected for so long? The short answer is, then, as now, some states were hostile to the idea of war crimes trials. In the United States and the United Kingdom, an interagency conflict (displaying a very modern feel) contested the UNWCC's work (see chapters 7 and 8).

The widespread public demand for a legal and military response to the actions of the Nazis came from political parties and religious organizations, from the governments exiled to London from Europe, from China and the pre-independence government of India, and from a few Anglo-American officials. Their combined efforts subsequently contributed to the creation of the International Military Tribunal (IMT) that tried the Nazi leadership at Nuremberg and the Universal Declaration of Human Rights and Genocide Convention.

The UNWCC's mostly secret work was overshadowed by the resources and publicity accorded to the trials at Nuremberg. Subsequently, the US priority of rebuilding Germany required the closure of the commission and sealing of its files. The accepted story was that the commission's ineffectiveness meant that it warranted little more than a footnote in any account documenting the development of international criminal justice.

Cold War rivalries following World War II prohibited any revival of international criminal justice for decades, despite the efforts of nongovernmental groups such as the Russell Tribunals that were established in response to the Vietnam War. When the international community determined to add a legal and trial-based component to its actions in response to the Balkan wars of the 1990s, the model that presented itself was Nuremberg. Samantha Power, in her discussion of the foundations of the International Criminal Tribunal for the former Yugoslavia, commented that it drew so heavily upon the "memory of Nuremberg" that even the architecture, judicial pomp, and physicality of the courtroom in which trials took place "seemed deliberately chosen to harken back to the UN tribunal's functional parent."[5] The commission's work went unnoticed.

Creation of the United Nations War Crimes Commission

The UNWCC was created through the initiative of the states that had been victims of Nazi invasion and aggression in order to provide an international system of justice to reinforce and legitimate the actions of these countries after liberation. There was a need for some glimmer of warning to perpetrators and hope to victims that justice would be done. This alone is a useful example for our own time. Moreover, with respect to contemporary debates, a number of precedents stand out and can be headlined. As already demonstrated, rape was prosecuted routinely, albeit unevenly. Legal responsibility for criminal acts was

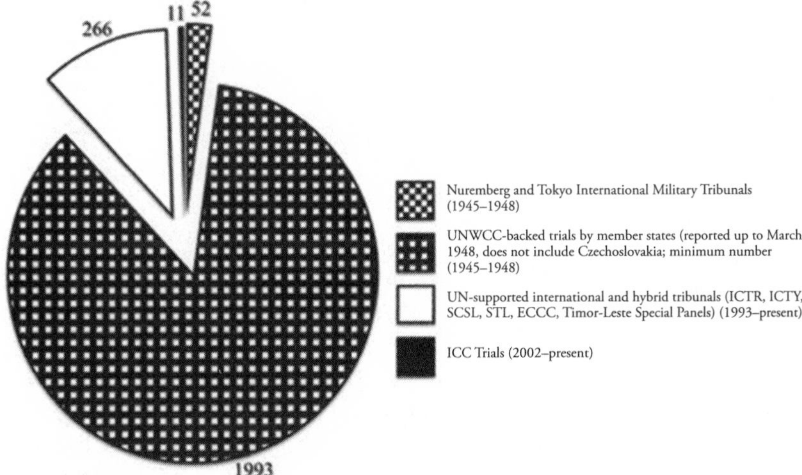

FIGURE 2.1. Number of Trials Carried Out by International Military Tribunals, by Post–World War II UNWCC-Supported Tribunals, and by UN-Supported Post–Cold War Judicial Bodies

Source: UNWCC, *Complete History of the United Nations War Crimes Commission and the Development of the Laws of War* (London: Her Majesty's Stationery Office, 1948), 3, 518; Francis Pakes, *Comparative Criminal Justice* (London: Routledge, 2014), 198; ICTY, *Key Figures of ICTY Cases* (January 20, 2015), available at http://www.icty.org/x/file/Cases/keyfigures/key_figures_en.pdf; ICTR, "Key Figures of ICTY Cases" (accessed November 26, 2015), available at http://www.unictr.org/sites/unictr.org/files/publications/ictr-key-figures-en.pdf; SCSL and "No Peace Without Justice Gender and Human Rights Program," *Impact and Legacy Survey for the Special Court for Sierra Leone* (August 2012), available at http://www.rscsl.org/Documents/NPWJ_SCSLImpactLegacyReport_04OCT12.pdf; STL, "The Cases" (accessed November 26, 2015), available at http://www.stl-tsl.org/en/the-cases; ECCC, "Caseload" (accessed November 26, 2015), available at http://www.eccc.gov.kh/en/caseload; http://www.trial-ch.org/en/resources/tribunals/hybrid-tribunals/special-panels-for-serious-crimes-timor-leste/main-cases.html (Timor Leste data); and "Situations and Cases" (accessed November 26, 2015), available at https://www.icc-cpi.int/en_menus/icc/situations%20and%20cases/Pages/situations%20and%20cases.aspx.

attributed to commanders who gave the orders, to whole groups, such as the Gestapo, that carried them out, and to named foot soldiers who fired the guns and did the torturing.

A uniform system of collecting facts and evidence about war crimes was developed and implemented. Prosecutions took place in the states where they occurred and were pursued with urgency and economy.

The UNWCC was comparatively inexpensive. Lord Wright frequently stated that the UNWCC was the least expensive international commission known in history—a fact in the 1940s that remains compelling today. The UNWCC's total annual expenditures were:

> October 10, 1943–March 31, 1944: £730
> April 1, 1944–March 31, 1945: £4,238
> April 1, 1945–March 31, 1946: £12,462
> April 1, 1946–March 31, 1947: £15,137
> April 1, 1947–March 31, 1948: £15,388[6]

In current pounds this equals around £1.7 million, or US$2.6 million *total*, clearly a small fraction of the usual operating budget of many international organizations.[7] By contrast, Stuart Ford, the former assistant prosecutor at the ECCC in Cambodia (which itself has spent over $200 million to convict only three defendants[8]) estimates that by the end of 2015, UN member states spent approximately $6.3 billion total on the ICC, on the International Criminal Tribunals for the former Yugoslavia and for Rwanda, on the ECCC, and on the Special Court for Sierra Leone. As Ford has remarked, "It is well understood by scholars and practitioners that trials at international criminal courts are expensive, at least compared to the average domestic criminal prosecution."[9]

In many ways the direct financial comparison is unfair because the UNWCC was not a trial or prosecutorial structure but rather a mechanism by which domestic trial structures could be coordinated and given further authority. The UNWCC provided a way for prosecutors to draw upon expert legal advice, get support in their early planning, and exchange information about the disposition of prisoners and evidence. The true cost of the postwar criminal justice project would have to include costs across the various jurisdictions and countries where the commission was active. But, rather than trying to handle thousands of cases and defendants on its own, the commission was able to distribute this burden across a wide range of other jurisdictions and legal systems. Nonetheless, the juxtaposition is striking because it demonstrates what could be done by taking advantage of existing systems and providing them with the support and legal coordination they lack in order to avoid duplication and unnecessary expense.

In brief, the political debates of the 1940s resonate today. State-interest pragmatists in Washington and London at the time were unsuccessful in preventing an international court to try the enemy leadership, and it was eventually created at Nuremberg.

Official Resistance to Prosecuting War Crimes

How would we fare today without the legacy of Nuremberg? The International Military Tribunal that was eventually established at Nuremberg stands as a single shining light. However, Nuremberg did not stand alone. It was the jewel in the crown of a whole range of wartime efforts to bring justice. But it was a jewel that was almost never cut for Nuremberg nearly never happened.

As US ambassador Herbert Pell alleged at the time, despite years of official statements that the Nazis would face justice, there was no political will in Washington for war crimes trials until the spring of 1945. Only through the efforts of a coalition of small states, civil society, and leading actors, notably President Franklin Roosevelt, were any war crimes processes created; eventually an inescapable momentum was imposed onto the new administration of President Harry Truman.

Before surveying the commission's central operations in London, it is important to present a few caveats. Some of the conventions of the time, notably the use of the death penalty, are not practices that fit easily with twenty-first century international standards. Peace did not break out across Europe with the Nazi surrender. It was a time of chaos, vigilante violence, and temporary mob rule. Retribution against collaborators was often unjust and inevitably politically charged. This book does not examine the problem of collaborator crimes and is confined to international war and high crimes. For example, what we now call "ethnic cleansing" was at that time—an earlier incarnation of liberal internationalism—regarded as a "good thing" and was described with the more innocuous term "population transfer." Its advocates proposed this transfer as a means of producing what they hoped would be stable and ethnically unified states. Germans were expelled forcibly by the millions from what is now Polish and Czech territory. It is not the intention of this book to sanitize the conduct of governments and peoples in the postwar period.

However, this book does show that, from early on in the war, the exiled governments anticipated the problem of mob justice against the defeated enemy and they organized an international judicial response to anticipate and (largely) prevent indiscriminate retribution by citizens. What is remarkable is that in that most extreme circumstance of total world war, countless peoples and states devoted enough energy to create a significantly effective system of international criminal justice.

The commission's remit was limited and could only support prosecutions of enemy personnel for offenses committed against the citizens of UN member states during World War II. It had no mandate to address the actions of those citizens against others. It also sought jurisdiction over crimes committed by the Germans against their own people, notably the Jews, but it was unsuccessful (although this unsuccessful pressure contributed to the adoption at Nuremberg of the notion of crimes against humanity, a term used by the UNWCC more than a year earlier in the spring of 1944).

Chinese and Indian Leadership

There is a tendency to view international criminal law, indeed international human rights in general, as a Western or even an Anglo-American invention.[10] The records of the UNWCC show a very different picture, however. Of the "big four" powers (United States, Great Britain, China, and Russia), China was the first and only one of them to support the foundational declaration, "Punishment for War Crimes," articulated by the exiled governments in London in January 1942.[11] (Held at St. James's Palace, here this declaration will be referred to as the "St. James's Declaration.") China went on to become a founding and prominent member of the UNWCC. It proposed and created in Chunking the Far Eastern Sub-Commission that indicted thousands of Japanese nationals for crimes committed in China. Chinese representatives proposed that the use of narcotics to subdue a population be considered a war crime, and helped lead in the effort to create a crime of aggression and crimes against peace.[12]

The Chinese role in developing the UNWCC was led by Ambassador Wellington Koo who, beginning in 1943, sought to create the subcommission in China to prosecute Japanese aggressors (the subject of more detailed attention in chapter 4). China's legal response to atrocities has been the subject of a number of recent studies, which confound the notion of international criminal law as a Western concoction and emphasize the Confucian roots of Chinese policy and diplomatic practice as it relates to the debate on the creation of the UN Universal Declaration of Human Rights in 1948.[13]

China was taking part in decisions primarily concerning international criminal law in Europe. Week after week, throughout the course of the war and its aftermath, the Chinese ambassador debated international law and devised strategies that affected policy in London and Washington for lawfully holding Axis soldiers and officials to account. From a twenty-first-century perspective it is hard to imagine the revolutionary nature of these actions, and the evidence flies in the face of centuries of racial prejudice. Ambassador Pell, the US representative on the commission, spoke in glowing terms of the role of Ambassador Koo, whom he had known in America. Nevertheless, the actions of the Chinese government took place against the backdrop of its own country's crumbling nationalist regime and in the face of the Japanese attack, the rise of the communists, and the US demands on China's military priorities.[14]

India's role—though still somewhat limited by its just-still-imperial status—was also unprecedented. The representatives of the imperial government of India sat alongside their British and Dominion colleagues on the UNWCC in London and in China, often taking different positions from the British. India continued its role in the UNWCC after independence and argued successfully for the UNWCC to consider Ethiopian cases.[15]

Military tribunals are a lasting legacy of the work of the commission. One Indian official at the London meetings, Niharendu Dutt-Majumdar, wrote the first draft proposal for joint military tribunals working closely with Pell and drawing on US experience going back to the Civil War.[16] Dutt-Majumdar's work began the process.[17] This form of justice is best known today under the names of the notorious concentration camps where the trials were held: British trials at Belsen and American trials at Dachau.

Chinese and Indian judges were also active in tribunals across the Pacific and on mainland China. The debate over Asian involvement in the post–World War II trials usually goes no further than to note the rejection of the crime of aggression as imperial hypocrisy by Indian judge Radhabinod Pal at the Tokyo trial. From the earliest moments, however, the ideas and practices of international criminal justice that exist today had significant and at times leading input from the representatives of non-Western states.

Chinese support for developing the legal foundation for the crime of aggression was rooted in its century-long experience of multiple imperialisms;[18] indeed, it was built on a long history of Chinese legal process and provides strong evidence that contradicts the views of a single Indian judge at Tokyo.[19] Scholars who rely exclusively on Pal to support their arguments might explain why they are justified in overlooking the concurrent position of the Chinese state, which has been a matter of public record for over seven decades. The Chinese nationalist government used the experience of World War II to draw a legal line against further aggression—in parallel to its successful efforts to overturn the unequal treaties governing many Western concessions in China.

A Global System of Complementary Justice

The lack of a system in which international bodies support national legal efforts to tackle war crimes is one of the key problems in twenty-first-century international criminal justice. This approach, dubbed "complementary justice," is one of the foundations of the International Criminal Court. The ICC mainly has a role when nations are unwilling or unable to bring their own nationals to trial. Even so, when a state is struggling to implement its own legal measures, there is no global system of support. The varied circumstances of Cambodia, Rwanda, and Libya illustrate this difficulty. While the ad hoc tribunals created in response to events in Africa and the Balkans had UN mandates and set important precedents, these mandates were limited and are coming to the end of their usefulness.[20] Although the ICC has a mandate to develop a system that supports national jurisdictions and exists to prosecute cases when national legal systems fail to prosecute, it has thus far failed to perform a broad supporting role.

The UNWCC was created by its member states to provide international legitimacy to local processes by giving legal, political, and administrative support for trials that they wished to conduct themselves. Unlike the ICC, however, it was never accorded a full judicial function by its members. The declaration by the three great powers (the USSR, the US, and the UK) in Moscow of November 1943 mandated that, aside from Nazi leadership, war criminals would face justice in the territories where they had committed their crimes.[21] In contrast, today's ICC trials are conducted in the Netherlands even when the accused are not from within the highest levels of government.

The Hague is remote, both geographically and culturally, from the site of modern war crimes. The *gacaca* trials in Rwanda, according to national practice, echo the intent of Allied practices in World War II.[22] The UNWCC provided legal and practical advice to national jurisdictions, and legal legitimacy, even authority, to national legal processes—a useful model of "complementarity" for the twenty-first century. The process in 1944 was that a country would send to the commission proposed charges to determine whether there was a case to answer—that is, on *prima facie* grounds—and after receiving the commission's endorsement, a trial would ensue. This process was used across Europe and the Far East, with over eight thousand dossiers under consideration against more than thirty-six thousand persons.[23] On this basis, weak states today might bring details of cases to the ICC for validation of their own processes rather than simply handing them over to the court. Regional organizations like the Arab League and the African Union—where currently an important pushback against an emphasis on African cases can be seen—might develop regional courts that similarly operate with the voluntary endorsement of the ICC. Indeed, the African Union enabled this by adding criminal jurisdiction to the African Court in 2014.

In the 1940s states large and small, from the United States to Luxembourg, considered it necessary and important to obtain international support for their national actions. This precedent should lend weight to authorizing such a relationship for our own era. UNWCC member states were Australia, Belgium, Canada, China, Czechoslovakia, Denmark (after liberation), France, Greece, India, Luxembourg, the Netherlands, New Zealand, Norway, Poland, the United Kingdom, the United States, and Yugoslavia. South Africa was present at the commission's creation but never became involved further.[24]

The commission did not appear out of nowhere. It had important historical, intellectual, and organizational predecessors. Mark Lewis has very usefully described the link between World War I–era legal processes and those of World War II.[25] The 1919 Commission on Responsibilities at Versailles developed ideas for international war crimes trials and formalized a number of key debates on international law. There were unsuccessful attempts to try the defeated German kaiser, to hold the Turks to account for the massacre of Armenians, and to task German courts with prosecuting German soldiers. These failures discouraged some British officials from revisiting the issue of war crimes and, for its part, the US State Department continued to oppose the concept of crimes against humanity—a concept that a number of states had wished to use to try Turkish officials for the Armenian Genocide of 1915.[26]

The London International Assembly (LIA) of exiled governments of continental Europe created a body to consider war crimes issues. During 1942 and 1943 it compiled a four-hundred-page report, "Punishment for War Crimes," intended to be used by a future formal international investigative and prosecuting body.

Many LIA members went on to represent their countries on the UNWCC, a body they had worked to create. Notably, though, neither the American nor British governments joined Russia in sending an observer to the LIA, though the assembly lists among its members some legal experts of these three countries and also the consul of Brazil, Luiz Felippe de Rego Rangel.[27]

The British government is often characterized as finding the exiled governments a nuisance with little to offer militarily and too much time on their hands. But this is too glib. One need only mention the role of Poland's air crew in the Battle of Britain or Norway's merchant shipping fleet in the Battle of the Atlantic to recognize the early and vital contribution of both to Britain's survival during the war. As we will see regarding the war crimes issue, British derision was simply a smoke screen for differences of policy.

When the commission first met it was chaired by senior British officials; though Roosevelt had expected that the US ambassador would chair the body, officials in the State Department made assurances to the British, with whom they had close relations, that they would do so instead. The first British chair, Sir Cecil Hurst, legal advisor to the Foreign Office, had been part of the British delegation to the Hague in 1907 and was an eminent and foundational architect of international law through the League of Nations. The British government formally recognized the commission's diplomatic status as an international organization while Hurst was chair. He was succeeded by a career foreign ministry official, Sir Robert Craigie, and then by Lord Wright of Durley. Durley, a very senior British judge and member of the Inner Temple of the Bar, had a reputation for creating sound if somewhat drily written legal precedents.

The first and only senior commissioner from the United States was Herbert Pell. Pell had been a college classmate of Roosevelt and came from the same social class of families in the Northeast that had been wealthy since before the American Revolution. Pell had been elected to Congress and then served as a US ambassador, first to Portugal and then to Hungary, before the bombing of Pearl Harbor. After having seen the impact of Nazism through these roles he consistently warned of the threat posed by Nazism and a German people who had not experienced invasion in the war of 1914–1918.

The commission members from continental Europe were among their country's most senior legal experts, judges, and foreign diplomats. The Belgian member, Marcel de Baer, went on to become his country's attorney general. The Czech delegation was especially strong, including the country's future president, Eduard Benes, as well as Bohuslav Ečer, Herbert Mayr Harting, and Egon Schwelb. Schwelb later had a distinguished career as deputy director of the UN's human rights division. French representatives included René Cassin, who was awarded the 1968 Nobel Peace Prize for his role in the creation of the Universal Declaration of

Human Rights, and André Gros, a member of the French team at Nuremberg. All had fled their countries in fear of their lives, with some having been interrogated by the Gestapo and been on the receiving end of some of the crimes they then prosecuted.

The commission had three specific duties: to investigate and record the evidence of war crimes; to report to the governments involved on cases that appeared to have adequate evidence to support a prosecution; and to make recommendations to member governments concerning questions of law and procedure in order for them to be able to conduct trials.[28] The UNWCC had three committees that met weekly in the British Royal Courts of Justice on the Strand in central London to implement these mandates: Committee 1, Facts and Evidence; Committee 2, Enforcement; and Committee 3, Legal Affairs. After the war the commission moved offices, first to Church House in Westminster and then to Lansdowne House.

Member states set up "national offices" within their governments to liaise with the commission, to coordinate investigations, to collect evidence, and to create new legal structures to handle war crimes where necessary.[29] All national office staffs interacted directly with the main UNWCC headquarters in London as they conducted investigations and constructed lists of suspected war criminals for review. This process began in early 1944 and continued until the end of 1948 when the commission closed. A National Offices Conference (NOC) was held in London in May and June 1945, which discussed policy and practices for the pursuit and trial of war criminals and its surviving papers document a number of national statutes for war crimes trials.[30]

The UNWCC conducted the only comparative analysis of the different national practices to take place during this time, in a report to the UN Economic and Social Council (ECOSOC) in 1948.[31] Until recently, virtually no additional research on the work of the many national offices has been conducted; in many cases the documents of these offices have only just been released to the public (for example, via the ICC Legal Tools Archive).

In addition to setting up national offices, some governments created legislation that enabled war crimes courts. For example, by August 1943 Belgium and the Netherlands had both passed laws creating courts to try war crimes in their own countries following liberation.[32] These are listed and sometimes reprinted in the NOC minutes and in the report to the UN ECOSOC. This ability to create new national laws while the war continued and their homelands were under occupation is further indication that the laws that were applied to perpetrators were not retroactive.

Through its committee structure the UNWCC supported the national offices in conducting investigations and in some cases investigated on its own, through the work of a small staff team that also liaised with governments through the

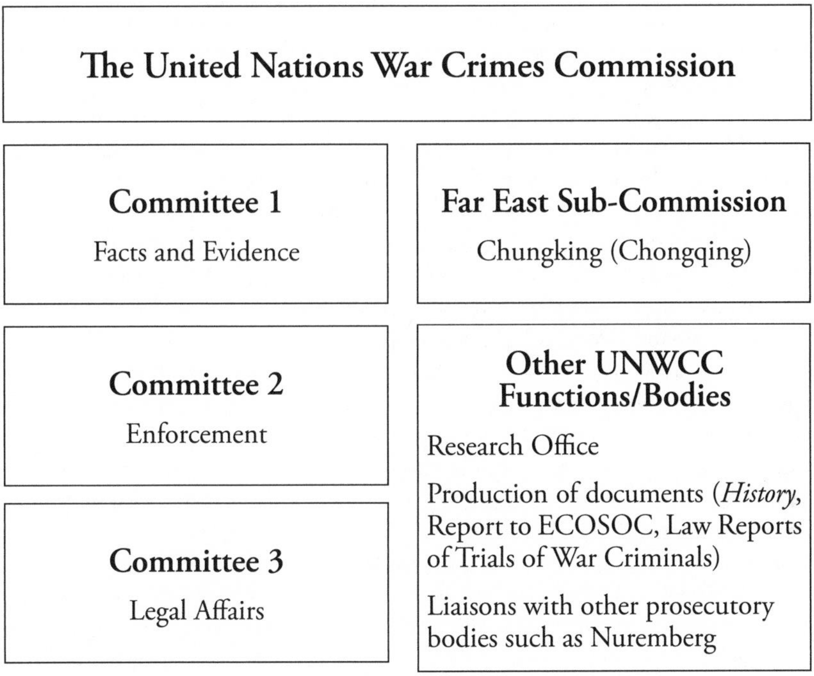

The United Nations War Crimes Commission

Committee 1
Facts and Evidence

Far East Sub-Commission
Chungking (Chongqing)

Committee 2
Enforcement

Committee 3
Legal Affairs

Other UNWCC Functions/Bodies
Research Office
Production of documents (*History*, Report to ECOSOC, Law Reports of Trials of War Criminals)
Liaisons with other prosecutory bodies such as Nuremberg

FIGURE 2.2. The Structure of the UNWCC

offices.[33] The UNWCC was ultimately responsible for issuing *prima facie* decisions on the cases brought to it by the national offices.[34]

Great Britain provided facilities to house the commission but the staff was international and all member states contributed to its funding on the same basis, as had been agreed to by the forty-four-nation UN Relief and Rehabilitation Administration created in November 1943.[35] However, the United States and United Kingdom, both of which had the resources, limited the commission's annual budget to around $60,000 each (in 1940 dollars).[36]

When national prosecutions resulted from UNWCC support, states were encouraged to send trial reports to be recorded by Committee 1. Seventy of these cases were selected by the commission and published in the fifteen volumes of the Law Reports.[37] This was done to explicitly complete the process by which legal precedents are typically established in the Anglo-Saxon legal tradition. The process of law reporting in some countries was not fully formed by the time of the UNWCC's closure in 1948, thus many countries were unable to finish and process their reports in time to be included in the commission's publications. Nevertheless, over two thousand trials were recorded by the commission and thousands more cases await publication. The efforts by the national offices and Committee 1 were complemented by the enforcement work of Committee 2, which initially was led by Ambassador Pell.[38]

In the spring of 1944, through the work of Committee 2, the commission developed proposals for the Allies to create mechanisms for war crimes offices in the territories of defeated enemies[39]—a proposal that contributed to the creation of the Central Register of War Criminals and Security Suspects (CROWCASS) under the supervision of Gen. Dwight D. Eisenhower, supreme commander of the Allied Expeditionary Force.[40] Other initiatives include a detailed proposal for mixed military tribunals under the major Allied commands that was later adopted by many UNWCC member states.[41] Discussions within the UNWCC on how to bring accused war criminals to trial—largely led by India and the United States—resulted in the issuing of the British Royal Warrant, which gave legal authority to war crimes tribunals, and the creation of the British War Crimes Executive, according to an official briefing for new political leaders following the Labour Party victory in July 1945.[42] This British practice was followed in Australia and Canada.

As the commissioners developed proposed structures for international criminal justice in 1944, their priority was to create an international criminal court, which had been a goal of legal activists since 1919. It had been debated throughout the interwar period in the context of the League of Nations and within the London International Assembly. Hersch Lauterpacht's proposed organization for International Penal Reform also contributed to the debate over such a court. As William Schabas has demonstrated, the essentials of the proposed court by the UNWCC anticipated the Rome Statute of the International Criminal Court of 1998 by half a century.[43] An international criminal court in 1944 was vetoed by British and American foreign ministry officials and was pursued but with no results during the postwar period. The work was then left in limbo as an aspiration of the UN in association with the Universal Declaration, but the effort engaged few people outside the International Law Commission until the successful revival of the concept in the 1990s.

Committee 3 received complex legal questions from the different participating countries in order to generate debate and ultimately arrive at decisions and recommendations for the practice of the national offices. Crimes addressed by national military tribunals included crimes that did not have specific geographic locations, crimes committed against Allied nationals in Germany, and crimes that had occurred across parts of the Far East under various forms of colonial administration.[44] The military authorities, primarily from the United States and the United Kingdom, were also responsible for aiding their respective nations in conducting investigations and holding trials. The integration of military authorities was also an effort to have trials proceed "without waiting for the initiative of any one Government on the matter."[45] Collectively, Allied military authorities conducted a large number of trials around Europe and in the Far East.[46]

Contemporaneous jurists, including US Supreme Court justice Robert Jackson and UK solicitor general David Maxwell Fyfe, were clear in their belief that the UNWCC played an import judicial role and helped develop the London Charter for Nuremberg. Justice Jackson sent his staff to meet with the commission and they did so at various times through the spring and summer of 1945.[47] He himself once came with Maxwell Fyfe to discuss the way the UNWCC could contribute to the IMT. For commission members, this was welcome input, though it fell short in creating the large international criminal court some had wanted.

When Jackson and Fyfe met with the commission in July, Jackson noted that he already knew most the members from earlier informal discussions but carefully warned the commissioners on the record that the effort to create the IMT might fail—in which case US efforts might be confined to trying individuals for crimes against US prisoners of war:

> Mr. Justice Jackson ventured to say that work was being diligently and successfully carried on in respect of the plan for an international tribunal for the trials of the designers of a great series of wrongs. He hoped and believed that it would be successful, but if not, there were enough charges against those men and he could assure the meeting that there would be very active pursuits made—insofar, at least, as crimes against American prisoners of war were concerned.[48]

The Development of Key International Legal Principles

The commission and national governments responded to two detailed requests for evidence that Jackson had sent in early July. In the end, though, the Nazi leaders' own documents condemned them more effectively than much of the evidence that had been gathered so painstakingly by commission members. (Later chapters include detailed discussions of whether criminal charges and court processes, especially regarding crimes against humanity, were applied fairly.)

Aggression

A discussion of the crime of aggression was present in the commission's debates from the very outset. The *Complete History of the United Nations War Crimes Commission and the Development of the Laws of War* notes: "By far the most important issue of substantive law to be studied by the Commission and its Legal Committee was the question of whether aggressive war amounted to a criminal act."[49] Faced with thorny questions related to the underdeveloped and highly contentious topic in the complex context of World War II, the commission sought legal ground in the Kellogg-Briand Pact of 1928. The first two articles of the pact sought to address the concept of aggressive war, explicitly stating that the contracting parties "condemn recourse to war for the solution of international controversies" and that they must agree that settlement and solution for all disputes and conflicts should be sought only through peaceful means.

The *Complete History* makes the case that in the context of the World War II, "there are clear precedents for the rule that it is an unlawful act to start and wage an aggressive war. It has indeed been long held by humanity that he who does such a thing is guilty of a supreme offense."[50] Despite the seemingly clear legal basis for concluding that launching and waging a war of aggression is against international law, the politics of the time limited the advancement of this principle, just as it does today. Not until after the London Charter was concluded in August 1945 was the principle of aggressive war endorsed by the commission.[51]

The August 1946 trial of Japanese military commander Takashi Sakai conducted by the UNWCC-supported Far East Sub Commission, however, provides evidence of the commission's support for the concept on legal grounds. Sakai was charged with crimes against peace and crimes against humanity. His indictment for numerous acts of atrocity against Chinese civilians is directly referenced in the trial report. He was found guilty "of participating in the war of aggression" and sentenced to death.[52]

Following the debate within the commission and the Sakai trial, Lord Wright stated: "I am quite satisfied that in the future, even though other forces may temporarily and on occasion prevail, the nations of the world will not let the principle go."[53] It is clear, however, that issues surrounding the crime of aggression continue to be contested, as demonstrated by the ambiguous nature of the conclusions of the Kampala Conference in 2010 that presented the ICC with the opportunity to incorporate the concept into the Rome Statute. While a historic agreement was reached on the adoption of a definition of the concept, the ICC will not be able to enforce the crime until 2017 at the earliest.[54]

The Sakai trial does not provide an indisputable precedent on the crime of aggression; it does, however, represent support for the adoption of the principle that remains relevant today. Additional precedents may be found in the national legislation for war crimes tribunals and in national practice. A question for further historical research is whether China pursued cases other than the Sakai case on the basis of the charge of making aggressive war or committing crimes against peace. Both the Yugoslav and Greek courts were empowered to pursue these types of cases by their own laws, for example.[55] The London Charter for the IMT influenced the subsequent drafting of US military tribunals and the US and Allied regulations in operation in the Pacific and China.[56] These examples of national practice indicate a wider acceptance and inclusion of crimes against peace than is usually assumed.

Superior Orders

The question of the validity of the defense of superior orders was also debated throughout the duration of the UNWCC, whose members unanimously agreed that "the mere fact of having acted in obedience to the orders of a superior does not of itself relieve a person who has committed a war crime from responsibility."[57] The UNWCC did not, however, seek to impose this view on its members. Many individuals accused in national trials pleaded the defense of superior orders. Such attempts were often anticipated by the members of the commission and highlighted in numerous debates seeking to address "the extent to which persons pledged by law to obey orders of their superiors, in particular those issued by heads of State and Governments, were to be held personally responsible for acts committed by them in subordinate positions."[58] The issue was viewed as significant enough that Committee 3 appointed a subcommittee to address it.

Historical disagreements about the issue complicated the commission's efforts to clarify the principle. There is at least one instance—the Leipzig War Crimes Trials of the 1920s—when an officer was acquitted for his role in sinking a hospital ship on the grounds that he had obeyed orders from a superior. German law at that time held that such a defense was valid.[59] After numerous debates, the commission's official statement was that "civil and military authorities cannot be relieved from responsibility by the mere fact that a higher authority might have been convicted of the same offence. It will be for the court to decide whether a plea of superior orders is sufficient to acquit the person charged from responsibility."[60] Along these same lines, another of the key issues that the UNWCC addressed was the legal conundrum presented by traditional standards of immunity for state officials and their ubiquitous practice of issuing orders to subordinates to engage in illegal actions. This contention is echoed in the commission's report to the UN ECOSOC in 1948.[61] This report also discusses criminal liability for keeping watch while a crime is being committed, passing on orders, participating in lynching, and instigating crime and common design.[62] Ultimately, Wright expressed this in his introduction to the *Complete History:* "I think it can now be taken as settled that [the] plea is not a sufficient defense but that it may have effect by way of extenuation."[63]

Collective Responsibility

Justice Jackson decided that the United States should adopt the commission's recommendations regarding collective responsibility; for example, he believed membership in the Gestapo could be considered a legitimate form of criminal responsibility in the charter for the IMT.[64] The subsequent use of this form of responsibility at Nuremberg set important precedents. But the broad and thorough consideration of the issue by the UNWCC had a substantial impact and should be used today.

The importance of using historical precedents for group responsibility for international crimes had been analyzed by Kip Hale and Donna Cline of the American Bar Association.[65] They have explored a number of recent cases and legal practices and conclude that there is much to be learned from the UNWCC-supported trials, especially because some of them have already been used to support modern trials.[66] As they write, "Most importantly, these [World War II] cases are perfect examples of how the newly released trove of UNWCC archival material can have a significant impact on the work of today's judges, legal scholars, and practitioners who are seeking further clarification on Joint Criminal Enterprise or other legal issues."[67] Hale and Cline also argue for the relevance of the UNWCC's effort to the interpretation of the collective responsibility provisions of the ICC statute, which applies criminal responsibility to an individual for both co-perpetration and indirect perpetration.[68] This language is similar to the UNWCC's recommendation to member states that they "commit for trial, either jointly or individually, all those who, as members of these criminal gangs, have taken part in any way in the carrying out of crimes committed collectively by groups."[69] Hale and Cline have urged that "ICC judges and practitioners would be well advised to research the Commission's debate on this provision as well as investigate any national jurisdictions that applied this provision at trial. The interpretative and precedential value is manifest." (These issues are more fully explored in chapter 6.)

Conclusion

It is not easy to change our way of thinking to match new evidence. Nevertheless, the quality and the intellectual and political breadth and depth of the commission demands it and the effort is worth it. For, rather than being an American-centered focus on elite criminals based on the wisdom of a few intellectual giants of international law, we now have a culturally richer and more democratic tradition on which to base our pursuit of justice. Now having established the relevance and scope of the new paradigm, we need to see how the UNWCC's work was connected to what is in many ways the defining event of that age: the Holocaust.

The commission did not begin its work until late in 1943. To understand the political pressures that led to the commission's creation—two years before the Nuremberg trials—it is necessary to review the Allied response to Nazi atrocities and especially to the extermination of Europe's Jews in the early years of the war.

Notes

1. Richard Goldstone, foreword to "The United Nations War Crimes Commission Symposium," in *The United Nations War Crimes Commission: The Origins of International Criminal Justice*, ed. William Schabas et al., special double issue of *Criminal Law Forum* 25, no.1–2 (2014): 9–15. Dan Plesch and Shanti Sattler, "Changing the Paradigm of International Criminal Law: Considering the Work of the United Nations War Crimes Commission of 1943–1948," International Community Law Review 15, no.2, (2013): pp. 203–223; Dan Plesch and Shanti Sattler "A new paradigm of customary international criminal law," in Criminal Law Forum 25 no. 1 (2014): pp. 17–43; Dan Plesch and Shanti Shattler, "Before Nuremberg: Considering the Work of the United Nations War Crimes Commission of 1943-1948," in Bergsmo, Morten and Cheah, Wui Ling and Yi, Ping, (eds.), Historical origins of international criminal law. (Brussels, Torkel Opsahl Academic EPublisher, 2014): pp. 437–473; Dan Plesch, "Building on the 1943-48 United Nations War Crimes Commission", in Wartime Origins and the Future United Nations, (Oxford, New York: Routledge, 2015), pp. 79–98; Dan Plesch, Thomas G. Weiss, and Leah Owen, "UN War Crimes Commission and International Law: Revisiting World War II Precedents and Practice," in Global Community: Yearbook of International Law and Jurisprudence 2015. (Oxford: Oxford University Press, 2016):71–112.
2. UNWCC, "Minutes of Last Meeting of Commission held on Wednesday, March 31, 1948," 15–26.
3. Leonard Baker, *Brahmin in Revolt: A Biography of Herbert C. Pell* (New York: Doubleday, 1972), 266–68.
4. (London) *Times*, June 20, 1944.
5. Samantha Power, *A Problem from Hell: America and the Age of Genocide* (New York: HarperCollins, 2002), 484.
6. UNWCC, *Complete History of the United Nations War Crimes Commission and the Development of the Laws of War* (London: Her Majesty's Stationery Office, 1948), 3, 134.
7. Dan Plesch and Shanti Sattler, "A New Paradigm of Customary International Law: The UN War Crimes Commission of 1943–1948 and Its Associated Courts and Tribunals," *Criminal Law Forum* 25, no. 1–2 (2014): 17–23.
8. Charlie Campbell, "Cambodia's Khmer Rouge Trials Are a Shocking Failure," *Time* magazine, February 13, 2014, available at http://time.com/6997/cambodias-khmer-rouge-trials-are-a-shocking-failure/.
9. Stuart Ford, "How Leadership in International Criminal Law Is Shifting from the United States to Europe and Asia: An Analysis of Spending on and Contributions to International Criminal Courts," *Saint Louis University Law Journal* 55 (2011): 956–1257.
10. To varying degrees, and in different ways, depending on the author. See, for example, Stephen Hopgood, *The Endtimes of Human Rights* (Ithaca, NY: Cornell University Press, 2013) for a perspective that stresses the difference between grassroots

"human rights" and Western-stressed "Human Rights"; see also Raimundo Panikkar, "Is the Notion of Human Rights a Western Concept?" *Diogenes* 30, no. 120 (1982): 75–202, for an exploration of what the Western historical origins of human rights actually mean for non-Western polities; and Nico Krisch, "International Law in Times of Hegemony: Unequal Power and the Shaping of the International Legal Order," *European Journal of International Law* 16, no. 3 (2005): 369–408, for an exploration of the role of unequal power relations in the development of international criminal law.

11. US Department of State, "Foreign Relations of the United States: Diplomatic Papers, 1942, general; the British Commonwealth; the Far East," vol. 1 (1942), 45. See https://history.state.gov/historicaldocuments/pre-truman.
12. The Inter-Allied Information Committee, "Punishment for War Crimes: The Inter-Allied Declaration Signed at St. James's Palace London," January 13, 1942, 16.
13. Wen-Wei Lai, "China, the Chinese Representative, and the Use of International Law to Counter Japanese Acts of Aggression: China's Standpoint on the Period Covered by UNWCC Jurisdiction," *Criminal Law Forum* 25, no. 1–2 (2014): 111–232; Anja Bihler, "Late Republican China and the Development of International Criminal Law: China's Role in the United Nations War Crimes Commission in London and Chungking," in *Historical Origins of International Criminal Law,* vol. 1, ed. Morten Bergsmo, Cheah Wui Ling, and Yi Ping, 507–40 (Brussels: Torkel Opsahl Academic EPublisher, 2014).
14. Rana Mitte, *China's War with Japan, 1937–1945: The Struggle for Survival* (London: Penguin, 2013).
15. UNWCC, "Minutes of Meeting of Commission Held on Wednesday, September 24, 1947 at 3.00 p.m.," September 24, 1947, 6.
16. UNWCC, "Minutes of Thirty-Fourth Meeting Held on October 3rd 1944," comment of Marcel de Baer, 5.
17. UNWCC, "Proposal for a United Nations Military Tribunal (Mr. Dutt's Proposal as Amended by a Drafting Committee)," DN II/26, August 1, 1944; and Proposal for United Nations Military Tribunals, DN II/26/1, August 16, 1944.
18. Inter-Allied Information Committee, "Punishment for War Crimes," 16.
19. See Shi Bei, Zeng Siqi, and Zhang Qi, "Chinese Confucianism," 141–270; and Bihler, "Late Republican China."
20. Martin J. Burke and Thomas G. Weiss, "The Security Council and Ad Hoc Tribunals: Law and Politics, Peace and Justice," in *The Security Council as Global Legislator*, ed. Vesselin Popovksi and Trudy Fraser, 241–65 (London: Routledge, 2014).
21. United Nations Information Organization, "Moscow Declaration on Atrocities, by President Roosevelt, Mr. Winston Churchill and Marshal Stalin," issued on November 1, 1943, available at http://avalon.law.yale.edu/wwii/moscow.asp.
22. Tens of thousands of *génocidaires* languished in Rwandan prisons in the late 1990s, awaiting domestic prosecution by the country's underresourced criminal justice system. To expedite trials the government turned to a local system of informal arbitration called *gacaca*. Villages have traditionally convened such assemblies to settle

disputes over issues on property, marriage, and theft, with the participation of members of the community through resolutions acceptable to both parties. The *gacaca* courts for genocide have operated since 2006 and have attempted to combine reconciliation and justice although, unlike traditional *gacaca*, they are formal institutions established by law and have the ability to impose sentences of up to thirty years in prison. These courts combine elements of criminal justice and restorative justice in a local alternative to the strictly criminal approach of the ICTR. While views on their effectiveness have been mixed, they at least provide an alternative to many years in jail for the thousands awaiting trial and they constitute only one element in the country's transitional justice regime. See, for example, Phil Clark, *The Gacaca Courts, Post-Genocide Justice and Reconciliation in Rwanda: Justice without Lawyers* (Cambridge: Cambridge University Press, 2010); and Eric Stover and Harvey Weinstein, eds., *My Neighbor, My Enemy: Justice and Community in the Aftermath of Mass Atrocity* (Cambridge: Cambridge University Press, 2004).

23. UNWCC, *Complete History of the UNWCC*, 150.
24. The brief membership of South Africa and the late entry of Denmark account for membership being variously referred to as of sixteen or seventeen states.
25. Mark Lewis, *The Birth of the New Justice: The Internationalization of Crime and Punishment* (Oxford: Oxford University Press, 2014).
26. Donald Bloxham, *The Great Game of Genocide: Imperialism, Nationalism, and the Destruction of the Ottoman Armenians* (Oxford: Oxford University Press, 2005); Gary Jonathan Bass, *Stay the Hand of Vengeance: The Politics of War Crimes Tribunals* (Princeton: Princeton University Press, 2000); Lewis, *Birth of the New Justice*; Vahakn N. Dadrian, *Warrant for Genocide: Key Elements of Turko-Armenian Conflict* (Piscataway, NJ: Transaction, 1999).
27. London International Assembly, *Reports on Punishment of War Crimes* (London, 1942) 1.
28. UNWCC, *Complete History of the UNWCC*, 3.
29. The Netherlands laws authorizing the trial of war criminals, for example, were enacted in 1943; French ones were passed in 1944.
30. Minutes and papers of the UNWCC National Offices Conference, 1945, available at cisd@soas.ac.uk.
31. UNWCC, "Information Concerning Human Rights Arising from Trials of War Criminals," report to the UN Human Rights Division, UN DN E/CN.14-AM9, 1948, 125–245 and appendix, available at http://www.unwcc.org/documents/.
32. UNWCC, "Information Concerning Human Rights." For the Netherlands, see Netherlands Extraordinary Penal Law Decree of December 22, 1943 (statute book D. 61), 130, and the decrees of December 22, 1943 [statute book D. 62]; for Belgium, see page 291.
33. UNWCC internal memo, April 18, 1945.
34. Some criticism of this has been that it was based on hearsay evidence, a matter discussed by the UNWCC itself. See UNWCC, "Information Concerning Human Rights," no. 1. The colloquial sense of "hearsay" as gossip has been used to denigrate

the work of the UNWCC as a whole. Also see the UN ARMS application package for the UNWCC.

35. Dan Plesch, *America, Hitler and the UN: How the Allies Won World War II and Forged a Peace* (London: I. B. Tauris, 2011), 124–225.
36. UNWCC, UNWCC Budget for the Fourth Fiscal Period April 1, 1947–March 21, 1948, Statement A: Actual Expenditure for 1946–1947, £15,137, DN C258.
37. UNWCC, *Law Reports of Trials of War Criminals,* vols. 1 –15 (London: Her Majesty's Stationery Office, 1947), 2.
38. See Graham Cox, "Seeking Justice for the Holocaust: Herbert C. Pell versus the US State Department," *Criminal Law Forum* 25, no. 1–2 (2014): 77–210.
39. UNWCC, "Minutes of Twenty-First Meeting Held on June 6th 1944," 3, and the accompanying document, UNWCC, "Establishment in Enemy Territory of War Crimes Offices –Draft Report by the Commission submitted by Committee II," May 30, 1944. See also UNWCC, "Minutes of Twenty-Second Meeting Held on 13 June 1944," 3, and the accompanying document, UNWCC, "Recommendation Regarding the Establishment in Enemy Territory of an Appropriate Agency to Assist the Commission in Its Work Adopted by the Commission on 13 June 1944," June 15, 1944.
40. UNWCC, "Minutes of Thirty-Second Meeting Held on 19th September 1944," 2–2. Also see UNWCC, "Recommendation in Favour of the Establishment by Supreme Military Commanders of Mixed Military Tribunals for the Trial of War Criminals," September 26, 1944.
41. UNWCC, "Minutes of Thirty-Second Meeting." The commission approved the adoption of a proposal for a United Nations War Crimes Court. See the accompanying documents to this proposal: UNWCC, "Draft Convention for the Establishment of a United Nations Joint Court—Memorandum by the Drafting Committee," DN C49, September 22, 1944; UNWCC, "Convention for the Establishment of a United Nations Joint Court–Draft Presented by Committee II," DN C50, September 22, 1944; UNWCC, "Explanatory Memorandum to Accompany the Draft Convention for the Establishment of a United Nations War Crimes Court," October 6, 1944.
42. Memorandum from the Treasury Solicitors Office for the Attorney General, July, 1945. Part of the document is held in the National Archives of the United Kingdom, "Note to the Attorney-General on Procedure; Miscellaneous Papers Regarding Charges; List of British Subjects of European Extraction Killed in the Philippines," archival reference TS 26/897.
43. William Schabas et al., "The United Nations War Crimes Commission and the Origins of International Criminal Justice," *Criminal Law Forum* 25, no. 1–2 (2015): 1–2.
44. See the October 1945 trial of Kapitanleutnant Heinz Eck and Four Others, who were accused of killing crew members of the Greek steamship *Peleus* in the British "Military Court for the Trial of War Criminals."
45. UNWCC, "Minutes of Thirty-Third Meeting held on 26th September, 1944."
46. The UNWCC's reliance on military authorities was due in part due to the UNWCC's commitment to providing justice that was swift and effective. The meaning of "swift and effective" was debated among members throughout the existence of the

UNWCC. The internal document "Recommendation in Favour of the Establishment by Supreme Military Commanders of Mixed Military Tribunals for the Trial of War Criminals," dated September 26, 1944, declared that the strategy would be used "so that no criminals escape trial and punishment because of the inability to effect a speedy trial" (UNWCC DN C.52(1)). In hesitation, French representative M. Gros addressed the idea in a written statement submitted at the UNWCC's thirty-first meeting of September 12, 1944: "Although the notion of swift justice is found in manuals of military law, 'justice' is something that does not admit of qualifying adjectives." Also see UNWCC, *Complete History of the UNWCC,* 5.

47. See, for example, UNWCC, "Minutes of Sixty-Third Meeting held on 1 June 1945"; UNWCC, "Minutes of Seventieth Meeting held on 18 July 1945."
48. UNWCC, "Minutes of Seventieth Meeting held on 18 July 1945," 2.
49. UNWCC, *Complete History of the UNWCC,* 180.
50. Ibid., 17.
51. UNWCC, "Minutes of Seventy-Seventh Meeting held on 29 August 1945." See also earlier discussions in UNWCC, "Minutes of Thirty-Fifth Meeting held on 10 October 1944," 3–23; UNWCC, "Minutes of Thirty-Sixth Meeting held on 17 October 1944," 3–20; UNWCC, "Minutes of Forty-First Meeting held on 6 December 1944," 4–2.
52. Trial of Takashi Sakai, Chinese War Crimes Military Tribunal of the Ministry of National Defence, Nanking, CN 83, August 29, 1946, found in UNWCC, *Law Reports of Trials of War Criminals,* vol. 16 (London: Her Majesty's Stationery Office, 1949), 1–2.
53. UNWCC, *Complete History of the UNWCC,* 10.
54. The Kampala Conference defined the crime of aggression as "the planning, preparation, initiation or execution, by a person in a position effectively to exercise control over or to direct the political or military action of a State, of an act of aggression which, by its character, gravity and scale, constitutes a manifest violation of the Charter of the United Nations."
55. UNWCC, "Information Concerning Human Rights" (no. 5), 288, 295–97.
56. Ibid., 158.
57. UNWCC, "Report to the Governments on the Plea of Superior Orders," DN C86, M54, 2.
58. UNWCC, *Complete History of the UNWCC,* 263.
59. See the case of Lt.-Com. Karl Neumann, commander of the submarine *U67,* and the case of the sinking of the hospital ship *Dover Castle* on May 26, 1917.
60. UNWCC, *Complete History of the UNWCC,* 138.
61. UNWCC, "Information Concerning Human Rights," UN DN E/CN.14-AM9, 1948, 217–36.
62. Ibid., 212–16.
63. UNWCC, *Complete History of the UNWCC,* 11.
64. UNWCC, Minutes of Seventieth Meeting held on 18 July 1945, DN M70, 1945, 8.

65. Kip Hale and Donna Cline, "Holding Collectives Accountable: The UNWCC's Undervalued Role in Developing Collective Responsibility, Yesterday and Today," *Criminal Law Forum* 25, no. 1–2 (2014): 261–90.
66. As in the Tadić case before the ICTY, for example. ICTY, Prosecutor v. Tadić, Appeals Judgment, CN IT-94–2-A, July15, 1999, paras. 142, 194, 197, 198.
67. Hale and Cline, "Holding Collectives Accountable," 288. Examples of such content are widespread throughout the commission's archives; one definition the commission agreed upon and issued to Allied governments can be found at UNWCC, "Collective Responsibility for War Crimes: Recommendation to the Governments," adopted by the commission on May 16, 1945, Commission DN C105(1).
68. Stefano Manacorda and Chantal Meloni, "Indirect Perpetration versus Joint Criminal Enterprise: Concurring Approaches in the Practice of International Criminal Law?" *Journal of International Criminal Justice* 9, no. 1 (2011): 159–278.
69. UNWCC, "Collective Responsibility for War Crimes: Recommendation to the Governments," by Professor André Gros, March 28, 1945.

3

WHEN THE ALLIES CONDEMNED THE HOLOCAUST

In 1942 the American, British, and Soviet governments led all the United Nations members in a public declaration that explicitly condemned Hitler's ongoing extermination of European Jews. This UN declaration was the most formal and multinational of a series of statements on Nazi atrocities, with the first stretching back to 1940 and others going forward beyond the Nuremberg trials of 1945–46. This official condemnation of human rights violations in the early 1940s—far stronger than commonly believed—provides a strong precedent for action today and helps combat Holocaust denial. But it also places a greater responsibility on governments that did speak out then and yet did so little to help the victims.

Raul Hilberg, a great historian of the Holocaust, has written: "The Allied powers . . . did not think of the Jews. The Allied Nations who were at war with Germany did not come to the aid of Germany's victims. The Jews of Europe had no allies. In its gravest hour Jewry stood alone, and the realization of that desertion came as a shock to Jewish leaders all over the world." Hilberg speaks of "the periods of total silence from 1941 through 1942 and the subsequent generality of language" condemning atrocities in general but not acts against the Jews in particular.[1]

In their book, *Atrocities on Trial*, Patricia Heberer and Jürgen Matthäus go so far as to declare that, "during the war, there was not even a word to properly describe the murder of the European Jews by Germany and its allies, other than the bizarre euphemism [Final Solution] coined by the perpetrators."[2] In his book *The Abandonment of the Jews*, David Wyman also observes: "The UN declaration [of 1942] was better publicized in the American press than most developments connected with the Holocaust."[3] Wyman is one of the few scholars to mention this declaration or other similar condemnations of the extermination of the Jews and other groups during World War II, though he gives it little attention himself. The recent volume by Michael David-Fox, Peter Holquist, andAlexander M. Martin, *The Holocaust in the East: Local Perpetrators and Soviet Responses*, provides a fresh and much more detailed and nuanced account of Soviet political and legal responses to the Holocaust than has been previously understood and provides a useful counterpart to this.[4]

Early Allied Condemnations of the Holocaust and Nazi Atrocities

The Czech and Polish governments released a joint statement in November 1940 concerning the unprecedented nature of Nazi atrocities—the first governments to make this claim in a national statement.[5] A statement from the Polish government alone was released shortly thereafter, which informed the public about the Nazi attempt to eradicate Polish national identity.[6] In the following months other governments began to speak out too. In October 1941 Franklin Roosevelt and Winston Churchill released parallel statements promising "retribution." Churchill emphasized that atrocities were occurring "above all behind the German fronts in Russia." He continued by adding: "Retribution [for] these crimes must henceforward take its place among the major purposes of the war."[7] While robust and judicial in tone, none of these statements made specific reference to the plight of the Jews.

The Soviet Foreign Ministry issued notes regarding German atrocities to all nations it had diplomatic relations with in November 1941 and again in January 1942.[8] These statements, published by the British government in London, included descriptions of numerous Nazi pogroms, particularly those that had occurred at Lvov. One document, for example, included this description: "On June 30 1941 the Hitlerite bandits entered Lvov, and on the very next day arranged a massacre under the slogan 'Kill the Jews and Poles." Another related that

> A horrible massacre and pogrom were perpetrated by the German invaders in the Ukrainian capital, Kiev. Within a few days the German bandits killed and tortured to death 52,000 men, women, old folk and children, dealing mercilessly with all Ukrainians, Russians and Jews who in any way displayed their fidelity to the Soviet Government. Soviet citizens who escaped from Kiev gave an agonizing account of one of these mass executions: "A large number of Jews, including women and children of all ages, was gathered in the Jewish cemetery of Kiev. Before they were shot, all were stripped naked and beaten. The first persons selected for shooting were forced to lie face down at the bottom of a ditch and were shot with automatic rifles. Then the Germans threw a little earth over them. The next group of people awaiting execution was forced to lie on top of them, and shot, and so on."

It appears that of all the states at war with Nazi Germany, the Soviet Union was the first to specifically mention the mass murder of Jews. These statements and other statements like it are important because they contradict the established account of total silence by the Allies on the murder of the Jews. (They do not, however, rehabilitate the general reputation of Stalin and Soviet institutional antisemitism.)

On January 13, 1942, British foreign secretary Anthony Eden, along with the US and Soviet ambassadors, attended a meeting at St. James's Palace to make a statement committing themselves to achieving "punishment for war crimes"—a meeting that had been initiated by the exiled governments of continental Europe. These ambassadors declined, however, to sign a statement issued that same day by representatives of Belgium, Czechoslovakia, France, Greece, Luxembourg, the Netherlands, Norway, Poland, and Yugoslavia. Among the leaders who *did* sign were Gen. Charles de Gaulle, leader of the "Fighting French," Gen. Władysław Sikorski of Poland, and the future secretary-general of the United Nations, Norwegian foreign minister Trygve Lie. The Chinese government—through its representative Wunsz King—soon gave its support. The Soviet Union, the United Kingdom, and United States, however, appear never to have signed the document, as their attention turned to the creation of a weaker general investigative commission.

The signed document, entitled "Punishment for War Crimes," is short, and appears in its entirety here:

> Whereas Germany, since the beginning of the present conflict which arose out of her policy of aggression, has instituted in the Occupied countries a regime of terror characterised amongst other things by imprisonments, mass expulsions, the execution of hostages and massacres,
>
> And whereas these acts of violence are being similarly committed by the Allies and Associates of the Reich and, in certain countries, by the accomplices of the occupying Power,
>
> And whereas international solidarity is necessary in order to avoid the repression of these acts of violence simply by acts of vengeance on the part of the general public, and in order to satisfy the sense of justice of the civilised world,
>
> Recalling that international law, and in particular the Convention signed at The Hague in 1907 regarding the laws and customs of land warfare, do not permit belligerents in Occupied countries to commit acts of violence against civilians, to disregard the laws in force, or to overthrow national institutions,
>
> (1) affirm that acts of violence thus inflicted upon the civilian populations have nothing in common with the conceptions of an act of war or of a political crime as understood by civilised nations,
>
> (2) take note of the declarations made in this respect on 25th October 1941, by the President of the United States of America and by the British Prime Minister,

> (3) place among their principal war aims the punishment, through the channel of organized justice, of those guilty of or responsible for these crimes, whether they have ordered them, perpetrated them or participated in them,
>
> (4) resolve to see to it in a spirit of international solidarity that those guilty or responsible, whatever their nationality, are sought out, and handed over to justice.[9]

The document's release was accompanied by speeches by representatives of the signatory states, but the simple message was clear. It spoke of the unprecedented nature of the Nazi atrocities and of the coming need for an international legal process to restore civilization after victory. Sikorski specifically recognized that the benefit of what they were doing would be slight for both the victims and their persecutors—given that the event took place at the height of the war—but he explained that the purpose was to create new international law to deal with the new international crimes.

On January 20, 1942, Nazi officials met in secret at Wannsee outside Berlin to plan the extermination of the Jews in what they called the "Final Solution." Despite the Nazis' attempts at secrecy, the Polish resistance was soon gathering the dreadful data on the operation as the Nazi plans went into operation.

On July 9, 1942, British information minister Brendan Bracken hosted a press conference alongside Polish government representatives in London. The subject was the "German terror in Poland." The Polish government had issued a document detailing Nazi atrocities in communities and in concentration camps across their country.[10] While this action of the Polish government is known in some scholarship, it remains unnoticed by important and authoritative works. This document was also distributed to the press in the United States by the Roosevelt Administration and the Allied Information Service in New York. A fuller, 750-page account of German atrocities, later published in Poland as the *Black Book*, provided background material to the press.

The press package from July 9th contains extensive evidence and describes what later became known as the Holocaust. The full report was submitted by Polish minister of home affairs Stanislaw Mikolajczk. The following passage provides some particularly significant details that deserve presentation in full:

> The existence of 23 concentration camps where Poles are confined is known to us: Belzec, Buchenwald, Ciechanów, Dachau, Dobraya, Dyle, Działdowo, Dzisionta, Flossenburg, Grossrosen, Grudziadz, Hamburg, Hohenbrueck, Mathausen, Nasielsk, Oranianburg, Oswiecim, Plonsk, Ravensbrueck, Sierpe, Stutthof, Trawniki, and Treblinka. . . .
>
> In all places throughout the length and breadth of Poland there are executions, murder and terror.

The Jewish situation is still worse. That of the ghetto in Warsaw is already well known—where hunger, death, sickness are systematically exterminating the Jewish population. In Lublin and the vicinity on the night of March 23 and 24, the Jewish population was simply driven out of their homes and the sick and the infirm were killed on the spot. 108 children from the age of two to nine in the Jewish orphanage were taken outside the town together with their nurses and murdered. Altogether that night, 2,500 people were massacred and the remaining 2,600 Jews in Lublin were removed to the concentration camps of Belzec and Trawniki. 8,000 people were deported from Izbica Rujawska to an unknown destination. In Belzec and Trawniki, murder is carried out by means of poison gas.

Mass murders occurred on such a large scale at Rawasuka and Bilgoraj that Jewish communities have ceased to exist. In Wawalnica near Kazimierz on March 22 the Gestapo shot 120 Jews in the market place and an unknown number of Jews was led out of town and slaughtered. On March 30, Jews were driven from Opol to Nalcozow. 350 were killed on the way and the rest were put into freight trucks which were sealed and departed to an unknown destination.

In Mielec about 1,300 Jews were slaughtered on March 9; in Mir 2,000 Jews were killed; in Nowogrodek 2,500; in Wolozyn, 1,800; in Kajdanow, 4,000 were killed. Thirty thousand Jews from Hamburg were deported to Niask where they were all murdered. Jews slaughtered in Lwow amount to 30,000; in Wilno, to 50,000; in Stanislawow, 15,000; Tarmopol, 5,000; Sloczow, 2,000; and Erzezany, 4,000. Reports have been received that Jews have been murdered in Tarnow, Rudom, Zborowa, Kelomyja, Sambor, Stryj, Drohchyoz, Zbaruz, Brody, Przemyal, Kelo, and Domo. They are forced to dig their own graves and then are mown down with machine guns, hand grenades, and are poisoned with gas. These are methods daily applied to annihilate the Jewish population. In Lwow the Jewish Council had to provide victims themselves.

The number of Poles executed, murdered and tortured to death during nearly three years of German occupation amounts today to 200,000 and the number of massacred Jews exceeds 200,000.

The births recorded from January to June 1939 among Christians were 7.7% and for Jews 10.1% during the same period. For the same period in 1941 the birth rate for Christians was 6.4% and for Jews 3.8%. Deaths recorded among Christians from January to June in 1939 were 5.9% and among Jews 5%. For the same period in 1941 the death rate was 9.6% for Christians and 24.3% for Jews. There were 131 cases of typhus in Warsaw in 1939.

One week later, on July 17, 1942, FDR wrote publicly to Rabbi Stephen S. Wise:

> Citizens, regardless of religious allegiance, will share in the sorrow of our Jewish fellow-citizens over the savagery of the Nazis against their helpless victims. The Nazis will not succeed in exterminating their victims any more than they will succeed in enslaving mankind. The American people not only sympathize with all victims of Nazi crimes but will hold the perpetrators of these crimes to strict accountability in a day of reckoning which will surely come.[11]

The president repeated his concerns not long after meeting with Polish resistance fighter Jan Karski on July 28, 1942, though he made no instructions for a rescue effort other than to win the war as quickly as possible. Winning the war was more hope than expectation at that point. Nazi armies were approaching Cairo from Libya and the British seemed unable to keep them from breaking through to occupy the oil fields of Iraq and take Jerusalem. Roosevelt had sent an emergency supply of tanks to the British, but these did not arrive until the fall. The Soviet Union also seemed doomed to defeat. Domestically Roosevelt faced opponents within the US military and Congress who thought that the war against Hitler should be placed on the back burner until the Japanese had been defeated—a notion he rejected in favor of the defeat of Nazism as quickly as possible. Despite this resistance, on August 21, 1942, FDR declared:

> The United Nations are going to win this war. When victory has been achieved, it is the purpose of the Government of the United States, as I know it is the purpose of each of the United Nations, to make appropriate use of the information and evidence in respect to these barbaric crimes of the invaders, in Europe and in Asia. It seems only fair that they should have this warning that the time will come when they shall have to stand in courts of law in the very countries which they are now oppressing and answer for their acts.[12]

By the fall of 1942 pressure grew on the American and British governments to take some action in response to the atrocities.[13] British organizations in support of action had sent US ambassador John Gilbert Winant over two hundred petitions, pleading for engagement.[14] In response to pressure organized by Jewish organizations within the United States and from Ambassador Winant in London, Roosevelt agreed to issue a statement, in coordination with the British, expressing his support for a commission to investigate war crimes. On October 7, 1942, Roosevelt said:

> I now declare it to be the intention of this Government that the successful close of the war shall include provision for the surrender to the United Nations of war criminals.

> With a view to establishing responsibility of the guilty individuals through the collection and assessment of all available evidence, this Government is prepared to cooperate with the British and other Governments in establishing a United Nations Commission for the Investigation of War Crimes. . . .
>
> It is not the intention of this Government or of the Governments associated with us to resort to mass reprisals. It is our intention that just and sure punishment shall be meted out to the ringleaders responsible for the organized murder of thousands of innocent persons and the commission of atrocities which have violated every tenet of the Christian faith.[15]

In deference to Jewish and Muslim concerns, the British version omitted the reference to Christianity in favor of a human rights–based wording. This, and FDR's other statements and actions supporting a legal response to war crimes, belie the oft-repeated claim that his only planned intervention on the matter of war crimes was his toying with the idea of mass executions of some fifty thousand Nazis (a claim based on a report of a conversation with Stalin and Churchill at Tehran).

The Soviet Union also responded to the creation of a war crimes commission with a clear expression of support. In their diplomatic communications Soviet officials called for the immediate trial of Rudolf Hess as a war criminal. Hess, then Hitler's deputy, had flown to Britain in 1941 on a peace mission and had been in custody ever since. The British would not agree.

The Declaration

A large part of the public and national pressures on and among the United Nations was rooted in concern for the fate of the Jews. Jewish organizations, the Anglican Church in England, and representatives of European states in London (including the Polish government-in-exile) pursued a call for a public condemnation of the extermination of the Jews and for a commitment to try all accused war criminals.

In early December 1942 Jewish representatives met briefly with FDR. Following the meeting, in a State Department communication reported in the media the US government endorsed the view that two million Jews had already been killed and a further five million were at risk of death.[16]

The fate of the war was turning in these weeks in late 1942. The Soviet Union had encircled but not yet destroyed the Nazis at Stalingrad. Anglo-American armies had landed in Africa and were negotiating peace with the Vichy French leadership there.

The State Department's report, "Foreign Relations of the United States," gives the published record of the US version of the diplomatic discussion on the persecution of the Jews that took place that December.[17] These records show that telegrams were sent back and forth between London, Moscow, and Washington on a proposed declaration on atrocities. In one telegram to Ambassador Winant, British foreign secretary Anthony Eden accompanied a draft declaration with an observation of his discussions with Winant and Ivan Maisky, the Soviet ambassador to London:

> We discussed whether any steps could usefully be taken by the United Nations to make clear their condemnation of these horrors and possibly to exercise a deterrent effect on their perpetrators. We agreed that, although little practical effect could be expected, it might be useful for the United States and Soviet Governments to join with His Majesty's Government in condemning these atrocities and in reminding their perpetrators that certain retribution awaits them.

The US State Department chose not to include Roosevelt's reference to the huge numbers of victims and so it was left to the Soviet government to add a sentence to the declaration that specified that the number of victims at that time amounted to "many hundreds of thousands." Consequently, the statement was issued as the "United Nations Declaration on the Persecution of the Jews," with the initial support of these three states and the nine governments-in-exile. These twelve signatories were later joined by the remainder of the then-twenty-eight-member United Nations.

The declaration, issued on December 17, 1942, is the first public multinational recognition and condemnation of the fact that Hitler was implementing a program to exterminate the Jewish population in Europe.[18] It is worth presenting the statement in its entirety, especially as it is often ignored in scholarly discourse that examines when and how much the Allies knew about the Holocaust.[19]

In response to a question in the British Parliament by (MP) Sidney Silvermann about German plans regarding the deportation and extermination of the Jews of occupied Europe, Anthony Eden read the declaration:

> Yes, Sir, I regret to have to inform the House that reliable reports have recently reached His Majesty's Government regarding the barbarous and inhuman treatment to which Jews are being subjected in German-occupied Europe. They have in particular received a note from the Polish Government, which was also communicated to other United Nations and which has received wide publicity in the Press. His Majesty's Government in the United Kingdom have as a result been in consultation with the United States and Soviet Governments and with the other Allied Governments directly concerned, and I should like to take this opportunity to communicate to the House the text of the following declaration which is being made public to-day at this hour in London, Moscow and Washington: "The

> attention of the Governments of Belgium, Czechoslovakia, Greece, Luxembourg, the Netherlands, Norway, Poland, the United States of America, the United Kingdom of Great Britain and Northern Ireland, the Union of Soviet Socialist Republics and Yugoslavia, and of the French National Committee has been drawn to numerous reports from Europe that the German authorities, not content with denying to persons of Jewish race in all the territories over which their barbarous rule has been extended, the most elementary human rights, are now carrying into effect Hitler's oft repeated intention to exterminate the Jewish people in Europe. From all the occupied countries Jews are being transported, in conditions of appalling horror and brutality, to Eastern Europe. In Poland, which has been made the principal Nazi slaughterhouse, the ghettoes established by the German invaders are being systematically emptied of all Jews except a few highly skilled workers required for war industries. None of those taken away are ever heard of again. The able-bodied are slowly worked to death in labour camps. The infirm are left to die of exposure and starvation or are deliberately massacred in mass executions. The number of victims of these bloody cruelties is reckoned in many hundreds of thousands of entirely innocent men, women and children. The above mentioned Governments and the French National Committee condemn in the strongest possible terms this bestial policy of cold blooded extermination. They declare that such events can only strengthen the resolve of all freedom-loving peoples to overthrow the barbarous Hitlerite tyranny. They re-affirm their solemn resolution to ensure that those responsible for these crimes shall not escape retribution, and to press on with the necessary practical measures to this end."[20]

Following the reading of the declaration, members of the British Parliament who were present stood in silence in respect for the dead. This is something that had previously only ever occurred following the death of a monarch. In Moscow the declaration was read on the radio by Foreign Minister Vyacheslav Molotov. The British Broadcasting Corporation (BBC) transmitted the declaration in more than twenty languages and in the United States it received media publicity, including an editorial in the *New York Times*.

The US Congress did not follow the example of the British Parliament of standing in silence when it returned from recess in early January, and the address does not appear to have been read out by the president or secretary of state on the radio. The congressional record for the period reveals no statements from the leadership of either the Democratic or Republican parties similar to those of the president in the preceding months.

It is worth reviewing some of the key points in the declaration. It could not have been more explicit: it informs the world that German authorities "are now carrying into effect Hitler's oft repeated intention to exterminate the Jewish people in Europe" and that Poland "has been made the principal Nazi slaughterhouse." The declaration also spoke of the denial to the Jews of their most basic human rights by the Nazis. Almost a year earlier, in the declaration by the United Nations, the Allies had committed themselves to the support of human rights; now they declared their intention to bring retribution to those who would deny human rights to the Jews.

In the days following the declaration the Inter-Allied United Nations information operations units—first in London and then in New York—issued supplemental information on each country under Nazi rule.[21] The additional member states of the United Nations Information Organization (UNIO) were Australia, Canada, China, India, New Zealand, the Philippines, and South Africa.

George Schommer, chairman of the Inter-Allied Information Committee in London, wrote the document's introduction and issued follow-up information in London on December 18, 1942, and in New York on January 15, 1943. This statement provided accompanying analysis of the fate of the Jews in each of the nations under Nazi occupation, including Germany itself. It also received some publicity following promotional work by the UNIO in New York. During this period, however, the major newspaper organizations were highly conservative in their politics and the material was rarely given prominence, if it was printed at all.[22]

Schommer wrote that many of the details of what went on in Europe during these days of World War II was "shrouded in death itself."[23] The Allies were, however, in agreement that there was "a continent-wide consistency of the persecution." In continuation of their protest, the Allies warned the people responsible "that punishment will be inevitable and severe."

As part of the description of the persecution, the report stated: "Finally, in the middle of the year 1942 . . . evidence was forthcoming of a plan of extermination which transcends anything in history, a plan which was revealed and formulated by Ley and by Rosenberg at a meeting of the Reich Chamber of Labor in November . . . that destruction is proceeding—among other methods, by shootings and by lethal gas. And it is not isolated in one country but is continent wide."

The report cited the US State Department estimate—released in December 1942—which claimed that some two million Jews had been killed or deported in Axis-controlled Europe starting in 1939, and that a further five million were "in danger of extermination." This statement followed the presentation to the US government of what is known as the Riegner Telegram—a document sent from Switzerland and compiled by Jewish organizations of all the reliable data they had on the extermination program.

The accuracy of this account—together with the US State Department estimate of seven million at risk of extermination—is noteworthy for two reasons. First, gas is singled out, alongside gunshots, as a main method of execution; and second, the total number of people estimated to be at risk of extermination is seven million.

Both observations tally closely with modern histories of the Holocaust—in the methods of execution and in the modern broadly historically agreed-on estimate that a little under six million Jews died in the Holocaust.

The accounts given in summary for each nation under occupation stand up surprisingly well to comparison to those established by academic and historical study in the twenty-first century. Here we may consider the brief account of events that occurred in Poland. These include the following two assertions. First: during a visit to Warsaw in March 1942, leading member of the Nazi party Heinrich Himmler gave orders that half of Poland's Jews were to be killed within a year. Second: a special "Vernichtung Kommando" (extermination commando) had been trained in Germany for the purpose of killing half of the Polish Jewish population, and that places of execution were organized at Chelm and Belzec. Methods for committing the executions included shooting, electrocution, and lethal gas. The conclusion was that "the Germans have, in fact, transformed Poland into one vast center for murdering Jews, not only those of Polish nationality but those of other European nationalities, also."

The United Nations Review, an official allied publication published in New York, was sent to newspapers, newsreel services, and radio stations across the United States and other countries; it followed Schommer's introduction, with summaries of the extermination under way in each country, provided by the government of that country. The Belgian government reported: "It was not until May, 1942, that the actual extermination of the Jews was decided upon. . . . On the 15th of May, 1942, the German governor published a decree tantamount to an order for the extermination for all Jews residing in Belgium." The Czechoslovak government detailed the persecution, concentration, and deportation of 72,000 Jews to Poland by October 1942. General De Gaulle's government reported that "a great round-up of Jews in France, during which the most hideous atrocities were committed, began on the night of July 12th, 1942. . . . By September, 1942, it was estimated that 10,000 had already been deported to Germany from concentration camps at Rivesaltes, Vernet, Pau, Perpignan, and Marseilles. . . . Before the deportation began, Vichy had over a period of two years passed a great deal of anti-semitic legislation." Press reports from the Greek resistance noted the opposition of the Orthodox Church to proposed deportations and the rounding up of some 8,000 Jews in Salonika into mountain concentration camps in Macedonia in late 1942. The Yugoslav government reported that "the vast majority—99%—of the Jugoslav Jews, and those who had taken refuge in Jugoslavia, are now dead." The special section of the Gestapo in Serbia "carried out its last task by exterminating by lethal gas the few scores of remaining Jewish women and children kept in Safmiste camp. In March, with pomp and ceremony, its offices too were closed, its mission had been accomplished." The Grand Duchy of Luxembourg reported that there were around 3,000 Jews at the time of the German occupation. While some 2,000 or so were helped to escape from Luxembourg with the help of American relief organizations, in the end "the Jewish community was finally liquidated by deportation of the remaining 300 Jews on July 28th, 1942, to the fortress of Theresienstadt in Bohemia-Moravia."

The Dutch section detailed the fate of the 180,000 Jews in Holland, recording strong acts of resistance by the overall population that were sparked especially by the deportation of 1,200 Jews in March 1942 to Mathausen; within a few weeks 800 had died from working in the sulfur mines without protective equipment. By the autumn of 1941 more than 70,000 Jewish businesses across the Netherlands had been seized. But it was on July 13, 1942, that "the Germans adopted a still more infamous policy. On that day a start was made with a scheme which will in time clear the Netherlands of Jews. Sixty thousand Jews between the ages of 18 and 40 were to be deported at the rate of 600 per day." The tiny prewar Norwegian Jewish population was around 1,400. The Nazi persecutions came to a head on November 23, 1942, when some 900 of those Jews were shipped to Poland—this just a few weeks before the United Nations declaration was made and the background paper United Nations Review was issued.

The Polish account is short and does not repeat the details given earlier. It details the appalling conditions of some 500,000 people in the Warsaw ghetto, commenting that:

> the purpose of the regulations in enforcing these conditions is clear: to liquidate the Jews in cold blood in accordance with the stated principles of Nazi policy. . . . Actual data concerning the fate of the deportees is not at hand, but the news is available—irrefutable news—that places of execution have been organized at Chelm and Belzec, where those who survive shootings are murdered en masse by means of electrocutions and lethal gas.

The report described the support offered by the Christian population and the way that the resistance had gathered information on the extermination and sent it to the government in London. [24]

FDR continued to periodically make statements concerning the coming trials of war criminals. For example, during his radio broadcast of July 28, he told Americans that war criminals would be "punished for their crimes against humanity."[25] However, nearly a full year passed after the international condemnation of the Holocaust in December 1942 before anything concrete was done to try to bring the perpetrators to justice. In late 1942 the major powers had agreed on the creation of a UN commission to investigate atrocities; political disagreements within national bureaucracies and between the governments, however, slowed its creation. In the end, the United Nations War Crimes Commission was created on October 20, 1943. A few days later the foreign ministers of Britain, China, the United States and the Soviet Union met in Moscow and issued a number of statements on the war. These included a declaration from President Roosevelt, Prime Minister Churchill, and Premier Stalin that set out their countries' general approach to war crimes made on behalf of the United Nations alliance:

> The United Kingdom, the United States and the Soviet Union have received from many quarters evidence of atrocities, massacres and cold-blooded mass executions which are being perpetrated by Hitlerite forces in many of the countries they have overrun and from which they are now being steadily expelled. The brutalities of Nazi domination are no new thing, and all peoples or territories in their grip have suffered from the worst form of government by terror. What is new is that many of the territories are now being redeemed by the advancing armies of the liberating powers, and that in their desperation the recoiling Hitlerites and Huns are redoubling their ruthless cruelties. This is now evidenced with particular clearness by monstrous crimes on the territory of the Soviet Union which is being liberated from Hitlerites, and on French and Italian territory.
>
> Accordingly, the aforesaid three Allied powers, speaking in the interest of the thirty-two United Nations, hereby solemnly declare and give full warning of their declaration as follows:
>
> At the time of granting of any armistice to any government which may be set up in Germany, those German officers and men and members of the Nazi party who have been responsible for or have taken a consenting part in the above atrocities, massacres and executions will be sent back to the countries in which their abominable deeds were done in order that they may be judged and punished according to the laws of these liberated countries and of free governments which will be erected therein. Lists will be compiled in all possible detail from all these countries having regard especially to invaded parts of the Soviet Union, to Poland and Czechoslovakia, to Yugoslavia and Greece including Crete and other islands, to Norway, Denmark, Netherlands, Belgium, Luxembourg, France and Italy.
>
> Thus, Germans who take part in wholesale shooting of Polish officers or in the execution of French, Dutch, Belgian or Norwegian hostages or Cretan peasants, or who have shared in slaughters inflicted on the people of Poland or in territories of the Soviet Union which are now being swept clear of the enemy, will know they will be brought back to the scene of their crimes and judged on the spot by the peoples whom they have outraged.
>
> Let those who have hitherto not imbrued their hands with innocent blood beware lest they join the ranks of the guilty, for most assuredly the three Allied powers will pursue them to the uttermost ends of the earth and will deliver them to their accusors [*sic*] in order that justice may be done.

> The above declaration is without prejudice to the case of German criminals whose offenses have no particular geographical localization and who will be punished by joint decision of the government of the Allies.[26]

This joint statement was not followed by joint action which included the Soviet Union. Disputes between the Western and Soviet governments over the representation of the Soviet Republics as independent states in the UNWCC, however, ultimately kept the Soviet Union out of the organization. The Soviet Union also criticized the UNWCC's terms of reference for not going far enough, especially for not clearly identifying the commission of a war of aggression and crimes against humanity as war crimes.[27] The Soviet Union pursued its own war crimes process in Kharkov from 1943 on, and its tribunals considered war crimes and collaborator cases in communities soon after they were liberated from Nazi occupation. Stalin was doubtless keen not to open up a process that might bring his own actions into the spotlight.

Abandonment of the Jews Nonetheless

The declaration on the extermination of the Jews and the work to create the commission did not result in major changes of humanitarian policy toward those fleeing extermination. As a balance to the overall discussion here regarding the strained attempts to implement justice, consider this statement by Viscount Cranbourne, one of Churchill's ministers. He commented in March 1943—not long after the declaration was made—that the Jews should not be regarded as a special case and that the British Empire was so full of refugees that it could barely take any others because those fleeing extermination could not be guaranteed an adequate diet. His lack of urgency in the face of the slaughter is indicative of the indifference and hostility that the Jews faced from some British officials. "The noble Lord must not regard this as a Jewish problem. Every nation in Europe is being tortured by the Germans, and the noble Lord will only do the Jews themselves harm by taking that attitude," scolded Cranbourne. He went on: "The present situation in East Africa, from the food point of view, is not a happy one. It is a very difficult one, and I understand, having made careful inquiries, that it is really undesirable to take any more refugees into East Africa at present." Cranbourne continued to make similar excuses for the rest of the British Empire.[28]

In the presence of such a policy emanating from Churchill's government, the creation of the UNWCC could only ever be a small recompense, if indeed it could not be seen as an insult. We should, however, consider what the commission *did* achieve. This discussion includes details of the energetic people who gave the commission life and how their achievements resonate today. Another writer who focused on this is Arieh Kochavi, in his book *Prelude to Nuremberg*.[29]

Indeed, to get any attention paid to the issue in the United States required an official memorandum from US Treasury officials to the president in January 1944, which detailed the State Department's obstruction of efforts to help the Jews.[30] An Anglo-American conference on refugees in the Bahamas in April 1943 also failed to achieve any substantial progress. In late 1944, however, Roosevelt established the US War Refugees Board, which enabled the escape of some Jews from Europe, even though by this time most of the killing had been completed. There was no effort, especially from within the US Congress or among State Department officials, to fund or support escape routes—through, for example, Hungary, Romania, Bulgaria, Italy, Vichy France (before November 11, 1942), or Spain, none of which were under direct Nazi control or shared the same degree of exterminationist Nazi antisemitism.

Conclusion

In practical terms, continental Europe at the end of 1942 was in the grip of the Nazis and the Western Allies were doing all they could to send supplies to help at Stalingrad. Nevertheless, at the highest political levels all the allies—United Nations—paused for a moment to publicly condemn the extermination of the Jews. They did so in response to the facts at hand and to internal political pressure in the West.

The modern implications of that international condemnation of the Holocaust include strengthening the foundation of postwar human rights, combating Holocaust denial, and furthering Holocaust research and education. Postwar revulsion at the Holocaust is a strong basis for determining "never again." But we must acknowledge that public opinion, national governments, and resistance fighters found the voice both to condemn the Holocaust at the same time that it was happening and to warn of legal retribution.

A fuller understanding of the reality of this crime against humanity, including official condemnation and planning for retribution, adds to the challenge for states that are reluctant to implement the demand "never again" in the twenty-first century. The precedent of the Holocaust can no longer be understood as "We (the American and British governments) did not really know much and did not do much." Rather it should be "We did know, we said we knew, we warned of retribution, and yet we still stood by and did almost nothing"—a situation that is all too familiar today.

It is beyond the scope of this book to assess why the public condemnations of the extermination of the Jews do not prominently appear in the public and scholarly historical narrative of the Holocaust. A few preliminary possibilities come to mind, however. The first relates to the fact that significant parts of the governments in the United States and the United Kingdom were directly opposed to doing anything to help the Jews or to support war crimes prosecutions. Can it be assumed that the current lack of attention to these statements is an expression of institutional continuity? Furthermore, given that Stalin endorsed the UN declaration of December 1942, did others consequently consider this document to be too tainted to be mentioned? Did the Soviet criticism of antisemitism, pogroms, and extermination jar with common anti-Soviet narratives and a contemporary narrative that equates Soviet repression with Nazi antisemitism? Is the neglect of UN wartime statements merely part of a wider conservative nationalist agenda that is opposed to the ideas and politics of the UN during and after the war, as I have argued elsewhere?[31] "We did not know" is often the excuse—expressed by the Germans and Allies alike—for not doing more to combat the tragedies of the Holocaust. Given the account provided here, which suggests that the Allies were very much aware of the Holocaust, how do we interpret this inaction?

"Forgetfulness" also extends to the operations of the UN War Crimes Commission, which finally began its inexplicably controversial task of bringing war criminals to justice in early 1944, a full two years after nine European states and China had set out the need for an international judicial process to achieve justice. The next chapter explores the worldwide operations of the UNWCC.

Notes

1. Raul Hilberg, *The Destruction of the European Jews* (New Haven, CT: Yale University Press), 1129, 1138.
2. Patricia Heberer and Jürgen Matthäus, "Introduction: War Crimes Trials and the Historian," in *Atrocities on Trial: Historical Perspectives on the Politics of Prosecuting War* Crimes, ed. by Patricia Heberer and Jürgen Matthäus, xiii–xxx (Lincoln: University of Nebraska Press, 2008), xiv.
3. David S. Wyman, *The Abandonment of the Jews: America and the Holocaust* (New York: Pantheon, 1984), 75.
4. Michael David-Fox, Peter Holquist, and Alexander M. Martin, eds., *The Holocaust in the East* (Pittsburgh: University of Pittsburgh Press, 2014).
5. The *Times* (London), November 12, 1940.
6. The *Times* (London), December 12, 1940.
7. M. E. Bathurst, "The United Nations War Crimes Commission," *American Journal of International Law* 39, no. 3 (1945): 565–68.
8. Her Majesty's Stationery Office for the Soviet Embassy, *German Atrocities* (London: Her Majesty's Stationery Office, November 7, 1941, and January 6, 1942). See also US Department of State, "Punishment for War Crimes," in *Foreign Relations of the United States: Diplomatic Pape*rs, *1942*; "General: The British Commonwealth, vol. 1: The Far East," 1942, 45, at https://history.state.gov/historicaldocuments/pre-truman; and UNWCC, *Complete History of the United Nations War Crimes Commission and the Development of the Laws of War* (London: Her Majesty's Stationery Office, 1948), chap. 5.
9. US Department of State, "Punishment for War Crimes."

10. Michael Edwards has described the flow of information from the Polish government in Poland to London about Nazi atrocities as well as the general resistance to using the materials by Anglo-American officials and media outlets. See http://www.cambridge.org/gb/academic/subjects/history/twentieth-century-european-history/auschwitz-allies-and-censorship-holocaust.
11. Quoted in Theodore S. Hamerow, *Why We Watched: Europe, America, and the Holocaust* (New York: W. W. Norton, 2008), 319.
12. US Department of State Bulletin, August 22, 1942, 710.
13. Arieh Kochavi, *Prelude to Nuremberg: Allied War Crimes Policy and the Question of Punishment* (Chapel Hill: University of North Carolina Press), 33–34.
14. US Department of State, *Foreign Relations of the United States: Diplomatic Papers, 1942*, 54–55.
15. US Department of State Bulletin, October 10, 1942, 797.
16. Quoted in the *Times* (London), "Persecution of the Jews," December 21, 1942, 3.
17. US Department of State, *Foreign Relations of the United States: Diplomatic Papers, 1942*, 67–70.
18. Royal Institute of International Affairs, "Declaration on Persecution of the Jews, 17 December 1942," in *United Nations Documents 1941–1945* (London: Royal Institute for International Affairs, 1946).
19. Elizabeth Borgwardt, *New Deal for the World* (Cambridge: Harvard University Press, 2005), 218–20.
20. House of Commons Official Report, London, December 17, 1942.
21. UNIO, "Persecution of Jews," *United Nations Review* 3, no. 1 (1943): 1–4. The UNIO archive is publicly available at the UN Archives and Records Administration in New York.
22. The website newspaperarchives.com is a portal into a huge number of US regional newspapers for the period. Based on a search conducted in June 2015, barely two hundred of them reported the persecution of the Jews in late December 1942 and January 1943.
23. Georges Schommer and Inter-Allied Information Committee, *Conditions in Occupied Territories No.6: The Persecution of the Jews* (London: Her Majesty's Stationery Office, 1942).
24. UNIO, "Joint Protest on Jewish Wrongs," *United Nations Review* 3, no. 1 (1943): 1.
25. Franklin D. Roosevelt, "Fireside Chat on Progress of War and Plans for Peace, July 28, 1943," in *The Public Papers and Addresses of Franklin D. Roosevelt*, ed. Samuel Irving Rosenman (New York: Harper & Brothers, 1950), 327–28.
26. "Joint Four-Nation Declaration—Statement on Atrocities," the Moscow Conference, October 1943. Quoted in US Senate Committee on Foreign Relations, *A Decade of American Foreign Policy: Basic Documents, 1941–49* (Washington, DC: US Government Printing Office), 13.
27. Kochavi, *Prelude to Nuremberg*, 222–30.
28. House of Lords, "Hansard Parliamentary Debates: House of Lords," vol. 126 (March 23, 1943), column 848.

29. Kochavi, *Prelude to Nuremberg*.
30. Randolph Paul and the Foreign Funds Control Unit of the US Treasury Department, "Report to the Secretary on the Acquiescence of this Government in the Murder of the Jews," PBS, America and the Holocaust Primary Sources. Available at http://www.pbs.org/wgbh/amex/holocaust/filmmore/reference/primary/somereport.html.
31. Dan Plesch, *America, Hitler, and the UN: How the Allies Won World War II and Forged a Peace* (London: I. B. Tauris, 2011).

4

PURSUING WAR CRIMINALS ALL OVER THE WORLD

Courtroom 5 of London's Royal Courts of Justice has hosted countless trials. At the end of May 1945, three weeks after the Nazi surrender, newsreel cameras rolled and photographers' flashbulbs popped as Lord Wright—the chairman of the UNWCC—rose to deliver the opening address to the National Offices Conference of the UNWCC. The conference had brought together London-based commissioners, representatives from the organization's national offices, and observers from the Allied military commands.

This meeting remains the world's only multilateral meeting of war crimes prosecution agencies.[1] Early in the war many of those present had hoped to be part of an international criminal court that would try the Nazis, but this was not supported by enough member states. Now the commissioners and national representatives were meeting to compare notes on their individual war crimes processes and, by coming together, provide international momentum to meting out justice to war criminals.

This chapter lays out the global operation of the international criminal justice system supported by the UNWCC and its member states. It provides a statistical overview and demonstrates the global reach of the commission, beginning with the example of Ethiopia. It then surveys the work of the United States and United Kingdom, and follows with a look at the Polish and Dutch practices as examples of continental European processes. Finally the chapter examines operations in Asia, with particular attention paid to Chinese and Indian activities.

The May 1945 conference was a chance for the members of the commission to finally present its work to the global public. Until then it had operated in secret. In part this was an attempt to not incite Hitler to further reprisals, but the secrecy also served the interests of American and British officials who had never wanted an international war crimes process in the first place. However, because its work was conducted out of public view, the commission could not build public support and was open to charges of ineffectiveness that would have been better directed at the American and British foreign ministries.

All conference attendees in the courtroom were aware that President Harry Truman had finally announced US government support for an international tribunal to try the top Nazi officials. The negotiations between the Big Four on how to arrange for a trial had only just begun, however, and the discussions were held in secret; the outcome was uncertain even to those at the negotiating table. Observers at the National Offices Conference included two representatives sent by US justice Robert Jackson: Dwight Whitney, and Maj. John Monighan. Jackson had just accepted the assignment from Truman to convene the British, French, and Soviet representatives in order to work out how to try the Nazi leaders.[2] The British government had agreed with Truman's proposal. With Jackson's mission to Europe underway and the National Offices Conference due to start, Churchill addressed the British Parliament:

> Under the terms of the Moscow Declaration on German Atrocities, published on 1st November, 1943, those major war criminals whose crimes have no particular geographical localisation will be punished by a joint decision of the Governments of the Allies, and discussions are at present in active progress with a view to deciding the best procedure.
>
> As regards criminals who are accused of having taken part in specific war crimes against Allied nationals, the Moscow Declaration laid down that they should be sent back to the countries in which their offences were committed, in order that they might be judged and punished there by the Governments concerned. So far as concerns those who have been guilty of crimes against British subjects, the procedure is that the charges brought against them are examined by the United Kingdom National Office, of which the Treasury Solicitor is the head, and submitted by him to the War Crimes Commission. The Judge Advocate-General will be responsible for the collection of evidence against and the prosecution of these criminals before military courts. The Attorney-General exercises a supervisory role in matters relating to war crimes which concern His Majesty's Government, and, in particular, in prosecutions against persons who have committed alleged war crimes against British subjects. His fiat is required for any such prosecutions. In addition, as I have to-day told the House, he has been appointed as the United Kingdom representative for the prosecution of such war criminals as may be brought before the proposed Inter-Allied Military Tribunal.

> The functions of the United Nations War Crimes Commission were described by my right hon. and learned Friend the Lord Chancellor in his speech to another place on 7th October, 1942, when he proposed the establishment of this body. The Commission is principally concerned with the drawing up of lists of persons alleged to have committed war crimes, on the basis of material which is normally submitted to it by the various National Offices of the Allies represented upon it. Arrangements are being made for these lists to be forwarded to Allied commanders in the field, and the lists will, I am sure, prove of very considerable use to them in ensuring that all these criminals are detained as a preliminary to their appropriate disposal.
>
> The Allied Control Commission will, when established, be generally responsible for the administration of justice in Germany, but it is not at present envisaged that Control Commission courts will deal with war crimes against British subjects.[3]

Churchill made no mention of the issue of German crimes against fellow Germans—especially the Jews—which was of considerable public concern (discussed further in chapter 7).

In his speech opening the National Offices Conference, Lord Wright noted that the purpose of war crimes trials was to satisfy the desire for justice and serve as a deterrent to such crimes in the future. A key function of the commission was to provide an "impartial judgment at the international level, thus preventing criticism on the grounds that people were listed as criminals by the Commission on the partial unchecked statement of a single Government or nation." The conference brought together "those who have justice at heart." It was important, he argued, that future ages should be able to say that the "deep-seated common instincts of humanity had at last found expression in acts of just retribution."[4] These goals notwithstanding, the member states had contributed only enough money to support two legal officers on Wright's staff.

By May 1945 many victims of and witnesses to international crimes had already given legal testimony against their abusers. Commission member states had gathered (and continued to gather) testimony from their own officials and special investigators, had processed them in their national capitals, and had then forwarded the charges to London and Chungking with the aim of garnering international support for trying the legal cases and tracking down the accused.

Lord Wright gave a first public account of the cases that had been referred to the commission (in Europe) by its member states at the time of the Nazi surrender, several months before the four-power agreement on the London Charter for the International Military Tribunal at Nuremberg. He explained that as of May 1945, 2,524 Germans, 110 Italians, 17 Bulgarians, 39 Hungarians, and 2 Romanians faced internationally supported indictments.

A Global Achievement

In its official history the commission published summary statistics of the indictments and trials that had taken place up to and including early 1948. Overall, the commission approved over eight thousand pretrial dossiers of charge files, which included cases against more than 36,000 individuals as well as individual members of specific military, paramilitary, or police units. Trials before a variety of legal bodies began to take place in late 1945. Thus, in addition to the international military tribunals established at Nuremberg and Tokyo, UNWCC members established a variety of courts for the trial of accused war criminals following the commission's recommendation to create such tribunals.

The commission surveyed the operation of the various legal processes in its own history, in the minutes of the NOC, and in its report to the UN ECOSOC in 1948.[5] The Americans and British operated military tribunals in those parts of the world where they had been fighting. The British acted as a central statistical clearinghouse for cases from Australia, India, and New Zealand and included their allies in cases of concern to them as judges and court officials. These were Greeks and Poles in European trials and Indians in both Europe and Asia. Both the Australians and Canadians operated tribunals under national laws based on the British Royal Warrant of June 1945. The British, French, Soviets, and Americans operated zones of control in Germany using legal authority derived from

TABLE 4.1. Total Number of Persons Charged by the Governments and Listed by the UNWCC

	War Criminals	*Suspects*	*Material Witnesses*	*Total*
Albanian	9	29	–	38
Bulgarian	402	20	–	422
German	22,409	9,339	2,522	34,270
Hungarian	62	3	4	69
Italian	1,204	69	13	1,286
Japanese	363	60	17	440
Romanian	4	–	–	4

Note: Additional charges brought against persons already charged by the same government and already included in the list are not counted a second time; this total equals 2,156 persons. When the description of a charged person reads "XY head of . . . or his successor or successors at the material time," the case has been counted as involving only one person. Persons listed as "unknown" by name are included. When the description of a group of persons includes an unspecified number of persons who are unknown by name but who held official positions in a number of unspecified different places of the same administrative district or region, the group has been counted as a unit. Japanese totals do not include nationals identified by the Far East Sub-Commission nor nationals listed independently by American, Australian, British, Dutch, or other military authorities in the Far East.

Germany's unconditional surrender. They operated a range of military courts in their zones.

Some states operated temporary civil and military tribunals and military courts. Belgium, the Netherlands, France, and Poland are examples of states that operated decentralized tribunals at the provincial level. The Netherlands and France operated parallel processes at home and in their overseas colonial territories.

By the spring of 1948 the commission had approved a total of 8,178 cases and provided all available data on the trials and their outcomes; a selection of its summary tables is reproduced here, and provides a glimpse of the scope and scale of the UNWCC process.[6]

TABLE 4.2. Number of German Persons Charged by the Governments and Listed by the UNWCC

	Total	*War Criminals*	*Suspects*	*Material Witnesses*
Australia (see note)				
Belgium	4,592	2,471	1,422	699
Canada	30 (see note)	22	1	7
China	1	1	–	–
Czechoslovakia	1,543	1,103	428	12
Denmark	159	1,148	11	–
France	12,546	7,483	4,291	772
Greece	339	310	22	7
India (see note)				
Luxembourg	90	81	9	–
Netherlands	2,423	1,343	319	761
New Zealand (see note)				
Norway	209	191	13	5
Poland	7,805	5,445	2,270	90
United Kingdom	1,709	1,598	60	51
United States	828	695	98	35
Yugoslavia	1,926	1,454	391	81
UNWCC	70	64	4	2
	34,270	22,409	9,339	2,522

Note: All Australian, Indian, and New Zealander cases against German war criminals were submitted through the UK National Office and are included in UK figures. Some Canadian cases other than those indicated were submitted through the UK National Office and are included in UK figures. UNWCC cases were listed on the commission's own intiative.

TABLE 4.3. Number of Italian Persons Charged by the Governments and Listed by the UNWCC

	Total	*War Criminals*	*Suspects*	*Material Witnesses*
Australia (see note)				
Canada (see note)				
Ethiopia	10	8	2	–
France	85	80	5	–
Greece	191	179	11	1
India (see note)				
New Zealand (see note)				
United Kingdom	188	170	9	0
United States	3	3	–	–
Yugoslavia	809	764	42	3
	1,286	1,204	69	13

Note: A number of the cases listed under the United Kingdom were submitted by the UK on behalf of the Australian, Canadian, Indian, and New Zealand national offices.

Despite the closure of the commission in 1948, national governments continued to bring new cases to court well into the 1950s, but these lacked the added legitimacy of international endorsement. At the time of this writing, a full inventory of trials by UNWCC member states has not yet been created. Many of the documents necessary for such an inventory are currently in the archives of member states and are often sealed to the public.

Commission Members and Court Structures

The presently available records of individual national courts are patchy and incomplete, and it is not the intention here to provide a comprehensive global history of all activities taken by UNWCC member states. Rather, the discussion will demonstrate the scale and, by example, the richness of the work.

Ethiopia

The global reach of the work of the UNWCC can be seen in the example of Ethiopia, the only state to have cases endorsed by the commission even though it was not a member of that body. It had infamously been among the first victims of fascist invasion, when Italy invaded in October 1935 and conquered the country in a year.[7] Italy later became the first Axis state to surrender. In September 1943, Mussolini was toppled after the Allied invasion and a new government was formed, led by the former fascist leader Pietro Badoglio and the reigning Italian king, Victor Emmanuel. On the initiative of the United States, by the end of 1944 the two had been ousted.

Ethiopia brought ten cases against Italian officials for prosecution on war crimes in the former country during and after the invasion in the 1930s, which were approved by the commission in March 1948.[8] These included charges against military leaders Badoglio and Gen. Rodolfo Graziani for their use of poison gas and other forms of bombardment against hospitals and Red Cross units, as well as torture, destruction of religious buildings, and pillage.[9] To bolster its efforts toward accountability, the Ethiopian government also produced a scalding dossier, "The Civilization of Fascist Italy in Ethiopia," which contained research of and photographs documenting Italian war crimes that had taken place following the invasion and occupation. The dossier was made public but was specifically presented to the UNWCC to bolster its cases.[10]

The legal basis for the charges is found in the peace treaty which Ethiopia and the other Allies signed with Italy in 1947.[11] The treaty gave the date of invasion by Italy in 1935 as the starting point for accountable war crimes, rather than the date of 1939 when the war in Europe started. The treaty also required Italy to assist in the arrest and extradition of accused war criminals.

By 1948 Ethiopia was still the only independent African state with governmental continuity dating to the precolonial era. (Jumping forward to the current era: There is a general sense in the twenty-first century that Africans have been unduly singled out for charges by the ICC. The ICC is perceived as a form of neocolonialism. However, Ethiopia's successful engagement with the UNWCC alters this misunderstanding of Africa's relationship to international criminal law. (Clearly the country was active in its own right in pursuit of justice and had gained support in principle from the seventeen members of the commission, even though the US representative, seemingly unaware of the provisions of the peace treaty, abstained based on the idea that a war prior to September 1939 was not within the purview of the commission's work.) In Washington, the State Department alleged that the UNWCC was going beyond its duties in seeking to implement the 1947 treaty, as another reason to attack its value.[12]

As Cherif Bassiouni has explored, however, the United Kingdom and the United States both supported the Italian government in resisting applications for the extradition of accused war criminals from a range of countries, including Greece, Libya, and Yugoslavia. These were in violation of several wartime and postwar agreements, including the Moscow agreement, the Italian armistice of 1943, and the peace treaty of 1947.[13]

These obstacles notwithstanding, it is clear that Ethiopia, spurned by the League of Nations in the 1930s, had found some support among its Commission of Jurists, which had collected exhaustively referenced legal evidence of war crimes. One account of the bombing of a Red Cross hospital in Ethiopian territory, for example, contained nearly fifty pages of careful accounts and intelligence data assessing the details and criminality of Italian actions, this account and others were used years later when Ethiopia filed its charges with the UNWCC.[14] Then, after the war, Ethiopia—which of all countries might have had cause to give up on the international system—brought charges to the commission, whereupon the seventeen member states considered and approved the charges following the usual recountings of accused war criminals, suspects, and material witnesses.

The rediscovery of Ethiopian engagement with international criminal justice does not remove the substance of contemporary problems. But it does show a historical case where an African state seeking agency against a European power did so with the support of many states. The experience of Ethiopia should, therefore, be added to our understanding of non-Western states that engaged in developing and using international criminal justice in the mid-1940s. China, and to a lesser extent India, were active in leading roles, and the Philippines and Ethiopia both built heavily on the UNWCC system. These are the reasons why the country survey begins with the Ethiopian example.

The United States

While some states (notably China and Poland) had created government offices to handle international crimes following quickly on the heels of the Declaration on Punishment for War Crimes signed at St. James's Palace in 1942, progress in the United States was much slower. Not until late in 1944 did Secretary of War Henry Stimson finally respond to the UNWCC's request to all governments (made in April of that year) to designate an office within their governments to be responsible for war crimes. The US agency was to act as liaison—alongside representatives of the State Department—with the commission's offices in London and the Far East Sub Commission. In September 1944 Stimson created the US National Office for War Crimes Investigation, based in the Army Section of the department's Office of the Judge Advocate General and led by a brigadier general. By the spring of 1945 this office had established a complex filing system for alleged crimes; at the NOC, the US representative proudly discussed the office's map department, which sported a map of the world with color-coded pins for different types of crimes.

While the incongruity of the US office's focus on stationery may seem a little odd today, it does nonetheless highlight the scale of wartime prosecutions. Col. Howard Brundage, an American representative, noted that "it was dramatic to see those pins stretching across the [theater] map," and he used this illustrative approach to connect war crimes to particular perpetrators.[15] The office coordinated efforts across the US government and employed some forty lawyers plus support staff and investigative teams in the field. Nevertheless, the United States did not bring its first indictment to the commission—a charge for the starvation and beating of US prisoners by the Germans—until late in 1945.[16]

The US Judge Advocate General teams worked under the authority of regional military commanders in Europe and in the Asia Pacific region. They administered national and joint inter-Allied military commissions, a practice stretching back to the Revolutionary War, but now it was carried out on an international scale with the support of the UNWCC.

The United States conducted a host of trials in addition to its leading role in the military tribunals conducted at Nuremberg and Tokyo. These included the subsequent prosecutions at Nuremberg and the Dachau concentration camp; military tribunals in the occupation zone in Germany under Control Council Law No. 10 in Italy; in the Pacific under the jurisdiction of Gen. Douglas MacArthur (trials held in Japan); and in the Philippines and numerous other locations, including Shanghai.

The US JAG's own history provides a useful insight into how that organization currently perceives the work it did at the time. The official history of the Army JAG, *Army Lawyer*, devotes just four pages to the JAG's work on war crimes during World War II, which belies a level of attention apparently echoed in the culture of the JAG following the war.[17] For example, very few of the theses produced at the JAG Legal Center and School even address the JAG's participation in the commission beyond a passing mention.[18] *Army Lawyer* records that 2,500 enemy nationals were tried by military commissions and military government courts[19]: "The Army trials were held from July of 1945 until July of 1948, involving a total of 489 cases and 1,672 defendants. There were 1,416 convictions; 244 death penalties were executed."[20] Durwood Riedel provides a useful discussion of these trials.[21] *Army Lawyer* is silent, however, on the twelve "subsequent proceedings" trials at Nuremberg and on all proceedings concerning Japan, although the case total of 489 appears to include prosecutions of Japanese nationals since the UNWCC includes some 150 US Army cases in Europe and some 250 cases against Japan up to March 1948.

The US trials in Nuremberg that followed the famous trial of the top twenty-four leaders were brought by the Germany-based European Office of the Army JAG, but these are largely overlooked in the office's official history beyond limited mentions of cases related to the Dachau and Mathausen concentration camps. The 12 subsequent proceedings at Nuremberg have only recently been the subject of a major study. This important work by Kevin Heller, who surveyed the 12 trials against specific groups of defendants, includes the prosecution of industrialists, civil servants, doctors, generals, and mobile execution units at the heart of the Nazis' criminal enterprise, and together they show the broader base of the American international legal response to cases.[22] The files of the UNWCC strengthen Heller's argument regarding the international legal and political significance of these 12 trials, since they show that cases were brought by the United States to the

UNWCC and that the prosecutions took place after the *prima facie* cases had been endorsed by the multinational body. Together, these facts strengthen the notion of international support for state prosecutions.

The UNWCC also approved a number of the US indictments for trials at the Nuremberg Military Tribunal, at Dachau, and at other locations in Germany. These include trials of officials at the I.G. Farben and Krupp companies, and within the German High Command.[23] The Dachau trials concentrated on actions by Germans against citizens of non-US members of the United Nations and by actions of certain air crews. The US Army also conducted many trials at Dachau and at other locations in Germany for actions against US prisoners of war, most of whom were US Army Air Force crews shot down over Germany.

These trials were founded on interrogations conducted and intelligence gathered by occupying forces, with information often shared and coordinated between different UNWCC member states. In an ironic twist of history, the affidavits for one case of mass murder of partisans are marked as having been gathered by Henry Kissinger, who—upon learning that one low-level perpetrator he was interviewing as part of his work in the US counterintelligence corps had been involved in war crimes—handed the case to his US superiors, who thus facilitated a Yugoslav indictment.[24] In the Asia-Pacific region, US trials were prosecuted against Japanese personnel for actions against US prisoners of war and, in the Philippines, against civilians on US territory (the Philippines was, at the time, a US possession).

The US appears to have been among the most assiduous of the member states in reporting trial results. The commission's official records include the full transcripts and final outcomes of over 800 US trials, several of which were mentioned earlier for their inclusion of sexual violence as a war crime. These have yet to be published by the US government as authoritative texts needed by lawyers who wish to use them in court.

United Kingdom

The United Kingdom conducted trials in both Europe and Asia. In Europe, these were initially focused on German crimes against British prisoners of war. In response to the growing awareness of the scale of the concentration camps, however, the UK office also initiated trials of the camp staff at the Belsen concentration camp beginning in September 1945—before the opening of the first major war crimes trial at Nuremberg. The Belsen trials were the subject of an extensive report in the UNWCC's Law Reports series of 1948.[25]

The UK office continued to conduct trials for crimes that had been committed against other persons who, though not British citizens, were nonetheless members of Allied states—and thus United Nations citizens. For example, starting in April and May 1946, charges were brought against the staff of Neuengamme concentration camp;[26] one prosecution was of the civilian managers of the firm that the camp inmates were working for.[27] Shortly after this, the first charges were brought against the staff of the concentration camp for women at Ravensbruck.[28] A supplemental charge concerning a further eighteen staff at Ravensbruck was accompanied by a telling note from the British Judge Advocat General official: "This is the usual concentration camp case. Thousands of internees were brutally ill-treated or murdered." Other "usual cases" included actions at Stocken and Ahlem, at Hildsersheim, at Luneberg, and at Sasel.[29] In the Sasel case, Bruno Tesch (the director of the firm Tesch and Stabenow) and Karl Weinbacher (the firm's manager) were sentenced to death by a British military court in Hamburg for the manufacture of poison gas while knowing it would be used for killing German Jews.

One unusual indictment concerned the killing not of UK or Allied personnel, but of neutral citizens. These were five Irish merchant seamen at Bremen Farge, among a group of one hundred Irish whom the Nazis had failed to turn into active supporters of the Reich.[30] This case may raise a question of the jurisdiction of the tribunals regarding crimes against neutral citizens.

Liberated Europe

For many of us the picture of life in Nazi-occupied Europe has been formed by classic movies showing heroic resistance fighters taking on the brutal occupiers with meager weapons or agents parachuting in from London, where Churchill's Special Operations Executive was charged with "setting Europe ablaze." Resistance fighters, facing torture and execution, wreak havoc on the occupiers, who respond with the mass execution of civilian hostages. Recent attention has been given to Nazi collaborators and the prevailing sense of public inertia and inaction among occupied peoples. A further dimension needs to be added to this perception.

Resistance groups and their coordinating governments gathered and sent evidence against Nazi organizations and individuals to London in order to support a legal process for retributive justice. The St. James's Declaration and the later creation of the UNWCC came about in part because of public pressure on the American and British governments. These public international voices provided the opportunity for the public to pursue international legal actions against invaders. Many citizens took up the opportunity to provide legal evidence even while they were under Nazi occupation. Once the UNWCC finally began its work in early 1944, the exiled governments began to file charges against their tormentors.

Many states passed new laws to create war crimes tribunals and processes in anticipation of liberation. By the time D-Day finally came, the Belgians, Dutch, French, Poles, and Yugoslavs, among others, had created the legal mechanisms for postwar justice.

Each liberated nation, including those of Eastern Europe and the Soviet Union, also conducted large numbers of trials of those accused of collaborating with the invaders. In the often-violent aftermath of the war many summary executions and other acts of revenge occurred, at times linked with large-scale population transfers (e.g., in Poland and the Sudetenland). While it is beyond the scope of this book to examine this aspect of the postwar era, when considering the pedigree of the internationally supported war crimes trials it is important to be aware of the background of devastation and political conflict taking place across the continent at the time. The widespread adherence to a founding principle of the St. James's Declaration—that states should come together to provide international legitimacy for individual countries' war crimes trials—is in itself a powerful commitment to the value of retributive justice within each of these states.

National involvement in the commission appears to have been little influenced by the emerging capitalist-communist split in Europe. The Polish and Yugoslav governments of the war years were replaced by far more leftist regimes. The Greeks had a consistently Royalist government that by the end of the war had become embroiled in its own civil war. In general, exiled governments in London tended to be more conservative than the ones that arose in the country following the war. Nevertheless, while the letterheads and national symbols may have changed, the numbers of charges brought and the engagement in debates by the commission appears to have been little influenced by the political hue of the specific government concerned. Holding the Nazis accountable before national tribunals was a significant part of the restoration of legitimate governments in many of the states that had been invaded. A larger issue became the cessation of prosecutions and the early release of the convicted (discussed in chapter 8).

The European Allies compiled documented charges against suspected criminals long before liberation. The Polish government, which had led the creation of the St. James's Declaration, compiled charges from evidence partly sent in secret by the underground government in Poland, and drafted charges and smuggled these to London.[31] By the end of May 1945 the Polish government in London had submitted thirty-nine charges; these included large-scale accusations against German leaders, midlevel officials, and low-level soldiers and police. A good many of these were compiled by Poland's office in Scotland. From there, and from London, the government collected eyewitness accounts from Polish soldiers who had fought alongside the Western Allies and from the thirty-thousand Poles who had been forced into the German Army and then captured as the Allies advanced. By mid-1945 nearly one thousand witness statements of this type alone had been gathered.

The priority given to retributive justice for the underground movements in countries under Nazi occupation—particularly Poland, where the repression was most severe—serves as an inspiration and example for the twenty-first century. It also contradicts those who may argue that it is impossible to collect evidence of atrocities in conflicts today, where—whatever the conditions of repression—the ability of external actors to help is incomparably greater than it was in the 1940s. In contemporary conflicts in the Middle East and Africa, help of some kind is often discovered across national boundaries. In occupied Europe of the 1940s, a free country was far away and, until late in the war, often no country was in a position to help.

After liberation, most returning governments accelerated their searches for evidence of war crimes. The Dutch commissioner, Commander M. W. Mouton, described the typical process happening across liberated Europe: "There would be a National Office in Holland with a branch in London and there would be a large number of sub-offices in different parts of the Netherlands. Flying squads of investigation officers would be sent by the Chairman of the NO to these places where investigations were particularly required."[32] By 1948 the Dutch had brought nearly six hundred cases to the commission. Even after the commission's closure, the Netherlands continued to send translations of trial outcomes, including appeals, to the office of the new UN Human Rights Division in London's Russell Square.[33]

States announced their war crimes prosecution policies through local government organizations, and sometimes even in newsprint; one such advertisement appeared in a paper that was pointed out to the National Offices Conference by Belgium and Luxembourg. Denmark, which did not fight the occupiers and maintained a government in Copenhagen in uneasy relationship with the Nazis, did not join the commission until after liberation and then moved quickly to bring cases forward.

The Czechoslovak government-in-exile was among the most active in the commission and in postwar prosecutions. As Benjamin Frommer has shown, the effort resulted in trials of some one hundred thousand individuals as either enemy war criminals or collaborators.[34] Frommer argues persuasively that these were not communist show trials but rather a genuine if flawed attempt to use retributive justice to bring closure to internal and external conflict. After a draconian start involving public executions that were carried out within a few hours of conviction and witnessed by large crowds, the Czech processes evolved into a fairer process.

Asia

The war crimes trials across Asia were conducted under a range of national legal authorities, all of which brought their cases to the UNWCC for pretrial approval either through the Far Eastern Sub-Commission in Chungking or through the commission's London office. As in Europe, these legal processes were accompanied in some countries with trials of collaborators and the trial systems varied according to culture and political circumstances.

In contrast to the still-sparse academic study of war crimes trials in the countries of Continental Europe, a stream of studies concerning such trials in Asia have appeared. The following analysis draws upon and seeks to build on these findings. They include Yuma Totani's *Justice in Asia and the Pacific Region,*

TABLE 4.4. Number of Japanese Persons Charged by the Governments and Listed by the UNWCC

	Total	*War Criminals*	*Suspects*	*Material Witnesses*
Australia	94	82	3	9
China (see note)				
France	3	3	–	–
India (see note)				
New Zealand (see note)				
United Kingdom	120	84	28	8
United States	223	194	29	–
	440	363	60	17

Note: Figures do not include Japanese nationals who were listed independently by the American, Australian, British, Dutch, or other military authorities in the Far East. Chinese cases were listed by the FESC. Some of the UK cases were submitted by the United Kingdom on behalf of the Indian and New Zealand national offices.

1945–1952,[35] a study of British trials at Hong Kong by Suzannah Linton; of Australian trials by Georgina Fitzpatrick and by Narelle Morris;[36] and of Chinese trials and processes by Anja Bihler, Barak Kushner, Wen-Wei Lai, and Zhang Tiangshu.[37]

The overall theme of the intersection of war crimes trials and decolonization has been explored in a major research project led by Kerstin von Lingen.[38] Her study examines the war crimes trials under American and British jurisdiction as well as those in the Dutch East Indies, French Indochina, and the Philippines. As in other parts of the world, war crimes trials following World War II were an instrument by which defeated states were able to renew their legitimacy through a demonstration of law and justice. In the colonial setting it was far more problematic, given the theoretical impossibility of democratic legitimacy within a colony. Table 4.4, like those included earlier, is sourced from Appendix 4 of the UNWCC's own history.[39]

China

Important evidence exists that contradicts the prevailing view of the weakness or indeed total absence of China in international criminal law in this period. China's role at the International Military Tribunal for the Far East—the "Tokyo Trials"—was notoriously weak and lackluster, so focusing on its performance and representation would support the idea that the development of international criminal law is a Western monopoly.[40] The idea is compounded by widespread corruption within Chiang Kai-shek's nationalist government, which was subsequently defeated by Mao Zedong's communist forces in the civil war of 1945–48.

Taken together these would seem to consign the political actions of the nationalist regime to the dustbin of history.

A consideration of China's role in the UNWCC's organizational and ideological development and implementation of the commission's ideas through war crimes trials, however, makes it clear that China has a foundational role in the development of International Criminal Law. This role has been obscured, but an increasing number of revisionist assessments of this period of Chinese history have appeared. Several scholars have noted the Confucian roots of Chinese government engagement with international law.[41] A greater appreciation of the country's role in the UNWCC would further enrich this growing reappraisal of nationalist China.

In January 1942 China became one of the first states to support a new international legal process to prosecute suspected war criminals and declared that it supported the international process. The Chinese government set up a structure within the Foreign Ministry in the spring of 1942, years before other leading powers.[42] By mid-1944 the UNWCC was operating the Chungking division office—the Far East Sub Committee—and China became highly active in engaging with it. In common with practice in Europe, the Chinese government used its local government and national press to make the public aware that they could report as war crimes any actions taken against them by the Japanese. This was highly successful: Dr. Wang Hua-Cheng, one of the Chinese representatives at the National Offices Conference, announced that it had enabled them to gather information on "about three thousand" cases to be submitted to the Sub-Commission. [43] While he did note that the scale of Japanese war crimes in China and the long duration of the conflict meant that this number was a small fraction of crimes committed during the war, it nonetheless represents a significant popular mobilization effort and engagement with the international system.

Wen-Wei Lai has discussed how the process developed in China.[44] The need for an office was laid out by China at the founding meeting of the UNWCC, while its anticolonial intent was clear from the start. Any British official reading mention of the use of narcotics to subdue the population as a putative war crime would have detected an uneasy resonance with Britain's own forcing of opium imports on China at gunpoint during the nineteenth century.

By the time of the Japanese surrender, the Chinese government had had some three hundred indictments endorsed by the UNWCC Sub-Commission.[45] Chinese officers, who appear prominently in the newsreel report of the National Offices Conference, described the Chinese government's efforts to use local governments and the press to obtain complaints; by the time of the conference China had already created its own national war crimes law.[46] Kushner references the burden on the Chinese to submit reports to the UNWCC in London but does not discuss the interaction between the Chinese government and the subcommission office (a multilateral legal institution with diplomatic status that was in large part the UNWCC's own creation).[47] This initiative to create the FESC was effective in garnering international support for Chinese national action but the value internationally was diminished since all other states chose to process their Asian cases through the main court in London.

The Chinese government described its efforts in a letter of March 13, 1945:

> The Chinese National Office is under the direct control of the Executive Yuan and is organized in the form of a commission whose membership includes representatives of the Ministry of Justice, the Ministry of War, the Ministry of Foreign Affairs, and the Ministry of the Interior. The Office has a Standing Committee of three, one of whom is the Minister of Justice. There is a Secretary-General, assisted by two secretaries. Under the Standing Committee are three sections in charge respectively of (1) the investigation of war crimes; (2) the compilation of lists of war criminals; and (3) the translation of cases of war crimes into foreign languages and the maintenance of contact with international agencies concerning war crimes, e.g. the Sub-Commission of the United Nations War Crimes Commission.
>
> The head of the National Office, namely the Chairman of the Standing Committee, is Dr. C. T. Wang. The Secretary-General is Mr. Kuan Yu.
>
> . . . (d) The procedure followed in carrying out investigations is through instructions issued to local authorities for the investigation of war crimes. The general public is also advised by appropriate means to report cases of war crimes, together with the necessary evidence.
>
> (e) The general result is highly satisfactory. The Chinese National Office is in possession of a great number of cases including also those where Chinese nationals were victims of Japanese war crimes abroad, and those where foreigners were victims in China.
>
> (f) About 3,000 cases have been investigated and are being prepared for presentation to the Sub-Commission.
>
> (g) Up to date 48 cases have been submitted to the Sub-Commission.[48]

The FESC was closed at China's request on March 4, 1947, on the basis that no more new charges were reported. In this period typical attendance at the weekly or biweekly meetings included representatives of Australia, Belgium, China, Czechoslovakia, France, the Netherlands, Poland, the United Kingdom, and the United States.[49]

The Chinese reported only one case to the commission directly, against the officer Sakai, though by the time of this reporting the commission had considered over twelve hundred charge files. While Kushner mentions that according to Japanese sources 883 Japanese nationals came to trial, there is some evidence that the number was far higher.[50]

In October 1946 the Chinese government reported to the FESC that it had received 160,000 complaints of war crimes, 30,000 of which were serious enough

TABLE 4.5. Far East Sub Commission Lists of Japanese War Criminals

Total number of War Criminals and Material Witnesses (Sub-Commission Lists Nos. 1, 2, 5–26)	3,028
Total number of War Criminals and Material Witnesses (Sub-Commission's Lists Nos. 3 and 4)	130
Total	3,158

Source: Lists prepared and adopted by the FESC and reproduced by the commission as list nos. 17–23, 33–37, 46–49, and 68–77. See UNWCC, *Complete History of the United Nations War Crimes Commission and the Development of the Laws of War* (London: Her Majesty's Stationery Office, 1948), 514.

to bring to the commission, and that 70,000 less serious cases were being considered by the Chinese independently; that left 60,000 cases for further investigation.[51] The FESC had one update from China in January 1947.[52]

Over 4,000 accused war criminals had been brought to court by May 1947, according to a statement by the Chinese minister of justice in May 1947. The document implies these accused and the further 1,500 said to be awaiting trial were serial offenders responsible for the vast majority of the 150,000 reported crimes.[53] Other sources give a far lower figure: 145 death sentences and no more than 500 total convictions prior to 1949.[54] The truth is unlikely to ever be known for certain. At the time of writing neither the Chinese charge files nor trial outcomes are available.

For political reasons the war crimes processes were highly contested, both within China and between China and Japan. The then-insurgent communists accused the nationalist Kuomintang (KMT) government of inaction on war crimes, and it is certain that the KMT employed Japanese army units and commanders in its fight against the communists. For their part the Japanese soldiery had always been told that they were fighting on behalf of "genuine" Chinese interests. It is easy to assume that Western skepticism of the Chinese trials was a correct view.

What stands out is that in China, the government sought international legitimacy for national legal actions all while pursuing legal action against those it considered traitors. Through its national trials and its participation in the FESC, and as demonstrated by its role in the commission in London, China established itself as an equal partner at the international level including in decisions on European legal cases.

Australia

The Australian delegation to the NOC took the opportunity to explain their country's planned case-gathering process: the commissioner of the national office, supported by a legal staff, would take evidence under oath. The Australian military planned to arrange for questionnaires to be read out to all relevant military units and patrol officers would go out to communities in New Guinea seeking evidence of Japanese crimes. Where it was found, the evidence was recorded in writing and signed by a witness and a commissioner. By that point in time the Australian national office had submitted 21 cases to the UNWCC in London and withdrawn 1 case. It anticipated a total of 300 cases.[55]

Narelle Morris discusses how 812 Japanese were brought to court through approximately three hundred trials in Morolai, Wewak, Labuan, Manus, Rabaul, Darwin, Singapore, and Hong Kong.[56] Morris and other authors provide an erudite account of a number of aspects of these trials. As with other national processes taken by UNWCC members, the trials were generally of cases that had first been approved by the commission in London. Thus both the Australian and the New Guinea actions can be considered international processes.

India

While India's role in the commission was not as substantial as China's, its representatives had significant responsibility for pushing forward international criminal law in the 1940s even while still part of the British Empire.[57] As discussed earlier, India's participation in the UNWCC from the outset and its contribution to the development of the proposal for military tribunals was key. Now we turn to the role of pre-independence judges within the military court system, especially since this role continued after independence.

India provided judges for the British military tribunals in Asia. In more than twenty trials, one and sometimes two of the judges were Indian, a sample of which can be found in Table 4.6.

These cases began in 1946 and continued until after independence, according to UNWCC records. For example, in July 1947, a military tribunal in Kuala Lumpur sentenced a Japanese soldier to four years in prison for mistreating 7 Malay civilians. An Indian officer was among the three-man tribunal. Indian judges continued to hear cases after the commission's closure.

Conclusion

A global system of international criminal justice that was both grassroots and government-sponsored, and that began to process charges as early February 1944, emerges from the often brief and dryly written documents submitted by the national bodies to the commission's offices. This movement for justice was thus a reality more than a year before the London Charter for the Nuremberg Trials was agreed on in August 1945. A short reading of the commission's documents helps clarify the fact that the image of immediate postwar human rights is not merely incomplete, but an utterly inadequate recognition of the practical vision and actions of tens of thousands of people all over the world who sought not merely revenge, but justice too.

TABLE 4.6. Joint Trials Conducted in East Asia by British and Indian Judges

Trial	*Court membership*	*Date*	*Location*	*Crime*	*Verdict / Sentence*
Lt. Yamaguchi Akuni and 4 others, all of the Japanese Army	1 Indian, 2 British	February 21–26, 1946	Singapore	Planning, preparing, aiding, and/or failing to prevent the arrest and ill-treatment of several civilian residents of Singapore, in consequence whereof the said persons suffered injuries which caused or contributed to their deaths.	Verdict: Not guilty: 1; Guilty: 4 Sentence: Death by hanging.
Capt. Matsuo Kobayashi and Interpreter Masao Fujita, both of the Japanese Army	1 Indian, 2 British	May 20–23, 19146	Singapore	Being concerned, together and severally, in the ill-treatment of civilian residents of Nancowry.	Verdict: Guilty, 2 Sentences: Kobayashi: Imprisonment for 4 years; Fujita: Imprisonment for 3 years. Findings confirmed and 5 months emitted from each sentence.
Nikei Yamanie	1 Indian, 2 British	April 10–26, 1946	Singapore	Ill-treatment of a civilian resident of Port Blair, thereby causing the death of the said person.	Verdict: Guilty. Sentence: Imprisonment for life. Sentence confirmed.
Susumi Yoshida	1 Indian, 2 British	April 10–26, 1946	Singapore	Ill-treatment of a civilian resident of Port Blair, thereby causing the death of the said person.	Verdict: Guilty. Sentence: Imprisonment for life. Sentence confirmed.
Yoshinobu Takayanani	1 Indian, 2 British	March 3, 1946	Singapore	Being concerned in the ill-treatment of a civilian resident of Port Blair.	Verdict: Guilty. Sentence: Death by hanging. Sentence confirmed.

(continued)

TABLE 4.6. Joint Trials Conducted in East Asia by British and Indian Judges (*Continued*)

Trial	*Court membership*	*Date*	*Location*	*Crime*	*Verdict / Sentence*
Maj.-Gen. Itzuki Toshio, 12 other members of the Japanese Army and 3 members of the Japanese Navy	1 Indian, 2 British	March 11–26, 1946	Singapore	*Joint*: Torture and ill-treatment of civilian residents of Car Nicobar in consequence whereof 6 died. *Against Itzuki Toshio and Ueda Mytsharu only*: Being concerned together in the unjust trial and judgment of civilian residents of Car Nicobar, as a result of which 49 were condemned to death and executed. *Against Itzuki Toshio and Sakagami Shigero only*: Being concerned together in the unjust trial and judgment of civilian residents of Car Nicobar, as a result of which 22 were condemned to death and executed. *Against Itzuki Toshio and Sakagami Shigero only*: Being concerned together in the unjust trial and judgment of civilian residents of Car Nicobar as a result of which 12 were condemned to death and executed.	Verdict: Not Guilty, 1; Guilty, 15. Sentences: Death by Hanging: 5; Death by Shooting: 1; Imprisonment for 15 years: 1; Imprisonment for 12 years: 2; Imprisonment for 10 years: 5; Imprisonment for 3 years: 1. Sentences confirmed.
Noboru Goda of the Japanese Navy.	1 Indian, 2 British	May 23–24, 1946	Singapore	Ill-treatment of civilian inhabitants of Port Blair, thereby causing the death of 1 person.	Verdict: Guilty. Sentence: Death by hanging. Sentence confirmed.

Trial	*Court membership*	*Date*	*Location*	*Crime*	*Verdict / Sentence*
Renji Tanaka, Harumi Nakayama, and Takeo Fujie, all of the Japanese Navy	1 Indian, 2 British	May 30–31, 1946	Singapore	Ill-treatment of a civilian resident of Port Blair, as a result of which the said person died.	Verdict: All guilty. Sentences: Death by hanging, 3. Sentences confirmed.
Suefusa Sakamoto of the Japanese Navy	1 Indian, 2 British	June 3, 1946	Singapore	Being concerned in the killing of a civilian resident of Port Blair.	Verdict: Not guilty.
Iwao Mizukani of the Japanese Navy	–	June 3–5,1946	Singapore	Ill-treatment of Indian civilian residents of Port Blair, causing the death of 1 person and physical suffering to 3 others.	Verdict: Not guilty.
Noboru Kuboki, civilian attd. to the Japanese Navy	–	June 5–6, 1946	Singapore	Ill-treatment of 4 Indian civilian residents of Port Blair, causing the death of said persons.	Verdict: Guilty. Sentence: Death by hanging. Sentence confirmed.

Source: All cases taken from "Document C.255: Fourth Supplement to the Synopsis of Trial Reports," DN C.204, April 30, 1947.

Leaders including Eleanor Roosevelt, Raphael Lemkin, Hersch Lauterpacht, Robert Jackson, and William Shawcross are all rightly honored for their part in the development of human rights after 1945, but these people were not acting alone in turning the mood of the age into actual courtroom convictions and treaty drafts. Rather, they helped distill and carry forward the work of many courtrooms and thousands of witnesses and investigators. In the mid-1940s, when people's very nations were being obliterated, thousands worked for what then must have seemed far-off justice.

Twenty-first century academics debate the pragmatism and romanticism of international justice; lawyers take their fees and justices write judgments the length of an airport novel. The label "romantic" is an ignorant insult and "pragmatic" an argument in the tradition of those who opposed action for justice following the Armenian Genocide of 1915 and who would have preferred to end World War II by simply getting on with rebuilding Germany after a firing squad for Hitler and his closest henchmen. However, those who worked for international justice in those worst of times following World War II are best honored when we, who enjoy the luxury of advanced society, pursue justice.

Notes

1. Footage of the conference can be found here: British Movietone, "War Crimes Commission" (no sound), May 31, 1945, http://tinyurl.com/nationalofficesconference.
2. UNWCC, "National Offices Conference—First Session, Thursday, May 31st, at 11.30 a.m.," May 31, 1945, 12.
3. House of Commons, "Hansard Parliamentary Debates: House of Commons," vol. 411, May 29, 1945, columns 36–37.
4. UNWCC, "Conference First Session," 3.
5. UNWCC, *Complete History of the United Nations War Crimes Commission and the Development of the Laws of War* (London: Her Majesty's Stationery Office, 1948), 461–76.
6. Ibid., 508–18.
7. States and peoples had been invading each other for millennia, but the political responses to World War I and the creation of the League of Nations were intended to usher in a new era in world affairs.
8. I have written incorrectly that these were not approved in my book *America, Hitler and the UN: How the Allies Won World War II and Forged a Peace* (London: I. B. Tauris, 2011). Further analysis of commission documents and charge files referred to in the present text demonstrate that they were.
9. E.g., UNWCC, "Ethiopian Charges against Italian War Criminals," RN 7878/E/It/1, CN 1 A-D, and RN 7887/E/It/10, CN 10 A-B, February 28, 1948.
10. Ethiopian Government Press and Information Office, *La Civilisation de l'Italie Fasciste en Ethiopie,* vols. 1 and 2: 1948 (Addis-Ababa: Berhanea Selam, 1948).

11. Treaty of Peace with Italy, signed in Paris, February 10, 1947, available at http://www.loc.gov/law/help/us-treaties/bevans/m-ust000004–0311.pdf. See articles 38 and 51.
12. Christopher Simpson, "Shutting Down the United Nations War Crimes Commission," *Criminal Law Forum* 25, no. 1–2 (2014): 141.
13. M. Cherif Bassiouni, *Crimes Against Humanity in International Criminal Law* (Dordrecht: Nijhof, 1992), 227–28.
14. UNWCC, "Ethiopian Charges against Italian War Criminals," RN 7878/E/It/1, CN 1, A-D (February 16, 1948).
15. UNWCC National Offices Conference Minutes of the Second Session, Thursday, May 31, 1945, 14.
16. UNWCC, "United States Charges against German War Criminals," RN1628/US/G/1, CB 1, (October 6, 1945).
17. JAG, "Army Lawyer: A History of the Judge Advocate General's Corps, 1775–1975," available at http://www.loc.gov/rr/frd/Military_Law/pdf/lawyer.pdf.
18. Based on an online search of the thesis collection database of the JAG Legal Center and School at http://jag.iii.com:2082/search~S2, accessed June 1, 2015, as well as an online search at http://www.loc.gov/rr/frd/Military_Law/theses.html.
19. JAG, "Army Lawyer," 181.
20. Ibid., 184.
21. Durwood Riedel, "The U.S. War Crimes Tribunals at the Former Dachau Concentration Camp: Lessons for Today," *Berkeley Journal of International Law* 24, no. 2 (2006): 554–609, available at http://scholarship.law.berkeley.edu/cgi/viewcontent.cgi?article=1315&context=bjil.
22. Kevin Jon Heller, *The Nuremberg Military Tribunals and the Origins of International Criminal Law* (Oxford: Oxford University Press, 2011).
23. UNWCC, "United States Charges against Krupp War Criminals," RNs 5917/US/G/209, 5918/US/G/210, 5919/US/G/211, 5920/US/G/212, 5921/US/G/213, 5922/US/G/214, 5923/US/G/215, 5924/US/G/216, 5295/US/G/217, 5296/US/G/218, 5927/US/G/219, 5928/US/G/220, 5929/US/G/221, and 5930/U/G/222, CNs 453, 454, 455, 456, 457, 458, 460, 461, 462, 463, 464, 465, 466, all July 17, 1947. UNWCC, "United States Charges Against I. G. Farben War Criminals," RNs 5198/US/G/181, 5628/US/G/200, CN 437, 443, May 21, 1947, and June 20 1947.
24. Memorandum for the Sub-Regional Chief, April 26, 1946, in UNWCC, "Yugoslav Charges against German War Criminals," RN 4895/Y/G/284, CN R/N/284 (March 21, 1947).
25. UNWCC, *Law Reports of Trials of War Criminals,* vol. 2 (London: Her Majesty's Stationery Office), 1947.
26. One of the Belsen charges can be found at UNWCC, "United Kingdom Charges against German War Criminals," RN 3031/UK/G/528, CN UK-G/B 530, April 17, 1946. One of the Neuengammer Camp charges can be found at ibid., RN 3032/UK/G/529, CN UK-G/B 531, April 17, 1946.
27. UNWCC, United Kingdom Charges against German War Criminals, RN 4186/UK/G/607, CN UK-G/B 585, October 22, 1946.

28. Ibid., RN 4160/UK/G/605, CN UK-G/B 586, October 5, 1946.
29. RN 3022/UK/G/519, CN UK-G/B 520, April 17, 1946; RN 4050/UK/G/601, CN UK-G/B 580, September 19, 1946; RN 3023/UK/G/520, CN UK-G/B 521, June 17, 1946; RN 3034/UK/G/531, CN UK-G/B 533, June 17, 1946.
30. Ibid., RN 3290/UK/G/560, CN UK-G/B 559, June 17, 1946.
31. UNWCC, Conference Second Session, 11.
32. Ibid., 8.
33. Letter from Joyce Sweeney to Dr. J. J. Litawski, September 2, 1949, in UNWCC Archive, reel 61.
34. Benjamin Frommer, *National Cleansing* (Cambridge: Cambridge University Press, 2005).
35. Yuma Totani, Justice in Asia and the Pacific Region, 1945-1952: Allied War Crimes Prosecutions (New York: Cambridge University Press, 2015).
36. Georgina Fitzpatrick, "War Crimes Trials, 'Victor's Justice' and Australian Military Justice in the Aftermath of the Second World War," in *Historical Origins of International Criminal Law,* vol. 2, ed. Morten Bergsmo, Cheah Wui Ling, and Yi Ping, 327–54 (Brussels: Torkel Opsahl, 2014); Narelle Morris, "Obscuring the Historical Origins of International Criminal Law in Australia: The Australian War Crimes Investigations and Prosecutions of Japanese 1942–1951," in ibid., 355–94.
37. Barak Kushner, "Chinese War Crimes Trials of Japanese, 1945–1956: A Historical Summary," in *Historical Origins of International Criminal Law,* vol. 2, ed. Morten Bergsmo, Cheah Wui Ling, and Yi Ping, 243–65 (Brussels: Torkel Opsahl, 2014), and Zhang Tiangshu: "China's Post–Second World War Trials of Japanese War Criminals, 1946–1956," in *Historical Origins of International Criminal Law,* vol. 2, ed. Morten Bergsmo, Cheah Wui Ling, and Yi Ping, 270–300 (Brussels: Torkel Opsahl, 2014); Anja Bihler, "Late Republican China and the Development of International Criminal Law: China's Role in the United Nations War Crimes Commission in London and Chungking," in *Historical Origins of International Criminal Law*, vol. 1, ed. Morten Bergsmo, Cheah Wui Ling, and Yi Ping, 507–40 (Brussels: Torkel Opsahl, 2014).
38. Kerstin von Lingen, "Rethinking Justice? Decolonization, Cold War, and Asian War Crimes Trials after 1945" Paper presented at Cluster of Excellence: Asia and Europe in a Global Context Conference, Heidelberg University, October 26–29, 2014.
39. UNWCC, *Complete History of the UNWCC*, 510.
40. Barak Kushner, *Men to Devils, Devils to Men: Japanese War Crimes and Chinese Justice* (Cambridge, MA: Harvard University Press, 2015).
41. Shi Bei, Zeng Siqi, and Zhang Qi, "Chinese Confucianism and Other Prevailing Chinese Practices in the Rise of International Criminal Law," in *Historical Origins of International Criminal Law*, vol. 1, ed. Morten Bergsmo, Wui Ling, and Yi Ping, 141–70 (Brussels: Torkel Opsahl, 2014).
42. UNWCC Conference Second Session, 8.
43. Ibid.
44. Wen-Wei Lai, "China, the Chinese Representative, and the Use of International Law to Counter Japanese Acts of Aggression: China's Standpoint on UNWCC Jurisdiction," *Criminal Law Forum* 25, no. 1–2 (2014): 111–32.

45. UNWCC, "Minutes of the Thirteenth Meeting of the Far Eastern and Pacific Sub-Commission of the United Nations War Crimes Commission," September 28, 1945, 1.
46. British Movietone, *War Crimes Commission* (film, no sound), May 31, 1945, available at http://www.aparchive.com.
47. Kushner, *Men to Devils*, 142.
48. UNWCC Conference Agenda, May 16, 1945, annex 1, 2–3.
49. UNWCC, "Minutes of the Thirty-Eighth Meeting of the Far Eastern and Pacific Sub-Commission of the United Nations War Crimes Commission," March 4, 1947, 1.
50. Kushner, *Men to Devils*, 246.
51. Letter from the Australian Department of External Affairs to Australian Legation, Nanking, October 31, 1946, in National Archives of Australia, Files A1067–UN46 and WC 14–194101.
52. UNWCC, "Minutes of the Thirty-Sixth Meeting of the Far Eastern and Pacific Sub-Commission of the United Nations War Crimes Commission," January 14, 1947, 2.
53. Judicial Report by Dr. Hiseh Kwan-sheng [the Chinese minister of justice], May 22, 1947, reprinted in Australian Government, *Information Office Daily Bulletin* No. 14, June 17, 1947.
54. Shi Bei, Zeng Siqi, and Zhang Qi, "Chinese Confucianism and Other Prevailing Chinese Practices in the Rise of International Criminal Law," in *Historical Origins of International Criminal Law*, vol. 1, ed. Morten Bergsmo, Wui Ling, and Yi Ping, 141–66 (Brussels: Torkel Opsahl, 2014), 161; Justin Jacobs, "Preparing the People for Mass Clemency: The 1956 Japanese War Crimes Trials in Shenyang and Taiyuan," *China Quarterly* 205 (2011): 153; Weng Youli, "Comments on the National Government's Disposal of Japanese War Criminals," in *Journal of Southwest China Normal University: Philosophy and Social Science Edition* 6 (1998): 112.
55. UNWCC Conference Agenda, May 16, 1945, annex 1.
56. Narrelle Morris, "Obscuring the Historical Origins of International Criminal Law in Australia," in *Historical Origins of International Criminal Law,* vol. 2, ed. Morten Bergsmo, Wui Ling, and Yi Ping, 355–83 (Brussels: Torkel Opsahl Academic EPublisher, 2014), 355.
57. Asoke Mukerji, "Statement by Ambassador Asoke K Mukerji, Permanent Representative of India to the United Nations at the Panel Discussion on 'United Nations War Crimes Commission Records: Past, Present and Future,' UN Headquarters," in Edith Lederer, chair, "UNWCC Records (1943–1949): Past, Present, and Future" panel discussion, UN Live, United Nations WebTV, November 11, 2014, available at http://webtv.un.org/%E2%80%8Bmeetings-events/watch/united-nations-war-crimes-commission-records-1943–1949-past-present-and-future-panel-discussion/3886628590001#full-text.

5

THE HOLOCAUST INDICTMENTS

PROSECUTING THE "FOOT SOLDIERS OF ATROCITY"

Hundreds of Germans were indicted for the extermination of the Jews—while the Holocaust was still underway—by the states where the crimes took place. This reality leaps from the pages of the UNWCC's records of the thousands of indictments made against the Axis powers by their victims. It also contradicts the accepted truth that the Allies made only negligible attempts to prosecute the executioners of the Holocaust and certainly no attempts while the extermination progressed.

This chapter analyzes, country by country, the indictments made against the German "foot soldiers of atrocity": ordinary soldiers, low- and mid-ranking military and police officers, and superiors who were involved in the extermination of the Jews. Bulgarians, Hungarians, and nationals of other states were also indicted, but this study focuses only on the Germans. These indictments began to be made early in 1944. The first case to mention Jews was one submitted by Poland on February 23, 1944; it dealt with the systematic mistreatment of prisoners and shootings of Jews in a Nazi camp near Danzig.[1] National indictments of Germans for crimes against Jews continued to be endorsed by the commission right up to its final meetings before the commission was closed down in March 1948. These indictments appear to have been unknown to scholars for the last seventy years.

The main organizations that these foot soldiers belonged to were the Wehrmacht (armed forces) and three overlapping military and security organizations of the Nazi state: the Schutzstaffel (SS); the Sicherheitsdienst (the German Security Service and SS intelligence agency, or SD); and the Geheime

Staatspolizei (the Secret State Police, known as the Gestapo). I have chosen in this chapter to focus on indictments against low- and mid-level participants in the extermination of the Jews because their actions were such an important part of Nazi crimes and because the general assumption is that there was very little attempt by the victorious Allies to take legal action against those who exterminated the Jews.

Elizabeth Kolbert's 2015 *New Yorker* article, entitled "The Last Trial," described three phases of Holocaust prosecution.[2] These three phases were the first and subsequent proceedings at Nuremberg; prosecutions by the German government in the 1950s; and then, after the 1961 Eichmann case, the desultory trials of aging death camp guards beginning in the 1980s. This view represents the general scholastic understanding of post–World War II prosecutions, although specialists have written about isolated prosecutions in a number of countries.

Kolbert described the case against Oskar Groening, "the accountant of Auschwitz." What she knew was that as far back as 1947, Groening was indicted by Poland for collective responsibility for the crimes at the camp. The case against him was approved as far as listing him as a suspect by the commission. Groening's name appeared on the final series of charges against camp staff first brought by Poland in 1944.[3]

Kolbert's summary echoes that of other specialist writers on post–World War II war crimes trials in Europe, including three edited volumes: one by István Deák, Jan Gross, and Tony Judt titled *The Politics of Retribution in Europe: World War II and Its Aftermath*; another by Patricia Heberer and Jürgen Matthäus titled *Atrocities on Trial*; and a third by David Bankier and Dan Michman titled *Holocaust and Justice*.[4] All three are examples of great scholarship regarding the trials of war criminals. They do not demonstrate an awareness of the UNWCC or its work, however.

Donald Bloxham's important study of Jewish witnesses in war crimes trials of the postwar era begins with trials in the second half of the 1940s. In common with the consensus among scholars, Bloxham's discussion implies strongly that the famous IMT at Nuremberg, the twelve subsequent proceedings at Nuremberg led by Brig. Gen. Telford Taylor, and the trials at Dachau and Belsen by US and British militaries were the only legal efforts by the Allies to prosecute the Holocaust.[5] Elsewhere, Bloxham has argued that "Nazi Jewish policy was not subjected to systematic judicial examination directly after the war," and that it was rare indeed for attacks on the Jews to be the subject of trials.[6]

None of these studies mention the formation of the UNWCC nor its interaction with Jewish agencies, nor the indictments made of crimes against the Jews by the exiled governments before the commission. The UNWCC records indicate that, in all states where the Holocaust occurred and which were members of the commission, there was a substantial effort to prosecute the exterminators of the Jews, both while these exterminations were still underway and immediately after.

Hundreds of cases against thousands of perpetrators of the Holocaust were drawn up and presented to the UNWCC, the great majority of which were endorsed by the commission as presenting sufficient evidence that there was a case to answer—what is called a *prima facie* case.

Across Europe charges were drawn up against the organizers of Jewish deportations, the staffs of concentration and transit camps, and, in Poland, the staffs of the death camps. A number of states also sought to bring prosecutions against the Nazis concerned with the death camps in Poland. After the war Britain and the United States brought to the UNWCC for approval many cases they pursued after the surrender of Germany under the allied law Control Order 10, which included crimes against the Jews.

Table 5.1 provides a summary of approved indictments that specifically mentioned crimes against Jews. It compares these to the total number of approved indictments for each country, to give an impression of the degree to which commission members addressed this issue in their own indictments. For example, some 24 percent of Polish cases concerned Jews. We can learn from these percentages that a significant proportion of war crimes cases concerned crimes against Jews, whereas until now it has been thought there were only few and isolated prosecutions. However, not too much should be read into a comparative analysis of these percentages since some cases concerned the theft of Jewish property while others the deaths of millions, plus the cases shown are only those supported by the commission. Rejected and adjourned cases appear in the commission's files but are not the subject of this study.[7] As such, any case described here was supported by all the national representatives on the commission.

Some of the documents discussed in this chapter may be well known to scholars because they appear in charges brought at Nuremberg and elsewhere. For example, a description of the Treblinka death camp, which includes the comment, "There are terracotta floors in the chambers which become very slippery when wet," appears in a document used eighteen months later in London by the IMT prosecutor at Nuremberg of the "Major War Criminals."[8]

The following country-by-country account of indictments for crimes against Jews is intended as an illustration. In each case, both the first and last indictments are highlighted to indicate the continuity of indictments from wartime occupation to peacetime government. A systematic study of all these cases is an important task for Holocaust studies but is far beyond what can be achieved in this volume.

Belgium

The Belgian government in London had been at the forefront of the political effort in 1942 and 1943 that led to the creation of the UNWCC (with Belgian jurist Marcel de Baer playing a leading role). It was quick to bring cases to the commission. Crimes against the Jews were included among the first few cases

TABLE 5.1. Charges Brought for Anti-Jewish Persecution Submitted by UNWCC Member States

	Number of Jewish-Related Cases	*Total Number of Cases*	*Percentage of Cases*
Australia vs. Japan	0	19	0%
Belgium vs. Germany	18	399	5%
Canada vs. Germany	0	11	0%
China vs. Germany	0	1	0%
Czechoslovakia vs. Germany	52	246	21%
Czechoslovakia vs. Hungary	3	8	38%
Denmark vs. Germany	14	192	7%
Ethiopia vs. Italy	0	10	0%
France vs. Germany	91	2,231	4%
France vs. Italy	2	30	7%
France vs. Japan	0	1	0%
Greece vs. Albania	0	1	0%
Greece vs. Bulgaria	4	140	3%
Greece vs. Germany	12	140	9%
Greece vs. Italy	0	131	0%
Luxembourg vs. Germany	4	97	4%
Netherlands vs. Germany	110	584	19%
Norway vs. Germany	9	80	11%
Poland vs. Germany	372	1,564	24%
United Kingdom vs. Germany	21	672	3%
United Kingdom vs. Italy	1	114	1%
United Kingdom vs. Japan	1	28	4%
United Kingdom vs. Romania	0	2	0%
United States vs. Germany	4	258	2%
United States vs. Italy	0	3	0%
United State vs. Japan	1	241	0%
Yugoslavia vs. Albania	0	1	0%
Yugoslavia vs. Bulgaria	3	40	8%
Yugoslavia vs. Germany	30	561	5%
Yugoslavia vs. Hungary	7	11	64%
Yugoslavia vs. Italy	2	241	1%
Total	761	8,057	9%

it brought. German army general Alexander von Falkenhausen, based in Brussels for much of the occupation, was charged with various offenses, including the confiscation of Jewish property in 1944.[9] Early charges also concerned the commander and staff of Breendonk, a Nazi concentration camp housed in an old fort near Antwerp. Several individual charges of detention, maltreatment, torture, murder, systematic terrorism, and deportation to the East were brought against camp staff for their role in persecuting Belgium's Jewish population.

Obersturmbannführer Philipp Schmitt, the SS officer commanding the Breendonk camp, was tried, convicted, and sentenced to death in 1949.[10] After the war the Belgian government organized a prosecution of Belgian citizens who had operated the camp, including members of the SS unit of Belgian volunteers. The evidence provided by local officials and former inmates was initially smuggled out of the country to London by the resistance until liberation late in 1944.

After their country had been liberated, the Belgians also brought charges against a wider range of low-level guards at the Auschwitz, Mauthausen, and Majdanek concentration camps and at the camps at Anvers and Breendonk, from which Jews were sent East. Charges were brought against nine SS soldiers who had operated Anvers. These charges specified that 25,441 Jews had been deported to Auschwitz-Birkenau and that of these only 1,195 had survived. Charges included those against a German Jewish "kapo," Sternberg Siegfried, for his mistreatment of fellow inmates of the Greditz camp.[11]

The fact that the Belgian government prosecuted the persecutors of the Jews—both as a government-in-exile and on its return— appears to have gone unnoticed by scholars until now. In a 2010 study for Yad Vashem, Nico Wouters argues that Belgian authorities consistently failed to recognize the special nature of the attack on the Jews even when trials of collaborators and Belgian members of the SS were conducted in the later 1940s.[12] He is particularly critical of the behavior of the Belgian government-in-exile in London and its actions after it was restored to office in Brussels following liberation.

This view needs to be balanced by information now available from the UNWCC archive. By March 1945 the UNWCC had endorsed Belgium's proposed prosecutions for the mistreatment of Belgian prisoners at Auschwitz-Birkenau:

> <translation>"Assassination of numerous Belgians (exclusively Jews, it seems) transported to these camps where they were gathered together in specially designed chambers where gas was circulated that led, after a very brief delay, to the death of the victims. The bodies were then burned in crematoria. Furthermore, in 1944 the Belgians were forced to forced labor under absolutely inhuman conditions, being the subject of much abuse."[13]

The list of those accused by Belgian authorities began with Adolf Hitler and ran down the Nazi command chain and into the camp itself, to include female members of the SS, the camp doctors, and a number of prisoners classified as ordinary criminals and political prisoners who had participated in the functioning of the camp. The same charge files went on to level charges that, while familiar today, were shocking to contemporary observers:

> The concentration camps of Oswiecim (Auschwitz) and Rajsko (Birkenau) were true camps of extermination. The Germans systematically murdered hundreds of thousands of victims there, mostly civilians transported to the camps from all parts of Europe. The Germans made them sick by giving them injections. Moreover, they proceeded to exterminate very large numbers of victims by groups, making them pass into gas chambers. The bodies were then burnt in special ovens. The Germans indulged in many acts of brutality in these camps against internees who they forced to work. These acts were endured by the most diverse range of people. It will be necessary to refer to the many reports which have been produced, notably by the executive officer of the President (War Refugee Board of Washington) and by the Polish government.[14]

Czechoslovakia

Czechoslovakia was not liberated until the spring of 1945, and yet by then its exiled government in London had already brought hundreds of indictments against the Nazis and their allies. These charges were based partly on information on executions that the Nazis had published proudly in the local newspapers and partly on information gathered and transmitted by the underground government in Czechoslovakia. A considerable number of these were for crimes against Jews.

In December 1944 the Czech government charged 124 individuals, from the Nazi leadership through midlevel officials and commanders all the way down the ranks to SS guards, with a range of crimes.[15] These concerned the deportation of Czech citizens, including Jews, to Buchenwald and the maltreatment, torture, and murder of these citizens in the camp. In January 1945 the Czech government brought similar charges against a comparable number of Nazis for crimes against Czech citizens in other camps. These camps included Dachau, Natzweiler, Theresienstadt, and Auschwitz-Birkenau.[16] The names of the Nazi leaders and senior officers running the occupation of their country were publicly known, but the names of responsible lower-level SS and Gestapo staff had to be collected and transmitted to London, on pain of torture or murder if those collecting and communicating the information were discovered.

The behavior of the Nazis in response to acts of resistance was terrifyingly and intentionally plain. In response to the killing of SD leader Reinhard Heydrich by Czech and British fighters in a 1942 ambush, for example, the Nazis murdered the entire population of the village of Lidice.

After liberation, the Czech government brought many more cases to the commission, and these, too, included indictments for the extermination of Jews. Indeed, some of the last cases to be brought before the commission just before it was closed in March 1948 were charges against the staff of Einsatzkommando 14, for the killing of some 2,030 people, including Gypsies, Jews, Slovaks, and two US air crew over the winter of 1944 to 1945.[17]

Denmark

There was strong social and governmental support for Jews in Denmark and a comparatively lenient approach by the Nazis. Consequently, over 99 percent of the country's Jewish population survived, not least because the Germans themselves sent warnings of their planned arrests of the Jews.[18]

The Danish government joined the commission after liberation and brought 192 cases to it over the following two and a half years. Fourteen of these concerned crimes against Jews, beginning with the third case submitted. In contrast to the Czech practice, the Danes brought separate charges against individual Nazis for the arrest and deportation of Jews, citing their "zeal and brutality" and "barbaric ill-treatments and murder of Jews." The Gestapo chief, Dr. Rudolf Mildner, was, for example, charged with the "deportations of Danish communists and Jews" in the autumn of 1943.[19] The accused also included a Major Thyssen in the German army, who was charged with the arrest and subsequent deportation of two Jews in the town of Aalborg on October 1, 1943.[20] In the closing months of the war a member of the Gestapo in Aalborg, Oberscharführer Unger, was charged with various tortures and murders of members of the resistance and the blowing up of the premises of a dentist Jacobsen, "because he was a Jew."[21] In February 1948 charges were brought against SS officer Rolf Günther, who was alleged to have been sent from Berlin in the autumn of 1943 to "carry through an action at which so many Jews as could be got hold of were sent to Concentration Camps in Germany."[22]

France

Antisemitism was widespread in France and collaboration with the Nazis, the official policy of the government established after the surrender in 1940 in the spa town of Vichy. Until late in 1943 the Nazis did not occupy southern or western France, but the Vichy government nevertheless supported Nazi anti-Jewish policies and actions. The French government and many citizens assisted in the destruction of Jews in France, not only targeting Jews who were French citizens but also refugees from other parts of Europe who had fled there before the invasion, seeking refuge.

It is therefore startling to find that among the first charges brought to the commission by General de Gaulle's exiled Committee of National Liberation in London concerned the persecution of Jews. On February 1, 1944, France brought charges against SS officer Alois Brunner "and all his subordinates" for crimes committed in the "Jewish concentration camps" [underlining part of original file] of Pithivier, Compiegne, Drancy, Beaune-La-Rolande etc.," for a list of crimes including "murder and massacre of civilians, execution of hostages, torture of civilians, forced prostitution, deportation of civilians, internment of civilians in inhumane conditions and use of asphyxiating gases." Parallel charges were brought against other SS personnel at Drancy at the same time and against others later in 1945. The original charges were supported by affidavits from French police at Drancy and supplemented by others given in London on July 18, 1944 (before the liberation of Paris).[23] Brunner survived the war, emerging in the US zone of occupation and escaping to live abroad, despite attempts by the communist government in East Germany to extradite him in the 1980s.

The total of around ninety cases involving Jews brought by France provides a wide range of other examples. In the dossiers of thirty-five charges against accused Germans submitted in March 1944 (signed off on and compiled by the eminent human rights campaigner René Cassin), France addressed conditions in Stalag 325 Rawa-Ruska, a prisoner of war camp in Galicia (then part of Poland) in 1942 and 1943. These detailed a range of crimes, not just against French prisoners of war but also against other targeted populations, including Jews.

On August 2, 1944, charges were brought against the Gestapo staff at St. Etienne (Loire) for the torture, on December 18, 1943, of three seventeen-year-old schoolchildren for being Jews and for supporting the Gaullist resistance. The indictment records that, among other measures, they were tortured by having their hands crushed in a press.[24]

In February 1948 France brought some final cases to the commission for approval, including accusations against Gestapo members based in Nancy. These included a number of crimes against Jewish families, including deportation.[25]

Greece

In November 1944 the Greek government-in-exile in London indicted SS brigade leader Jürgen Stroop for ordering the persecution of the Jews, citing his public order of October 3, 1943, for the registration of all Jews on pain of death.[26] Later the Greek government filed charges with the commission in the spring of 1946 against SS general Walter Simana for his actions during the occupation in 1943 and 1944.[27] The charges began by stating that, "As C. in C [commander in chief] in Greece in 1943–1944 he issued orders and regulations for the arrest and execution of hostages, for the mass execution of civilians without trial, for the extermination of Jews[,] etc." This account specifically included the "persecution of Jews in Greece": "Out of 75,477 Jews living in Greece, 65,000 were exterminated in Greece or during their transportation to Poland, Germany etc., under the most inhuman conditions." The charges were supported by 12 affidavits.

In December 1946 charges were laid against Lieutenant Hildebrandt, an officer in the German Army, for actions against Jews in Castoria and Clissoura in 1944.[28] He was accused of the mass execution of the Jews of Castoria and of a mass murder in Clissoura, whose victims included 250 women and children. Also in December 1946 SS officer Wiessliscennyi and twenty-two accomplices were charged with organizing the deportation to Auschwitz of the Jews of Salonika.[29]

In November 1947 Maj.-Gen. Ulrich Kleemann, then in US custody at Nuremberg, was charged with the murder of 1,200 Jews from Rhodes by means of sending them to sea on barges and then opening the vents in the barge floors to let the sea in and drown the prisoners who were aboard.[30] This case was based on a witness statement from a German political prisoner in the penal unit of the German army; it indicated that the crimes were committed by ordinary German soldiers, since only two SS troops were stationed in Rhodes at that time. This account appears to supplement the existing historical narrative, which records almost all the Jews of Rhodes as dying at Auschwitz.[31]

Luxembourg

The Luxembourg government was not left behind in the effort to indict the Nazis for war crimes, including for the Holocaust. For example, in October 1945 it brought charges against Nazi officials Josef Ackermann and Willy Brauckmann for a range of crimes, including deportations of Jews to Poland and the confiscation of the fortunes of Jewish refugees.[32]

The Netherlands

The twelfth charge brought by the Netherlands to the UNWCC came in May 1944 and included deportations of Jews in September 1943 on the orders of SS officer Hanns Rauter.[33] These deportations were to camps within Holland, including Westerbork and Vught. The latter charge noted the role of the Dutch police in helping the Nazis conduct the rounding up of Jews.

In August 1944 the Netherlands brought charges against the commander of the Mauthausen camp, an SS officer named Etlinger, for a wide range of war crimes between 1940 and 1943.[34] The worst atrocities listed the execution of around 10,000 Jews in a nearby quarry, the torture and poison gas–related medical "experiments" that were conducted, and starvation to death. The case was primarily based on an affidavit from an escaped prisoner, one Dr. Sjoerd Theunis from Liège, whose lengthy statement was taken by Maj. F. J. van der Kroon of the Dutch police for the Dutch government in London in April 1944. Theunis was a member of the resistance who was captured and deported in November 1940—first to Mauthausen and then to a subsequent internment camp, from which he escaped in 1943. Other charges concerned events at Dachau[35] and Theresienstadt.[36]

In 1947 the Netherlands brought charges against the SS staff at Westerbork.[37] These included the camp's commandant, Albert Gemmeker, and eight others, of whom six were already in Dutch custody at the time of the indictment. The very specific charge in this case was for the murder of four young Jews for attempting to escape from the camp on September 7–8, 1944—only a few days after Anne Frank and her family and friends had themselves been transported from Westerbork to Auschwitz. The Netherlands also brought more general charges against SS officers Deppner, Dischner, Gemmeker, and others for their roles at Westerbork from 1942 to 1944.[38]

Another figure from Anne Frank's Amsterdam also appears in the Dutch charge files. Ferdinand Aus der Funten—an SS hauptsturmführer responsible for the deportation of Dutch Jews, including Frank—was indicted along with his command staff in early January 1947 for his role in deporting the inhabitants of a children's home and a mental health institution (1,200 in all) to concentration camps in Germany.[39] The Dutch continued to include crimes against Jews in cases brought to the commission until it was closed. In a charge issued in January 1948, a group of German army personnel and Nazi administrators in the Hague were accused of murder, deportations, and the pillage and destruction of property, specifically targeting Jews.[40]

Trial Reports

In discussions over several years with judges, government researchers, foreign and justice ministry officials, and academics in the Netherlands, I have found no one with a prior awareness of Dutch involvement in the UNWCC, or the systematic approach of the Netherlands national war crimes office of investigations and subsequent trials (with the notable exception of Lisette Schouten, a doctoral student at Heidelberg). Dutch scholarship since the war is largely silent on the scale of the Dutch judicial response to German crimes.[41]

This lack of energy in the Netherlands for taking up and commemorating the work of the Netherlands with the UNWCC is a wasted opportunity. The country's third largest city, The Hague, takes pride in being a global "City for Peace and Justice." It is home to the International Criminal Court and other international legal and judicial institutions. A greater awareness of the extent that the Netherlands prosecuted war crimes (in general) and the Holocaust (in particular) can be of important educational value among the public as a means of increasing support for the Dutch role in international criminal justice. It should be of some international educational value to demonstrate that there was, in the 1940s, an official Dutch effort to prosecute those involved in the system that sent Anne Frank to her death.

Norway

Norway was invaded and occupied in April 1940. The Norwegian government fled to London and from there supported a resistance movement against the Nazis and their collaborationist government under Maj. Vidkun Quisling. The Norwegian government-in-exile in London committed to the Allied cause what resources it had, notably a large merchant fleet.

As a founding member of the commission, Norway began bringing charges forward in early 1944. One of the first was a very broad set of charges against the Nazi commander in Norway, Josef Terboven. This indictment included a number of Terboven's crimes against Jews.[42] Of particular note was his organization of the deportations of Jews to Poland, the first of which was of 500 to 600 Jews aboard the ship *Donar* in November 1942; the second was of 120 Jews the following February. Two indictments against dozens of defendants concerned concentration camps in Norway, at Falstad near Trondheim and at Grini outside Oslo.[43]

Norway was not liberated until the final weeks of the war and, since Hitler feared that the Allies would launch a landing from the sea to provide a direct link with Russia, a very large army of occupation was stationed there until the very end of the war. Nonetheless, many Norwegians escaped to neutral Sweden across the long land border or narrow seas.

In Stockholm, Norwegian officials took hundreds of witness statements that concerned Falstad and Grini; these extracts were used to support numerous cases and provided mutually supporting evidence of crimes against Jews (and others) on a scale not possible for other countries. Norway continued to make use of the commission and, as late as March 1947, brought charges against two SS men for actions at Halden that included the torture and ill-treatment of a group of Jewish men who had tried to flee the country.[44]

Poland

The Nazi invasion of Poland in September 1939 opened unprecedented suffering for the population and intense repression by the Soviet Union in the eastern Poland area that it occupied. Notoriously, the Soviet Union executed tens of thousands of captured Polish military officers in the woods at Katyn. The Polish government fled to London, while Stalin also backed his own exiled government. Poles fought in large numbers in Polish military units, with both the Anglo-Americans and the Soviet Union. In Poland itself the "Home Army" organized resistance and sent information to London.

The antisemitism of non-Jewish Poles toward their fellow citizens during the prewar period was more extreme than what occurred in France. The disinterest (at best) of many Poles toward the Jews is an established part of the general Holocaust narrative. Postwar accounts of Polish prosecutions for crimes against Jews generally refer to a few cases, conceived after liberation, although Alexander Lasik's research has shown that some 700 of 6,500 known guards at Auschwitz were convicted before Polish courts.[45] Nevertheless, as discussed earlier, the Polish government in London took the lead in raising the issue of Nazi atrocities in Europe and in their own country in particular, including for crimes against Jews.

The UNWCC records demonstrate that the Polish government brought 1,535 cases against Germans and other Axis nationals for war crimes to the UNWCC (only France brought more), and about 372 of these included or were focused on crimes against Jews. The Polish delegation to the NOC in May 1945 explained that they had created a specialist section dedicated to developing war crimes charges for crimes against Jews.[46] In April 1944, in one of the first cases submitted by Poland and among the first 80 considered by the commission, Poland brought charges concerning the death camp at Treblinka.[47] This was several months before Treblinka's liberation by the Red Army that summer.

Charges were brought against Dr. Hans Frank, governor of central and southeastern Poland; five Nazi governors; and a "Reichkommisar of Districts" in Poland, one SS captain Sauer, "commander of the camp for Jews at Treblinka B" from "summer 1942 till the end of 1943" (see appendix D for the entire document).

Thus, by this point in the war—months before the D-Day landings at Normandy on June 6, 1944, and more than a year before the London Charter for the IMT at Nuremberg—sixteen states had endorsed the extermination of the Jews at Treblinka as international war crimes.

This first charge includes a firsthand account of what happened at Treblinka, which can only have come from either escaped prisoners, anti-Nazi members of the local population, or both. The Treblinka charge and those related to the other death camps in Poland provide a revoltingly vivid yet restrained contemporary account of the internal operations of the killing centers. As such, these death camp–related charges deserve a prominent place in international public education, scholarship, and Holocaust memorialization.

In June 1944 the UNWCC endorsed a further set of charges against twenty-one Nazis for the extermination of Jews at Belzec, Majdansk, Sobibor, Kosow Podlaski, Chelmno, and Oswiecim-Auschwitz, beginning in early 1942 until the end of 1943.[48] The "Short Statement of Facts" at the front of the dossier of charges states that it is indicting suspected war criminals because:

> In connection with the liquidation of the Jewish ghettos throughout Poland during 1942–1943 and in order to facilitate and speed-up the mass-killing of Jews[,] several special camps for the extermination of Jews were established by the Germans in Poland in which more than one and a half million Polish Jews were murdered as well as large numbers of foreign Jews were exterminated by means of mechanized methods i.e. electric current and gas. . . . "Among the most notorious of these camps the horrible memory of

> which will live for ever in the history of mankind the first place is held by the 'death camp' of Treblinka, which has been the subject of a separate charge."[49]

The charge went on to describe the activities of each of these camps, those that "were established for the only purpose of the extermination of Jews and were originally not intended for any other use" and those, such as Majdanek and Auschwitz, "which were adapted to accommodate the demand for murder." The charge claimed that by the end of 1943, 2.7 million of the original population of 3 million Jews in Poland had been killed.

In September 1944 the UNWCC approved Polish charges against ninety-five Nazis and complicit prisoners at Auschwitz-Birkenau, covering the period June 1940 through 1943.[50] Jews there were subjected to "unimaginable persecution and pitiless extermination." The indictment goes on to note that "the fact that the Germans as early as April 1940 started with the erection of a crematorium makes it obvious that they were bent on quiet mass-killing of the internees of the camp." The charges provide a month-by-month summary of events in the camp, numerous details of the fate of other groups—notably Romany "gypsies" and Catholic priests—and a description of the organizational development of the camp.

In January 1945 Poland brought charges against Hitler and twenty-three other members of the Nazi political and military leadership for "having signed, and issued, during the years 1939 to 1943 numerous laws, decrees and regulations which were designed to outlaw persons defined as Jews, and eventually became an instrument which, through a complete 'capitis deminutio' of such persons, facilitated the achievement of the German Reich's final aim: the biological extermination of Jews in Poland."[51] This led the Polish representative to the UNWCC to make several broader observations, which were included as part of the war crimes charge file:

> Present day Germany had from the very inception of the new regime adopted a special attitude to human beings which are from the point of view of race, creed, nationality and religion described as Jews.
>
> The attitude can be defined as attack against Jews as human beings. It is really irrelevant from a purely legal point of view why this has been done and for what reasons this point of view has been adopted. To ask for a reason means to seek for explanation and no reasonable explanation can justify this whole complex of measures taken against Jews.
>
> The guarantee of human rights has for a long time become the fundamental principle of civilized nations. Since the foundation stone was laid for the development of modern International Law in the centuries passed by: guarantee of man's fundamental rights has become part and parcel of the community of nations. The way to its general adoption led from the Magna Carta 1215, through the Petition of Right 1628, [and] the Bill of Rights 1789 to what can be described as [a] milestone in world history: the Act

> of Religious freedom introduced by Thomas Jefferson before the General Assembly of Virginia 1785. Proudly it announced to the world: "Whereas, Almighty God has created the mind freed; that all attempts to influence it by temporal punishment, or burthens, or by civil incapacitation, tend only to beget habits of hypocrisy and meanness." It went on saying: "That our civil rights have no dependence on our religious opinions any more than our opinions on physics and geometry."
>
> It enacted therefore that: "All men shall be free to profess, and by argument to maintain their opinions, in matters of religion, and that the same shall in no wise diminish enlarge or affect their civil capacities."
>
> Then came the French Declaration of the Rights of Men and Citizen 1789; it declared that: "The exercise of the natural rights of every man has no other limits that those which are necessary to secure to every other man the free exercise of the same rights."
>
> These two documents have in fact put into concrete form the very fundamental principles which were maturing in mankind for ages past. Once [*sic*] they become common property of the civilized world and part of both the written and unwritten International Law. Out of them has arisen the institution of the "intervention d'humanité." It is the right of any foreign State to intervene with a State or Government in all cases where these sacred principles were violated. Great Wheaton declares such an intervention as justified "when the human rights are violated by a barbarous and cruel Government."
>
> The "intervention of humanity" was several times applied in the course of the XIXth and XXth centuries. It was applied in spite of the strict principles of sovereignty guarded and watched by every state as symbol of its independence. The inference is simple and plain. It does not require any further elucidation: all human beings are born free, they have the right to enjoy full liberty with all others—irrespective of their race, creed or religion. It is therefore legally inconceivable and inadmissible to outlaw human beings only on account and because of their origin, the language they use, the faith they confess or the God they believe in.

The Polish government in London, and later its communist-dominated successor in Warsaw, continued to bring national cases to the UNWCC for endorsement, including the case against Rudolf Hoess, the commandant of Auschwitz.[52] In March 1948 Poland submitted its final two cases for approval. They both concerned atrocities in the camps.[53] In some instances the street addresses of the accused in Germany were given. The last case added to the list of the accused hundreds of camp staff from Auschwitz, Stutthof, Sobibor, Plaszow, and Majdanek.[54] In its submission to the UNWCC the Polish government recognized that shortage of time had prevented the creation of separate evidence files for each individual and asked that they be listed as suspects in cases already approved concerning these camps, which the commission allowed.

To assist readers in making their own evaluation of the indictments brought by Poland, I have included a full charge file here in its original form. This charge, from June 1944, followed one already brought concerning Treblinka and addressed the whole death camp system in Poland (see appendix E).

After the war a number of high-profile trials took place in Warsaw and Krakow. These included that of Auschwitz commander Hoess and of Amon Goeth, commander of Plaszow concentration camp. (Goeth's role has since come to particular prominence in popular awareness of the Holocaust; he was the antagonist in the Steven Spielberg film *Schindler's List.*) The chain of institutional and bureaucratic efforts that these trial efforts were based on, however, has often gone unremarked. Even a recent study of Goeth's trial in Krakow in 1948 does not mention the broader and early effort by the Polish government to indict the Nazis for the extermination of the Jews and to explicitly bring charges against the organizers of the entire extermination effort in Poland over the duration of the war.[55]

In a 1994 study Alexander Lasik describes how some one thousand SS guards were tried, resulting in some six hundred of them being convicted.[56] Polish activity in addressing and prosecuting these "foot soldiers of atrocity" is also corroborated by the Polish representative's own submissions to the commission. A 1947 letter from Dr. Marian Muszkat to Lord Wright describes Poland's efforts to pursue prosecutions of more low-level personnel following the pursuit of more high-profile figures such as Artur Greiser, Amon Goeth, and Rudolf Hoess. Despite the fact that preparations for these trials were still ongoing, Muszkat mentions that Poland had already "received [by extradition; they were seeking more] up to the present moment about 250 war criminals [from among Auschwitz personnel], and hope to find some others from this camp, and then those responsible for the camps in Treblinka, Plaszow, Majdanek, Sztutow and those who ordered the executions carried out by Gestapo men in Warsaw, Radom, and other Polish cities."[57]

In considering the importance of the indictments of Nazis for the extermination of Jews in Poland, it is again worth reminding ourselves of the current conventional wisdom on the topic: that the extermination of the Jews was never publicly denounced by the Allies at the time it was taking place, that the discovery of the death camps at the end of the war was a shock to the world (or at least confirmation of scandalous reports previously seen as propaganda), and that (with the exception of Nuremberg) the judicial response was fragmentary and tailed off in the trials of aged SS guards in the early twenty-first century. Regarding Poland, the indictment and prosecution of death camp staff by the Polish government adds an important dimension to a history that will remain dominated by a broadly felt antisemitism among the Christian Polish public and government.

More than 370 cases against Nazis for crimes against Jews were prepared by the Polish wartime government in London and then after the war in Warsaw. The exterminators were subject to criminal indictments supported by the international community. The charges were not merely "Polish"; they carried the weight and approval of Poland's Western Allies, including that of some of the most eminent jurists of the age. It is clear that the Holocaust had been documented to the point that indictments could be made against the SS staff in the killing centers. The international indictments of the Holocaust, submitted in early 1944, rips away the arguments of those in and around the British and US governments that "we did not really know." From 1942 onward these interests had downplayed the information available on the destruction of the Jews and they sought to prevent and then curtail the activities of the commission. The efforts of FDR through his ambassador, Herbert Pell, were accompanied by obstruction rather than support from the political and official leadership in the US State and War Departments.

The Polish cases are also important evidence to use in combatting Holocaust denial and in serving as a historical record. There are detailed contemporary accounts of the destruction of Europe's Jews and of the wider population of Poland, often from the firsthand experiences of escapees. The evidence from these contemporary legally certified cases reinforces that which is already known: the processes and institutions, including the actions of the Nuremberg tribunal, gathered by Yad Vashem, the Wiener Library, the Simon Wiesenthal Center, the United States Holocaust Memorial Museum, and other research centers. What the public can now see in the newly released UNWCC documents are the huge numbers of internationally endorsed legal indictments against the Nazis for exterminating the Jews of Europe in Poland.

Considerable attention of historians has rightly been given to the antisemitism of non-Jewish Poles and of their government. Indeed, the classification and recognition of "Jew" as a separate category from "Pole" in the presented charges has this element within in it. One charge file states that one of the measures used by the Nazis as a presumed persecution inflicted on Catholic priests was to put them in with Jews.[58]

While Polish antisemitism and sometime collaboration with the Nazis in the persecution of the Jews has been given prominence in Holocaust scholarship, the international indictments of the Nazis by the Polish government for perpetrators of both large-scale and individual actions has not been given its due. It should now be.

It is clear that the Polish government spent much effort and scarce resources in gathering evidence of the Nazi terror against both Jewish and non-Jewish Poles under conditions of constant terror. The government used its fragile communications system with London to convey the evidence to the UNWCC. Such behavior contradicts a blanket assumption of official Polish antisemitism.

Yugoslavia

In April 1941 Yugoslavia was overrun by German forces, who had intermittent support from Bulgarian, Hungarian, and Italian forces. The resistance was divided on political-ethnographic and religious lines, and there was significant organized collaboration, especially by the pro-Nazi Ustaše regime in Croatia. The Royalist government of Yugoslavia participated in all the efforts leading to the creation of the Commission, but by the time that its operations were in full swing in mid-1944, the Allies had decided to back Josip Broz Tito's communist partisan-led forces, who continued to support the Commission.

Among the first few cases brought to the Commission by Yugoslavia before the end of the war were those concerning crimes against Jews.[59] One case from November 1944 concerned the killing of an estimated 50,000 Yugoslav Jews at Auschwitz, for example. The case illustrates co-operation within the US government and between the US government and its allies. The Yugoslav indictment for Auschwitz was based on witness statements from escapees from Auschwitz, including Polish Major Krankenbau (this is likely a pseudonym to protect the witness' name; it means "sickbay" in German, and locations at Auschwitz were accordingly named Krankenbau) and two unnamed Slovak Jews. The indictment states that the five page summary of German actions at Auschwitz was compiled by "US services" and given to Yugoslavia by the US representative on the Commission, who was Herbert Pell at this time. It appears that this may be the same data used by the US War Refugees Board. Other cases brought by Yugoslavia after the war addressed persecutions, arrests, and deportations to camps in Germany and across Europe. Many of these included persecution of Jews as a central element, including some of which were concerned with the focused attacks on Jews in towns and cities including Zagreb, Belgrade, and Sarajevo. Charges were supported not only by witness statements, but also by publications in the Nazi controlled newspapers. These routinely spoke of hostages or resistance fighters as being communists and Jews, though whether in fact the victims were either or both was not established given the lack of a Nazi trial process.

United Kingdom

Neither the Americans nor British (save for the Channel Islands) had direct experience of Nazi occupation, so their experience of the Holocaust was distant. The terms of the Moscow Declaration had been constructed to place general responsibility for prosecutions on the victimized states rather than on the Allies in general, limiting the role of the United Kingdom and the United States in prosecuting antisemitic crimes. In postwar Germany, though, both powers initially bowed to public pressure and prosecuted some cases concerning the camps even when their own nationals were not involved. These prosecutions inevitably encompassed

Jews. Other cases involved Jews who were members of the American and British armed forces and prisoners of war of Germany.

Often British Jews incarcerated as prisoners of war reported particularly poor treatment due to the fact that they were Jewish.[60] One account concerning a POW camp near Hamburg specifically mentions a group with "Indian and Jewish" blood being singled out for particularly poor treatment, underlining the racial aspect to the persecution. Another case noted that a British prisoner already singled out for particular ill-treatment by camp guards concealed his religious identity in order to avoid receiving even worse treatment, possibly even being killed.[61] In short, UK indictments show a clear recognition of the racialized character of Nazi persecution.

In addition to these, however, British prosecutors also brought charges concerning the concentration camps to bring justice on behalf of Allied (United Nations) nationals persecuted by the Germans. The United Kingdom began vigorous prosecutions of Germans for actions in the concentration camps, including Auschwitz, Bergen-Belsen, Natzweiler, Sasel, and Neuengamme, in September 1945. The UNWCC records for these indictments often contain sections specifically regarding crimes against Jews (see chapter 4).[62]

United States

For many of the same reasons as the United Kingdom, the lack of direct experience of occupation meant that the United States had limited opportunities to bring trials of Nazis for persecuting Jewish Americans. Nonetheless, the United States brought a number of important cases concerning Jews in the trials it conducted at Dachau and at Nuremberg in the later 1940s. The study by Kevin Heller provides an overdue and exemplary account of the twelve trials at Nuremberg, which the US military conducted in Germany after the trial of the Nazi leadership by the International Military Tribunal.[63] There was an intense debate, however, within the US government over whether German government crimes against German citizens could be considered a prosecutable crime. The key issue was, and remains to this day, how far the political leaders of states can be held legally accountable by the international community for actions they commit against their own citizens.

Conclusion

A question arising from the study of the large number of international prosecutions launched across Europe over the extermination of the Jews is, Why has this information not been given greater prominence in academic and popular scholarship? According to Patrick Treanor, a full copy of the UNWCC's records was produced and disseminated to the Israeli government at the request of Benjamin Netanyahu while he was Israeli ambassador to the UN in the late 1980s; the records were kept by Yad Vashem.[64] Treanor is a former member of the US Department of Justice Office of Special Investigations charged with investigating Kurt Waldheim, who had appeared in the UNWCC's list of suspects. If Treanor is correct, the records do not appear to have been used in public research and education.

In addition, the official statement by the commission about the existence of charges concerning crimes against Jews published by the British government does not appear to have been noticed these past decades. The official history of the UNWCC (also published by the British government), states that non-governmental organizations also played a role in the prosecutions. The Jewish Agency for Palestine prepared and attempted to file with the commission about 500 cases involving atrocities committed by the Nazis against the Jewish population in Poland.[65] Here, the UNWCC's "Committee 1 (Facts and Evidence)" regretfully refused to assume jurisdiction and suggested to the agency that these cases be submitted by one of the member governments. Many of these cases were later submitted by the Polish National Office which had, in the meantime, assumed responsibility for investigating and preparing many of the original Jewish Agency cases that had arisen out of atrocities in Poland.

No one should think that these indictments fulfilled the impossible task of providing an adequate response to the Holocaust. It is beyond this study to look at the role of the local population in assisting the Nazis in each country or at the quality of trials and extra-judicial punishment of alleged collaborators. We also do not yet have access to a comprehensive set of the records of the trials that occurred as a result of the indictments. While some countries have made their records publicly available through their national archives and have digitized them for ease of access, many trial records are held still in their respective government archives as secret. In the United Nations, the documents of the Human Rights Division created in 1945 are also still largely secret.

Nevertheless, some direct conclusions can be drawn from what information is available. There was a categorical official multilateral condemnation of the extermination of the Jews and from early 1944 there followed a multilaterally endorsed set of indictments against the executioners and the organizers of the extermination system. It is plausible to think that had the commission been permitted to come into existence by the American and British governments in October 1942 when they initially agreed to its creation, rather than in early 1944, the indictments would have flowed earlier too.

Poland brought a comprehensive and cumulative set of indictments related to the death camps and to a great number of the persecutions that occurred across the rest of the country. All the other governments of invaded European members of the commission brought indictments for individual acts against the Jews as well, for the concentration camp and deportation systems in their countries and for the deaths of their citizens at the death camps in Poland, in Germany, and in other parts of Europe.

The public condemnation of extermination by the United Nations alliance in 1942 and the extensive contemporary international legal effort by Allied legal staffs make even more apparent the lack of effort to save the Jews. The commonly heard line of argument—that "we did not really know and this explains why we did not do more to help"—becomes increasingly weak when it is clear that the Allied governments did know, did condemn, and did have sufficient legal footing and firsthand evidence to approve hundreds of criminal indictments, yet they still did not help the Jews. The lack of effort and interest in helping the Jews is often placed as a responsibility on the strongest Western Allied governments, namely the Americans and the British. An examination of the various legal and political efforts, however, suggests that there were important members of each of these governments, and especially those associated with the UNWCC, who were pressing for more action as far as their positions allowed. Moreover, the representatives and governments-in-exile of continental Europe were not merely "sounding the alarm" about Nazi atrocities; they were also bringing charges against their oppressors for crimes against their citizens, whether nationalist or communist, Christian or Jew.

Perhaps the most searing condemnation of indifference in the US Congress and the State Department, in the British Parliament and Foreign Office, is contained in the pages of the charges themselves. Any sense that claims of German atrocities were exaggerated is immediately overwhelmed by the vivid, poignant, contemporary accounts that, in a number of critical examples, come from eyewitness escapees of the death camps. These accounts were recorded by resistance groups acting under conditions of Nazi terror, they were transmitted to London, and they were officially endorsed by member states. Perhaps some American and British officials never sent reports to their capitals. Nevertheless, it is clear, not least in the 1944 Yugoslav case, that some American officials were supplying their allies with evidence to support a case about Auschwitz at a time when the US State Department was defying the president's expressed intent and doing as little as possible.

These accounts of the extermination examined here for the first time require more attention. In Holocaust education we listen to accounts given by aged survivors. But the officially examined, endorsed, and recorded statements written during and shortly after the war express a freshness in the gruesome detail that turns the stomach. These accounts demand to be heard widely, now that they have finally been released from archival prison. They add to other well-known material, notably the extensive documents that the Nazis wrote about their murders which were used so effectively at Nuremberg and which also form a large part of the huge documentation of the 1940s UN records of displaced persons across Europe recorded by the International Tracing Service, which was itself only recently made public.

The UNWCC archives now provide to the seventeen member states and the institutions to which they belong a fresh and huge foundation for their work on human rights, predating later work by the UN such as the 1948 Universal Declaration of Human Rights. The indictments of the 1940s demonstrate that in this extreme crisis of Nazi occupation, peoples and governments sought legal redress as well as military victory. In each country there are now available for research a stack of indictments presented by the governments of the 1940s for the crimes of the Holocaust. These original accounts can be added to the postwar evidence of survivors, of forensic archeology, and of the Nazis' own documents to combat Holocaust denial.

It appears clear from these documents that the values placed on human rights as it emerged in Europe after the war and that found expression in the European Convention on Human Rights were not simply produced by a general public revulsion at Nazism, with legal expression only at Nuremberg. Rather, in each country the legal process envisaged in the Declaration at St. James's Palace of 1942 and focused by the Moscow Declaration of 1943 was implemented by states through the UNWCC. They were able to create large-scale legal processes for the trial of suspected war criminals all over Europe in the years following the war.

The same processes provided a systematic foundation that produced the great international agreements of the later 1940s: the UN charter, the four Geneva conventions, the genocide convention, and the Universal Declaration of Human Rights. Most accounts of the creation of these accords describe them as emanating from the general revulsion at the behavior of the Nazis—revulsion that was only turned into action at the trial of the Nazi leadership at Nuremberg. A history of human rights where the immediate post–Second World War understanding is limited to Nuremberg and the achievements of the legal activists who lobbied for these subsequent agreements—such as Raphael Lemkin and Hersch Lauterpacht—is too easy to dismiss as insubstantial. The global effort to bring justice to war criminals through the UNWCC provided a much more substantial and lasting base for the ensuing agreements. The diplomats and lawyers at the UN and in the national capitals of UNWCC member states were all aware of their respective nation's role in the broader UNWCC process.

Donald Bloxham argues that, "Nazi Jewish policy was not subjected to systematic judicial examination directly after the war" and that it was rare indeed for the attack on the Jews to be the subject of trials after the war.[66] The files of the UNWCC reveal indictments and cases brought to trial in every country where the Holocaust occurred and that the resistance movements and the governments in London combined in their efforts to bring justice to the victims.

Notes

1. UNWCC, "Polish Charges against German War Criminals," RN 29/P/G/9, CHN 9, (February 23, 1944).
2. Elizabeth Kolbert, "The Last Trial," *New Yorker*, February 16, 2015.
3. The charge file naming Groening as a suspected war criminal can be found in UNWCC, "Polish Charges against German War Criminals," RN 4771/P/G/139, CHN 139, March 6, 1947. The specific naming of Groening is found on p. 1967.
4. István Deák, Jan T. Gross, and Tony Judt, eds., *The Politics of Retribution in Europe* (Princeton: Princeton University Press, 2000); Patricia Heberer and Jürgen Matthäus, *Atrocities on Trial: Historical Perspectives on the Politics of Prosecuting War Crimes* (Lincoln: University of Nebraska Press, 2008); David Bankier and Dan Michman, eds., *Holocaust and Justice: Representation and Historiography of the Holocaust in Post-War Trials* (Jerusalem: Yad Vashem, 2011).
5. Donald Bloxham, "Jewish Witnesses in War Crimes Trials of the Postwar Era," in *Holocaust Historiography in Context*, ed. David Bankier and Dan Michman, 539–54 (Jerusalem: Yad Vashem, 2008).
6. Donald Bloxham, "Prosecuting the Past in the Postwar Decade," in *Holocaust and Justice: Representation and Historiography of the Holocaust in Post-War Trials*, ed. David Bankier and Dan Michman, 23–43 (Jerusalem: Yad Vashem, 2011), 32–33.
7. In total there were 461 cases withdrawn (for a range of reasons) by the member states of the UNWCC. They are listed in reels 30 and 31 of the original UNWCC archive.
8. "Trial of Major War Criminals," part 2, December 14, 1945, 416 document 3311-PS, exhibit USA 293.
9. UNWCC, "Belgian Charges against German War Criminals," RN 274/B/G/16, CHN 9, September 4, 1944.
10. Breedonck and its related camps spawned a wide range of charges that were submitted by Belgium against the camp's officials and leaders. The following are a sampling of these, all found within the compilation of "Belgian Charges against German War Criminals," produced by the UNWCC: RN 86/B/G/2, CN 4, 9–18, May 2, 1944; RN 87/B/G/3, CN 5, May 3, 1944; RN 88/B/G/4, CN 6, May 3, 1944; RN 89/B/G/5, CN 7, May 3, 1944; RN 91/B/G/7, CN 8. May 6, 1944; RN 92/B/G/8, CN 9, May 6, 1944; RN 93/B/G/9, CN 10, May 6, 1944; RN 98/B/G/10, CN 13, May 13, 1944; RN 630/B/G/24, CN A.G. Breedonck, March 18, 1945.
11. UNWCC, "Belgian Charges against German War Criminals," RN 6383/B/G/374, CN 581/589, 1,171–1,178, August 18, 1947.
12. Nico Wouters, "The Belgian Trials (1945–1951)," in *Holocaust and Justice: Representation and Historiography of the Holocaust in Post-War Trials*, ed. David Bankier and Dan Michman, 219–44 (Jerusalem: Yad Vashem, 2011). See also Martin Conway, "Justice in Postwar Belgium," and Luc Huyse, "The Criminal Justice System as a Political Actor in Regime Transitions, the Case of Belgium, 1944–1950," both in *The Politics of Retribution in Europe*, ed. István Deák, Jan T. Gross, and Tony Judt, 133–56 and 157–72, respectively (Princeton: Princeton University Press, 2000).

13. UNWCC, "Belgian Charges against German War Criminals," RN 628/B/G/22, CN 4 (London), March 4, 1944. Original French text: "Assassinat de nombreux Belges (exclusivement Juifs semble-t-il) transportés dans ces camps où ils étaient réunis dans des chambres spéecialement aménagées et où l'on faisait circuler des gaz entrainant a trés bref délai la mort des victimes. Les corps étaient ensuite brulés dans des fours crematoires. D'autre part, en 1944 des Belges ont été contraints au travail forcé dans des conditions absolument inhumaines, étant l'objet de nombreux mauvais traitements."
14. Original French text: "Les camps de concentration de Oswiecim (Auschwitz) et Rajsko (Birkenau) etaient de véritables camps d'extermination. Les Allemands y ont systematiquement assassiné des centaines de miliers de victimes, en géneral des civils transportés dans ces camps de toutes les régions d'Europe. Les Allemands achevaient les malades en leur donnant des piqures. D'autre part, ils procédaient a l'extermination par groupes de trés nombreuses victimes qu'ils faisaient passer dans des chambres de gaz. Les corps étaient ensuite brulés dans des fours speciaux. Les Allemands se sont livrés dans ces camps à de nombreux actes de brutalité à l'égard des internés qu'ils faisaient travailler. Ces actes ont revêtu les caractères les plus divers. Il y aura lieu de s'en référer aux nombreux rapports qui out été établis notamment par l'executive officer of the president (War Refugee Board of Washington) ainsi que par le gouvernement polonais."
15. UNWCC, "Czech Charges against German War Criminals," RN 423/Cz/G/9, CN Z 11/44, December 5, 1944.
16. UNWCC, "Czech Charges against German War Criminals," RN 465/Cz/G/15, CN Z 15/44, January 2, 1945.
17. UNWCC, "Czech Charges against German War Criminals," RN 7706/Cz/G/234, CN 83, 1,658–1,662, February 18, 1948.
18. Michael Ignatieff, "One Country Saved Its Jews; Were They Just Better People? The Surprising Truth About Denmark in the Holocaust," review of Bo Lidegaard, *Countrymen: The Untold Story of How Denmark's Jews Escaped the Nazis*, in *New Republic*, December 14, 2013, available at http://www.newrepublic.com/article/115670/denmark-holocaust-bo-lidegaards-countrymen-reviewed.
19. UNWCC, "Danish Charges against German War Criminals," RN 2897/D/G/31, no case date in original file.
20. UNWCC, "Danish Charges against German War Criminals," RN 2917/D/G/51, no case date in original file.
21. UNWCC, "Danish Charges against German War Criminals," RN 5314/D/G/131, no case date in original file.
22. UNWCC, "Danish Charges against German War Criminals," RN 7680/D/G/189, no case date in original file.
23. UNWCC, "French Charges against German War Criminals," RN 4/F/G/4, CN 8, February 1, 1944; RN 7/F/G/7, CN 35, March 7, 1944; RN 8/F/G/8, CN 10, 804–808, March 7, 1944; and RN 13/F/G/13, CN 7, 818–840, February 1, 1944.
24. UNWCC, "French Charges against German War Criminals," RN 192/Fr/G/50, CN 54, August 2, 1944.

25. UNWCC, "French Charges against German War Criminals," RN 7555/Fr/G/2209, CN 2442, February 9, 1948.
26. UNWCC, "Greek Charges against German War Criminals," RN 385/Gr/G/7, CHN 8, November 7, 1944.
27. UNWCC, "Greek Charges against German War Criminals," RN 348/Gr/G/1, CHN 5/137/46, May 1, 1946 (redrafted).
28. UNWCC, "Greek Charges against German War Criminals," RN 4345/Gr/G/51, CHN 206/G/52, December 5, 1946.
29. UNWCC, "Greek Charges Against German War Criminals," RN 4348/Gr/G/54, CHN G/55 III/46, December 5, 1946.
30. UNWCC, "Greek Charges against German War Criminals," RN 6903/Gr/G/132, CHN GR/G/136, November 6, 1947.
31. The USHMM, for example, records comparatively few Jews dying at sea, arguing that almost all were killed at Auschwitz. See USHMM website, Special Focus section, "The Holocaust in Greece: Rhodes," available at http://www.ushmm.org/information/exhibitions/online-features/special-focus/holocaust-in-greece/rhodes.
32. UNWCC, "Luxembourg Charges against German War Criminals," RN 1599/L/G/22, CHN12, October 5, 1945.
33. UNWCC, "Dutch Charges against German War Criminals," RN 144/Nl/G/12, CHN 1, June 28, 1944.
34. UNWCC, "Dutch Charges against German War Criminals," RN 240/Nl/G/20, CHN 10, August 18, 1944.
35. UNWCC, "Dutch Charges against German War Criminals," RN 386/Nl/G/32, CHN 35, November 7, 1944.
36. UNWCC, "Dutch Charges against German War Criminals," RN 960/Nl/G/44, CHN 117, June 29, 1945.
37. UNWCC, "Dutch Charges against German War Criminals," RN 4426/Nl/G/347, CHN 423, January 6, 1947.
38. UNWCC, "Dutch Charges against German War Criminals," RN 4979/Ne/G/403, CHN 479, April 18, 1947.
39. UNWCC, "Dutch Charges against German War Criminals," RN 4585/Nl/G/365, CHN 441, January 23, 1947.
40. UNWCC, "Dutch Charges against German War Criminals," RN 7308/Nl/G/577, CHN 654, January 9, 1948.
41. See, for example, Dutch Holocaust historians Abel Herzberg, Jacques Presser, Loe de Jong, and Guus Meershoek, *Dienaren van het gezag: De Amsterdamse politie tijdens de bezetting* (Amsterdam: Van Gennep, 2003) (in Dutch); Ido de Haan, *Na de Ondergang: De herinnering aan de Jodenvervolging in Nederland (1945–1995)* (The Hague: Sdu Uitgevers, 1997), 87 (in Dutch); Manfred Gerstenfeld, *Europe's Crumbling Myths* (Jerusalem: JCPA, Yad Vashem, and World Jewish Congress, 2003), 72–79; Isaac Lipschits, *De Kleine Sjoa: Joden in Naoorlogs Nederland* (Amsterdam: Mets & Schilt, 2001), 10 (in Dutch); Joel S. Fishman, in "The Netherlands: Majority-Minority Relations, The War Orphan Controversy," in *Dutch Jewish History*, vol. 1:

Proceedings of the Symposium on the History of the Jews in The Netherlands, ed. Jozeph Michman and Tirtsah Levie, 219–44 (Jerusalem: Tel Aviv University, Hebrew University of Jerusalem, and Institute for Research on Dutch Jewry, 1984), 431; Elma Verhey, *Om het joodse kind* (Amsterdam: Nijgh & van Ditmar, 1991) (in Dutch); Manfred Gerstenfeld, "Jewish War Claims in The Netherlands: A Case Study," *Jewish Political Studies Review* 12, no. 1–2 (2000): 55–95; Speech given at the International Symposium on the Occasion of the Thirty-Year Jubilee of CIDI [Center for Information and Documentation on Israel]. These references can all be found in the endnotes of Manfred Gerstenfeld, review of *De Drie van Breda: Duitse oorlogsmisdadigers in Nederlandse gevangenschap 1945–1989* by Hinke Piersma, *Jewish Political Studies Review* 18, no. 1–2 (2006), available at http://www.jcpa.org/phas/phas-piersma-06.htm.

42. UNWCC, "Norwegian Charges against German War Criminals," RN 131/N/G/4, CHN 1, June 13, 1944.
43. UNWCC, "Norwegian Charges against German War Criminals," RN 216/N/G/7, CHNs 13–24, August 6, 1944 and RN 391/N/G/12, CHNs 37–61, November 22, 1944.
44. UNWCC, "Norwegian Charges against German War Criminals," RN 4898/N/G/77, CHNs 535–536, March 28, 1947.
45. Alexander Lasik, "Postwar Prosecution of the Auschwitz SS," in *Anatomy of the Auschwitz Death Camp*, ed. Yisrael Gutman and Michael Berenbaum, 219–44 (Bloomington: Indiana University Press, 1994).
46. UNWCC, "Information Supplied by the National Offices as to Their Organisation and Operation," May 22, 1945, 11.
47. UNWCC, "Polish Charges against German War Criminals," RN 79/P/G/16, CHN 15, April 24, 1944.
48. UNWCC, "Polish Charges against German War Criminals," RN 123/P/G/21, CHN 20, June 3, 1944.
49. Ibid., p. 2d of the original dossier.
50. UNWCC, "Polish Charges against German War Criminals," RN 304/P/G/30, CHN 30, September 1, 1944.
51. UNWCC, "Polish Charges against German War Criminals," RN 473/P/G/34, CHN 34, January 5, 1945.
52. UNWCC, "Polish Charges against German War Criminals," RN 304/P/G/30, CHN 30, September 1, 1944.
53. UNWCC, "Polish Charges against German War Criminals," RN 7866/P/G/1563 and RN 7867/P/G/1564, March 3, 1948.
54. Ibid., cont. p. 1.
55. Edyta Gawron, "Amon Goeth's Trial in Cracow: Its Impact on Holocaust Awareness in Poland," in *Holocaust and Justice: Representation and Historiography of the Holocaust in Post-War Trials*, ed. David Bankier and Dan Michman, 281–98 (Jerusalem: Yad Vashem, 2011).
56. Lasik, "Postwar Prosecution."

57. UNWCC, "Polish Progress Report and Plans Relating to War Criminals," letter from Dr. Marian Muszkat to the Rt. Hon. Lord Wright, UNWCC Ref. No. A.38, March 11, 1947.
58. UNWCC, "Polish Charges against German War Criminals," RN 111/P/G/20, CHN 21, 816–832, September 1, 1944.
59. UNWCC, "Yugoslav Charges against German War Criminals," RN 321/Y/G/4, CN R/N/4, 246–60, September 25, 1944; and RN 380/Y/G/7, CN R/N/7, 275–84, November 4, 1944.
60. UNWCC, "British Charges against German War Criminals," RN 1910/UK/G/316, CN UK-G/B 319, November 19, 1945; RN 2430/UK/G/429, CN UK-G/B 431, February 13, 1946; and RN 6045/UK/G/645, CN UK-G/B 623, July 30, 1947.
61. UNWCC, "British Charges against German War Criminals," RN 2740/UK/G/478 CN UK-G/B 480, March 28, 1947.
62. UNWCC, "British Charges against German War Criminals," RN 6045/UK/G/645, CN UK-G/B 517, May 3, 1946; RN 3027/UK/G/524, CN UK-G/B 525, February 24, 1947; and RN 3264/UK/G/556, CN UK-G/B 554, June 12, 1946.
63. Kevin Jon Heller, *The Nuremberg Military Tribunals and the Origins of International Criminal Law* (Oxford: Oxford University Press, 2011).
64. Edith Lederer, chair, "UNWCC Records (1943–1949): Past, Present, and Future" panel discussion, UN Live, United Nations WebTV, November 11, 2014, available at: http://webtv.un.org/%E2%80%8Bmeetings-events/watch/united-nations-war-crimes-commission-records-1943–1949-past-present-and-future-panel-discussion/3886628590001#full-text.
65. UNWCC, *Complete History of the United Nations War Crimes Commission and the Development of the Laws of War* (London: Her Majesty's Stationery Office, 1948), 483.
66. Bloxham, "Prosecuting the Past," 32–33.

6

FAIR TRIALS AND COLLECTIVE RESPONSIBILITY FOR CRIMINAL ACTS

The United Nations War Crimes Commission achieved fair standards in the legal systems it facilitated, as demonstrated by the following analysis of the statistical and documentary evidence it produced along with recent studies of national trials. The tribunals held at Nuremberg and Tokyo that tried national leaders have already been discussed extensively in the literature. However, the role the UNWCC played in pursuing these national leaders for major crimes has been given little attention. These crimes include crimes against humanity, genocide, and aggressive war.

This chapter also considers lower-level criminals and crimes, specifically the statistical evidence of them, and then includes a review of the global system administered by the commission, the types of actions that could be judged criminal, and the quality of trials held by national governments. The statistics include how many cases were withdrawn after being submitted by states to the commission, how many people accused of war crimes were found by the commission not to warrant being charged as war criminals, and how many people tried in resulting cases reported to the commission were judged innocent. As has been mentioned, the UNWCC closed its operation before many trials were complete and many states did not report all of their trials even before its closure.

Legal issues will also be reviewed, including the process of trials, the types of crime committed, and the types of responsibility assigned for committing certain crimes. A number of arguments are considered, including the general argument of victors' justice, the issue of trying people for offenses that were not ruled as crimes at the time they were committed, the issues of "hearsay" evidence, and the defense of "only obeying orders," or "only giving orders." A particular set of issues relate to how far individual responsibility can arise from being part of a criminal group.

The UNWCC set out criteria advising member states how to present charges in one of its first actions in December 1943.[1] These included a requirement for information concerning both the defense and the prosecution; the international and national laws that had been broken; a short statement of facts and supporting documents; and that the offender be identified by name, rank, and position. States were also asked to demonstrate the level of responsibility of the accused for the alleged crime, how far the accused acted on his or her own initiative, and how far the accused had acted in obedience to orders or according to a court order. The list of criteria concluded with a request for a summary of a likely defense and the likelihood that any trial would produce a conviction.

The commission produced an outline form under these headings, which at first glance has the routine bureaucratic impact of a traffic ticket: offense charged, date, name of accused, international and national crime, and so forth. Member states all used this form of presentation to bring their cases to the commission.

The administration of this uniform system for the presentation and consideration of cases was implemented in thousands of pretrial case dossiers and rebuts any notion that it was a random, arbitrary process. It also shows that from the outset issues surrounding the defense were included and considered.

The commission's own statistics reveal that it was far from automatic for states to have the UNWCC's approval in charging suspects as war criminals. To begin with, some 5 percent of the 8,000-plus charge files brought to the commission—454 in all—were either rejected by the commission's Committee 1 (Facts and Evidence) or adjourned or withdrawn entirely by the state that had brought the charge(s).[2]

Of the 95 percent of cases that were accepted, nearly a third of the people charged were not listed as indicted war criminals.[3] For example, states brought charges against 34,270 enemy citizens and units. Of these, 22,409 were listed as accused war criminals, 9,339 were listed as suspects, and 2,522 as material witnesses. Oskar Groening, for instance—the "accountant of Auschwitz"—was charged by Poland in 1947 as a member of a group of 300 SS staff at the camp.[4] The commission only charged him as a suspect in the "common design" of the SS in the camp, however, not as an indicted war criminal. The downgrading of a large portion of those charged, from "war criminal" to "suspect," shows an important aspect of due process was implemented by the commission within the legal processes of member states.

A comparable respect for process can be found in the outcomes of the subsequent trials. The number of people found not guilty is an equally important indicator of whether the operations of a court are fair or simply a venue for the powerful to hold "show trials" of those whose only crime is to be an enemy. While in individual cases factors other than the quality of process may influence the judgment (that is, acquittal or not), overall the high proportion of acquittals is evidence of the quality of the process.

Some 15 percent of the war criminals who faced trial as part of the UNWCC system were acquitted. In its *Complete History*, the UNWCC provides a snapshot of the 1,993 trials whose outcomes had been reported to it from across Asia and Europe as of March 1, 1948.[5] Of the 2,794 accused, 415 were acquitted (see Table 6.1). This compares favorably to the acquittal rate of the International Criminal Tribunal for former Yugoslavia (ICTY), which was also 15 percent.[6] The fairness of the UNWCC's proceedings and the trials conducted within countries is demonstrated in the fact that large numbers of cases were subject to international legal review and some cases were rejected; furthermore, of those that came to trial, a significant number produced acquittals. This evidence strongly supports the idea that the overall process was fair. But was there adequate attention to fairness in the trials themselves?

TABLE 6.1. Progress Report of War Crimes Trials from Data Available as of March 1, 1948

Crimes in Europe	*Cases tried*	*Number of accused*	*Sentenced to death*	*Sentenced to imprisonment*	*Acquitted*	*Remarks*
Czechoslovakia	–	18,496	362	13,969	4,165	as at January 11, 1946
France	117	427	151	234	42	as at January 2, 1948
Greece	6	11	3	7	1	as at January 6, 1947
Netherlands	2	2	2	–	–	as at January 3, 1948
Norway	74	74	18	48	8	as at January 3, 1948
Poland	–	296	75	173	8	as at January 1, 1948
United Kingdom	274	909	214	437	258	as at January 3, 1948
United States	489	1,672	426	990	256	January 3, 1948
Yugoslavia	5	79	63	16	48	as at January 5, 1947
Total	967	21,963	1,314	15,874	4,786	

(continued)

TABLE 6.1. Progress Report of War Crimes Trials from Data Available as of March 1, 1948 (*Continued*)

Crimes in Europe	*Cases tried*	*Number of accused*	*Sentenced to death*	*Sentenced to imprisonment*	*Acquitted*	*Remarks*
Crimes in the Far East						
Australia	259	769	138	397	234	as at January 3, 1948
Netherlands East Indies	175	308	102	199	7	as at January 3, 1948
United Kingdom	388	1,143	305	718	120	as at January 3, 1948
United States	202	574	140	380	54	as at February 5, 1947
Total	1,024	2,794	685	1,694	415	

Note: Czechoslovakia's numbers include both war criminals and collaborators.
Source: UNWCC, *Complete History of the United Nations War Crimes Commission and the Development of the Laws of War* (London: His Majesty's Stationery Office, 1948), 518.

The Fundamentals of Fair Trials

The fundamentals of a fair trial are laid out in the Statute of the International Criminal Court,[7] as well as in other internationally agreed-on documents and treaties, such as the European Convention on Human Rights.[8] Some of these rules are: court should be founded in law, take place in public, and be both independent and impartial; the accused should have the opportunity to prepare a defense, have access to translation where needed, and face trial without undue delay; the accused shall be presumed innocent until proven guilty; and evidence shall generally be given in person but may be given through written testimony.

A number of these issues can be settled straightaway in regards to the work of the UNWCC. The national trials the commission supported did take place in public—there is no evidence of secret national trials within the records of the commission. There was a presumption of innocence in the criteria established by the commission, defendants were allowed to prepare their defenses, and translation services were available. In some cases the adequacy of translation and the time given for defense were raised as problems, but in general the legal legitimacy of the courts and trials was accepted by the defense. As an example, Mark Ellis, the executive director of the International Bar Association, quotes the example of

Japanese Lt. Gen. Ito Takeo, who, despite initial trepidation about the fairness of the court, soon "began to feel more at ease with the President and the members of the Court because of the way the trial has been conducted."[9]

The UNWCC sought to support fair trials through its working procedures. First, as laid out in the St James's Declaration of January 1942, member states considered international support an important insurance against accusations of mob rule and victors' justice.[10] This was a key motive of states in the creation of the UNWCC, as Lord Wright highlighted at the opening of the NOC in London. States chose to seek international support for their legal actions. Each state received the support of sixteen other nations for the charges being brought, which provided against the accusation of partiality.

No state in the twenty-first century considers it beneficial to act in this multilateral manner. Yet, in the 1940s four major powers and now permanent members of the UN Security Council (China, France, the United Kingdom, and the United States) chose to do this, along with many of their allies. The accusation of victors' justice is countered both by officials' determination to have international support for their cases and the fact that cases did not automatically receive their full support.

In forming the UNWCC the Allies were seeking to put their enemies on trial for actions they had taken outside accepted standards of warfare; they were not seeking to judge their own actions and they had internal processes governing the conduct of their governments and armed forces. Nor did the Allies think that the Germans or Japanese could be relied on to try their own people (plus it could not have involved neutral states such as Sweden or Switzerland, who would have considered such a process as a violation of their neutrality).

One of the criticisms leveled at post–World War II justice is that it was unilateral. The Nuremberg and Tokyo IMTs were concluded by victorious states on behalf of the wartime United Nations and Allies, respectively, but without wider engagement. In addition, the military trials carried out by the four powers in their zones of occupation in Germany—the prosecutions under occupation authority Control Order 10—were, it is often claimed, entirely unilateral.[11] In fact, it was general national policy among the Americans, British, and French that Control Order 10 indictments went to the UNWCC for approval prior to trial, and it is well known that the UN General Assembly endorsed the legal basis for the IMTs.

It perhaps needs restating: in general, all national trials had first been approved by the UNWCC. This includes trials conducted by the United States at Dachau, by the Australians at Darwin, by the British at Singapore, by the French at Marseilles, and by the Norwegians at Oslo. This is often not clear to scholars examining trial documents, since the correspondence with the commission took place before and after the trials and by a central government department.

This is true only generally because the records of the commission are incomplete and the records of member states are dispersed around the world and in some cases still classified. Nevertheless, it is clear that a minimum of 1,991 trials took place following presentation to and approval by the UNWCC. Thus, any discussion of trials conducted by the Americans, Australians, British, French, or Poles that took place prior to mid-1948 should include the point that these trials were supported by the weight of an international body that had determined that the accused had a case to answer.

There is a charge of hypocritical victors' justice in that accusers were ostensibly up to the same sort of actions as those being accused. Dresden, Hiroshima, and Nagasaki provide prime examples. In the Pacific War, prolonged face-to-face fighting produced a mutual dehumanization of the enemy. Likewise, there are also cases of the shooting of prisoners that went unpunished and apparently condoned as Anthony Beevor reminds us in his book on the Battle of the Bulge.[12]

Is the incineration of people in cities a war crime, or a crime against humanity? The "Versailles list" of war crimes that was used by the UNWCC and the Hague Convention both outlawed the bombing of undefended places.[13] But all the cities mentioned above were being defended. Luftwaffe generals and pilots were not charged with war crimes for blitzing London or Rotterdam. It has even been argued, with some evidence provided by Japanese government archives, that it was the Soviet invasion of Manchuria and not the atom bombings by the United States that finally produced surrender from Japan.[14]

War is always gruesome and the member states of the commission were deeply concerned with pursuing what was clearly beyond the pale. I am inclined to leave the issue with Ambassador Pell, who commented ruefully that he had been part of commission debates that concluded that bombing cities was not a crime while they themselves were sitting being bombed at the very moment, "shaking the building like a tree in the wind."[15]

"It Wasn't Illegal When the Action Was Taken"

A common accusation against war crimes prosecutions following World War II is that they could not be considered criminal because there was not a recognized assemblage of international criminal laws at the time the offenses were committed. The commission and UNWCC member states recognized this problem long before any charges were brought and worked out several means of demonstrating that there were international legal standards in place before World War II broke out. (Chapter 7 discusses this issue in relation to aggressive war and crimes against humanity.)

First of all, the statements made by Allied leaders (detailed in chapter 3) explicitly placed perpetrators on warning that they would face trial. However, while these statements spoke of atrocities of various kinds, they did not make explicit reference to laws. The UNWCC and its nongovernmental predecessors—the London International Assembly and the Cambridge Commission—considered various crimes. The UNWCC adopted at its fifth meeting the list of thirty-two crimes agreed on by the 1919 Paris Peace Conference's Commission on Responsibilities (figure 6.1). The UNWCC argued that Japan had agreed to them and Germany had accepted them.

In addition, many member states also made use of the Hague Convention on the Rules of Land Warfare agreed in 1907;[16] and, in addition, the Geneva Convention on Prisoners of War of 1929.[17] The commission also required member states to specify which laws—national and international—had been violated as

(i) Murder and massacres—systematic terrorism.
(ii) Putting hostages to death.
(iii) Torture of civilians.
(iv) Deliberate starvation of civilians.
(v) Rape.
(vi) Abduction of girls and women for the purpose of enforced prostitution.
(vii) Deportation of civilians.
(viii) Internment of civilians under inhuman conditions.
(ix) Forced labour of civilians in connection with the military operations of the enemy.
(x) Usurpation of sovereignty during military occupation.
(xi) Compulsory enlistment of soldiers among the inhabitants of occupied territory.
(xii) Attempts to denationalise the inhabitants of occupied territory.
(xiii) Pillage.
(xiv) Confiscation of property.
(xv) Exaction of illegitimate or of exorbitant contributions and requisitions.
(xvi) Debasement of the currency and issue of spurious currency.
(xvii) Imposition of collective penalties.
(xviii) Wanton devastation and destruction of property.
(xix) Deliberate bombardment of undefended places.
(xx) Wanton destruction of religious, charitable, educational, and historical buildings and monuments.
(xxi) Destruction of merchant ships and passenger vessels without warning and without provision for the safety of passengers and crew.
(xxii) Destruction of fishing boats and of relief ships.
(xxiii) Deliberate bombardment of hospitals.
(xxiv) Attack and destruction of hospital ships.
(xxv) Breach of other rules relating to the Red Cross.
(xxvi) Use of deleterious and asphyxiating gases.
(xxvii) Use of explosive or expanding bullets and other inhuman appliances.
(xxviii) Directions to give no quarter.
(xxix) Ill-treatment of wounded and prisoners of war.
(xxx) Employment of prisoners of war on unauthorised works.
(xxxi) Misuse of flags of truce.
(xxxii) Poisoning of wells.

FIGURE 6.1. The "Versailles List" of War Crimes Used by the UNWCC

Source: Report of Subcommittee (1) of the UNWCC, as adopted on December 2, 1943, chap. 1, p. 4.

part of the charge submission process. It is clear, then, that member states declared repeatedly in advance that perpetrators of war crimes would face trial and that the charges were based upon international agreements that preceded the war and which the aggressor states had either been party to or had accepted.

The St. James's Declaration also anticipated in principle the issues of command responsibility, obedience to orders, and indirect responsibility. The declaration stated that people be held responsible for crimes "whether they have ordered them, perpetrated them or participated in them."

Hearsay

An accusation made against the UNWCC was its use of written statements without the witnesses themselves being present. Indeed, when I first encountered UN legal experts to discuss accessing the UNWCC archives, an official expressed the view that its work was dangerously misleading and useless because it was based on so much hearsay evidence.

This use of the word "hearsay" is itself misleading. In normal conversation it means something unsubstantiated—gossip, even—rather than a statement based on direct knowledge. In legal parlance, however, "hearsay" has a technical meaning: that the witness was not present at the site of the crime. The commission recognized the dilemma.[18] Lord Wright cited, with approval, the British argument in the Belsen trials that justice would not have been done had affidavits not been allowed into evidence. This was an acknowledgment that in many cases the witnesses had gone home after the war, often after having been demobilized from their armed forces—a common and unavoidable situation in the circumstances of a world war and its aftermath.[19] In Continental civil law legal systems, the use of evidence without a witness present is quite normal, so the Anglo-American issue of hearsay does not arise.

Finally, it is important to remember that the UNWCC was not acting as a court but as a pretrial validation process. Less-stringent standards of evidence were needed to satisfy the requirement that a case to answer existed. The UNWCC process is comparable to that of a US grand jury or of an investigating magistrate in the Continental legal tradition. With respect to the issue of hearsay in trials themselves, Kevin Heller provides a useful discussion in his study of the Nuremberg military tribunals.[20]

The Rights of the Accused

The human rights of the accused in war crimes trials following World War II were discussed in the commission's 1948 report to the UN Human Rights Division; specifically mentioned were the implications for human rights of trials that were then underway. A quarter of this report—90 of some 360 total pages—are concerned with this topic, which is striking given that this was less than three years after the war had ended. These discussions included considerations of areas where the rights of victims and accused conflicted and where the rights of the accused might be directly affected. Lord Wright also addressed many of the same issues in the final volume of the *Law Reports of Trials of War Criminals*, including fifteen categories of defense arguments.[21] A number of the more important of these are discussed below.

The right of appeal following imposition of a sentence is an issue where trials related to the commission might be criticized. Lord Wright discusses this in the *Law Reports*.[22] It is clear that the military courts and tribunals did not generally operate an appeal system of the type existing in civilian courts, then or now, which is an issue for which the IMT at Nuremberg has also been criticized. Nevertheless, the nationally conducted trials usually had some form of appeals process and usually meant the sentence had to be confirmed at a higher level and the convicted had a period of a few days to make submission. However, death sentences had to be approved at the highest level of military command, not via some low-level office. In the US case, approval came from the commanders of US European forces and US Pacific forces. Appeals processes existed in national trials in France, Norway, and the Netherlands, for example.

Attention to the rights of the accused is further evidence that those working in and through the commission intended to provide fair standards.

Command Responsibility

The commission's report to the UN ECOSOC began with a review of national legal provisions concerning the responsibility of commanders for the actions of their troops. It noted the many provisions in national (municipal) war crimes laws governing the issue of command responsibility. The report surveyed many trial results concerning German and Japanese officers. This is not the place for a detailed survey of the development of law across these cases; rather, it is the overall picture that comes across: national courts were not implementing a near-uniform set of convictions against commanders for responsibility for the actions of their troops. In case after case complex prosecution charges and final judgments are leveled against infamous figures, including SS officer Josef Kramer of Belsen, Luftwaffe general Kurt Student, Luftwaffe field marshal Erhard Milch, and Gen. Tomoyuki Yamashita, among others. The UNWCC concluded that there was now considerable legal precedent to show that some actions by subordinates could be placed at the foot of commanders—but not all, by any means.

General Student was acquitted of responsibility for the actions of his subordinates, since they were seen as isolated occurrences. In the trial of Japanese officer Takashi Sakai, however, repugnant conduct by lower-level troops was so widespread as to be presumed to be Sakai's responsibility as their commander. The commission also reported that some national trial conviction practices led those who aided and abetted crimes to be found guilty of the murder of Allied prisoners, but not to the same extent and so not warranting equal penalties to those directly responsible.

Courts must balance the human rights of the accused and those of the victims. What is significant is the attention given to the human rights of the accused by the UNWCC and its staff, despite their having witnessed one of the greatest mass assaults on human rights in modern times.

Superior Orders

The argument "I was only following orders" might be used as a reinforcing and exonerating opposite to "I only *gave* the orders." As a concept, this was discussed extensively by the courts and their officials and by the commission itself, both in its history and in its report to the UN.

In forming its advice on the matter, the commission drew on input from both the London International Assembly and the Cambridge Commission. It reviewed national legislation and international law.[23] Again, the mere fact that substantial attention was being paid to the topic shows as a falsehood the idea that the commission and its associated procedures were administering show trials and kangaroo courts. The International Military Tribunal at Nuremberg, apparently commenting in its judgment on Article 8 of its charter, remarked: "The true test, which is found in varying degrees in the criminal law of most nations, is not the existence of the order, but whether moral choice was in fact possible."[24]

The Commission report presents a number of influential cases in which the plea of superior orders was accepted by the court.[25] The first of these, the acquittal of a Nazi civilian judge in Alsace, was based on the grounds that he was instructed clearly by his superiors on what penalties he should hand out. The second comes from the Supreme Court of Norway, where a sentence on an SS officer was reduced to twenty years in prison because it was accepted that, had the officer refused orders concerning the deportation of 521 Jews, he would himself have been killed. The report notes two other cases where lesser sentences were given to Germans who were "only" indirectly involved in the killing of US prisoners.

These judgments did not appear at random or in isolation. The commission's summary includes over 10 pages of international debates originating in the Versailles Commission on responsibilities.[26] The issue engaged the two main nongovernmental organizations at work in Britain during the war: the International Commission for Penal Reconstruction and Development and the London International Assembly.

The Versailles Commission on Responsibilities agreed unanimously that the "mere fact" of the accused having received an order did not provide exoneration.[27] Rather, it was up to individual courts to make decisions on each case—which is what did occur. In this respect the system supported by the UNWCC acknowledged the complexity of the issues and in doing so was working toward fairness.

Group Responsibility

Can a person be guilty of a war crime only because he is a member of a group that commits crimes? This is still a crucial issue in law—at its worst, this principle leads to the idea of "guilt by association." On the other hand—as US commissioner Herbert Pell pointed out—should the troops who massacre innocent villagers escape justice simply because the survivors or witnesses did not know their names and only knew the military or police unit to which the perpetrators belonged? Leonard Baker has quoted Ambassador Pell on the subject:

> It seems obvious that if you are in a room and a group of foreigners in foreign uniforms come in, shoot at you and your companions, your only chance of survival is to fall to the ground and hope that you will not bleed to death before they've gone. Clearly you cannot be expected to give the identification of a particular serjeant who fired the shots as you would in civilian life. You would not expect to get the quality of evidence that would be necessary to convict a boy of stealing cabbages in the suburbs. . . . We could find out what the regiment was that was there, who the German commanding officers were, and we knew that no punishments had been given by the Germans for the outrage.[28]

As we have seen, the commission's view was influential in the development of the Nuremberg trials. However, the legal debate extended beyond the commission's offices in London and the courtrooms in Nuremberg to our own time. The following discussion only touches on the complex issues and offers some suggestions from UNWCC-related practices.

The answer to this question by the commission, by the Nuremberg Tribunal, and by today's International Criminal Court has been that group membership can be assumed to involve committing war crimes in *some* circumstances.

In law there is a clear difference between the act of a crime and the forms of responsibility for that crime. Conspiracy can be considered a crime in itself, while "common design" or "joint enterprise" are forms of responsibility. "The difference between a charge of conspiracy and one of acting in pursuance of a common design is that the first would claim that an agreement to commit offences had been made while the second would allege not only the making of an agreement but the performance of acts pursuant to it."[29] The commission and its member states implemented crimes and responsibility in forms that can support enforcement today.

In the twenty-first century the issue has been handled cautiously and with little reliance on historical cases. Within the statutes of the International Criminal Court, the concept is quite limited as well. According to Article 25(3)(a), "a person shall be criminally responsible and liable for punishment for a crime within the jurisdiction of the Court if that person: (a) commits such a crime, whether as an individual, jointly with another or through another person, regardless of whether that other person is criminally responsible."[30] That is to say, "joint" action, and action "through" another person are both forms of liability. In addition, the IMT has introduced a type of mixed liability, or the doctrine of "indirect co-perpetration" involving membership of a hierarchical organization with intent to commit crimes (i.e., *mens rea*).[31] This concept was developed in the *Katanga and Ngudjolo* case.

The Role of the UNWCC in Developing Forms of Group Responsibility

Justice Robert Jackson credited the commission with developing a position on group responsibility that shaped the eventual position of the United States. Kip Hale and Donna Cline document the extensive debates between states and subsequent legal opinions of the Legal Committee 3 of the UNWCC.[32] These provide a body of international legal opinion in an area of law where such resources are thought to be in particularly short supply.

Conspiracy and common design, discussed below, were among the legal concepts developed at the Nuremberg IMT and have continued to develop since. As applied at Nuremberg, the provisions in Article 6 of the London Charter only concerned conspiracy to invade other countries—the crime of aggression, and the closely related crimes against peace.

Conspiracy and Common Design

French courts made use of the concept of conspiracy—"association des malfaiteurs"—in a number of cases leading to convictions. For example, on April 15, 1948, Henri Stadelhofer was convicted at a court in Marseilles of membership in the Gestapo. Similarly, Horst Hebersteidt was convicted of SD membership at a court in Toulouse on March 25, 1947.[33] The Netherlands pursued conspiracy charges against German nationals.[34] Nevertheless, the US NMTs clearly rejected the concept in a joint ruling in 1947, arguing that the concept was too loose to warrant being regarded as crime in itself.

Complicity and Joint Enterprise

By contrast, the US NMTs and the military government courts made widespread use of complicity and joint enterprise as legal concepts, favoring the term "common design" to describe them.[35] British military courts in Germany did as well. In trials at Essen and at Wuppertal the accused were convicted of being "concerned in the killing."[36] In the Zyklon B case, convicted war criminals were executed for "arranging" the supply of the chemical, not actually doing the supplying, with the knowledge it would be used in illegal killing.[37] Complicity was made illegal in the US Pacific Regulations for War Crimes. In French trials the *Law Reports* mention that, "complicity is often involved"; conspiracy to commit war crimes was likewise also included in French and Norwegian laws.[38]

The commission's approval of the charge provides a previously unknown level of international legal opinion supporting a variety of forms of group responsibility for international crimes. Even the incomplete trial records provided to the commission in London show that more than thirty trials were held, prosecuting charges for various forms of group responsibility. Thirty-two can be taken as the minimum number of trials in this category, while the number of individuals charged was very much larger. For example, numerous individuals, such as Oskar Groening, were charged with common design in cases brought by Poland. Of the thirty-two cases, a number included several forms of group liability. Twenty-four were US trials, five were French, two were Polish, and one was British.[39]

Reprisals and the Execution of Hostages

In 1944 the commission had accepted a Polish recommendation that states should consider including the mere taking of hostages as a war crime in itself, even when there was no clear purpose for the taking.[40] A number of cases can be brought into a discussion of reprisals within the commission's report to the UN. Here "real reprisals," as they are called, are regarded as formal, organized, and public and include the killing of civilians and the destruction of property in order to change the behavior of a population or of armed groups. In contrast, almost invariably these actions are characterized as acts of mere revenge and not deserving of legal protection. The distinction seems almost bizarre today, but in an era of terror-based colonial punitive expeditions it may have seemed "normal."

In speculating why the rules of warfare are not more respected, Brig.-Gen. Telford Taylor remarked that:

> Another reason is that the partial codifications of the laws of war are silent or ambiguous on many important matters. The Hague Conventions, for example, say nothing explicit about the taking or execution of hostages in occupied territories; international penal law on this subject can be, and is, applied today where it is quite clear the atrocities quite beyond the bounds of military necessity have been committed, but in closer cases we are left largely to the speculations of legal scholars, without much practical guidance. From the standpoint of internal penal law, we are not much better off.

> The American military manual, for example, tells us that hostages may be executed, but does not give the soldier much guidance as to when and under what circumstances such executions may be legitimate. The internal military law of other important countries is silent on this fundamental question.[41]

The abolition of the legal right to execute hostages as part of a formal "legal" process of reprisals in American and British military law after World War II may be counted as a significant change in stated practices of the leading powers in the post–1945 era. Even the harshest critics of Anglo-American conduct in Iraq and Afghanistan do not accuse them of state-sanctioned executions of hostages as an act of reprisal against a violently rebellious population.

Securing the Rights of the Accused

At the end of an extensive discussion, the commission argued that "the rules relating to evidence and procedure which are applied in trials by courts of the various countries, and by the International Military Tribunals in Nuremberg and Tokyo, when viewed as a whole are seen to represent an attempt to secure to the accused his right to a fair trial while ensuring that the obviously guilty shall not escape punishment because of legal technicalities."[42] A review of the evidence available today fully supports this conclusion.

A number of leading scholars have examined the issue of fairness in post–World War II trials. Mark Ellis, in assessing the commission's work, concluded that on the basis of the some five hundred documents he had considered, general fairness was largely apparent. Ellis notes that—despite some flaws—many of the fair trial protections in modern-day law were at work in UNWCC-supported trials.[43] Two writers on Australian and British trials in Southeast Asia and the Pacific reached the same conclusion: Suzannah Linton analyzed the British trials in Hong Kong and Georgina Fitzpatrick surveyed Australian trials of Japanese.[44] Fitzpatrick cites the comment of a convicted Japanese officer in support of the fairness of Australian courts. She notes that earlier studies had been strongly critical of the Australian process but they were based on very few cases where, in any case, the alleged flaws were not as apparent.

German defense lawyers concerned with British military trials appear to have been more than satisfied with the standards of fairness. A British officer reported to the commission on "German opinion of fairness of trials":

> At the end of the Neuengamme trial the chief German counsel got up and said that he spoke on behalf of all the German counsel in that Court, and that they were all of the opinion that real justice had returned to Germany at last. Since 1933 many of them had risked their lives pleading, but now they felt that they could really say everything they wanted without fear of

personal consequences. This is a very general attitude amongst the German counsel, who frequently express gratitude for the help and latitude given to them by our military courts.[45]

Conclusion

The UNWCC and its member states set out to achieve fair trials after the war. The record of its own work, of national charges and prosecutions, provides a clear record of success. Some practices—particularly an impatience with technicalities and a sense of urgency that occasionally overrode careful and fulsome trial proceedings—can be criticized. However, these need to be set against the commission's success in convicting large numbers of the guilty through due process and in providing an obvious sense that in the face of huge injustice some important legal retribution had been achieved.

In taking its work forward, the commission and member states successfully innovated in applying forms of group responsibility to international crimes, in particular in applying the concepts of complicity, joint enterprise, and "association de malfaiteurs." These precedents and legal practices and multinational legal opinions should be used in international criminal justice processes today. At even a basic level they provide a great deal more support for the prosecution of responsibility arising from being part of a group than is normally assumed by those engaged in legal processes today.

Here we can note that Kevin Heller's conclusion appears to be consistent with those of Fitzpatrick and Linton and that it reinforces Mark Ellis's initial conclusion of considerable fairness. Heller argues that the prosecutors, defense attorneys, and judges all sought to provide fair trials, and they overwhelmingly did so. If anything, the leniency of sentencing, early release of the convicted, and findings of innocence suggest that the balance of injustice tipped too far to the defendants' side.[46] (See chapter 8 for a further discussion of issues of fairness in relation to the ending of prosecutions and the early release of the convicted, especially with relation to US military trials.)

A full study of the conduct of trials at the national level is not possible. In many cases trial records are simply not available and in many jurisdictions the full transcripts of proceedings or the reasoning of judges is not open to scrutiny. It would, for example, be helpful if the US government itself were to publish the records of the US trials so that these could be formally published and analyzed.

Defendants in war crimes cases and their political supporters often argue against "victors' justice" principally on the grounds that everyone does much the same in the grim business of war. But the UNWCC's record indicates clearly that charges and convictions brought by the Allies were directed at specific crimes outside of normal accepted practices of war. Is this also true of high crimes—of crimes against humanity, of invasion, of genocide, and of the responsibility of national leaders? These complex issues, which many government leaders believed touched the core interests of their nation-states, are the subject of the next chapter.

Before moving on from the issue of fairness it is import to be aware that twenty-first century legal processes are not immune to charges of unfairness. Among the criticisms leveled at modern international criminal trials the question of fairness remains, despite their long duration and enormous costs. UNWCC-supported trials rarely lasted more than a few days, and yet both contemporary and recent reviews support their fairness.

Notes

1. UNWCC, "Report of the Sub-Committee," December 2, 1943, 3 (paras. 14–16), and annex 2, *First Report of Committee 1 (Facts and Evidence): Preparation and Presentation of Cases of War Crimes to the Commission* C7, February 18, 1944, 22.
2. UNWCC, *Complete History of the United Nations War Crimes Commission and the Development of the Laws of War* (London: Her Majesty's Stationery Office, 1948), table 9.
3. Ibid., appendix 3 tables.
4. UNWCC, "Polish Charges Against German War Criminals," RN 4771/P/G/139, CN 139, March 6, 1947.
5. UNWCC, *History*, 518.
6. Ibid.
7. Fair trial provisions are present throughout the Rome Statute of the ICC; examples of key protections (against self-incrimination, presumption of innocence, right to appeal, and so on) are found in articles 54, 55, 66, 67, 69, 81, and 84. See Rome Statute of the International Criminal Court, DN A/CONF.183/9, July 17, 1998 (as amended, up to January 16, 2002), available at http://www.icc-cpi.int/nr/rdonlyres/ea9aeff7–5752–4f84-be94–0a655eb30e16/0/rome_statute_english.pdf.
8. A broader elaboration on Article 6 can be found at European Court of Human Rights, *Guide on Article 6: Right to a Fair Trial (Civil Limb)* (Strasbourg: Council of Europe and European Court of Human Rights, 2013), available at http://www.echr.coe.int/Documents/Guide_Art_6_ENG.pdf.
9. Quoted in Mark Ellis, "Assessing the Impact of the United Nations War Crimes Commission on the Principle of Complementarity and Fair Trial Standards," *Criminal Law Forum* 25, no. 1–2 (2014): 221. Available at http://www.unwcc.org/wp-content/uploads/2014/11/Ellis1.pdf.
10. "Punishment for War Crimes," Inter-Allied Declaration signed at St. James's Palace, London, January 13, 1942.
11. See, for example, Jeremy Rabkin, "No Substitute for Sovereignty: Why International Criminal Justice Has a Bleak Future—And Deserves It," in *Atrocities and International*

Accountability: Beyond Transitional Justice, ed. Edel Hughes, William A. Schabas, and Ramesh Thakur, 98–132 (Tokyo: United Nations University, 2007), 103.

12. Anthony Beevor, *Ardennes 1944: The Battle of the Bulge* (New York: Viking, 2015).
13. UNWCC, *Report of the Sub-Committee*, December 2, 1943, 4; also "Convention (IV) Respecting the Laws and Customs of War on Land" (hereafter "Hague Convention IV"), and its annex, "Regulations Concerning the Laws and Customs of War on Land," The Hague, Switzerland, October 18, 1907, available at: https://www.icrc.org/ihl/intro/195.
14. Ward Wilson, "The Bomb Didn't Beat Japan . . . Stalin Did," *Foreign Policy*, May 30, 2013, http://foreignpolicy.com/2013/05/30/the-bomb-didnt-beat-japan-stalin-did/.
15. Leonard Baker, *Brahmin in Revolt: A Biography of Herbert C. Pell* (New York: Doubleday, 1972), 268.
16. Hague Convention IV.
17. Convention (III) Relative to the Treatment of Prisoners of War (Geneva IV), Geneva, Switzerland, August 12, 1949, available at https://www.icrc.org/ihl/intro/375?OpenDocument.
18. ECOSOC, "Information Concerning Human Rights Arising from Trials of War Criminals," UN DN E/CN.4/W/19, May 15, 1948, 269–72.
19. UNWCC, *Law Reports of Trials of War Criminals*, vol. 2 (London: Her Majesty's Stationery Office, 1947), 131–32; and UNWCC, *Law Reports of Trials of War Criminals* vol. 15 (London: Her Majesty's Stationery Office, 1949), 197, available at http://www.unwcc.org/wp-content/uploads/2013/03/Law-Reports-Volume-2.pdf and http://www.unwcc.org/wp-content/uploads/2013/03/Law-Reports-Volume-15.pdf, respectively.
20. Kevin Heller, *The Nuremberg Military Tribunals and the Origins of International Criminal Law* (Oxford: Oxford University Press, 2011), 157.
21. UNWCC, *Law Reports of Trials* 15, 155–88.
22. Ibid., 194–99.
23. The UNWCC's incorporation of legal thinking from a wide range of national sources is apparent throughout its work; the indexes of its meeting minutes and documents all provide extensive samples of its analysis of different approaches and interpretations of international law on superior orders. See United Nations Archives, "Index to Minutes and Documents of the United Nations War Crimes Commission," United Nations Archives RGN 11, October 17, 1949, 85; UNWCC, *Complete History*, 588; and its external reports at UNWCC, *Law Reports of Trials* 15, 157–60. See also ECOSOC, "Information Concerning Human Rights Arising from Trials of War Criminals," UN DN E/CN.4/W/19, May 15, 1948, 217–29.
24. ECOSOC, "Information Concerning Human Rights," 44.
25. Ibid., 230.
26. Ibid., 274–84.
27. Ibid., 275.
28. Quoted in Baker, *Brahmin in Revolt*, 277.
29. UNWCC, *Law Reports of Trials* 15, 97–98.

30. Rome Statute, Article 25(3)(a).
31. Kip Hale and Donna Cline, "Holding Collectives Accountable: The UNWCC's Undervalued Role in Developing Collective Responsibility, Yesterday and Today," *Criminal Law Forum* 25, no. 1–2 (2014): 261–90.
32. Ibid.
33. UNWCC, *Sixth Supplement to the Synopsis of Trial Reports—C.265,* February 6, 1948, 80.
34. UNWCC, Law Reports of Trials 15, 98, available at http://www.unwcc.org/wp-content/uploads/2013/03/Law-Reports-Volume-11.pdf.
35. UNWCC, Law Reports of Trials 15, 5 and 14; Heller, *Nuremberg Military Tribunals*, chap. 11.
36. UNWCC, *Law Reports of Trials* 15, 69–70 ("Trial of Franz Schonfeld and Nine Others—Proceedings of a Military Court for the Trial of War Criminals Held at Essen, Germany, on Tuesday 11 June 1946, Wednesday 12 June 1946, and Thursday 13 June 1946"), UNWCC RN R6/G/19/8A, BR.121.
37. UNWCC, *Law Reports of Trials* 15, 49.
38. Ibid., 56–57.
39. These numbers were gathered from a search of trial result summaries in UNWCC, "Synopsis of Trial Reports Received by the United Nations War Crimes Commission from National Authorities, including First to Ninth Supplements," March 31, 1949, compiled in UNWCC archive reel 50. These represent (including some duplicates) fourteen trials involving criminal organizations, seventeen involving common design, and thirteen involving conspiracy (with some fitting into multiple categories).

    Criminal "organisation/organization": 14 trials

    §253—Karl Brandt and 22 others, p. 137, United States;

    §255—Josef Altstotter and 15 others, p. 138, United States, UNWCC List 9, 7145/P/G/1301;

    §256—Oswald Pohl and 17 others, p. 138, United States, UNWCC List 7, 1803/B/G/157, 3266/UK/G/558, 1352/Fr/G/562, 1535/Cz/G/18, 1083/P/G/40, 1964/Cz/G/30, 1893/B/G/192, 795/PB/G/31, 785/P/G/37, 841/P/G/38, 841/P/G/38, 960/Nl/G/44, 952/Cz/G/17, 399/Cz/G/8, 423/Cz/G/9, 432/Cz/G/11, 463/Cz/G/13, 465/Cz/G/15, 628/B/G/22, 712/B/G/25;

    §337—Erwin Wilhelm Konrad Shienkiewitz, p. 199, Dachau trial, United States, 4758/US/G/148;

    §342—Ulrich Greifelt and 13 others, p. 201, Nuremberg, UNWCC List 7, CROWCASS 62380;

    §343—Otto Ohlendorf and 23 others, p. 201, Nuremberg, UNWCC List 7, CROWCASS 62460, 712/B/G/25, 960/Nl/G/44, 952/Cz/G/17, 795/B/G/31;

    §5—Artur Greiser, p. 207, Polish, UNWCC List 7, 110/P/G/19, 111/P/G/20, 123/P/G/21, 304/P/G/30, 591/P/G/35, 785/P/G/37, 850/P/G/39;

§6—Amon Goeth, p. 207, Polish, 3471/Y/G/149;
§107—Horst Hebestreit, p. 215, French, 3974/Fr/G/1615;
§375—Jurgen Stroop and 21 others, p. 229, United States, 4609/US/G/133, 4610/US/G/134, 4611/US/G/135, 4612/US/G/136, 4613/US/G/137, 4614/US/G/138, 4615/US/G/139, 1630/US/G/3 (addendum 1, 2);
§376—Tito Roncaglia, p. 229, United States, 5639/US/It/3;
§416—Ernst von Weizsäcker and 20 others, p. 235, United States;
§564—Erich Hinkel and Adolf Schmidt, p. 274, United States, 4753/US/G/143;
§684—Kurt Petersdorf and 4 others, p. 620, United States, 7091/US/G/245;

Common design 17 trials: ±48 trials
§ Mauthausen-Gusen trial—Hans Altfuldisch and 60 others, p. 50, United States;
§84-J—Eisaku Murakami and 3 others, p. 63 US/G;
§253—Karl Brandt and 22 others, p. 137, United States;
§255—Josef Altstotter and 15 others, p. 138, United States, UNWCC List 9, 7145/P/G/1301;
§256—Oswald Pohl and 17 others, p. 138, United States, UNWCC List 7, 1803/B/G/157, 3266/UK/G/558;
§339—Ernst Arzberger and 7 others, p. 200, United States;
§344—Alfred Krupp von Bohlen und Halbach, Owner and Directing Head, and 11 others, Officials of the Krupp Firm and Family Enterprise (trial not complete at time of writing), UNWCC List 7, 5923/US/G/215, 5296/US/G/218, 5925/US/G/217;
§366—Josef Wolfgang Barblick and 6 others, p. 205, United States, 7554/Fr/G/2208;
§373—Joseph Becker, Friedrich Becker, and 50 others, p. 228, United States, 3210/US/G/111;
§374—Frans Auer and 13 others, p. 229, United States, 3982/Fr/G/1646;
§375—Jurgen Stroop and 21 others, p. 229, United States, 4609/US/G/133, 4610/US/G/134, 4611/US/G/135, 4612/US/G/136, 4613/US/G/137, 4614/US/G/138, 4615/US/G/139, 1630/US/G/3 (addendum 1, 2);
§377—Karl Adami, Adolf Baltes, and 6 others, p. 229, United States, 2172/Fr/G/934;
§416—Ernst von Weizsäcker and 20 others, p. 235, United States, US/G;
§474—Wilhelm von Loeb, Hugo Sperrle, and 12 others, p. 244, United States (trial ongoing);
§535—Anton Bernhard Schloeter and 7 others, p. 269, United States;
§541—Arthur Kurt Andrae and 22 others, p. 270, United States;
§460—Eduard Hermann, Karl H. Schickler, and 2 others, 3204/US/G/105.

Conspiracy: 13 trials
§37-J—Gozawa Sadaichi and 9 others, p. 13, United Kingdom;
§146-J—Chosoto Oishi and 9 others, p. 122, United States;

§253—Karl Brandt and 22 others, p. 137, United States;
§255—Josef Altstotter and 15 others, p. 138, United States, UNWCC List 9, 7145/P/G/1301;
§256—Oswald Pohl and 17 others, p. 138, United States, UNWCC List 7, 1803/B/G/157, 3266/UK/G/558;
§82—Karl Ernst Herbert Ehrlich, p. 164, France, 3550/Fr/G/1570;
§84—Albert Maria Léon Raskin, p. 164, France, 4293/Fr/G/1738;
§344—Alfred Krupp von Bohlen und Halbach, Owner and Directing Head, and 11 others, Officials of the Krupp Firm and Family Enterprise (trial ongoing), UNWCC List 7, 5923/US/G/215, 5296/US/G/218, 5925/US/G/217;
§375—Jurgen Stroop and 21 others, p. 229, United States (trial not yet complete), 4609/US/G/133, 4610/US/G/134, 4611/US/G/135, 4612/US/G/136, 4613/US/G/137, 4614/US/G/138, 4615/US/G/139, 1630/US/G/3 (addendum 1, 2);
§416—Ernst von Weizsäcker and 20 others, p. 235, United States;
§474—Wilhelm von Loeb, Hugo Sperrle, and 12 others, p. 244, United States;
§85—Ernst Dunker, p. 318, France, 6670/Fr/G/2127;
§192—Marguerite Magno, p. 333, France.

40. UNWCC, "Proposal by the Polish Representative for Adding New Items to the List of War Crimes," Report of Committee 3, C.15 , May 9, 1944.
41. ECOSOC, "Information Concerning Human Rights Arising from Trials of War Criminals," 215.
42. Ibid., 250.
43. Ellis, "Assessing the Impact."
44. Suzannah Linton, "Rediscovering the War Crimes Trials in Hong Kong, 1946–48," *Melbourne Journal of International Law* 13, no. 2 (2012); Georgina Fitzpatrick, "War Crimes Trials, 'Victor's Justice,' and Australian Military Justice in the Aftermath of the Second World War," in *The Hidden Histories of War Crimes Trials*, ed. Kevin Jon Heller and Gerry Simpson, 327–47 (Oxford: Oxford University Press, 2013), 344–47.
45. UNWCC, "Copy of semi-official letter from Colonel G. R. Bradshaw C.B.E., Deputy-Director of Personal Services (C)., to Sir Robert Craigie, read at meeting of Commission on 19th June and circulated by request" (UNWCC DN A.7), June 20, 1946.
46. Heller, *Nuremberg Military Tribunals*, 401.

7

CRIMES AGAINST HUMANITY

THE "FREEDOM TO LYNCH" AND THE INDICTMENTS OF ADOLF HITLER

In early September 1944, US secretary of war Henry Stimson wrote:

> I have great difficulty in finding any means whereby military commissions may try and convict those responsible for excesses committed within Germany both before and during the war which have no relation to the conduct of the war. I would be prepared to construe broadly what constituted a violation of the Rules of War but there is a certain field in which I fear that external courts cannot move. Such courts would be without jurisdiction in precisely the same way that any foreign court would be without jurisdiction to try those who were guilty of, or condoned, lynching in our own country.[1]

The implication is clear: by permitting international courts to have jurisdiction in other countries the United States would open itself to the international prosecution of those who conducted lynching in the United States: and that could not be permitted. This was not a theoretical concern for the emboldened African American civil rights movement, which was campaigning at the time under the "Double V" slogan (and was the basis for a play by James G. Thompson, a contemporary writer, who used the "V-for-Victory" sign). Just as it signified a "victory over aggression, slavery, and tyranny," so the double-V would signify a victory for "colored Americans [over] those who perpetrate these ugly prejudices" within.[2] The ending of lynching was a prime concern of the American civil rights movement of the 1940s—but not Stimson's. Nevertheless, Stimson was a strong advocate of

(*For the Use of the Secretariat*)

0414

Registered Number.	Date of receipt in Secretariat.
424/Cz/G/10	15th December 1944

UNITED NATIONS WAR CRIMES COMMISSION

Czechoslovak CHARGES AGAINST German WAR CRIMINALS

CHARGE No. 7/44. /SONDERGERICHTE/.

Name of accused, his rank and unit, or official position. (*Not to be translated.*)	1. Adolf HITLER, 2. The members of the Reich Government, a/ Rudolf HESS, Stellvertreter des Fuhrers, Reichsminister / - 17.5.1941. b/ Joachim Freiherr von RIBBENTROP, Reichsaussenminister /5.2.38 - / c/ Dr. Wilhelm FRICK, Reichsinnerminister /1933 - 24.8.43/ d/ Heinrich HIMMLER, Reichsinnerminister /24.8.43/. e/ SCHWERIN-KROSIGK Graf, Reichsfinanzminister /1933 - /Continued, see Enc.1 page 2/
Date and place of commission of alleged crime.	The crimes were committed in Prague, Brno, Litoměřice, Cheb and Opava. The criminal activities of the Special Courts commenced with the coming into force of the Order of 21.2.1940 /R.G.Bl.I.p.405-V.Bl.R.Prot.p.118/, accordingly pursuant to para.39 of this order on 15.3.40. It has been continued ever since.
Number and description of crime in war crimes list.	I. Murder and massacres - systematic terrorism.
References to relevant provisions of national law.	Paras.5, 134, 135 /3/, 93 and 34, 136 Czechoslovak Penal Code, apply to the persons mentioned under 1-4. Paras.134, 135 /3/, 93 and 34, 136 Czechoslovak Penal Code, apply to the persons mentioned under 1-5.

SHORT STATEMENT OF FACTS.

See Enclosure 2.

TRANSMITTED BY DR. B. ECER Dec. 15th 1944

*Insert serial number under which the case is registered in the files of the National Office of the accusing State.

FIGURE 7.1. UNWCC supported indictment of Adolf Hitler, Rudolf Hess, Heinrich Himmler, and other Nazis.

trying the Nazis for war crimes in general and especially for the crime of aggressive war. It was a controversial issue then as it is now, though Stimson took a resolute stand dating from the start of his service as US secretary of state in 1932.

Regarding crimes against humanity, however, Stimson's view represented the traditionalist side of an argument that stretched back to at least 1919. It continues to be controversial in the twenty-first century. The focus now is on the right and duty of the UN to intervene in a state if that state has failed to exercise its "responsibility to protect" (R2P) its own citizens from gross violations of human rights. The plea by Poland for intervention to stop atrocities in the death camps made in a submission to the commission harkened back to nineteenth-century cases and provides a ghostly preview of modern-day R2P.[3]

The issue of prosecuting a state and specific individuals for crimes against its own citizens—that is, for crimes against humanity—is closely connected with other issues relating to the key powers held by states and leaders. The lost debate among the nations within the context of the UNWCC speak to issues in our own time.

Closely linked to crimes against humanity is the liability of heads of government (e.g., the German kaiser after World War I and Hitler in World War II); the crime of genocide; and the problem of what legal authority has jurisdiction over such crimes (which is in part solved by the concept that any legal jurisdiction has authority over such "piratical" crimes under the concept of universal jurisdiction).

The invasion of another country was established as a major international crime at the Nuremberg and Tokyo IMTs, but these judgments were not widely accepted as universal until an amendment was made to the statute of the International Criminal Court in 2010.

Crimes against Humanity

As Mark Lewis and others have explored, after 1919 a number of nations sought to prosecute Turkish leaders for the massacre—genocide—of their Armenian population during the First World War.[4] The United States, led by Secretary of State Robert Lansing, vetoed the proposal as impinging on the principle of state sovereignty. The matter rested until World War II.

In June 1943 Roosevelt appointed Herbert Pell as the US representative on the commission. Pell made it his mission to establish, indeed create, international law on this point. He had seen how Confederate veterans in the South had created for themselves a misty-eyed mythology about the US Civil War and was determined that the Nazis would not do the same. Pell's motivation was to prevent postwar nostalgia for the Nazis breeding more war: "In a small German village, the local member of the Gestapo will be the hero. . . . He will tell young boys . . . of the fun of shooting Jews in Poland, or the profit of looting France. . . . Presently will come someone hopeful of succeeding Hitler."[5]

Pell declared that, if necessary, he was willing to lose his reputation over a confrontation with the State Department and its narrow legal interpretations. He was influenced by Harvard University's Sheldon Glueck, whose book on the punishment of war criminals was read by Roosevelt, among others. Glueck argued that since all laws and courts had been invented at some point, now was the time to establish international law.[6] He voiced the same view expressed by the Polish prime minster, General Sikorski, at the meeting that resulted in the St. James's Palace Declaration in January 1942.[7] Glueck was a member of the London International Assembly and had written a joint proposal on the trial of war criminals with Belgian minister Marcel de Baer, later that year.[8]

Roosevelt sent into the thick of this controversial area of international policy a man who he knew would stir things up toward a broader view of international criminal acts that were in line with his own broad statements and who had been briefed by America's leading advocate of international criminal law enforcement.

State Department officials, heirs to the Lansing tradition on strong state sovereignty, were not to be set aside easily. Led by successive secretaries of state—Cordell Hull, Joseph Grew (acting), and Edward Stettinius—with strong leadership in the department from legal advisor Green Hackworth, they did all they could to sabotage Pell and undermine the work of the commission—especially on the issue of crimes against humanity and the establishment of a permanent international criminal court.

First they told Pell that he was not needed in London in 1943, when in fact the commission and US ambassador in London Gilbert Winant, were waiting for him to get going. Indeed, the UNWCC's first meetings in late 1943 were only ratified as authoritative following Pell's arrival. Once in London, Pell wasted no time. In March 1944, as charges began flowing from member states to the commission, he presented a document outlining the definition of crimes against humanity: "It is clearly understood that the words 'crimes against humanity' refer, among others, to crimes committed against stateless persons or against any persons because of their race or religion; such crimes are judiciable by the United Nations or their agencies as war crimes."[9]

By May 1944 the commission had considered a comprehensive policy summary to expand its terms of reference. In it the following categories of crimes were considered to be within the scope of the UNWCC's work:

1. The crimes committed for the purpose of preparing or launching the war, irrespective of the territory where these crimes have been committed;
2. Crimes committed in the Allied countries and crimes committed against members of the armed forces or civilian citizens of the United Nations abroad, in the air or on the sea, whatever may be the rank of the accused;

3. Crimes committed against any person without regard to nationality, stateless persons included, because of race, nationality, religious or political belief, irrespective of where they have been committed;
4. Crimes that may be committed in order to prevent the restoration of peace.[10]

The first point concerns preparation of an aggressive war and appears as a concept in the London Charter of the IMT at Nuremberg. The language was designed to include acts of preparation within Germany but could also include acts intended to increase the wealth of the Nazi state by stealing Jewish assets.

The second point, which makes charges possible "regardless of rank," was designed to include Hitler and his top aides. The Moscow Declaration of November 1943 had put disposal of the top leadership under the direct purview of America, Britain, France, and Russia. With no follow-up from these states, the commissioners were seeking to make sure that the Nazi leaders did not escape justice.

The issue of holding government leaders to account in law is still controversial in the present century. President Slobodan Milošević of the Federal Republic of Yugoslavia was tried by the ICTY and ultimately died in custody (before his trial ended). However, despite the indictment of some leaders by the International Criminal Court, notably Sudan's president Omar al-Bashir, many notorious individuals still travel the world with impunity. In 2004 UN secretary-general Kofi Annan declared the war in Iraq illegal but neither US president George W. Bush nor British prime minister Tony Blair have faced charges. This, despite the efforts of a London waiter to make a citizen's arrest of the former British leader and of a cross-party group of parliament members to open a process of impeachment against him in the period 2004 to 2006.[11]

Part of the problem can be traced back to the IMT at Nuremberg. Hitler was already dead and his successor, Adm. Karl Dönitz, and surviving entourage were in the dock. There was no indictment against Hitler, as it has always been assumed. In fact, Hitler was already an indicted war criminal at the time of his death in April 1945. In November 1944 the UNWCC determined that he could be held criminally responsible for the acts of the Nazis in the occupied countries.[12] By March 1945 the commission had endorsed at least seven separate indictments against him for war crimes.[13] Thus, prior to the decision to create the IMT and despite the best efforts of officials in the American and British foreign ministries, the then-sixteen-nation commission supported the indictment of the German head of state for war crimes. These states—which includes four current members of the UN Security Council and many member states of the European Union (EU)—should increase their support of the principle that heads of state can face international prosecution because these countries set their own precedent by indicting Hitler.

Hitler and his officials were charged with crimes for actions against Belgian and Czechoslovak peoples and property, all of which were supported by detailed dossiers. These encompassed death and concentration camps, forced labor, and looting. The details found in these indictments may even now serve to support contemporary efforts at indictments. Hitler was only listed in the commission's first list of war criminals issued in December 1944, following extensive debate within the commission and formal charges being brought by the Czechs. In 1944 the British government faced public outrage when it equivocated on declaring Hitler's actions to be criminal. Finally, on a motion from the Indian and Dutch representatives, the commission ordered that the "Major War Criminals"—Hitler included—must be included on lists of war criminals.[14] In the notes attached to the list, the commission recognized that the Moscow Declaration had assigned jurisdiction over these figures to the major powers. But it acknowledged that it would surely be helpful if members of the commission were to gather evidence on them in any case. The list included former deputy führer Rudolf Hess, who was then in British custody but not yet accused of any war crimes. The major powers had not announced any legal process against the Nazi leadership.

This remarkable meeting of the commission in December 1944 was presided over by Sir Cecil Hurst and attended by Ambassador Pell for the United States and representatives of eleven other Allied countries, including China. Czechoslovakia, one of the earliest victims of the Nazis and a weak new state fraught with internal nationalistic elements, was in at least this one form seeking to be taken seriously as a nation-state. On many issues the representatives debated, voted, and referred comments back to the national capitals for instructions. On this one occasion there was a prompt and unanimous decision to permit the indictment of Hitler (albeit one made in secret).

Recall the commission's paper itemizing points where it sought to expand its remit. The fourth point is directed at potential attempts to sow the seeds of a new war. It is the third point, however, that is most revolutionary: it declares to be criminal any acts that are committed (wherever and whenever) on grounds unconnected with the period of the war—so that crimes before September 1939 could be included, whether or not they were directly connected to the war effort. Thus crimes in concentration camps against Germans before the invasion of Poland could also be included. Political and religious motivations are included too—so crimes inflicted on communists, socialists, and Jews could be addressed as well. The paper clearly presents crimes against humanity as an international crime.

The London Charter for Nuremberg that was agreed in August 1945 is far more restrained; it states that the crimes had to have occurred in war time, with the war being defined as starting with Germany's invasion of Poland on September 1, 1939.

We can contrast the documents that emanated from the commission with other mainstream and authoritative accounts of the development of the idea of crimes against humanity. Samantha Power describes the concept as arising from the Allied reaction to the discovery of the concentration camps at the end of the war.[15] Geoffrey Robertson finds roots in the English Parliamentary case against King Charles I, in the writings of H. G. Wells, and in the UN Declaration of 1942.[16] There is also the contribution of Hersch Lauterpacht and his interactions with Justice Robert Jackson on the inclusion of crimes against humanity in the Nuremberg indictments.[17]

Missing from these accounts, however, is the political pressure that came from governments, from officials inside the American and British governments, and from civil society organizations aiming to establish a broad official and international definition of crimes against humanity. This development occurred long before the negotiations for the charter for the Nuremberg IMT and faced profound resistance from within the leading Allied powers. This intra-Allied political fight is critical to understanding the establishment and value of crimes against humanity as an international crime.

The vital role of the commission and its leading figures, including Herbert Pell, needs to be restored from "specialist" into "popular" history and thus into memory. The commissioners' views as state representatives carry greater weight than those of private individuals. The depth of these intergovernmental legal debates can be illustrated by considering just the index to the commission's records: "Crimes against Peace and against Humanity" has nearly three pages of entries.[18]

The connection of the commissioners to their own governments, and through these connections to Justice Jackson and to representatives of Britain, France, and the Soviet Union, provide channels through which the idea of crimes against humanity as an international crime was transmitted from the commission to the proceedings against the Nazi leaders at Nuremberg. The commission's own endorsement of Poland's indictments for the Nazi death camp system—especially the rousing essay of the condemnatory legal and political philosophies underpinning its 1944 charges concerning the death camps—shows a far greater international focus on these crimes in the early and mid-1940s than has been recognized for almost four generations.

Anglo-American Opposition to the Concept of Crimes against Humanity

Through the summer of 1944 Herbert Pell and his fellow commissioners continued to be blocked by the State Department and the Foreign Office in their attempts to widen and strengthen the Allied war crimes effort. In London, the Foreign Office delayed responding to the commission's carefully phrased request that it be allowed to consider crimes committed by the Germans wherever they had occurred. In Washington the State Department continued to block this point by ensuring that it wrote replies to Pell which he believed came from the president himself, even beginning each note with the salutation, "My Dear Bertie."[19] Pell continued in vain to seek instructions from the State Department on the issue of crimes against humanity. Worse still, official Washington had decided that no one would even receive the commission's paperwork.

On August 1, 1944, Pell cabled to Washington again seeking to know who should get the UNWCC material, as there were "a great many cases and a great amount of data." He received no response from either the State or the War department. At this point in the war the Nazis were in full retreat, Hitler had just survived an assassination attempt, and the Nazi government was expected to collapse at any time. Only now do we know that it took another nine months, until the following May, for surrender.

That August 1944, as the Allies raced for the Rhine, State Department official Fletcher Warren was the unhappy man who needed to find a bureaucratic channel for the work of the UNWCC in Washington. He found none. The War Department referred him back to the State Department and there, Green Hackworth and Katherine Fite (a senior State Department attorney) told him it was just a matter for the British.

Outraged, Warren left a note for the file warning that the public would be furious if they found out the truth.[20] That same month Henry Morgenthau, the US treasury secretary, was in London. Pell took the opportunity to meet with him and his staff. They were appalled, as they had assumed that matters were well in hand for trying the Nazis for crimes committed against Germans in Germany as well as for other crimes. On returning to Washington, Morgenthau took the issue to Roosevelt, to the State Department, and to Stimson at the War Department.

By the end of 1944 the US State Department and the British Foreign Office had lost patience with their own commissioners, perhaps because they saw that the war crimes issue needed to be fully suppressed prior to the Nazis' surrender. Sir Cecil Hurst, the commission's chairman, resigned. Under questioning in the House of Commons, Churchill's government claimed the resignation was on grounds of ill-health.[21] The press reported that the resignation was over the refusal of the government to support the creation of an international criminal court plus its refusal to define German-on-German crimes as international crimes.[22] Hurst lived on until 1963.

In Washington, Pell had returned for the wedding of his son, Claiborne, later to be US senator for Rhode Island. Pell later explained how Roosevelt had encouraged him to inject fresh energy into the commission on his return to London. The Nazi surrender was now perhaps only weeks away: Hitler's last gamble, in the Battle of the Bulge, had failed and downfall was upon him. Pell stopped by the offices of the State Department for the latest instructions before returning to London. He was told that he had been fired.

The elegant but treacherous device used by officials at State to get rid of Pell was to fail to request funding for the commission and for Pell's salary and then blame Congress for no funds. This, too, was an excuse, as there were many routes to funding and supporting projects in wartime Washington.[23] Roosevelt abandoned his friend for reasons that are unclear. He may no longer have supported a strong approach to war crimes and he began to vacillate on postwar policy toward Germany. He may have been too ill to realize what he was doing. Or, he may have calculated that confronting Stimson would be too costly, but knowing that Pell would surely make a fuss if he was fired. There is no evidence for this interpretation save that it fits FDR's reputation for deviousness and also that in November he had arranged for his former ambassador to the Soviet Union, Joseph Davies, to go to London to try to get to the bottom of what was happening about war crimes. At the time of FDR's death three months later, Davies was waiting for his travel arrangements to be made by the State Department office.

Thus, on the eve of victory the State Department was adamant in its policy of letting the Nazi leadership off the legal hook for what they had done to their own people. A history that simply records the creation of the London Charter as a natural result of public revulsion at Nazi crimes conveniently obscures the role of American legal and political conservatives in obstructing the prosecution of war criminals in general and of perpetrators of crimes against humanity in particular.

Pell was not to be pushed aside so easily, however, and he went public in early 1945. After articles in the *New York Times* claiming that Hurst and Pell had been sacked for wanting both an International Criminal Court and the Nazis to be tried for crimes against German Jews stirred things up, journalist Drew Pearson confronted a leading State Department official at a public briefing. He pressed and pressed on whether the department supported the president's policy of legal action against the Nazis for crimes against their own citizens. Every evasion brought a fresh and precise question. In the end Joseph Grew, the acting secretary of state, confirmed that the policy was to regard actions by the Nazis against Germans in Germany as criminal.

In an essay from 2014 Graham Cox quotes an exchange between Pearson and Grew over the subject of German nationals who were Jewish and whether the latter's statement that prosecutions would be brought against Germans for crimes against "minority elements" and "Jewish and other groups" would include prosecutions for crimes committed within Germany. Grew replied to Pearson's questions with exasperation, asking: "Is it absolutely necessary to mention the particular place?" But Pearson replied with, "Is it absolutely necessary to evade it?"[24]

Partly following Pearson's suggestion to include a clause stating that prosecutions would take place "wherever these minorities may be found," Grew, cornered, finally caved, passing the wording change on to a State Department official, with the final text promising to prosecute Nazi perpetrators "for the whole broad criminal enterprise devised and executed with ruthless disregard of the very foundation of law and morality, including offenses, wherever committed, against the rules of war and against minority elements, Jewish and other groups, and individuals."

Pell continued his campaign to get the US government to actively support a war crimes process against the Nazis throughout the spring of 1945, even after President Harry Truman had announced the appointment of Justice Jackson to the commission. On June 6, 1945, Pearson published the memo from Pell to Truman that had set out the whole sorry business. Later that day the White House issued the precise terms of reference for Jackson's work on what became the London Charter. One interpretation is that Pell and Pearson made fools of themselves by alleging that no action was being taken when in fact it was. Another is that Pell and Pearson were sufficiently well connected to press the administration as effectively as they had, and that Truman's action on June 6, 1945 came about, at least partly, to defuse the public pressure from Pell and Pearson. Indeed, it still took another four months for the United States to bring any charges to the UNWCC.

Both the title of the memo and Pearson's introduction to it are illuminating accounts of governmental noncooperation and demonstrate the failure during the Second World War of US officials in Washington to support the prosecution of war crimes:

> US Section of War Crimes Commission Has Not Yet Named for Trial a Single Nazi; Jackson Cannot Even Be Pinned Down to Chances of Convicting Any Group Before Christmas; Pell's Report Reveals Runaround by Some State Department Officials.
>
> Washington.—Despite all the ballyhoo about grandiose plans for the trial of war criminals, the real fact is that as of this writing not one Nazi has been listed for trial by the American section of the War Crimes Commission.
>
> The British have proposed names. The Russians have gone ahead with an undetermined number. And the U.S. Army has tried and punished various Nazis who have committed crimes against American soldiers. But not one name so far has been listed by the U.S. section of the War Crimes Commission under U.S. Supreme Court Justice Robert Jackson.
>
> Furthermore, at a secret meeting held in Washington a few days ago, Justice Jackson would not be pinned down to conviction of any large group of Nazis, such as the Gestapo or SS Elite Guard, before Christmas. He even said he wasn't sure they were guilty under international law.
>
> How peculiar the whole runaround regarding the trial of Nazi war criminals is, has just been emphasized in a confidential report to the White House by Herbert Pell, former Minister to Portugal and Hungary and until recently U.S. Chairman on the War Crimes Commission.
>
> Mr. Pell reveals in his report that some State Department officials did not agree with him that Hitlerites who beat up and killed innocent victims because of their religion should be considered guilty of war crimes. Pell

took a vigorous stand on this, and eventually his differences with the State Department caused him to be euchred out of the War Crimes Commission.

His confidential White House Report dated May 23, 1945, follows:

**Pell's Secret Report

—Late in June, 1943, I was appointed American member of the War Crimes Commission by President Roosevelt. I immediately went to the State Department, and in a few weeks was ready to sail. I was informed that the British Government did not want the American Commissioner to get to England until the Commission was ready to meet. I discovered afterwards that no such suggestion had ever been sent through the American Embassy in London.

I tried to get as assistant, Professor Sheldon Glueck of Harvard, who was willing to come, and a friend of mine, Paul Lienau. The Department sent neither of these gentlemen but preferred Mr. Lawrence Preuss. After a very short time in London I discovered that a part of Mr. Preuss' duties was to write private letters, mostly abusive to me, to Mr. Sandifer of the State Department, who in turn gave them to Mr. Hackworth, the Legal Adviser, whose division had charge of war crimes in the Department. When I discovered this I told Mr. Preuss that he should file his private letters of this character with the Commission's documents. He did file some of them but not all.

In February, 1944, I moved, in a Committee of the War Crimes Commission, that chimeras against whomsoever committed for reasons of race, religion, or political opinion should be treated as war crimes. Mr. Preuss, although officially subordinate to me, rose in Committee and opposed this suggestion.

A few weeks later a British general sent me by special messenger a document marked secret, for which I had to sign. Mr. Preuss asked to have some copies made of it. I refused to allow him but told him that he could see the original. Shortly thereafter he was discovered dictating a copy of this document. I confiscated the copies, the stenographer's notes, and the carbons and immediately reported to Ambassador Winant, representing the President, that I could not accept the responsibility of secret documents if anyone in my office could arrogate to themselves the privilege of making copies.

Mr. Preuss was immediately returned to the United States but to my surprise instead of being reproved for making private copies of military secret documents he was placed in honor in the State Department and has been maintained and is now in a responsible position in San Francisco. These facts are known personally to the Secretary of State.

—Religious War Crimes—

During the Summer of 1944 I was chairman of a Committee of the Commission. This Committee recommended that crimes committed because of race or religion should be treated as war crimes and a letter to that effect was sent to the British Foreign Office on the 29th of May and immediately thereafter to the State Department.

The British Foreign Office did not answer this letter and eventually Sir Cecil Hurst, chairman of the Commission, resigned because of the refusal of the British government to answer. In spite of a vigorous letter requesting adequate instructions on this subject I received none from the State Department.

About the close of the Summer we recommended the setting up of mixed military courts and the preparation of an organisation along the lines of the FBI to apprehend war criminals as soon as any part of Germany was occupied. The last of these recommendations were sent in October 1944.

I returned to the United States in December, 1944, and found that nothing had been done about any of them. In my opinion, had these recommendations been acted on there would today have been adequate machinery for the immediate trial of war criminals.

My protest in December resulted in the failure of Congress to appropriate $30,000 for the Commission and I was told not to return. The State Department, however, did find adequate money to maintain an office in London with an adequate staff of stenographers; in fact, everything that was needed except the salary of the Commissioner, amounting with allowance to about $6,000. I offered to serve free but this offer was refused.

—Roosevelt Gave OK—

This failure to appropriate money which prevented my return took place during the close of the last Congress, which adjourned December 19, 1944. The State Department was given notice of this fact but I did not hear of it until the 9th of January. On that day I had an appointment with the late President Roosevelt and having been in the United States for more than a month I went to the State Department and asked Mr. Hackworth if anything new had come up so I could be accurately informed when discussing the subject with the President. Mr. Hackworth told me the literal truth which had come in from London but said nothing about the failure of the Congressional appropriation.

I then went over to the White House where I discussed the matter with the President. The last words that he said to me were, "Go back to London as quickly as you can and make yourself chairman of the Commission."

That afternoon I went to the Secretary of State expecting simply to shake him by the hand, say good-bye, and return on the next boat. In the Secretary's office I found Mr. Hackworth and was informed that I could not return at all.

When I asked Mr. Hackworth, in the presence of the Secretary of State, why he'd allowed me to go over to the White House and discuss this matter

> with the President in ignorance of the fact that I could not return, thus making a fool of the President and me, he answered that it was none of his business to keep me informed and that in any case, "You are the President's appointee and not mine."
>
> Since then four months have gone by and nothing has been done. No courts have been set up and no system of law has been accepted for the trial of war criminals.
>
> The effect of this course by the United States is manifestly harmful to our prestige in Europe. There are more than a hundred million people in Europe who for four years have been living in terror, kept alive mainly by the hope of ultimate justice. Most of these people would prefer the leadership of the United State but if they can get nothing from us they will turn to the leadership of some other country. The importance of this subject from an international point of view can hardly [*sic*] overestimated.[25]

Had Pell gone quietly, there would have been no clear and publicly established policy that German-on-German crimes were considered criminal by the US government. Had Truman come to office with no clear public US policy on the issue of crimes against humanity, it is hard to see who else in official Washington would have been interested and influential enough to make accountability for German-on-German crime the clear public policy of the US government in the spring of 1945.

Pell was not entirely on his own within the US bureaucracy. As the Army Judge Advocate General's office gained momentum, the United States conducted many trials—foremost among them the trials led by Telford Taylor. A vital link between the JAG and the UNWCC was provided by relatively junior US officers.

After Pell was dismissed, his successor was Lt. Col. Joseph Hodgson. During the same meeting when Hodgson was elected chairman of Committee 2 (Enforcement) in May 1945, he submitted a terse report entitled "Problems Facing the Commission." Hodgson noted the contradictory tasks and expectations set on the Commission: while theoretically tasked with the role of chasing down war criminals and ensuring accountability, the same countries who ostensibly placed their hopes in it were also often responsible for denying any genuine investigatory, enforcement, or even personnel powers. He wanted his government in Washington to support a significant expansion of the commission's remit and capacity, including the establishment of a "Prosecuting Office charged with the task of preparing cases against the major war criminals."[26]

Soon after his appointment, Hodgson met with Justice Jackson to coordinate the work, exchange information, and avoid duplication of effort.[27] Eventually, overwhelmed with the scale of coordinating US war crimes policy with reporting to Washington, doing legal research across multiple countries, sitting on multiple government committees, reviewing cases, and a whole host of other roles—all with just one assistant—Hodgson petitioned to the US State Department for additional staff members just to handle the correspondence from other war crimes prosecution centers, all to no avail. His assistant, John Wolff, reportedly suffered a nervous collapse due to overwork shortly after the Nuremberg Tribunal began that autumn, and Hodgson tendered his own resignation a few weeks later (to be replaced by the still-recovering Wolff).[28]

The establishment of crimes against humanity was the greatest achievement of the Nuremberg IMT. The credit for this must extend beyond the immediate actors: Truman, Jackson, and the delegations of the four powers. The UNWCC commissioners and their supporters produced a campaign in and around their governments. But it was Pell, almost alone though with the strategic but flickering support of FDR and latterly of Morgenthau, that succeeded in taking action.

Within the US government, the baton of pursuing justice for war crimes then passed to Justice Jackson, whose work with the Allies to produce a legal basis for the trial of the Nazi leadership is well known. Both the commission and national governments acted immediately to build on the London Charter and the subsequent Nuremberg judgment's ability to apply crimes against humanity more broadly.

The development of treating crimes against humanity as an accepted norm was rapid. By 1947 five treaties—between the Allies and the Nazi satellites: Bulgaria, Finland, Hungary, Italy, and Romania—enshrined crimes against humanity in customary international law. It also became established in the war crimes legislation and constitutions of several states.

One result of the commission's debates in light of the work of the IMTs was that crimes against humanity were deemed a type of war crime. On January 30, 1946, the commission voted on the motion, "Crimes Against Humanity, as Referred to in the Four Power Agreement of August 8th, 1945, are war crimes within the jurisdiction of the Commission." Nine states voted in favor, six abstained, and none opposed. In favor were Australia, Belgium, Czechoslovakia, the United Kingdom, the Netherlands, Poland, Yugoslavia, India, and Denmark. Abstaining were the United States, Canada, China, Norway, New Zealand, and France.[29]

The Crimes of Aggression and Genocide

The deliberation over crimes against humanity was closely linked to the consideration of whether invading another state is an international crime. In his foreword to the UNWCC's *Complete History* Lord Wright stakes out a claim that the commission had played a great part in the development of the idea that aggression could be considered a crime—envisaged by the commission in May 1944—just as it eventually was enshrined in the London Charter more than a year later.[30]

In the twenty-first century the crime of aggression remains controversial. Only recently was it included in the statutes of the International Criminal Court, and that court is not fully recognized by a number of the world's most powerful countries. However, advocates of treating invasion as a criminal act have eminent supporters, not least Benjamin Ferencz, a key prosecutor in the trials at Nuremberg who is still active today on these issues.

However, the view expressed by the Indian judge sitting on the Tokyo tribunal, Radhabinod Pal, finds favor with many in Japan. His minority and dissenting judgment was that invasion was as old as history and much practiced by Western imperialists—not least in the Indian subcontinent—so to prosecute Japan for its success against the West was rank hypocrisy.

The contrasting view was not merely held by the suddenly vulnerable Western powers unexpectedly on the receiving end of invasion. There appears to have been a general sense among states and publics alike that war—total war—even in the still pre-atomic age—had become too self-destructive.

China's position stood in marked contrast to that of Justice Pal. For China, establishing international law and restoring its sovereign rights was a means of drawing a line and ending imperialist invasion. China successfully forced its Western allies to give up their territorial enclaves, save for Hong Kong and Macau, and, from 1942 onward sought to criminalize the acts of invaders.

A central tenet of international law in the 1940s related to the crime of aggression was the enforceability of the 1928 Kellogg-Briand Pact. This brief treaty specified:

> Article 1
> The High Contracting Parties solemnly declare in the names of their respective peoples that they condemn recourse to war for the solution of international controversies, and renounce it as an instrument of national policy in their relations with one another.
>
> Article 2
> The High Contracting Parties agree that the settlement or solution of all disputes or conflicts of whatever nature or of whatever origin they may be, which may arise among them, shall never be sought except by pacific means.

Since Germany, Italy, and Japan were signatories to the treaty, many diplomats argued that the leaders of these three countries could be charged as criminals for breaking its provisions. Others, notably France, through its representative for the French National Committee, André Gros, argued that since the treaty did not specifically state that the provision could be enforced or that breaking it was criminal, then it also could not be used as the basis to criminalize invasion.

The commission was deeply divided over the issue of whether World War II, or indeed any war, could be declared illegal. The UNWCC's *Complete History* devotes a substantial section to these at-times agonizing debates.[31] As with crimes against humanity, it required a reliance on the London Charter in order to be able reach a legal conclusion, which the states could then build on. Here Stimson took the advice of his advisor Col. Frederick Bernays Wiener that the tenets of the Kellogg-Briand Pact could be applied regardless of whether it included an enforcement provision. It is worth noting that at that time none of the Hague Conventions had enforcement provisions, yet they were generally regarded as legally enforceable.

A similar process concerned the commission's consideration of genocide, a concept closely related to crimes against humanity. The concept of denationalization—the removal of national identity—has roots in the debates in the London International Assembly and, before that, in the Hague Conventions.[32] By 1944 the term "genocide," coined by Raphael Lemkin, was beginning to be in general use, including at Nuremberg.

It is important to note, though, that at least beginning with the United Nations Declaration on the Persecution of the Jews of 1942, the term "extermination" of the Jews was in general use among the Allies and was an accepted concept within the commission. Thus, the key underpinning idea of genocide—extermination—was in general legal use, not necessarily as a crime in itself but certainly as a collective noun describing the mass murder of a people.

Universal Jurisdiction

The idea that individual states had an international legal right to try people accused of international crimes, regardless of the perpetrator's nationality or when or where the alleged offense occurred, stands in contrast to the above debates. But the commission had a clear view—clearer, perhaps, than is the case today. This excerpt from the commission's report to the UN ECOSOC is a prime example of this clarity:

> I. Legal Basis Under International Law
>
> 1. Insofar as a Court tries enemy nationals for war crimes committed against nationals of the country whose authorities have established the Court, the Jurisdiction of the Court is based on the undoubted right under international law of a belligerent to punish, on capture of the offenders, violations of the laws and usages of war committed by enemy nationals against the nationals of that belligerent.
>
> 2. Insofar as such a Court tries enemy nationals for war crimes committed against Allied nationals (or persons treated as such) other than nationals of the country whose authorities have established the Court, Jurisdiction may be based on either
>
> (a) the general doctrine called Universality of Jurisdiction over War Crimes, under which every Independent State has in International Law Jurisdiction to punish pirates and war criminals in its custody regardless of

> the nationality of the victims or the place where the offence was committed; or (b) the doctrine that a State has a direct interest in punishing the perpetrators of crimes if the victim was a national of an ally engaged In a common struggle against a common enemy.
>
> The doctrine called Universality of Jurisdiction, which has received the support of the United Nations War Crimes Commission and is generally accepted as sound, received exhaustive treatment by Willard B. Cowles in an article entitled *Universality of Jurisdiction over War Crimes* (California Law Review, Vol. 33 [1945], page 177), in which the learned author states: ". . . when it is a matter of doing justice in places where ordinary law enforcement is difficult or suspended, the military tribunals of the United States . . . have acted on the principle that crime should be punished because it is [*sic*] crime. They have no concern with ideas of territorial jurisdiction . . . No evidence has been found that any of the decisions just discussed were the subject of protest by the governments of the accused persons. Certain it is that in none of these United States cases is there any evidence of a consciousness on the part of the courts of any duty not to assume jurisdiction." The author then argued that "while the state whose nationals were directly affected has a primary interest, all civilized states have a very real interest in the punishment of war crimes," and that "an offence against the laws of war as a violation of the law of nations, is a matter of general interest and concern." He concluded that "every independent state has jurisdiction to punish war criminals in its custody regardless of the nationality of the victim, the time it entered the war, or the place where the offence was committed."[33]

This consensual view in support of universal jurisdiction in 1948, held by representatives of seventeen states, should provide some reinforcement to those with the courage to apply it in the twenty-first century.

Conclusion

The depth and breadth of the Allied effort to prosecute high crimes and, indeed, to indict Hitler, are a resource that can enrich efforts to tackle international crimes by government leaders in the present century. The unsavory tale of the struggle to prevent and repress these efforts from within the major Western states serves as a warning today. Had those fighting for justice not been successful in achieving what they did, the Nazi period very likely would have ended without any legal accountability for the wrongdoers. Faced with an influx of refugees in the early twenty-first century, ghoulish attitudes appear to be rising once again. But at least we are not faced with Nazi veterans regaling television audiences with the delights of shooting Jews.

The lessons for our global history and memory of the vast effort for international criminal justice in the mid-1940s would not be complete without understanding how this process came to a halt. Regrettably it became widely considered to be unnecessary to both history and memory little more than a decade after the war's end. This is the subject of the following chapter.

Notes

1. Henry Stimson, Memorandum for the President, September 9, 1944, 5, available at Franklin Delano Roosevelt Presidential Library website, http://docs.fdrlibrary.marist.edu/psf/box31/a297j16.html.
2. James G. Thompson, letter to the editor, *Pittsburgh Courier*, January 31, 1942, reprinted April 11, 1942.
3. UNWCC, "Polish Charges against German War Criminals," RN 473/P/G/34, CHN 34, January 5, 1945.
4. Donald Bloxham, *The Great Game of Genocide: Imperialism, Nationalism, and the Destruction of the Ottoman Armenians* (Oxford: Oxford University Press, 2005); Gary Jonathan Bass, *Stay the Hand of Vengeance: The Politics of War Crimes Tribunals* (Princeton: Princeton University Press, 2000); Mark Lewis, *The Birth of the New Justice: The Internationalization of Crime and Punishment, 1919–1950* (Oxford: Oxford University Press, 2014); Vahakn N. Dadrian, *Warrant for Genocide: Key Elements of the Turko-Armenian Conflict* (Piscataway, NJ: Transaction, 1999).
5. Leonard Baker, *Brahmin in Revolt: A Biography of Herbert C. Pell* (New York: Doubleday, 1972), 255.
6. Graham Cox, "Seeking Justice for the Holocaust: Herbert C. Pell Versus the US State Department," *Criminal Law Forum* 25, no. 1–2 (2014): 88.
7. Inter-Allied Information Committee, "Punishment for War Crimes: The Inter-Allied Declaration Signed at St. James's Palace London," January 13, 1942, 9.
8. Harold Nicolson, "Marginal Comment," *Spectator* (London), January 14, 1943, available at http://archive.spectator.co.uk/article/15th-january-1943/9/marginal-comment.
9. United Nations War Crimes Commission Committee 2, Resolution Moved by Mr. Pell, March 16, 1944, DN III/I.
10. UNWCC, "Extension of the Commission's Competence to Crimes Not Committed against United Nations Nationals: Recommendations to be Forwarded by Each Member of the War Crimes Commission to His Own Government," draft report, DN C16, May 4, 1944, 2–4.
11. Alice Philipson, "Tony Blair: Bar Worker Attempts Citizen's Arrest on Former PM at Trendy Tramshed Restaurant," *Daily Telegraph* (London), January 21, 2014, available at http://www.telegraph.co.uk/news/politics/labour/10585280/Tony-Blair-bar-worker-attempts-citizens-arrest-on-former-PM-at-trendy-Tramshed-restaurant.html; and "Blair Impeachment Campaign Starts," BBC News, August 27, 2004, available at http://news.bbc.co.uk/1/hi/uk_politics/3600438.stm.

12. See minutes of UNWCC Committee 1 meetings, November 22 and 29, 1944; UNWCC Meeting Minutes, DN M.40, November 22, 1944; "Czech Charges against German War Criminals," RN 424/Cz/G/10, CN Z 7/44./Sondergerichte/, December 15, 1944, 498.
13. UNWCC, "Czech Charges against German War Criminals," RN 389/Cz/G/6, RN 399/Cz/G/8, RN 424/Cz/G/10, RN 433/Cz/G/12, 465/Cz/G/15, CN 6/44, CN Z 10/44 "Dachau," CN Z 7/44 "Sondergerichte," CN Z 13/44 "Forced Labour," CN 15/44 "Terezin," November 17, and 28, 1944, December 15 and 19, 1944, and January 2, 1945, respectively. UNWCC, "Belgian Charges against German War Criminals," RN 628/B/G/22, and RN 797/B/G/33, CN not listed, 15 (London), March 17 1944, and December 6, 1944, respectively.
14. UNWCC, "Minutes of Thirty-Third Meeting Held on 26 September 1944," 3.
15. Samantha Power, *A Problem from Hell: America in the Age of Genocide* (New York: Basic, 2002).
16. Geoffrey Robertson, *Crimes against Humanity: The Struggle for Global Justice* (London: Penguin, 2006).
17. Martti Koskenniemi, "Hersch Lauterpacht and the Development of International Criminal Law," *Journal of International Criminal Justice* 2, no. 3 (2004): 811.
18. UNWCC, "Index to Minutes and Documents of the United Nations War Crimes Commission, 1945–1948," United Nations Archives Reference Guide 11, October 17, 1949, 31–33.
19. Cox, "Seeking Justice," 92.
20. Tom Bower, *The Pledge Betrayed: America and Britain and Denazification of Germany* (New York: Doubleday, 1982), 71.
21. House of Commons, "Hansard Parliamentary Debates: Commons Sitting" vol. 1407, January 17, 1945, column 145-7.
22. John MacCormac, "Big Three Divided on War Criminals: British Oppose US-Soviet Plan to Try Heads of State in International Court," *New York Times*, January 19, 1945; Bertram D. Hulen, "Pell Leaves War Crimes Board, He Favoured Wider Punishments: Pell Ends Service on War Crimes Job," *New York Times*, January 27, 1945.
23. Cox, "Seeking Justice," 99.
24. Quoted in Cox, "Seeking Justice," 104–7.
25. Pell's report can be found in "Drew Pearson's 'The Washington Merry-Go-Round' (June 6, 1945)," Digital Research Archive, available at http://auislandora.wrlc.org/islandora/object/pearson%3A15930?solr_nav[id]=9b71181b2533afd9d950&solr_nav[page]=0&solr_nav[offset]=5#page/1/mode/2up/search/herbert+pell.
26. UNWCC (1945), "Problems Facing the Commission," UNWCC Committee 2, Commission Ref. II/39, May 5, 1945.
27. Robert Jackson, *Report of Robert H. Jackson United States Representative to the International Conference on Military Trials* (Washington: US Government Printing Office, 1945).
28. Christopher Simpson, *The Splendid Blond Beast: Money, Law, and Genocide in the Twentieth Century* (Monroe, ME: Common Courage, 1993), 257.

29. UNWCC, "Minutes of Ninety-Third Meeting Held on January 30th 1946," 4.
30. UNWCC, *Complete History of the United Nations War Crimes Commission and the Development of the Laws of War* (London: Her Majesty's Stationery Office, 1948), available at www.cisd.soas.ac.uk/documents/un-war-crimes-project-history-of-the-unwcc,52439517.
31. Ibid., 232–60.
32. For more on the Hague Convention see UNWCC, *Draft Report of Committee 3 on the Criminality of "Attempts to Denationalise the Inhabitants of Occupied Territory" by the Secretary to Committee 3*, 3/17, September 24, 1945, para. 8., and the preamble of the Convention (IV), "Respecting the Laws and Customs of War on Land (Hague Convention IV)" and its annex, "Regulations Concerning the Laws and Customs of War on Land," The Hague, October 18, 1907.
33. ECOSOC, "Information Concerning Human Rights Arising from Trials of War Criminals," DN E/CN.4/W/19, May 15, 1948, 125.

8

LIBERATING THE NAZIS

Gestapo men arrested for the infamous "Great Escape" murders of Allied air crews were released without trial when Great Britain halted war crimes prosecutions of them in 1948. A few years later, key SS men convicted of mass murder by the United States and other nations walked free—after spending only a few years in prison even though they had originally been sentenced to death. These are just two examples of the "liberation" of the Nazis by the Allies.

This chapter examines the halting of the prosecution processes and the early release of convicted war criminals, which is necessary to explain both the end of the UNWCC and the overall termination of international criminal processes by the 1950s—and their obliteration from both history and memory in the Western world. Included is a review of the debate over the liberation and rehabilitation of the Nazis, in light of both the intensifying Cold War and the idea that Nazi crimes had been exaggerated, especially ones taken against Jews, and that ordinary German soldiers and leaders were of "honest" character. The chapter concludes with an overview of the contribution of retributive justice to the postwar world.

Forgetting the Nazi Past to Build a West German Future

The amnesia exemplified in Elizabeth Kolbert's *New Yorker* article of the prosecution of Oskar Groening ("The Last Trial") extends to and is in large part explained by the determined and successful effort to halt prosecutions of Nazis and to free those that were convicted or detained awaiting conviction.[1] A comparable process took place with respect to Japan that is beyond the reach of this current volume.

By examining the end of the international criminal justice process of the 1940s and 1950s we will see that the closure of prosecutions and then the early release of the convicted by the mid-1950s was the culmination of a political process in the West (and especially within the US government) that opposed the development of international criminal justice at every stage. While briefly eclipsed from 1945 to 1947, this effort had achieved resounding and near-permanent success by 1949. Forgetting this part of the past was essential for the political construction of the Cold War within the West. For those who opposed helping the Jews, the mere fact of the condemnation and prosecution of the Holocaust perpetrators was too damaging, not only to the villains but also to the project of rehabilitating the Germans as a bastion against communism—some 17 million of whom had voted for Hitler before he came to power in 1933.

The closure of the commission in 1948 occurred in parallel with the winding down of American and British war crimes processes and those of their Allies in continental Europe. Figure 8.1 shows the total number of persons and units listed as war criminals, as suspects, or as material witnesses in the five years of the commission's operation. What stands out is that in the last three months of its operation, the commission was considering individual and group cases at the same rate as it had done in the two previous years of 1946 and 1947: some 12,000 per year. Projecting from this data alone, and assuming just a further nine months of operation until the end of 1948, 9,000 more individuals and units would have been considered for prosecution by the commission.

The US State Department sought the end of the UNWCC and war crimes prosecutions beginning in February 1946, but it recognized that it did not have enough support at a time when the Nuremberg trial was still underway and US Army and Allied war crimes investigators and prosecutors were just getting into their stride. Author Chris Simpson has analyzed the closure of the commission in his book *The Splendid Blond Beast* and in an article for the *Criminal Law Forum*.[2]

TABLE 8.1. Individuals and Units Charged by National Offices, by Year

Year	*Individuals and Units*
1944	762
1945	8,442
1946	12,236
1947	11,822
1948 (to March 31)	3,548
	36,810

Source: UNWCC, *Complete History of the United Nations War Crimes Commission and the Development of the Laws of War* (London: His Majesty's Stationery Office, 1948), 508.

Early Protests against Prisoner Release

Even before the closure of the commission, many European representatives were uneasy and rankled by the widespread Anglo-American policy of release and leniency against those accused of war crimes and crimes against humanity. In Belgium the "Scandal of Wolfenbüttel" was a particularly controversial instance. Marcel de Baer, the Belgian representative, originally writing in September 1946, complained to Lord Wright that the Allied Control Commission was leaving it to the German courts to try military personnel who had been listed as accused war criminals for extremely minor charges, including "disciplinary offences against the penal regulations in force in German prisons," instead of handing them over to the Belgians and other member states for prosecution. The Belgian press and public were reportedly furious that Germans involved in killing Belgians at Wolfenbüttel, a major Gestapo execution center, were being released with a slap on the wrist. After initially being reassured by Wright that the commission was "looking into it," de Baer later determined that Belgian requests for extradition were being specifically blocked by the Great Powers on the (in fact) false pretext that the accused had already been tried for the crimes. De Baer issued a formal complaint to Lord Wright.[3]

De Baer's dissatisfaction with Anglo-American cooperation was shared among many of the member states and grew when the British and American representatives began to return war crimes suspects—as free men—to their countries of origin. One British document from November 1947, for example, noted that any "unclaimed" war crimes suspects would begin to be repatriated back to Germany with immediate effect.[4] While acknowledging that being listed by the UNWCC did represent an initial *prima facie* case against war crimes suspects—since nothing had changed on that front and the British would continue to allow states to use the UNWCC process to "claim" German war criminals there—this was still not encouraging to states who had cases that they still wished to pursue.[5] The Allied Control Commission had, in cases like the Wolfenbüttel trial, already demonstrated an unwillingness to comply with extradition requests and the commission as a whole would be closed down in four months' time, in any event.

Hostility to the Commission

The new US president, Harry S. Truman had been selected as Vice President by Roosevelt to shore up support among Southern Democrats for his 1944 election bid (running against Republican Thomas Dewey). Truman was both a strong supporter of US military engagement in the world and an opponent of both the Nazis and communism. As chair of the powerful Lend-Lease committee in the US Senate, Truman had overseen US supplies to the Allies. Notoriously he had been quoted on the front page of the *New York Times* in June 1941 as advocating US support for either the Soviet Union or the Nazis, depending on who was losing.[6]

With Germany defeated, anti-communism became the priority. Leading State department officials had long held the same view and now found a ready audience for their briefings. Acting Secretary of State Joseph Grew wrote to the president that war with the USSR was inevitable.[7]

When Truman took office, anti-Nazi sentiment was at its height, and he enthusiastically endorsed the creation and funding of the Nuremberg Trials. However, this enthusiasm came about in the wake of the reaction to the liberation of the camps and Pell's continuing campaign. Truman's enthusiasm was not sustained and he appears to have at least condoned the renewed pressure from the State Department to close the commission. Simpson has provided a compelling and documented narrative of the process.[8] The account below showcases his work.

Officials at the State Department faced problems in quickly changing US war crimes policy. The JAG offices in Germany, Japan, and the Pacific Islands were launching prosecutions against hundreds of accused war criminals. The Allies were as well, along with trials against those of their own citizens who had collaborated with the enemy in the case of previously occupied countries.

In February 1946 Assistant Secretary of State H. Freeman Matthews took the view that the UNWCC did not have "any very useful purpose," but he recognized that the smaller European allies took the opposite view.[9] Key US diplomats agreed that the closure had to be carried out in secret and ideally through the workings of the British. By December 1946 the British War Office was seeking a common position among its allies for an end date to all war crimes trials.

Then, in April 1947 the British then-chair, Sir Robert Craigie, proposed that the commission cease to consider new cases after just two more months. His colleagues were horrified and urged delay. Lord Wright tried to put the whole idea to one side and the commission agreed with Wright's proposal that closure should not even be considered again until November.

By the summer the Anglo-Americans had forced through the decision that the commission would close by the end of March 1948. Further pressure came in June 1947 as the State Department's Katherine Fite and J. N. Henderson of the British Embassy in Washington began to collaborate on the shutting down of the commission because of what Simpson described as "what might be called today legal 'activism' on the part of the commission on the recognition of human rights" and its zealous pursuit of "wartime Nazi quislings and collaborators."[10]

The State Department did not seek funds from Congress for the UNWCC in the new fiscal year starting April 1, 1948. US officials and US money would no longer be sent to the commission, thus ending US participation and, by agreement, participation of the British too. Without the support of these two governments the UNWCC could no longer survive. At the same time, US general Lucius Clay, commander of

American forces in Europe, announced that after November 1, 1947, the United States would cease to transfer accused war criminals to UNWCC member states.

A mere eight months earlier President Truman had expressed support for democracy in a speech laying out a policy that became known as the Truman Doctrine. But it is hard to match up Truman's avowed pledge to support democratic governments in the face of authoritarian governments with the ever-increasing momentum within his administration to let the Nazis go free.

Opposition to the Commission's Closure

Simpson has documented the litany of futile protests from the European states across the political divide. They include Poland, with a recently installed Soviet-controlled communist government; Yugoslavia, pursuing independent communism; Czechoslovakia, still democratic; royalist Greece, racked by civil war; and several democratic states of northwestern Europe, such as France, Belgium, and the Netherlands. All, with one voice and complementary arguments, protested the closure. Practically speaking, however, they had no power to stop it. Their economies were still in ruins and the Marshall Plan was gearing up to take effect. While individual states continued with some prosecutions for a while, it was clear that such actions would be frowned on by Washington.

The files of the British Foreign Office reveal a particularly clear picture of the Anglo-American pressure to dismantle the commission and the disdain for war crimes prosecutions. While ostensibly motivated by issues of cost and concerns over trial fairness, the records show that the commission itself was objectionable to British officials and suggest there were ideological rather than practical reasons for its closure.[11]

One document noted the "legalistic and pedantic view" of defenders of the commission's ongoing work, such as Marcel de Baer.[12] F. F. Garner, a Foreign Office official, commented on the activities of the UNWCC (which then included over twenty thousand indictments and several hundred commission-supported trials in Europe and Asia):

> Frequently embarrassing and a nuisance to us. Generally speaking they adopt a legalistic and unrealistic point of view on most questions and our military authorities have to waste a lot of time and trouble to show the Commission that the proposals that they bring forward from time to time are impracticable. They often bring up and discuss questions which are really not strictly their concern.[13]

The phrase "questions which are really not strictly their concern"—likely a reference to the commission's work to promote the idea of crimes against humanity—also seems to have been an issue for the Foreign Office. It likewise perceived the precedents that the Nuremberg trials were setting in motion as a risky innovation that should not be allowed to be codified at an international level and should certainly not be allowed to fall under the purview of the UNWCC, which might work on these with the new United Nations Organization which we know today as the UN, and thus prolong its own existence.[14]

A letter from Orme Sargent in the British Foreign Office acknowledged that several member states, such as Poland and Yugoslavia, had encountered "administrative difficulties" lingering from the devastating impact of German occupation and suggested that they were perhaps not trying hard enough—noting that an early closure date for the commission might be enough to spur a "real effort" to carry out and submit cases.[15] The British and Americans contacted their allies in order to assemble a like-minded consensus that would withdraw their support from the commission *en masse* and set a clear date for its closure.

This attitude continued to be evident after the commission was closed. In September 1948, when the Dutch sought to extradite a collaborator and traitor who was living in Britain (and covered under the same extradition policy even though he was not necessarily a war criminal), the British sought a number of excuses to not give him up and considered the question of how best to rid themselves of the "embarrassing responsibility" of handing over accused persons.[16] The Dutch request was eventually acceded to, but the Foreign Office did nonetheless complain about the precedent that it might set: "The Poles at any rate have made clear their feelings about war criminals by weighing in with yet another note."[17]

At the same time, dissenting voices arose from governments and individual staff members who strongly opposed the early closure of the commission. When approached to provide political support for the early closure in 1947, the Canadian government representatives responded negatively. Though Canada had submitted all of the cases that it was interested in, "It is mandatory for the Commission to report and publish the trials of war criminals." Noting that the UNWCC still had a major role to play in overseeing the remaining trials, and that Canada would help to expedite the commission's work, "so long as war crimes trials continue, it would be difficult to terminate the life of the Commission itself."[18] The British, for their part, curtly complained in an internal memo that "we feel however that it puts forward arguments against the early winding-up of the United Nations War Crimes Commission which are not covered by our despatch [*sic*] which was confined to the arguments <u>for</u> an early winding up," and deliberated how best to address the Canadians in such a way as to receive a supportive answer.[19]

Simpson likewise quotes a wide range of dismay and protest from continental European states that disagreed with the closure of the commission in 1948. The Netherlands protested that closing the commission before the thirty thousand suspects were transferred to member states and prosecuted risked "nullify[ing the] UNWCC's work." Poland expressed "astonishment" at the United Kingdom's failure to observe UNWCC-gathered evidence regarding atrocities when releasing suspects (even before the closure of the commission). The US ambassador reported that the Czech Foreign Office and Military Ministry offered "extended reasons" not to cease prisoner transfers for war crimes prosecutions.[20] An early advocate of the UNWCC, de Baer of Belgium was particularly vocal in his defense of the commission. As well as noting that "in view of the number of cases still pending in the National Offices [he could not see how] the Commission could possibly be wound up before the end of the year [1948]," he also captured his and other governments' broader attitude toward the value of the commission:

> My Government would very much regret a premature winding-up of the United Nations War Crimes Commission. They feel that the Commission is the only channel by which smaller nations have an opportunity of expressing their views on the policy and methods of punishment.[21]

In a letter to Lord Wright, de Baer went further in suggesting that it was "deplorable if a premature curtailment of the work of the United Nations War Crimes Commission were to result in an incomplete picture of Nazi criminality being presented to those who, in the future, will read the report of the Commission."[22]

Even some within the British Foreign Office expressed serious doubts about the early closure of the commission. Sir Robert Craigie, never the strongest supporter of the commission's ongoing work, agreed that trials should not be prolonged unduly but also warned against hurrying the trials or closing the commission prematurely. Craigie noted that the states being criticized for supposedly partial trials were "precisely [those] territories [where] the worst of atrocities were committed"; that Anglo-American and Dominion observers should be careful about minimizing the severity of the crimes in those places, especially out of a growing but misplaced sympathy for the defendants inculcated by not having directly experienced Nazi rule; and that, against the odds, he had "been favourably impressed with the apparent fairness of the trials taking place in Poland and Greece"—two countries that were supposedly tardy in resolving prosecutions and becoming increasingly politicized in their trials.[23] In addition, he noted that while the FESC may have already been closed down, it was not because it had finished its work (meaning, by extension, that the UNWCC proper was being overly slow): "For many months the authorities on the spot have failed to provide it with the provender on which to sustain its activities." Craigie recognized that the trials were being hampered by political reluctance rather than politicized abuse.

That there was much work still to be done at the time of closure is indicated by the notes of the final meetings of the Committee on Facts and Evidence, in March 1948. The committee both accepted and rejected a variety of charges against Italians for gassing and other actions in Ethiopia. Among the last Polish cases, the commission gave approval and referral to the British Army in Germany for the extradition of Obersturmbannführer Walter Schween, who had been responsible for SS operations in Warsaw for four years.[24] Then, on March 31, 1948, the process of international support for cases against war criminals ended.

Ongoing Prosecution of War Crimes

All was not yet lost. Decrees from the principal officials in Washington and London to end war crimes prosecutions had to overcome the energy that still remained among official activists for retributive justice and remain sensitive to public opinion. US Army JAG officers continued to bring cases to the commission as late as December 1947, which illustrates how far the administration's policy on war crimes established in the State Department was at odds with the increasingly isolated lawyers of the JAG's office in Germany. Among the final cases brought were those against a member of the Krupp Board for crimes against peace, war crimes and crimes against humanity,[25] as well as a stream of cases concerning the murder of unarmed US Army Air Force crewmen who had parachuted into Germany after their planes were shot down.[26]

Even as the trials of the major war criminals was ongoing at Nuremberg, staffs from the four powers had considered a second major trial, a proposal unsupported in Washington. In their zones of occupation the Allies conducted their own trials, empowered by their acquisition of sovereign rights to act for and on Germany following that country's unconditional surrender. Indeed, the British had launched the first trials concerning Auschwitz and Bergen-Belsen even before the IMT got started at Nuremberg.

Trials continued in both the US and the UK military governments in Germany, carried forward by the energy of the legal staffs in the military. Funded through the military budget, not that of the State Department, the JAG's office had far greater resources than the UNWCC. It also had a determined leader in Brig. Gen. Telford Taylor. The result was twelve subsequent trials. The US Army High Command acted to limit the prosecutions, however, and with the few exceptions of those who were executed, a series of reviews of sentences and early release programs began.

Prisoner Release

A parallel process occurred in Britain, where public sentiment and military prosecutors were overruled by a diplomatic policy written in Washington and increasingly by the emerging government of West Germany under Chancellor Konrad Adenauer. In the minds of the British public, the most outrageous example of leniency toward Nazis concerned an infamous set of murders. Stephen Davies has analyzed how the Royal Air Force police tracked down a considerable number of Nazis who had executed fifty escapees from Stalag Luft III at various locations in Germany. Some of those accused were tried, convicted, and executed. Some were held in British prisons in Germany but never had their day in court and were instead released. Following a British decision in 1948 to end all prosecutions, Walter Hampel (implicated in twenty-nine murders), Max Kilpe, Herbert Wenzler, Harold Witt, and Wilhelm

Nolle had all charges dropped, leading Davies to remark that "they walked away with blood on their hands as free men."[27] In 1986 the Canadian Commission of Inquiry on War Criminals published a British government telegram to seven Commonwealth states on July 13, 1948: "In view of future political developments in Germany envisaged by the recent tripartite talks we are now convinced that it is necessary to dispose of the past as quickly as possible."[28]

Detailed accounts of halted prosecutions, sentence reviews, and early releases by US authorities are provided by Frank Buscher and Kevin Heller.[29] Tom Bower's *Blind Eye to Murder* (a book that was initially serialized in the *Times* of London) provides a longer-term overview of Anglo-American policy.[30] For example, Buscher describes the case of Standartenführer (colonel) Martin Sandberger, who was convicted and sentenced to death at the NMT as one of the leaders of the Einsatzgruppen.[31] He had carried out exterminations of Jews and communists in Estonia and Russia. In September 1947 he was convicted of crimes against humanity, war crimes, and membership in criminal organizations. But Sandberg had a supporter in the United States Senate: the US Army paused his execution following repeated communications to the NMT on his behalf from Sen. William Langer of Illinois.

Sandberg's case came before the US military authorities as they began a series of reviews of convicted war criminals, and his sentence was commuted to life in prison in 1951. Two years later, in January 1953, he was released from the US military prison at Landsberg.

The process of his release arose from concerted lobbying against war crimes trials by almost all sections of German society, except the social democrats and the communists; many Germans attacked the entire war crimes program and saw Germany as a victim at war's end with no collective responsibility. The Catholic Church accepted no responsibility for the crucial support given by the (Catholic-dominated) Center Party to the Enabling Act passed by the Reichstag in March 1933, which transferred the Reichstag's parliamentary power to Hitler, who had just won 44 percent of the vote; nor did it regard German conduct in the war as requiring criticism. After the war the German Catholic Church was led by Cardinal Josef Frings and Bishop Johannes Neuhausler, the latter of whom was attached to the prison and campaigned on behalf of the convicted criminals held by the US at Landsberg. Frings had sermonized in 1946 that the Allies should not play God by judging the guilt or innocence of the Nazi leadership.

The Protestant hierarchy worked in parallel and concert with the Catholics. It was led by Theophil Wurm of Stuttgart and Bishop Hans Meiser of Munich, with strong support coming from the most senior Protestant clergyman, Berlin's Otto Dibelius, who was president of the German Evangelical Church Council.

Their efforts were echoed in the West German Parliament. Buscher concludes: "Most importantly, during the period between the creation of the Federal Republic and the attainment of sovereignty, the parliament stubbornly refused to accept any responsibility for Nazi Germany's atrocities and war crimes. Instead, legislators of almost all parties portrayed the Allies as villains and the violators of the law."[32]

One focus of this German lobbying effort against war crimes trials was over the alleged abuse of SS troops by US Army soldiers during their pretrial interrogations for the murder of US soldiers during the Battle of the Bulge. Leading the accusations in the US were Sen. Joseph McCarthy and Senator Langer. As a result of McCarthy's accusations, the Senate commenced investigatory hearings on April 18, 1949.[33]

In resigning from the Baldwin Subcommittee of the Senate Armed Services Committee (so named for Connecticut senator Raymond Earl Baldwin, the chair), McCarthy issued a damning, persuasive, and false account of the US Army's treatment of the SS men:

> I have listened to testimony and seen documentary evidence to the effect that accused persons were subject to beatings and physical violence in such forms as only could be devised by warped minds. They were subjected to sham trials, to mock hangings; and families were deprived of rations—all of which the prosecution justified as being necessary to create the right psychological atmosphere in which to obtain confessions. I am firmly convinced that innocent as well as guilty persons thus put in the right psychological atmosphere will confess to or make statements supporting anything. I want no murdering Nazis freed. I do want the innocent protected from the abuse of Hitlerian tactics, Fascist interrogation, and the communistic brand of justice. Consistently the evidence pointed to four interrogators. One in the course of his appearance before the subcommittee agreed to take a lie detector test as to whether or not brutalities were used in securing of confessions or statements. The chairman of the subcommittee objected to the use of the lie detector test. The subcommittee chairman submitted the question to the Armed Services Committee; but they also objected to the securing of the facts as would be developed by the lie detector test. I accuse the subcommittee of being afraid of the facts. I accuse it of attempting to whitewash a shameful episode in the history of our glorious armed forces. I accuse it of compounding a wrong, perpetrated by a few members, and impugning the fair name of the millions of men and women who served with valor and distinction in the armed services. I accuse it of sabotaging our efforts under the European Recovery Act.[34]

The subcommittee went on to conduct twenty-nine days of hearings and heard from more than a hundred witnesses (about the same number as were called in the trial of the Nazi leadership at Nuremberg). It found little to support the allegations of maltreatment. On the contrary, and besides the ample amounts of Bull Durham tobacco given to the accused, it found clear evidence of collusion and evidence fabrication by the SS troopers and their supporters outside the court, both in Germany and the United States.

In the end the Baldwin Subcommittee provided general support for the US Army's war crimes prosecutions in Germany and recommended that the UN adopt common standards for war crimes trials, and that the US retain a permanent staff to support such trials. It condemned those who used alleged problems in the prosecution of war criminals to serve the interests of revived German nationalism. Both Senators Langer and McCarthy had launched sustained attacks on the entire war crimes trial system to the benefit of their many ethnic German and anticommunist constituents.[35]

The final Baldwin report was too weak and came too late, however. Langer and McCarthy got a ready hearing in Germany, where the portrayal of US opposition to the trials gave support to German efforts to whitewash the Nazis' actions. In the early 1950s US policy moved toward complete closure of the war crimes process. This policy cannot accurately be attributed to the needs of postwar anticommunism, however. It was a culmination of policy against war crimes trials that from the early 1940s had been supported by leading figures in the US administration in Washington, and gained strategic direction in the heart of the administration in 1946 and gathered momentum thereafter.

The release of the Einsatzgruppen leaders is another good example of US policy in the 1950s. In this case the distinction of "pure Nazi" as opposed to alleged "honest German soldiers" was at its height and liberation was to be afforded even to those condemned to death for the most grievous crimes. Though McCarthy made the allegations, the political climate in Washington gave him space to do so.

By the early 1950s a series of escalating events of the early Cold War—such as the North Korean attack on South Korea, the Soviet test of an atom bomb, the Berlin blockade, and the communist violent coup d'état in Czechoslovakia in 1948—contributed to the decision, after months of debate in the White House, to support the creation of a West German armed force as part of a European defense against possible Soviet attack. But public opinion in Great Britain, western Europe, and large parts of the United States was very much opposed to doing this. In Germany, rearmament became an opportunity to seek an amnesty for war criminals and thereby continue the rehabilitation of the Nazi period as essentially an anticommunist crusade. Although German chancellor Konrad Adenauer and his government strongly desired the rebuilding of their country's military, they used the opportunity to press their new Western allies for concessions on the war crimes issue.

It is worth considering the eventually whitewashed career of Gen. Adolf Heusinger. He had fought in World War I and during World War II was a key staff officer in the central planning staff of the German armed forces (the Wehrmacht). But he never became a public figure. When the July 20, 1944, bomb exploded, he was standing next to Hitler as his acting chief of staff. Yet, following the war, he was able to rise to the very top of the North Atlantic Treaty Organization (NATO) and was chairman of NATO's Military Committee in the early 1960s. He also became an adviser to Chancellor Adenauer. It is difficult to see how the concepts of "common design" or joint enterprise would not have presented a *prima facie* case against Heusinger, had they been brought. His role in preparing for attacks by the Germans on the smaller nations of northwestern Europe—Belgium, Denmark, Luxemburg, the Netherlands, and Norway—are a particular case in point. His picture can be found in a Nazi publicity photo of Hitler standing with his generals in Russia. No country brought charges against him, however, which testifies to the clear view among the victorious allies that simply being a general on the losing side did not warrant charges.[36]

In early 1951 Adenauer sought a general amnesty for war criminals, but this was a step too far and too early. By the late summer of 1951 the last executions of condemned war criminals had taken place, including that of Oswald Pohl, director of the whole SS concentration system, on June 7. Pohl had been prosecuted successfully at the NMT by Telford Taylor.[37] However, the issue of war criminal release continued to be pressed by Adenauer and his officials through the early 1950s, which resulted in an acceleration of releases. Between December 1951 and June 1952 the number of convicted war criminals in US custody fell from 458 to 345 as the US Army continued to review sentences and release prisoners.[38]

Through the political drive of Dwight D. Eisenhower, then US president, and Prime Minister Winston Churchill, West Germany was brought into NATO, a military ally safely under Western command and control. In this context there was no Western fear of uncontainable revival of German nationalism.

Conclusion

On August 31, 1953, six days before elections in West Germany, Adenauer was able to announce that all remaining convicted war criminals in American, British, and French custody would be eligible to be granted parole and clemency.[39] In the 1980s British author Tom Bower revealed the Anglo-American "blind eye to murder" when he wrote, quite correctly, that those who fought for justice were "betrayed by their own side."

The federal German government continued to investigate and prosecute national socialist crimes until at least the time of writing in 2016. Not until the mid-1980s did it have (via Yad Vashem) the UNWCC charge files—which it then meticulously cross-referenced with its existing records system. Neither the United States nor any other member state of the UNWCC provided the German federal prosecutors with the UNWCC archive.

Notes

1. Elizabeth Kolbert, "The Last Trial," *New Yorker*, February 16, 2015, http://www.newyorker.com/magazine/2015/02/16/last-trial.

2. Christopher Simpson, *The Splendid Blond Beast: Money, Law, and Genocide in the Twentieth Century* (Monroe, ME: Common Courage, 1993); and Christopher Simpson, "Shutting Down the United Nations War Crimes Commission," *Criminal Law Forum* 25, no. 1–2 (2014): 133–46.
3. UNWCC, letter from Marcel de Baer to Lord Wright, UNWCC Ref. A.43/I, May 7, 1947; UNWCC RGN A.43/II, September 27, 1946.
4. UNWCC, "Repatriation of Prisoners of War from the United Kingdom Who Are at Present 'Frozen' as Suspect War Criminals," UNWCC RGN A.59, November 4, 1947.
5. UNWCC, "Extradition of War Criminals from the British Isles," UNWCC RGN A.60, November 24, 1947.
6. David McCullough, *Truman* (New York: Simon & Schuster, 1992), 262.
7. Simpson, "Shutting Down the United Nations War Crimes Commission," 137.
8. Ibid., and Simpson, *The Splendid Blond Beast.*
9. Ibid., 138.
10. Simpson, "Shutting Down," 140.
11. Letter from Robert Craigie to Orme Sargent, May 7, 1947, in UK National Archives, "Winding-Up of the United Nations War Crimes Commission, Code 73 File 58," RGN FO 371/66570; and Robert Craigie, "Winding-Up of the United Nations War Crimes Commission," January 28, 1947. Part of document held in The National Archives of the UK, "Winding-Up of the United Nations War Crimes Commission, Code 73 File 58," RGN FO 371/66570.
12. Craigie, "Winding Up," May 3, 1947.
13. F. F. Garner, "Future of the UNWCC," January 9, 1947, in UK National Archives, "Winding-Up of the United Nations War Crimes Commission, Code 73 File 58," RGN FO 371/66570.
14. "Cooperation of the UNWCC with the UN Human Rights Commission, Col. G. A. Ledingham," January 30, 1947, in UK National Archives, "Winding-Up of the United Nations War Crimes Commission, Code 73 File 58," RGN FO 371/66570.
15. Letter from Orme Sargent to Leslie Cameos, January 18, 1947, in UK National Archives, "Winding-Up of the United Nations War Crimes Commission, Code 73 File 58," RGN FO 371/66570.
16. Minutes of meeting, "Time Limit for the Extradition of War Criminals and Traitors from the United Kingdom," October 19, 1948, in UK National Archives, "Request by Dutch Representative of War Crimes Commission for Handing Over of Wilhelm Koning, Code 29, File 7520," RGN FO 371/73279.
17. Ibid.
18. Letter from Lester B. Pearson to Viscount Addison, July 5, 1947, in UK National Archives, "War Crimes Inter-Departmental Committee, Presided over by Lord Finlay, Winding-Up of United Nations War Crimes Commission," RGN LCO 2/2978.
19. Letter from J. A. Walsh to Joseph Garner, July 19, 1947, in UK National Archives DN FO 371/66570.
20. Quoted in Simpson, "Shutting Down," 142–43.

21. Letter from Marcel de Baer to Robert Craigie, January 30, 1947, in UK National Archives, DN FO 371/66570.
22. Letter from Marcel de Baer to Lord Wright, January 30, 1947, in UK National Archives, DN FO 371/66570.
23. Letter from Robert Craigie to Oliver C. Harvey, July 4, 1947, in UK National Archives, DN FO 371/66570.
24. UNWCC, "Summary Minutes of the Meeting of Committee 1 (Facts and Evidence)," March 31, 1948, DN M.141, 8.
25. UNWCC, "United States Charges against German War Criminals," RN 5930/US/G/222, CN 466, December 4, 1947.
26. UNWCC, "United States Charges against German War Criminals," RN 7104/US/G/258, CN 502, July 25, 1947.
27. Stephen R. Davies, *RAF Police: The "Great Escape" Murders* (Bognor Regis, UK: Woodfield, 2009), 141–42, 158.
28. Parliament of Canada, "War Criminals: The Deschênes Commission," CN 87–3E, October 16, 1998, available at http://www.parl.gc.ca/Content/LOP/researchpublications/873-e.htm#B.
29. Frank M. Buscher, *The U.S. War Crimes Trial Program in Germany, 1946–1955* (New York: Greenwood, 1989); and Kevin Jon Heller, *The Nuremberg Military Tribunals and the Origins of International Criminal Law* (Oxford: Oxford University Press, 2011).
30. Tom Bower, *Blind Eye to Murder: Britain, America and the Purging of Nazi Germany, A Pledge Betrayed* (New York: Doubleday, 1982).
31. Buscher, *U.S. War Crimes Trial Program*, 166.
32. Quoted in Peter Maguire, *Law and War: International Law and American History* (New York: Columbia University Press), 207.
33. United States Senate, *Hearings Before a Subcommittee of the Committee on Armed Services, United States Senate, 81st Congress, 1st Session, pursuant to S. Res. 42, Investigation of Action of Army with respect to Trial of Persons Responsible for the Massacre of American Soldiers, Battle of the Bulge, near Malmedy, Belgium, December 1944* (April 18, 20, 22, 29; May 4–6, 9–13, 16–20, 23–24; June 1–3, 6, 1949).
34. See, for example, "McCarthy Accuses Probers of Attempting 'Whitewash,'" *Daily Times-News* (Burlington, NC), May 20, 1949.
35. William Bosch, cited in Buscher, *U.S. War Crimes Trial Program*, 47; Glen H. Smith, *Langer of North Dakota: A Study in Isolationism 1940–1959* (New York: Garland, 1979), 148–50. Also see William Bosch, *Judgment on Nuremberg: American Attitudes toward the Major German War-Crime Trials* (Chapel Hill: University of North Carolina Press, 2011), 85.
36. Buscher, *U.S. War Crimes Trial Program*, 71.
37. Ibid., 70–71.
38. Ibid., 77.
39. Bower, *Blind Eye to Murder*, 83.

9

THE LEGACY UNLEASHED

How fortunate we are to have the ideas and work of the thousands of people who fought for justice as part of the Allied victory in World War II. We must seize the opportunity to use their legacy. The suppression of the UNWCC's achievements and its work should embolden us to use it as a model to the full, energized by outrage at its long-enduring loss.

This chapter first looks at current debates concerning the weakness and demise of human rights in the light of the work of the UNWCC and then places it in the context of the famous human rights agreements of the period: the UN Charter and especially the Genocide Convention and the Universal Declaration of Human Rights. This leads into a discussion of the heart of the relevance of the UNWCC to international criminal law in the twenty-first century, beyond the arguments made so far.

The People's Human Rights

There is an intellectual trend to write of "the end of human rights" and at the same time to place their origins in the postwar period, sometimes as late as the 1960s or 1970s. Such arguments can be found across a multitude of political and legal studies.[1] These various arguments state that the postwar agreements were worth little more than the paper they were written on, that the writers of the texts were in any case Western intellectuals, and that human rights have a singularly Western and modern source. Samuel Moyn maintains that the texts of Raphael Lemkin on genocide and Hersch Lauterpacht on crimes against humanity were stillborn creations that had to be reborn in the 1970s.[2] Lynn Hunt argues that human rights started with the American-French political enlightenment.[3]

Yet the Golden Rule—"Do unto others as you would wish them to do unto you"—encapsulates the core of human rights values and their importance in a just society. Step into any undergraduate classroom, or indeed any grade school class on religion and civics, and you are likely to find a chart showing how this precept is common to philosophies and religions around the planet. It is true that these precepts do not carry a legal reference, but they exist nonetheless, and they permeate social life all over the world.

Many writers have detailed these socially embedded universal values of human rights. Eric Helleiner and colleagues provide a through overview in "The Neglected Southern Sources of Global Norms."[4] The connection of non-Western thinking and participants in the postwar agreements mentioned above has also been illuminated in an elegant article by Bertrand Ramcharan, a former director of the UN Human Rights Division, who details the people from outside the West who shaped key components in the modern human rights agreements.[5]

We have seen that the UNWCC agreed on a definition of crimes against humanity as early as 1944, though it also failed to gain American and British support. In general terms, though, Anglo-American leaders had begun to speak of crimes against humanity in response to the Armenian massacres and then in response to the crimes of Nazi Germany. As described in chapter 3, the commission adopted the term "humanity" as a diplomatic replacement for "Christianity" in deference to Jewish and Muslim opinion in the 1940s. They echoed the actions of British and French diplomats in their 1915 response to the unfolding Armenian Genocide, who persuaded their Russian allies to replace the condemnation of crimes "against Christianity and civilization" with the universal term "against *humanity* and civilization" in order to be more sensitive to potential Muslim allies in the conflict.[6] Thus, on two occasions, when Anglo American officials had to form policy in response to atrocities, they found it necessary to move beyond Christianity to an all-encompassing description of humanity. There was a clear operational need to provide a universal discourse that required a shift in language from specific protection of "Christians" to a broader notion of "humanity." Furthermore, the foundational and operational role of China and India in the UNWCC's debates and decisions, as well as the engagement of Ethiopia and the Philippines in the discussion, provide a reinforcement of non-Western activism in agreeing and enforcing international human rights standards.[7]

As already discussed, the effort to add justice to victory was carried forward by democratic opinion and low-level officials around the world. This effort should be seen as an international, grassroots-driven campaign to formalize and enforce global norms.

There is another argument in connection with these actions, however, that needs to be tackled: that non-European officials and intellectuals are "not really" non-Europeans because they wrote and worked mostly in English, they have or had been educated by Western schools and universities, and so forth. It would be simple to respect the views denying non-Western input in human rights as part of the richness of academic debate. Perhaps they are just a form of the chauvinism of Western denigration of other cultures. To be less tactful and more forthright: the denial, in the face of the evidence, of non-Western foundational and ongoing engagement with human rights and their legal enforcement is simply bigotry and racism—unconscious or otherwise.

This denial, that scholars and politicians from the Global South (if only a small handful) have created and value human rights, is also extremely dangerous. It permits a flow of self-serving political thought among Western elites. Just as seriously, it provides legitimacy for repressive governments outside the West to denounce human rights as imperial impositions. I characterize the argument this way: "We are civilized, they are barbaric, so when faced with barbarism we, too, must, from time to time, lower our civilized standards—but we get to decide when that is." This is the road to water torture being used at Central Intelligence Agency–run black sites and it was part of the rationale for letting key Holocaust perpetrators go free on grounds of political expediency and the suppression of the records of the UNWCC.

In the 1940s the United States, largely in the form of the State Department, was at the forefront of the *prevention* of retribution for international human rights violations, rather than in the vanguard of its promotion. The efforts of Eleanor Roosevelt, Herbert Pell, Telford Taylor, and Robert Jackson were exceptions among US leaders.

But America was not exceptional in being affected by an internal conflict between those who sought justice and those who were either disinterested or downright opposed. All Allied states experienced a contentious development and application of human rights standards—especially in the form of international crimes. The efforts of Green Hackworth and Katherine Fite do not devalue the work of the Roosevelts, just as the corruption of the nationalist Chinese do not wipe out the work of Wellington Koo and the FESC.

There is another argument that justified setting aside the work of the UNWCC, as made by American postwar figures such as George Kennan, Joseph McCarthy, and the Dulles brothers.[8] Europe, especially Western Europe, began a remarkable period of reconciliation and development after 1945—driven by fear of the communist enemy—and did so even though the Americans had closed down the war crimes processes. This, surely (as the argument runs) shows that these two were linked and that postwar critics of the commission were right. Justice was an obvious obstacle to peace and reconciliation. This ingenious line of thought is twenty-twenty hindsight through lenses distorted by McCarthyism.

Across Europe, national days still mark the day of liberation from the Nazis. The four or five years of that experience still sear those nations' souls. Everywhere liberation brought some mob rule and some justice.[9] In the fraught years of the later 1940s, every liberated society decided to hold judicial processes for collaborators—a subject of controversy to this day—and sought to prosecute the crimes of the invaders. They did so with determination, in parallel with the processes that would, in time, produce the European Union, NATO, and ultimately the

European Convention on Human Rights. At the time, people regarded retributive justice as vital and protested its crushing by the United States. They were committed to holding the Nazis to account but were unable to continue in the face of US opposition. The consequences of not following through can be seen today.

Once again xenophobia, Holocaust denial, antisemitism, and anti-Muslim prejudice are on the march. Some proponents—as Herbert Pell feared—look back with nostalgia to the achievements of the Nazis. One might have hoped a political leader today might have invited refugees to occupy the homes of the 6 million dead Jews and point out that, if any part of Europe is mono-religious, it is only because all the Jews and Romany were killed. Long-suppressed indictments and forgotten trial records should provide every nation concerned with fresh and gruesome reminders of where these doctrines take us, and why the process of law is an essential part of the response.

The late 1940s saw the successful negotiation of three landmark international agreements: the Universal Declaration of Human Rights, the Genocide Convention, and the Third and Fourth Geneva Conventions (the latter two of which offered, respectively, revised protections for prisoners of war and new protections for civilians caught up in conflicts and in occupied territories). The history of the UNWCC and its associated tribunals provide an added dimension to the development of these legal documents. Many involved in them went on to occupy major roles in the early United Nations, such as Egon Schwelb, a key member of the UNWCC in London, who went on to become the deputy director of the UN Human Rights Division. The suppression of the international criminal process of the UNWCC occurred in parallel with these developments. What is rarely if ever discussed is that the high-level negotiations on agreements for the future were taking place at a time when the Western powers were burying the Nazi past with great determination.

The near-consensus that ancient men such as Oskar Groening should face trial comes in part from a righteous sense that not enough was done at the time. It is beyond irony that so much more was done (and even more attempted) to hold war criminals to account in the 1940s than has been recognized.

The UNWCC as an International Human Rights Agreement

A fundamental and positive shift in understanding the role and potential of human rights after Hitler comes from understanding the work of the UNWCC. Let us compare the UNWCC to the Nuremberg IMT, the UDHR, and the Genocide Convention:

- The Genocide Convention was put into cold storage by the major powers almost as soon as it was created in 1948. Only in recent decades has it provided the basis for a score of national—that is, intrastate—prosecutions and cases related to crimes in the Balkans, in Cambodia, and in parts of Africa and Latin America.

- The Nuremberg IMT tried twenty-four people and set the example for the subsequent trials at Nuremberg and for those conducted in the tribunals for crimes in Rwanda, Sierra Leone, and the former Yugoslavia and the eventual creation of the ICC.
- The UDHR provides a standard of norms and customary information law that human rights advocates can use.
- The UNWCC facilitated the conviction of some thousands of war criminals, developed a system of global criminal justice, and helped provide the intellectual, institutional, and political momentum that contributed to the creation of all three of the above, with exemplary economy of time and money.

For US officials opposed to binding human rights agreements the closure of the legally effective UNWCC was a success. The aspirational and non-binding agreements posed comparatively little threat to traditional abuses of power.

Consider the counterfactual: a well-resourced UNWCC continuing into the 1950s with the Genocide Convention in its arsenal, reinforcing the pursuit of all the indictments already processed by the commission. Would such processes have undermined democracy in West Germany and driven German elites into Stalin's arms? That is hard to imagine. It is far easier to see this encouraging the progress of human rights globally. FDR's anticolonial policy abroad and the related issue of African American rights could have grown from this too. During the war, African Americans had campaigned on the "Double V," signifying the victory of "Democracy at Home and Abroad." Membership of the National Association for the Advancement of Colored People had grown fifty-fold, reaching 500,000, and black voter registration in the South grew from 2 percent to 18 percent. The continuation of prosecutions outside America for human rights abuses would have likely fed back positively into US politics in the manner feared by Henry Stimson.

We should now recall the value of the UNWCC, having fished it out of the Orwellian "memory hole" into which its contemporary detractors cast it. We must reflect upon the missed opportunity of the last seventy years and bring its values and prototypes to life, using them to inspire a new generation. Are we to act as the heirs of Herbert Pell, the State Department chief law officer of the period, or Green Hackworth?

The international legal response to human rights abuses was, and can be, the achievement of victims and their witnesses. It was not and should not be the sole province of great powers, great leaders, and great thinkers. It was and can be the creation of normal people in abhorrently abnormal conditions.

Auschwitz was not, and should not be regarded as, beyond human response or as a negation of the human condition. Along with the other death camps, it was responded to as best as could have been by victims, and government officials high and low, in peril of their lives and in the relative safety of missile-bombarded London. "We" *did* know, "we" *did* condemn, "we" *did* indict, and "we" *did* prosecute. The argument that "we" did not know and so could not condemn or act until it was too late is shown conclusively to be a lie, which suits those who did not care and wished an opportunity to ally with the perpetrators against what they saw as the greater enemy: communism. The critiques of the 1940s human rights agreements as stillborn or as solely driven by the West are founded on a narrow view of that inheritance. That narrowness and depoliticization can be found in the Anglo-American sphere of scholarship; a sphere that we should now see as constructed by the ascendancy of conservative approaches to the UN and to human rights in the postwar world. Those approaches had been on the defensive in the war years but became ascendant and ensured the suppression of the UNWCC at an early stage.

As discussed in my book *America, Hitler, and the UN* and in subsequent research with Thomas G. Weiss, progressive liberalism and social democratic politics at home and abroad provided a crucial dynamic operating within the anti-Nazi political coalition.[10] The suppressed history and memories of the global effort toward international criminal justice demonstrates just how rich that wartime tradition can be as a source for future generations.

Critics of the historical development of human rights often take as their empirical foundation the narrow base of Nuremberg and Tokyo and the subsequent UN agreements. As we can now see, this narrow base is all that remained after the repressive intellectual and political efforts of Western conservatives in the later 1940s and 1950s. Liberal critics who claim to seek a human rights "high ground" are doing their opponents' job for them by attacking the origins of human rights on the basis of a false image of those origins.

A similar construction exists when we debate issues of transitional justice and peace versus justice. There is one major difference between the UNWCC-associated legal processes and most of those in recent decades: after World War II the Axis countries surrendered unconditionally (though in the case of Japan the ultimate political authority—the emperor—was granted immunity). In trials of recent years concerning major international crimes in Africa, the Balkans, and the Middle East, there have been no absolute winners or losers. The criminalization of opponents in a conflict hardens the resolve of the accused and makes the conflict worse. In such situations—more than in a postwar environment of political compromise, when amnesty laws and burying the past are considered necessary and financial and other compensation rather than prison is preferred—trials may serve to aggravate social wounds. No doubt there have been and will be occasions where such considerations may suit the best interests of victims, of wider society, and of international relations. But let us be clear: these were also the considerations of the 1940s. Today we have new challenges in the application of transitional justice and effective legal retribution for human rights abuses. In making balanced judgments on what to do, we draw on past experience. As we have seen, the experience of the UNWCC and its member states places an awesome weight in favor of justice.

A large and unifying theme that has not been explored yet concerns how the international community can help states in prosecuting major international crimes as the UNWCC did. The potential to develop new political and legal systems of necessity requires a somewhat more technical discussion from a legal perspective.

Complementarity and the UNWCC

One of the UNWCC's practices with the most power today was its role as a bridge between national and international law, especially in reinforcing national law and legal practices. For some commentators today, this role holds a greater legitimacy and a sounder basis for action than its international counterpart.[11]

The term "complementarity" describes this bridge in modern international law, especially with regard to the International Criminal Court. It was prefigured by the commission's work, as articles by Mark Ellis and Carsten Stahn make clear.[12] Many scholars have written on the topic of complementarity since the ratification of the Rome Statute for the ICC in 1998; studies range from critical forward-looking appraisals of the ICC's early existence; to overviews of the principle and its theoretical and practical implications; to appraisals of the practical implications for tribunals.[13] Rather than repeating ground covered elsewhere, we should instead briefly examine complementarity as it currently exists before teasing out the points where it overlaps with the ideas and approaches of the UNWCC. Could a resurrected commission-like body assist in the implementation of complementarity today?

The ICC is intended to be "complementary to national criminal jurisdictions," that is, a supplement to rather than a replacement of national courts.[14] Its role is most clearly defined in Article 17, which addresses the types of admissible cases. Noting that cases that are currently being investigated or prosecuted by a state that has jurisdiction over it are not the ICC's concern, unless the state in question is "unwilling or unable genuinely to carry out the investigation or prosecution." This unwillingness, discussed in Section 2, can be seen in attempts to shield the perpetrators, to cause an unjustified delay, or to conduct trials that are not impartial or independent and are inconsistent with the intent to bring the person concerned to justice. Section 3 describes this inability in terms of "whether, due to a total or substantial collapse or unavailability of its national judicial system, the State is unable to obtain the accused or the necessary evidence and testimony or otherwise unable to carry out its proceedings." In short, the ICC should be viewed as a court of last resort that exists to prosecute cases that would not be prosecuted or prosecuted fairly under national jurisdictions.

Today, just as in the 1940s, there is often reluctance to bring the accused to court. The case of Sudan's president, Omar al-Bashir, is a salutary example. Following the referral to the ICC by the UN Security Council in 2005 (and a period of pretrial arrest warrants and investigation), the court's chief prosecutor requested that Sudan arrest and surrender al-Bashir and that ICC member states do the same if presented with an opportunity.[15] For a variety of reasons—usually pointing to the impact on the peace process and the suitability of the ICC's approach—the Sudanese government did not hand over its president for trial and other African countries allowed him to visit without arresting him.[16] Similar problems exist in Syria, with calls for ICC action against President Bashar al-Assad that won't have any chance of success; he will likely never find his way into the court's jurisdiction, to say nothing of the political obstacles that such a prosecution would face. But the 1940s offer many examples of the difficulty—sometimes impossibility—of bringing prosecutions and, as we now know, far more was achieved than most believed. In consequence, we should pursue cases today from this larger foundation.

Then as now, the major powers had a sometimes negative impact on the development of international justice. In theory a small state in need of international legal assistance and legitimacy—and fearful of great powers—might take advice from a group of smaller credible states. This is but one example of badly needed innovation.

While the existence of an international body with an interest in assisting prosecutions might help to encourage willingness for trials and shift domestic political cultures away from acting with impunity, if a state is unwilling to cooperate with international criminal justice or try a sitting leader there is little to learn from the UNWCC's experience. Enforcement issues, noncooperation, and an unwillingness to participate would have torpedoed the efforts of the UNWCC's Committee 1, for example, which typically dealt with governments-in-exile that were engaged and enthused in the process of prosecution of war criminals while the war was still going on. The commission did not have to deal with fundamentally noncompliant states, though standards of compliance varied a good deal.

What about states that are willing but unable to prosecute major cases—that is, countries that are unable to prosecute because of disruptions to their legal systems (a common situation in the wake of major war crimes, crimes against humanity, and genocide)? Tom Fawthrop and Helen Jarvis note that under the Khmer Rouge, of the "legally trained personnel from the pre-1975 period, only seven remained" alive or in the country.[17] They propose that major cases for genocide and war crimes should be handled through a broader international framework that is not damaged by the same conflict that had had such a devastating impact on national courts. A number of writers, however, have suggested that questions of complementarity should go beyond the simple binary between states being able or not able to prosecute major war criminals to instead take a more cooperative and constructive approach. Contributors to Carsten Stahn and Mohamed M. El Zeidy's edited volume, *The International Criminal Court and Complementarity*, express a range of different opinions about how this might be established. Silvana Arbia and Giovanni Bassy draw upon their own experience working at the ICC and upon the conception of "passive" versus "proactive" complementarity defined in William Burke-White's contribution to the volume.[18] The ICC, Arbia and Bassy argue, could engage in efforts to assist and encourage trials; the registry of the court in particular could assist by strengthening and coordinating lists of legal representation for those involved, coordinating international and bilateral schemes of witness protection, and sharing the benefits of its "state-of-the-art" court management processes (including translating, archiving, and distributing documents). Burke-White elaborates on these ideas but remarks that the ICC, "has not formally taken [a range of trial improvement measures] . . . its policy with respect to positive complementarity is muddled at best, and its track-record for encouraging national prosecutions is decidedly mixed."[19] Carsten Stahn explores similar notions of "positive complementarity" and stresses the benefits of its more holistic nature and wide range of forms as well as its capacity to lead to fairer, more effective, and more legitimate trials.[20]

The "constructive" or "positive" or "holistic" aspects of complementarity should sound familiar from the discussion of the UNWCC, as should these authors' specific recommendations for a range of bureaucratic actions to support courts active in war-torn countries and international processes that provide legitimacy. While the UNWCC did not offer direct trial support that is sometimes desired by advocates of positive complementarity, its structure increased the capacity of states to carry out prosecutions by offering international legal backing for initial charges and pushing them to improve charges to the point that backing could be given.

Sadly, the ICC has done little about this opportunity. Indeed, the ICC's Bureau of Stocktaking explicitly places the court outside the provision of "capacity building, financial support, and technical assistance," suggesting instead that this would be an activity for member states to carry out on a voluntary basis.[21]

Nonetheless, Ellis cites several places where such assistance could be helpful: Kenya's enthusiasm to prosecute war crimes (combined with its still-fragile domestic legal system and reticence surrounding the ICC); Uganda's prosecutions of the Lord's Resistance Army (where some training has been provided, but still needs increased tailoring to specific domestic conditions); and mobile courts prosecuting sexual violence in armed conflict in the Democratic Republic of the Congo.[22] These sorts of projects have been fairly successful. For example, one United Nations Development Program (UNDP) assessment found that supporting mobile courts was an effective way of promoting accountability and justice for widespread crimes such as sexual violence. Because courts were roving and dispersed, people outside civic centers became more in touch with the courts, which in turned helped reduce the sense of justice as something only available in civic centers.[23]

This effort had a broadly positive effect from a complementarity-based perspective. It helped to develop legal skills among national jurist populations and led to successful prosecutions of international crimes in situations where political insecurity, lack of infrastructure, and remote location had made them legally unpromising.[24] The potential for complementarity-based systems across many African states was described in *Unable or Unwilling? Case Studies on Domestic Implementation of the ICC Statute in Selected African Countries*, a volume edited by Max du Plessis and Jolyon Ford. As the writers explained, the friction between support for the ideals of the ICC (regarding prosecution of international crimes) and skepticism over its practices and Western-dominated nature might be resolved by encouraging domestic courts to follow international criminal justice principles in their trial processes. It is essential, they suggested, to offer technical support toward this goal and involve regional bodies such as the African Union.[25] Non-African domestic trials for incidents of major crimes have taken place in areas as disparate as Kravica in Bosnia-Herzegovina and the Ixil municipalities in Guatemala. These trials drew upon the resources of international courts—such as referencing legal precedents established by prior courts and forming internationally supported truth commissions —but were carried out in a domestic environment.[26]

In many cases, the enthusiasm for prosecution combined with fragile judiciaries make conducting such cases difficult or lead to poorly conducted and unfair trials. This suggests a need for technical assistance, possibly of the sort the UNWCC offered. The UNDP review of technical support provided to mobile courts commented repeatedly about the positive results that international coordination among relevant UN and nongovernmental agencies could bring. Regularizing and broadening this cooperation will reap positive benefits. In addition, framing international support in terms of cooperative "assistance" rather than routinely referring cases to The Hague, might be a less-intrusive option and could help keep states more enthusiastic about international criminal justice. Du Plessis and Ford note, however, that it is important to ensure that any product of an international assistance system not "dilute or subvert universal values."[27] A complementary system of international legal assistance might risk being caught between failing to do its job and assisting (and thus legitimating) a trial process that violates human rights. It might also be difficult for countries today to accept putting up prosecutions for major cases before an international body for review, as was done with the UNWCC. Nevertheless, while such a move, even if voluntary, would appear to relinquish sovereignty and might return unwelcome results, linking support for broader justice and humanitarian and human rights concerns with necessary technical assistance might help make the relinquishment more palatable, and even desirable.

Another problem would be cohesion: a modern UNWCC-like entity would have to be sustained by normative structures and frameworks built up since 1945 rather than by the intense interstate bonds that existed among the Allies of the 1940s. That bond derived not only from a shared commitment to justice and human rights but also from the fact that they were joint participants in a military conflict against the Axis powers. Modern complementarity mechanisms would have to address the challenge of building mutual confidence and trust and replace the strong sense of anti-Nazi camaraderie with a desire for cooperation. One potential tactic could come from the technical, legal nature of legitimation—specifically an emphasis on using a diverse group of experts to provide advice instead of an intergovernmental arm providing deliberations and judgment. Another possible approach might be to encourage regional rather than global reviews. While rivalries and mistrust exist within a region, the shared identity that often exists among members of such groups could assist in fostering confidence and trust as a prelude to greater cooperation.

Toward a "UNWCC 2.0"?

One approach to creating a new system of international support for national war crimes processes revolves around dedicated legal support and technical assistance. Mark Ellis, the head of the International Bar Association (IBA) and former advisor on war crimes prosecutions in The Hague and Yugoslavia, has laid out his plan for an "International Technical Assistance Office" (ITAO) that would be responsible for the specific provision of services like those of the commission. Ellis's proposed organization would aim to satisfy twelve key goals; while these are too extensive to fully examine here, it is worth looking at how a commission-like approach could supply many benefits.

To reinforce the provision of "fair, impartial, and effective trials," for example, Ellis argues for a committee of judges, prosecutors, and academics from across the world who possess experience in handling major cases involving war crimes. These independent legal experts would be capable of providing briefs and other advice on the foundation of major trials as well as on the substantive legal and procedural issues that arise during the running of trials.[28] They would be able to present neutral, unbiased, and effective advice; as an international body their input would also be valuable in legitimating and accrediting a new trial system. The result would be to "give the new court access to the very best in establishing a newly promulgated domestic court."[29]

Ellis's recommendation to systematize this capacity could in fact draw upon the concrete experience of the UNWCC's committees 1 and 3, which successfully carried out similar work in institutionalizing trial structures, supporting tribunals, and providing legal expertise to resolve substantive legal questions. While the UNWCC did not carry out systematic detailed trial observations—and instead relied on transcripts that were sent to it by member states and on individual observations made by its members—it assessed the results of trials that it supported and produced valuable transnational studies of best practices, such as the ECOSOC report on human rights issues. That this worked (albeit in a narrower form) could be the spur to Ellis's proposed International Technical Assistance Organization (ITAO) and its playing a major role in trial oversight.[30] Other possible roles—such as training judges; supporting, coordinating, and protecting defense counsel (the last of which, Ellis notes, is a serious issue because defense lawyers sometimes face harassment while trying to carry out their work); running witness and victim support programs; and assessing post-trial sentencing—do not have precedents in the commission's history. Nevertheless, work that the UNWCC accomplished successfully during its brief existence was certainly the precursor to modern international jurisprudence.[31]

A second option for a "UNWCC 2.0" would be to look to the sheer scale and scope of prosecutions and indictments of war criminals by the UNWCC following World War II, and take that work as a challenge—and a model—for a more extensive, less "exceptional" approach to war crimes prosecutions today. One option would be to create a tribunal to deal with "ordinary" war crimes below the level of the ICC, that are adapted to local activities and actions. Such tribunals—carrying a UN mandate or attached to UN peace operations—would operate according to international standards but in accordance with local cost structures and procedures. The UNDP analysis of the value of local courts in Africa is one starting point.

In the case of Syria, the UN enclaves on Cyprus could provide a regional base for such legal operations. Some examples of these sorts of structures have occurred in the national prosecutions of "cases involving intermediate and lower rank accused [in] competent national jurisdictions," in the case of the ICTR and Rwandan national courts.[32] They offer a potentially productive way of approaching the issue of complementarity and addressing wider ranges of perpetrators in more "ordinary" legal settings, albeit one that so far has been used overcautiously and with too-high standards.[33] Complex conflict termination processes, widely varying national situations, and the requirements of formal justice have nothing trivial or easy about them, but the UNWCC's approach—providing a set of broadly-agreed-upon standards and arguments—might provide a useful model in standardizing and disseminating the ad hoc achievements of the ICTR to other locales. In any case, such an approach—with its ability to support and promote the trials of intermediate and low-level perpetrators—might help redress the current focus, which is almost entirely on the higher-level perpetrators.

Many of the problems confronted by the commission are still present. Allied states (often in exile) rose to the legal challenges of the time with a spirit of genuine multilateral cooperation and political innovation under extremely dire circumstances—in wartime London under attack, in occupied Europe at the height of the Holocaust, and in the conflict-ravaged political landscape of postwar

Poland. Even the four major powers that remain outside the International Criminal Court—China, India, Russia, and the United States—played leading roles in launching a global system of international criminal justice, whereas Britain—today an advocate of international criminal justice—played a direct role in sabotaging the UNWCC's work. It is possible to be optimistic. Crucial members of the original United Nations once vigorously cooperated on orchestrating an international scheme of accountability for major crimes, and should now do so again.

International criminal law practiced since the 1990s has been patterned after the events in Nuremberg and Tokyo—large-scale, expensive, drawn-out trials of leaders conducted by international (overwhelmingly Western) lawyers and officials. The UNWCC's system—which both postdated and predated the International Military Tribunals—offers a different approach characterized by building on, supporting, and coordinating already-existing institutions and groups in order to promote justice at the national, domestic, local levels through existing judicial systems. This finds its modern equivalent in notions of complementarity in the ICC—the notion that it is not a court of first resort, but a last resort. Rather than seeing fully internationalized trials as the be-all and end-all of international criminal justice, sitting at the opposite end of the spectrum from solely domestic trials, the UNWCC's work suggests that the value of blending the two takes advantage of existing domestic structures while bringing to bear international legitimation and technical assistance to ensure full and fair trials. Blending also helps to "domesticate" legal processes and thereby increase their traction with the public. We should recall that the UNWCC was multilateral and diverse in its constituents; it benefited from its ability to be "steered" toward areas of particular concern among its participants, such as attempted crimes of sexual violence in several European countries (particularly Greece and Yugoslavia) or aggression in China. While there is value in an internationally harmonized and consistent system of criminal justice for major atrocities, this more responsive, local approach is crucial.

We can also identify specific ways in which the legacy of the UNWCC can be carried forward with a variety of possible modern-day applications that are patterned on historical antecedents, such as that of the ITAO. Carsten Stahn notes that "international criminal justice is still in search of a 'UNWCC 2.0.'"[34] There is irony in modern-day academic debates and legal practices, which are only beginning to return to the intense burst of innovation in legal practices and organization that brought policymakers and jurists together in the 1940s. Modern policymakers would be served well by actively drawing upon this historical legacy to refine fledgling current international criminal legal structures. Complementarity and a system of hybrid international-domestic criminal justice for mass atrocity crimes represent a potentially productive and underinvestigated field of study as well as inspiration for contemporary action.

It will be challenging and difficult to create what Stahn has envisaged as a UNWCC 2.0, and hard to generate the necessary political will—but not nearly as difficult as it was to create the original UNWCC and present charges to it in the midst of a world war.

It is essential to rewrite sections of textbooks explaining the Holocaust, human rights, international criminal law, and a significant part of the political history of World War II and the rise of human rights as antibodies to fascism. It may be a bother to dig out and digitize the yet-to-be-unearthed records of the World War II trials held by more than a dozen states, but archivists often relish such a challenge. Similarly, many officials and politicians will welcome the reinforcement for policies they are trying to make today by pointing to the standards their governments once adhered to.

It is hoped that the legacy of the UNWCC will provide the additional moral courage and political arguments needed to revitalize the global human rights agenda in the present century—and we need it. The commissioners were not interested in processes divorced from politics. On the contrary, they saw effective implantation of human rights standards as an essential part of preventing "totalitarian warfare" where belligerents "were under no obligation to respect human rights, but were entitled to trample them underfoot wherever the military forces found them inconvenient for the waging of war."[35] This is, of course, part of the argument of the human rights community today. But it faces opposition from self-styled realists. Actual events of the last few decades, especially in the Middle East, show that setting aside human rights does not reduce conflict and violence—quite the contrary.

Our contemporary human rights debates are founded on a narrow history and memory of the use of human rights trials in response to Nazism. People fought against Hitler and for civilization, as exemplified in the Four Freedoms, the Declaration by the United Nations, the St. James's Declaration, and in countless political documents produced by populations that after the war voted en masse for liberal and socialist parties. They produced Keynesian-style social and political rights based on a consensus underpinning Western societies, at least until the 1980s. It is my hope that this discussion offers a start in recalibrating our history, memory, and thus our political direction. In parallel, the records of the United Nations War Crimes Commission provide ample material for drama, documentaries, exhibitions, memorials, and textbooks.

Conclusion

The UNWCC is a major and important historical source of reinforcement for the politics and law of international criminal justice today. It provides a rich, varied, and, until recently, largely unknown foundation for holding perpetrators of atrocities to legal account. After more than half a century of neglect, this lost wisdom, born in the worst years of modern civilization, can be of great practical import today.

The opportunity should not be lost again, and there are essential lessons to be learned about our approach to knowledge. The UNWCC's *Law Reports of Trials of War Criminals* and *Complete History of the United Nations War Crimes Commission and the Development of the Laws of War* have been in the public domain since 1948 but were almost completely unused as research tools despite the categorical demand from commentators at that time for such research. Leo Gross, an escapee from Nazi Germany and a leading academic of twentieth-century international relations and law, wrote a review of the *Complete History* in which he praised the commission for its "perseverance under adverse circumstances" and criticized governments that failed to make better use of it. Perhaps a little tragically, Gross concluded: "They may rest assured that their work, which is described by Lord Wright with characteristic understatement as 'little more than a preparatory study,' will become an indispensable source and guide for the study of the problems of war crimes in all their ramifications."[36]

The information exists. In deciding whether to explore it, we may ask ourselves who we are going to support. Will it be the narrow pragmatists who initially fought the creation of the UNWCC and the international military tribunals and who later succeeded at the end of the 1940s in halting the pursuit of international criminal justice? Or will it be the pioneers who strove to lay the foundations for such a system, many of whom were exiled to London from their native lands and sometimes forced to meet while be sheltered from Nazi bombs? Sadly there can be little comfort in the warming thoughts of political philosophers such as Steven Pinker, who see present society as continually improving, albeit with setbacks. Rather, the frightening lesson of the demise of the UNWCC and its documented work is how easily great successes can be lost. We may have a difficult task in rejuvenating international criminal justice today, but not in comparison to the difficulties faced by those under Nazi occupation and bombardment. As the violent hatred of foreigners arises again, and states leave the ICC in the early twenty-first century, the story of the UNWCC provides both a warning and a badly needed role model.

Notes

1. For an exploration of what the Western origins of human rights actually mean for non-Western polities, see, for example, Raimundo Panikkar, "Is the Notion of Human Rights a Western Concept?" *Diogenes* 30, no. 120 (1982): 75–102. For more on the role of unequal power relations in the development of international criminal law see Nico Krisch, "International Law in Times of Hegemony: Unequal Power and the Shaping of the International Legal Order," *European Journal of International Law* 16, no. 3 (2005): 369–408.
2. Samuel Moyn, *The Last Utopia: Human Rights in History* (Cambridge, MA: Harvard University Press, 2010).
3. Lynn Hunt, *Inventing Human Rights: A History* (New York: W. W. Norton, 2003).

4. These were contributions to "Principles from the Periphery: The Neglected Southern Sources of Global Norms": Eric Helleiner, "Southern Pioneers of International Development"; Martha Finnemore and Michelle Jurkovich, "Getting a Seat at the Table: The Origins of Universal Participation and Modern Multilateral Conferences"; Kathryn Sikkink, "Latin American Countries as Norm Protagonists of the Idea of International Human Rights"; and Amitav Acharya, "Who Are the Norm Makers? The Asian-African Conference in Bandung and the Evolution of Norms," all in a special section of *Global Governance* 20, no. 3 (2014): 359–418.
5. Bertrand Ramcharan, "Normative Human Rights Cascades, North and South," *Third World Quarterly* 37 (forthcoming).
6. Donald Bloxham, *The Great Game of Genocide: Imperialism, Nationalism, and the Destruction of the Ottoman Armenians* (Oxford: Oxford University Press, 2005), 137.
7. The Philippines, while not a member state of the commission, nonetheless launched several UNWCC-related trials, including that of Lt. Gen. Shigenori Kuroda. See Richard Goldstone and Adam Smith, *International Judicial Institutions: The Architecture of International Justice at Home and Abroad* (London: Routledge, 2015), 80.
8. Christopher Simpson, *The Splendid Blond Beast: Money, Law, and Genocide in the Twentieth Century* (Monroe, ME: Common Courage, 1995), 173; Jonathan Friedman, "Law and Politics in the Subsequent Nuremberg Trials 1946–1949," in *Atrocities on Trial: Historical Perspectives on the Politics of Prosecuting War Crimes*, ed. Patricia Heberer and Jürgen Matthaüs (Lincoln: University of Nebraska Press, 2008), 75–102; Kerstin von Lingen, *Allen Dulles, the OSS, and Nazi War Criminals: The Dynamics of Selective Prosecution* (Cambridge: Cambridge University Press, 2013); and Simpson, *The Splendid Blond Beast.*
9. Benjamin Frommer, *National Cleansing: Retribution against Nazi Collaborators in Postwar Czechoslovakia* (Cambridge: Cambridge University Press, 2005).
10. Dan Plesch, *America, Hitler, and the UN: How the Allies Won World War II and Forged Peace* (London: I. B. Tauris, 2011), 25; Dan Plesch and Thomas G. Weiss, "1945's Lesson: 'Good Enough' Global Governance Ain't Good Enough," *Global Governance* 21, no. 2 (2015): 197–204.
11. This section draws upon a forthcoming article by Thomas G. Weiss, Leah Owen, and the author entitled "UN War Crimes Commission and International Law: Revisiting World War II Precedents and Practice."
12. Mark Ellis, "Assessing the Impact of the United Nations War Crimes Commission on the Principle of Complementarity and Fair Trial Standards," *Criminal Law Forum* 25, no. 1–2 (2014): 191–222; Carsten Stahn, "Complementarity and Cooperative Justice Ahead of Their Time? The United Nations War Crimes Commission, Fact-Finding, and Evidence," *Criminal Law Forum* 25, no. 1–2 (2014): 223–60.
13. Louise Arbour and Morten Bergsmo, "Conspicuous Absence of Jurisdictional Overreach," *International Law Forum du Droit International* 1, no. 1 (1999): 13–19; Carsten Stahn and Mohamed M. El Zeidy, eds., *The International Criminal Court and Complementarity: From Theory to Practice* (Cambridge: Cambridge University Press, 2011); and Mark Ellis, *Sovereignty and Justice: Balancing the Principle of*

Complementarity between International and Domestic War Crimes Tribunals (Oxford: Oxford University Press, 2014).

14. Preamble to Rome Statute of the International Criminal Court, UN DN A/CONF.183/9, 2187 UNTS 90, July 17, 1998.
15. Gwen Barnes, "The International Criminal Court's Ineffective Enforcement Mechanisms: The Indictment of President Omar Al Bashir," *Fordham International Law Journal* 34, no. 6 (2011): 1603.
16. Ibid., 1607–13.
17. Tom Fawthrop and Helen Jarvis, *Getting Away With Genocide? Elusive Justice and the Khmer Rouge Tribunal* (Kensington, Australia: UNSW, 2005).
18. Silvana Arbia and Giovanni Bassy, "Proactive Complementarity: A Registrar's Perspective and Plans," in Carsten Stahn and Mohamed M. El Zeidy, eds., *The International Criminal Court and Complementarity* (Cambridge: Cambridge University Press, 2011), 52–67; William W. Burke-White, "Reframing Positive Complementarity: Reflections on the First Decade and Insights from the US Federal Criminal Justice System," in Carsten Stahn and Mohamed M. El Zeidy, eds., *The International Criminal Court and Complementarity* (Cambridge: Cambridge University Press, 2011).
19. Burke-White, "Reframing Positive Complementarity," 342.
20. Carsten Stahn, "Taking Complementarity Seriously: On the Sense and Sensibility of 'Classical,' 'Positive,' and 'Negative' Complementarity," in *The International Criminal Court and Complementarity* (Cambridge: Cambridge University Press, 2011), 262–70.
21. Ellis, *Sovereignty and Justice*, 242.
22. Ibid., 262–70.
23. United Nations Development Program, "Evaluation of UNDP's Support to Mobile Courts in Sierra Leone, the Democratic Republic of Congo, and Somalia," May 2014, 7, 13, 19.
24. Ibid., 22–23.
25. Max du Plessis and Jolyon Ford, "Recommendations," in Max du Plessis and Jolyon Ford, eds., *Unable or Unwilling? Case Studies on Domestic Implementation of the ICC Statute in Selected African Countries* (Pretoria: Institute for Security Studies, 2007), 123–25.
26. Alfredo Strippoli, "National Courts and Genocide: The Kravica Case at the Court of Bosnia and Herzegovina," *Journal of International Criminal Justice* 7, no. 3 (2009): 595; and Jan Perlin, "The Guatemalan Historical Clarification Commission Finds Genocide," *ILSA Journal of International and Comparative Law* 6 (1999): 389–414.
27. Du Plessis and Ford, "Recommendations," 123–25.
28. Ellis, *Sovereignty and Justice*, 250–54.
29. Ibid., 250.
30. Ibid., 256.
31. Ibid., 145.
32. W. Schabas, "Anti-Complementarity: Referral to National Jurisdictions by the UN International Criminal Tribunal for Rwanda," *Max Planck Yearbook of United Nations Law Online* 13, no. 1 (2009): 34.

33. Office of the Prosecutor, *Complementarity in Action: Lessons Learned from the ICTR Prosecutor's Referral of International Criminal Cases to National Jurisdictions for Trial*, UNICTR (2015), 56–58; and Schabas, "Anti-Complementarity," 58.
34. Stahn, "Taking Complementarity Seriously," 224.
35. UNWCC, "Information Concerning Human Rights Arising from Trials of War Criminals: Report Prepared by the UN War Crimes Commission In Accordance with the Request Received from the United Nations," DN E/CN.4/W.19 147, May 15, 1948, ii.
36. Leo Gross, "History of the United Nations War Crimes Commission and the Development of the Laws of War by the United Nations War Crimes Commission," *American Journal of International Law* 44, no. 2 (1950): 431–34.

APPENDIX A

TIMELINE OF THE ALLIES' PRINCIPAL POLITICAL RESPONSES TO AXIS ATROCITIES

November 1940	Polish and Czech governments issue a joint statement on Nazi atrocities, followed by a Polish statement on Nazi attempts to "eradicate Polish national identity."
September 1941–1942	London International Assembly of exiled governments and Cambridge Commission convene Allied experts to discuss war crimes prosecutions.
October 1941	Churchill and Roosevelt issue parallel statements declaring "retribution [for] these crimes must henceforward take its place among the major purposes of the war."
November 1941	Soviet Foreign Ministry issues notes on German atrocities, the first statement to specifically highlight attempts to exterminate Jews as a group.
January 13, 1942	Exiled European governments in London issue Declaration of St. James's Palace on Punishment for War Crimes; only China adheres.
July 9, 1942	UK Information Minister hosts a press conference on "German terror in Poland"; account is later expanded as the 750-page "Black Book of Poland."
August 1942	Roosevelt declares "each of the United Nations" will begin gathering evidence of the "barbaric crimes of the invaders in Europe and in Asia," specifically warning

	offenders that they will be held accountable in "courts of law."
October 7, 1942	Roosevelt and British officials declare that the Allies will establish "a United Nations Commission for the Investigation of War Crimes."
December 17, 1942	United Nations Declaration on the Persecution of the Jews issued by the United Kingdom, the Soviet Union, the United States, and exiled governments in London; declaration is subsequently endorsed by other Allies. The declaration accuses Germany of exterminating the Jews of Europe.
October 20, 1943	United Nations War Crimes Commission is established.
October 30, 1943	The United Kingdom, the Soviet Union, and the United States publish the Moscow Declaration. Its "Statement on Atrocities" sets out the rationale for disposing of Nazi leadership and trying accused war criminals in the countries where crimes were committed.
February 1944	UNWCC receives and approves its first indictments and charge files from member states.
May 16, 1944	Far Eastern and Pacific Sub-Commission is established, and Allied powers active in the area (particularly China) begin submitting cases.
September 1944	US Secretary of War Stimson creates the US National Office for War Crimes Investigations.
May 1945	Truman announces process that leads to the Nuremberg Trial.
May-June 1945	UNWCC National Offices Conference brings together Allied war crimes agencies for a multilateral discussion of war crimes policy and coordination.
August 8, 1945	London Charter (empowering the Nuremberg Tribunals) is issued.
November 20, 1945	International Military Tribunal at Nuremberg opens. It tries twenty-four leading Nazi figures for crimes against peace, war crimes, and crimes against humanity. Tribunal closes on October 1, 1946.
April 29, 1946	International Military Tribunal in the Far East is convened to try a large fraction of the Japanese leadership for war crimes and crimes against peace. It is adjourned on November 12, 1945.

September 5, 1946	To date, four thousand charge files submitted to UNWCC.
December 9, 1946	Growing tensions among the Allies prevent a second international military force. United States prosecutes (at least partially on the basis of UNWCC-gathered data) other war criminals in the subsequent Nuremberg Trials. Twelve trials (each with multiple defendants) are held, concluding on April 13, 1949.
March 4, 1947	Far Eastern and Pacific Sub-Commission closes.
March 31, 1948	UNWCC concludes. Overall it received 8,178 charge files and approximately 2,000 trial reports. Commission publishes its history along with fifteen volumes of trial reports.
May 15, 1948	United Nations Economic and Social Council receives the UNWCC's report, "Information Concerning Human Rights Arising from the Trials of War Criminals."
December 9, 1948	United Nations General Assembly adopts Convention on the Prevention and Punishment of the Crime of Genocide.
December 10, 1948	United Nations General Assembly adopts Universal Declaration of Human Rights.
August 31, 1953	After a period of prisoner releases and amnesties, West German chancellor Adenauer announces that all remaining convicted war criminals in American, British, and French custody would be eligible for parole and clemency.

APPENDIX B

A NOTE ON THE UNWCC'S ARCHIVES AND RELATED MATERIAL

The archives of the United Nations War Crimes Commission contain a wealth of material but it is often difficult to extract useful content out of the vast quantity of trial reports, meeting minutes, and charge files. The task is made harder by the poor quality of many scans in the archive. The following guide is designed to assist researchers and augment existing finding aids listed in the notes. The commission's own index to its minutes and documents is invaluable, as is the "finding aid" created by the UN Archives and Records Management Service in the 1940s.

The entire archive of the commission's documents as transmitted from London to the United Nations in 1949 is found in several places. It resides in hard copy, microfilm, and digital form with the UN Archives and Records Administration; it appears in digital form at the US Holocaust Memorial Museum in Washington, DC; and at least part of it is in the US National Archives. The government of Israel is said to have obtained a copy of the process used in the aftermath of the Waldheim affair, though if this is the case these do not appear to have percolated into the public domain. All these locations hold, or are understood to hold, both the commission's minutes and related documents as well as the eight thousand dossiers of charges filed against some thirty-six thousand people and units.

The whereabouts of the thousands of charge files endorsed by the Chungking Sub-Commission are unknown to the author, though the Sub-Commission's own minutes state that copies were to be retained by the Chinese nationalist government and sent to both the UNWCC in London and US prosecutors in Japan.

The commission's documents are held at the US Holocaust Memorial Museum and can in part be accessed online at www.unwcc.org and at the ICC Prosecutor's office's research collection: see https://www.legal-tools.org/en/go-to-database/ltfolder/0_28425/#results. Commission minutes and related documents exist both in whole and in part in the national archives of UNWCC member states. In the case of Australia and the United Kingdom, for example, these are accessible online or by ordering a paper version via http://www.naa.gov.au and http://www.nationalarchive.gov.uk, respectively.

Contents of the Archives

The documents generally fall into a number of broad categories.

Charge Files

These records come from both the eight thousand charges against multiple defendants that were submitted to the commission for review and approval and withdrawn cases. They contain information on the accused, the locations and dates of where their crimes were committed, descriptions of the crimes, and witness statements, as well as initial assessments of proposed defense strategies. Owing to the wide range of countries involved, the approaches to notation and documentation are not consistent. They largely appear in English, although some member states submitted large quantities of material in their native languages (mostly French, Danish, and Czech). Equivalent charge files of the Far East Sub-Commission are not archived together with these records.

Meeting Minutes

These include the meeting minutes and descriptions of the UNWCC's various bodies' activities, including discussions and deliberations. They are arranged in chronological order and grouped by body: minutes of the main commission meetings are listed as "M. (number)," while minutes of the various committee meetings are labeled either numerically or with a number and year.

UNWCC Documents

A wide range of material from the UNWCC's work can be found. Generally organized chronologically, "A" documents are usually associated with actions and progress reports submitted to the UNWCC, while "C" documents are associated with various committees. Each of the three main UNWCC committees produced a discrete set of documents associated with its particular work; these are labelled with the Roman numeral of the committee followed by its number: for example,

II/23 is the twenty-third document produced by the Enforcement Committee (Committee II). Other documents include weekly bulletins and information briefings produced by the Research Office, submissions of pamphlet-book-length reports by the various member states, material related to war crimes produced by military governments and authorities, and a broad range of "miscellaneous" documents that do not easily fit into a category. Owing to the confusing range of documents, it is strongly recommended that researchers use either a searchable electronic version of the archive or the October 1949 Index to UNWCC Minutes and Documents.

Correspondence between the UNWCC, Offices of Member States, and International Organizations

This apparently incomplete collection of correspondence includes correspondence between the commission's central office in London and the national offices of member states, as well as correspondence with the commission and international organizations such as the United Nations and the British Army of the Rhine.

Wanted Lists

Lists of wanted criminals come from a range of sources, including: CROWCASS (Central Registry of War Criminals and Security Suspects); the legal section of the General Headquarters of the Supreme Commander for the Allied Powers; the War Crimes Registry of the Allied Land Forces of the South East Asia Command; and military records from several member states. The documents show details of Axis-suspected war criminals, in some cases their service histories and in some cases grouped by their connection to specific concentration and death camps. The commission's archive also includes a list of index files with a brief summary of all criminals and suspects indicted by the commission, along with (in many cases) details of present circumstances and the results of trials.

Trial Reports

Member states were encouraged to submit reports of the progress of their war crimes trials, so the commission has a wide selection of trial reports from member states. These are usually written in the native language and they reflect standard trial-recording practices from the countries where the trials took place. Anglophone trials are copied out verbatim, French trials are reported in line with a formal set of questions, and so on. These reports represent only a fraction of UNWCC-supported cases that went to trial and reached verdicts, but they are the only ones that were formally submitted to the commission; searches of other historical documents, and cases mentioned elsewhere in the commission's archives (including the entirety of China's work in the Far East Sub-Commission) are not included but are attested to elsewhere, making this section of the archive only a sampling of the UNWCC's work. The UNWCC also produced a number of synopses of trial reports from the various trial reports received by the commission. It was updated regularly between 1945 and 1948, although following the closure of the commission this process became more intermittent.

To better navigate through the archive, it is best to use a combination of the UNWCC's own finding aid: http://www.unwcc.org/wp-content/uploads/2015/11/AG-042-1-UNWCC-finding-aid.pdf; and its index of committee discussions: http://www.unwcc.org/wp-content/uploads/2015/11/Reel-33-Index-to-UNWCC-minutes-and-documents-Oct-1949.pdf.

APPENDIX C

THE ROLE OF THE UNWCC IN OBTAINING ICTY VERDICTS

Even if the broader significance of the work of the UN War Crimes Commission has not yet been widely recognized, some small part of that work and the national tribunals it fed into have become a widely referenced component of international law. Below is a (likely incomplete) list of twenty-four cases in the International Criminal Tribunal for former Yugoslavia online record that draw upon the UNWCC's records or its fifteen volumes of law reports. These are listed by the specific original document and include references to the volumes.

Blaškić (IT-95-14)
Trial Chamber Judgement: http://www.icty.org/x/cases/blaskic/tjug/en/bla-tj000303e.pdf.

Delić (IT-04-83)
Pretrial Brief of Rasim Delić Pursuant to Rule 65*ter* (F): www://icr.icty.org/LegalRef/CMSDocStore/Public/English/Brief/NotIndexable/IT-04-83/.

Đorđević (IT-05-87/1)
Judgement: http://www.icty.org/x/cases/djordjevic/acjug/en/140127.pdf.

Erdemović (IT-96-22)
Separate and Dissenting Opinion of Judge Stephen: http://www.icty.org/x/cases/erdemovic/acjug/en/erd-asojste971007e.pdf.

Separate and Dissenting Opinion of Judge Cassese: http://www.icty.org/x/cases/erdemovic/acjug/en/erd-adojcas971007e.pdf.
Separate and Dissenting Opinion of Judge Li: http://www.icty.org/x/cases/erdemovic/acjug/en/erd-asojli971007e.pdf.
Joint Separate Opinion of Judge McDonald and Judge Vohrah: http://www.icty.org/x/cases/erdemovic/acjug/en/erd-asojmcd971007e.pdf.
Sentencing Judgement: http://www.icty.org/x/cases/erdemovic/tjug/en/erd-tsj961129e.pdf.

Galić (IT-98-29-T)
Appeals Chamber Judgement: http://www.icty.org/x/cases/galic/acjug/en/gal-acjud061130.pdf.

Hadžihasanović, Alagic, and Kubura (IT-01-47)
Separate and Partially Dissenting Opinion of Judge David Hunt, Command Responsibility Appeal: http://www.icty.org/x/cases/hadzihasanovic/acdec/en/030716so.htm.

Halilović (IT-01-48)
Trial Chamber Judgement: http://www.icty.org/x/cases/halilovic/tjug/en/tcj051116e.htm.

Karadžić (IT-95-5/18)
Pretrial Brief: http://www.icty.org/x/cases/karadzic/custom3/en/090629.pdf.
Preliminary Motion on Lack of Jurisdiction Concerning Omission Liability: http://www.icty.org/x/cases/karadzic/custom1/en/090325c.pdf.

Kordić and Čerkez (IT-95-14/2)
Trial Chamber Judgement: http://www.icty.org/x/cases/kordic_cerkez/tjug/en/kor-tj010226e.pdf.

Krstić (IT-98-33)
Appeals Chamber Judgement: http://www.icty.org/x/cases/krstic/acjug/en/krs-aj040419e.pdf.
Trial Chamber Judgement: http://www.icty.org/x/cases/krstic/tjug/en/krs-tj010802e.pdf.

Kunarac, Kovac, and Vukovic (IT-96-23 and 23/1)
Trial Chamber Judgement: http://www.icty.org/x/cases/kunarac/tjug/en/kun-tj010222e.pdf.

Kupreškić et al. (IT-95-16)
Trial Chamber Judgement: http://www.icty.org/x/cases/kupreskic/tjug/en/kup-tj000114e.pdf.

Kvočka et al. (IT-98-30/1)
Trial Chamber Judgement: http://www.icty.org/x/cases/kvocka/tjug/en/kvo-tj011002e.pdf.
Judicial Supplement 29: http://www.icty.org/x/file/Legal%20Library/jud_supplement/supp29-e/kvocka.htm.

Martić (IT-95-11)
Appeals Chamber Judgement: http://www.icty.org/x/cases/martic/acjug/en/mar-aj081008e.pdf.

Milošević (IT-02-54)
Amicus Curiae Submissions on the Law of Self-Defence as Stipulated in Parts (b) and (c) of the Order of the Chamber to the *Amicus Curiae* of December 11, 2002, CN IT-02-54-T, July 14, 2003: http://www.icty.org/x/cases/slobodan_milosevic/amicus/bcs/mil-amic030714b.htm.

Mucić et al. (IT-96-21)
Trial Chamber Judgement: http://www.icty.org/x/cases/mucic/tjug/en/cel-tj981116e.pdf.
Appeals Chamber Judgement: http://www.icr.icty.org/x/cases/mucic/acjug/en/cel-aj010220.pdf.

Naletilić and Martinović (IT-98-34)
Trial Chamber Judgement: http://www.icty.org/x/cases/naletilic_martinovic/tjug/en/nal-tj030331-e.pdf.

Orić (IT-03-68)
Trial Chamber Judgement: http://www.icty.org/x/cases/oric/tjug/en/ori-jud060630e.pdf.

Perišić (IT-04-81)
Appeals Chamber Judgement: http://www.icty.org/x/cases/perisic/acjug/en/130228_judgement.pdf.

Prlić et al. (IT-04-74)
Separate and Partially Dissenting Opinion of Presiding Judge Jean-Claude Antonetti: http://www.icr.icty.org/x/cases/prlic/tjug/en/130529-6.pdf.

Corrigendum to Appellant's Brief of Valentin Ćorić: http://www.icty.org/x/cases/prlic/custom6/en/160322_1.pdf.

Šainović et al. (IT-05-87)
Decision on Dragoljub Ojdanic's Motion Challenging Jurisdiction—Joint Criminal Enterprise: http://www.icr.icty.org/x/file/Legal%20Library/jud_supplement/supp41-e/milutinovic-a.htm.

Stakić (IT-97-24)
Appeals Chamber Judgement: http://www.icr.icty.org/x/cases/stakic/acjug/en/foot2.htm.

Strugar (IT-01-42)
Appeals Chamber Judgement: http://www.icty.org/x/cases/strugar/acjug/en/080717.pdf.

Tadić (IT-94-1)
Appeals Chamber Judgement in Sentencing Appeals: http://www.icty.org/x/cases/tadic/acjug/en/tad-asj000126e.pdf.
Decision on the Prosecutor's Motion Requesting Protective Measures for Victims and Witnesses: http://www.icty.org/x/cases/tadic/tdec/en/100895pm.htm.
Trial Chamber Opinion and Judgement: http://www.icty.org/x/cases/tadic/tjug/en/tad-tsj70507JT2-e.pdf.
Appeals Chamber Judgement: http://www.icty.org/x/cases/tadic/acjug/en/tad-aj990715e.pdf.

APPENDIX D

AN EARLY UNWCC CHARGE FILE AGAINST A GROUP OF GERMANS INVOLVED IN THE TREBLINKA DEATH CAMP

Appendix Source: Polish Charges against German War Criminals (Reel 14), RN 79/P/G/16, CHN 15, April 24, 1944.

(*For the Use of the Secretariat*) 0788

Registered Number.	Date of receipt in Secretariat.
79/P/G/16	24 APR 1944

UNITED NATIONS WAR CRIMES COMMISSION

P O L I S H CHARGES AGAINST G E R M A N WAR CRIMINALS

CHARGE No. 15.*

Name of accused, his rank and unit, or official position. (*Not to be translated.*)	1. Dr.Frank Hans, Governor General of Central and South-Eastern Poland /the so called General Gouvernement/ 2.Dr.FISCHER Ludwig, Governor of the Warsaw District 3.KUNDT,Ernst, Governor of the Radom District 4.ZÖRNER Ernst, Governor of the Lublin District 5.Dr.WENDLER Richard, Governor of the Kraków District 6.Dr.WÄCHTER /-/, Governor of the Lwów District 7.KOCH Erich, Reichskommissar of the Białystok District 8. SAUER /-/, SS.Captain and commander of the camp for Jews at Treblinka B.
Date and place of commission of alleged crime.	From summer 1942 till the end of 1943 at Treblinka near Małkinia /at the railway line Warsaw-Białystok /
Number and description of crime in war crimes list.	I. Murder and massacres - systematic terrorism III.Torture of civilians.
References to relevant provisions of national law.	Criminal Code /1932/ art.225, 246 and 248. War Crimes Responsibility /Decree 1943/art.2, 3, 4 and 10.

SHORT STATEMENT OF FACTS.

See Continuing Page 1.

Dr.J.Litawski
Officer in charge

TRANSMITTED BY Polish War Crimes Office

* Insert serial number under which the case is registered in the files of the National Office of the accusing State.

(26352) Wt.P.1505 1120 500 1.44 A.& E.W.Ltd. Gp.685
(26924) Wt.P.1817 P.1139 5,000 3.44 " "

Page 2

PARTICULARS OF ALLEGED CRIME

0789

In 1940 the German authorities established in the village of Treblinka ,near Malkinia close to the railway-line Warsaw - Bialystok ,a concentration camp for Poles who refused to deliver contingents of agricultural products ordered by the German administrative authorities.In November 1941 the District Governor of Warsaw Dr.FISCHER proclaimed this camp as a general concentration camp for the whole district of Warsaw and ordered all Poles to be deported there who some way or other contravened against the orders or prohibitions of the German authorities .Later on this camp was named "Treblinka A ".

In March 1942 the Germans began to erect another camp "Treblinka B" / in the neighbourhood of "Treblinka A" /intended to become a place of torment for Jews.

The erection of this camp was closely connected with the German plans aiming at a complete destruction of the Jewish population in Poland which necessitated the creation of a machinery by means of which the Polish Jews could be killed in large numbers.Late in April 1942 the erection of the first three chambers was finished in which these general massacres were to be performed by means of steam.Somewhat later the erection of the real "death-building "was finished which contains ten death chambers.It was opened for wholesale murders early in autumn 1942.

It may be mentioned here that there were several phases in the development of the persecution of the Jews in Poland.During the first period /till October 1940 / the Germans were aiming only at the moral degradation and complete pauperisation of the Jews by all kinds of restrictions of their rights, by the confiscation of their property etc., but later on they turned to their gradual annihilation and destruction as a nation.This change of policy is apparent in their treatment of the ghettos , first they had only to isolate the Jews from the Aryans but later on they were /the ghettos / the very means of their physical annihilation.

Healtheir and stronger Jews were deported for forced labour whilst those who remained in the Ghettos were decimated by starwation and epidemics.As these methods did not produce the desired results more drastic measures were adopted.Wholesale massacres were organized in the Ghettos and , finally' a complete annihilation of the Ghettos was decided upon.

The Jews had simply cease to exist.Special camps were established for this purpose where the destruction of human lives was carried on by mechanized means.The best known of these death camps are those of Treblinka, Belzec and Sobibor /in the Lublin district /.In these camps the Jews are put to death in thousands by new hitherto unknown methods ,gas and steam chambers as well as electric current areemployed on a large scale. The victims were recruited chiefly from the General Gouvernment, and particulary from the following districts: Warsaw, Radom, Lublin, Kraków and Lwów , bu t Jews from outside the General Gouvernment were also sent there ,particularly from the Bialystok district where the Ghettos were maintained for a long time and where in the summer months of 1943 about 10.000 Jews were rounded up and transported to Treblinka for extermination.

The main part of the "work" was done in summer and autumn 1942. Winter 1942 and the year 1943 were used for "mopping up operations "i.e.for the extermination of those who managed to dodge the main round-up and, of those younger Jews who were employed in war industry.To indulge in their lust for destruction the German did not hesitate to put to death even those younger Jews although their man power was badly needed and their loss-as admitted by the Germans themselves - was a serious handicape for the war effort.

It is apparent from this short summary that the persecution of the Jews was carried out after a carefully prepared plan with the only obvious objective:the complete extermination of the Jewish race.In this summary we describe only the last phase of the realisation of this plan and especially the atrocities perpetrated in Camp B in Treblinka.Other charges will be presented and the names of those responsible for the crimes wil be given in separate cases.

Continuing Page 1. **0790**

SHORT STATEMENT OF FACTS.

a/ The accused Dr.FRANK Hans as chief of the General Government, and the accused Dr.FISCHER Ludwig as chief of the District of Warsaw, established in March 1942 in connection with the liquidation of the Jewish Ghettos in Poland a death's camp at Treblinka intended for a mass-killing of Jews by means of a mechanised procedure consisting in the suffocation of people in steam-filled chambers.

b/ The accused ad 2, 3, 4, 5, 6 as District-chiefs in the General Government, acting as executors of orders, received from the accused ad 1/, took part in the mass-killing of Jews by ordering the deportation of Jews from the respective Districts and Ghettos to the camp of Treblinka ,in which hundreds of thousands of Jews were consequently killed.

c/ The accused ad 7/ as chief of the District of Białystok ordered in summer 1943 during the liquidation of the Białystok Ghetto the deportation of about 10.000 Jews to the camp of Treblinka in which they were killed in the way mentioned above.

d/ The accused ad 8/ as commander of the camp at Treblinka B carried out the mass-murder of hundreds of thousands of Jews by killing them with steam in special chambers.He also shot dead a large number of Jews and tortured Jews conducted to the steam-chambers by flogging their naked bodies.

Continuing Page 2. **0791** a/

The Camp B of Treblinka is situated in a hilly,wooded country. It covers an area of about 5.000 ha /-8 sq.miles / and is fenced off by hedges and barbed wire ./1/It is bordered in the North by a young forest,/2/in the West by a railway-escarpments whilst low hills shut it off from the East and South. There are several observation posts inthe camp for the camp guard /Lagerschutz/ as well as searchlights used for securing the camp during the hours of darkness. A side track/3/leads from the main railway track on to a loading platform ,/4/ adjoining a large open place /5/ fenced off by barbed wire ,/6/where several thousands persons can be accomodated at the same time. To the North stands a large barrack /7/, and in the south-western corner an observation post/8/.The place to the South of th the barbed wire fence was used for sorting out pieces of clothes of the victims, which were fit for further use /Lumpensortierungsplatz /-/9/Farther to the South is the place of execution and a mass grave /10/.A gate /11/opens from the place /5/ to a road leading to the buildings /13/and /15/.Building No.13 is divided by a narrow corridor into two parts and measures approx.40 yards by 25 yards.On each side of the corridor are situated 5 chambers whose height is about 6 and a half feet. There are no windows.The doors can be shut hermetically.

The second building /15/ consists of 3 chambers and a boiler-room /16/. The steam generated in the boilers is led by means of pipes to the chambers. There are terracota floors in the chambers which become very slippery when wet. Along the southern wall of the building /15/ runs a loading platform where the bodies of the victims were piled up after execution.A well /18/ is situated near the boiler-room.

Behind the building /15/ and separated from the rest of the camp by barbed wire /19/ stands a barrack /20/and a kitchen /21/destined for the grave diggers.On both sides of these buildings are situated observation posts /22,23/. No.10,24,25 are mass graves.As the executions grew in numbers ~~the~~ mass graves were dug out by motor driven machines and not by hand and shovel as in the beginning.

The camp was guarded by Germans of the SS.detachments and by Ukrainians.The officer to whom this guard was subordinated was the SS.Captain SAUER.This garrison /Lagerschutz/performed also the duties of executioners,whilst menial services had to be performed by the inmates of the camp themselves so e.g. the unloading of the trucks ,the stripping of the victims and sorting out of their clothes and shoes /Lumpensortierung /the emptying of the death chambers and the burrying of the bodies.When a new transport arrived some of the Jews were picked up to do this work ,so long until they broke down morally under the impression of this organized and mechanized mass murder.Then they had to dig their own graves and take up their position at them,whereupon they were shot ,one by one by SAUER personally.Their last duty before dying was to push the body of the preceding victim into its own grave.A new party was then chosen to continue their work in the camp.The sadism of SAUER in enjoying the shooting personally sounds incredible ,but his guilt has been established beyond any doubt.

The average number of Jews dealt with at the camp in summer 1942 was about two railway transports daily,but they were days of much higher efficiency. From autumn 1942 this number was falling.

After unloading in the siding /4/all victims were concentrated in place /5/ where men were separated from women and children.In the first days of the existence of the camp the victims were made to believe that after a short stay in the camp necessary for bathing and desinfection they would be sent farther East,for work.Explanations of this sort were given by SS.men,who assisted at the unloading of the transport and further explanations could be read in notices stuck up on the walls of the barracks.But later,when more and more transports had to be dealt with the Germans dropped all pretences and only tried to accelerate the procedure.

All victims had to strip off in barrack /7/their clothes and their shoes /which were collected afterwards in place /9/, whereupon all victims ,women and children first,were driven into the death chambers.Those too slow or to weak to move quickly were driven on by rifle butts,by whipping and kicking ,often by SAUER himself.Many slipped and fell,the next victims ,pressed forward and stumbled over them .Small children were simply thrown inside.After being filled up to capac the chambers were hermetically closed and steam was let in.

Continuing Page 2 . **0792** b/

In a few minutes all was over.The Jewish menkials had to remove the bodies to the platform /17/ and to bury them in mass graves.By and by, as new transports arrived,the cemetary grew extanding in Eastern direction.

From reports sent to the Polish Government from Poland it may be assumed that several hundred thousands of Jews have been exterminated in Treblinka B.Exact figures are impossible to obtain as the Germans did not bother to keep any records concerning the number of Jews deported to this camp and killed there. It will be even impossible to establish some correct figures after the liberation of Poland ,because as early as Spring 1943 the Germans began to exhumate the bodies and to burn them ,so as to destroy all evidence of the crimes perpetrated.These exhumations continued until summer 1943 ,when the victims were able to start a mutiny and to kill some of the guards enabling thus several hundred Jews to escape from the camp.

The above description of the mass massacres in Treblinka give only a faint idea of the horrors prevailing in the camp B.It is practically impossible to imagine the sufferings in the camp and to grasp the full extent of the atrocities.For the victims transported to the camp in cattle trucks and exposed for several days to the most cruel sufferings of body and soul , death in the steam chambers must have come as a welcome relief.Their only crime consisted in belonging to a race condemned by Hitler to death.

The responsibility for these crimes must be borne by all who devised and developed the plan of exterminating the Jews.Here we confine ourselves to a few persons whose names and exploits could be established by ample proof. Those accused under I-VII are directly responsible for the liquidation of the Ghettos and for giving orders to transport the Jews to the Death Camp.Those accused under I-II are,besides,responsible for establishment and organisation of the Camp where all these horrors have taken place.The heaviest responsibility lies with SAUER who as the commanding officer of the camp issued orders to murder hundreds of thousands of Jews and who personally took part in their maltreatments and their executions.

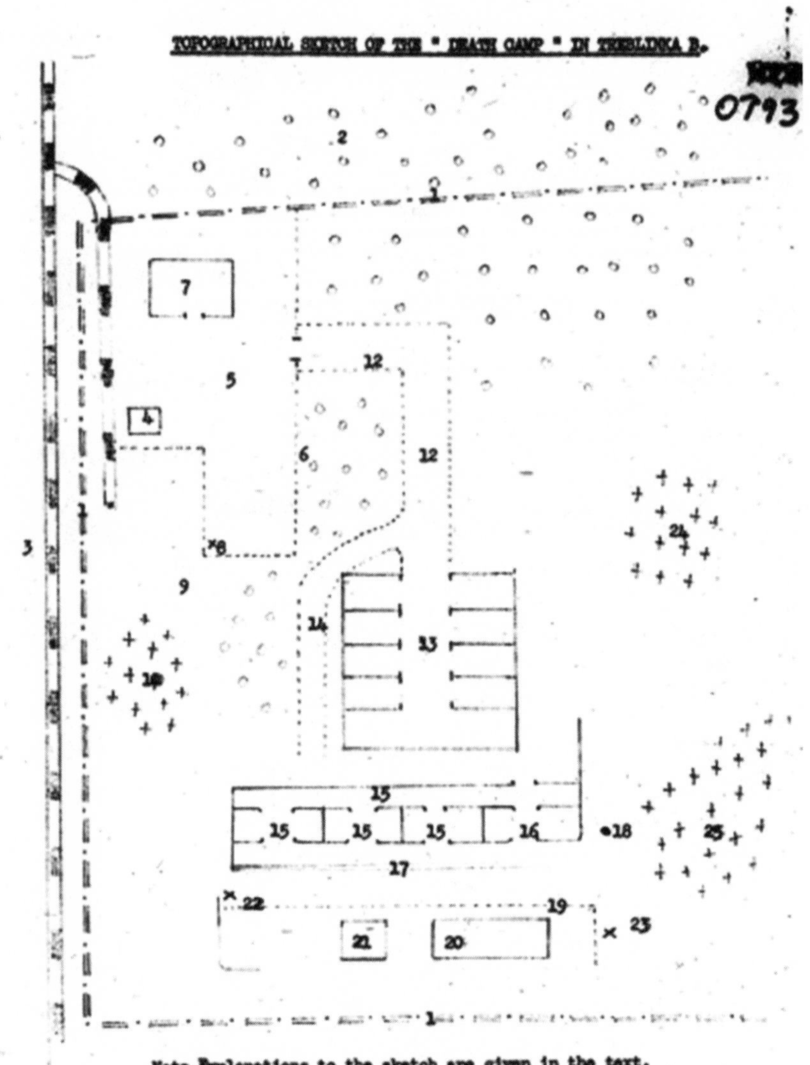
TOPOGRAPHICAL SKETCH OF THE " DEATH CAMP " IN TREBLINKA B.
0793
1
2
3
4
5
6
7
8
9
10
12
12
13
14
15
15
15
15
16
17
18
19
20
21
22
23
24
25
Note. Explanations to the sketch are given in the text.

Page 3

PARTICULARS OF EVIDENCE IN SUPPORT **0794**

1. Statement of above facts and other particulars were contained in the confidential reports form the Polish Government's Plenipotentiary residing in Poland ,addressed to the Polish Government in London.

2. The original communications from the Plenipotentiary are in the possesion of the Polish Ministry of the Interior in London.

3.Topographical sketch of the camp for Jews at Treblinka B /enclosed /.

4. A large number of witnesses will be available after the cessation of hostilities.

Page 4

570 NOTES ON THE CASE 0795

(Under this heading should be included the view taken as to (*a*) the degree of responsibility of the accused in view of his official position, e.g., was offence committed on the offender's own initiative, or in obedience to orders, or in carrying out a system approved by authority or a legal provision ; (*b*) the probable defence ; (*c*) whether the case appears to be reasonably complete.)

1 / The above mentioned offences were committed by the accused /I/ and /II/ partly on their own initiative and partly in carrying out the Reich's general policy of persecution of Jews aiming at their complete extermination in Poland. This later motive was deciding for the accused /III/ till /VII/ ,too.

The accused /VIII/ was acting on his own initiative so far as ill-treatment, wanton shootings and beating of Jews are concerned , whilst the mass-killing of Jews in the steam-chambers was committed by him in obedience to orders received from superior authorities.

II / The accused /I/ to /VII/ will probably defend themselves by stating that they were acting in accordance with the general policy of the Reich ,as fixed by the supreme German authorities.

The accused /VIII/ will probably defend himself by stating that he was compelled to obey the order received and will also, probably, deny the offences committed by ill-treatment and beating of Jews, thus taking advantage of the difficulty to adduce proofs.

APPENDIX E

AN EARLY POLISH CHARGE FILE AGAINST A GROUP OF GERMANS INVOLVED IN THE CONCENTRATION CAMP SYSTEM

Appendix Source: Polish Charges against German War Criminals (Reel 14), RN 123/P/G/21, CHN 20, June 3, 1944, 834–43.

(*For the Use of the Secretariat*) **0834**

Registered Number.	Date of receipt in Secretariat.
123/P/G/21	3rd June 1944

UNITED NATIONS WAR CRIMES COMMISSION

POLISH CHARGES AGAINST GERMAN WAR CRIMINALS

CHARGE No. 20 *

Name of accused, his rank and unit, or official position. (*Not to be translated.*)	See continuing page 1
Date and place of commission of alleged crime.	From the beginning of 1942 up to the end of 1943 in the following localities : a/ Bełżec, in the district of Lublin, b/ Majdanek near Lublin, district of Lublin, c/ Sobibór near Włodawa, district of Lublin, d/ Kosów Podlaski, district of Warsaw, e/ Chełmno, near Koło, in the "Reichsgau Wartheland" f/ Oświęcim /in German "Auschwitz"/, "Gau Oberschlesien"
Number and description of crime in war crimes list. References to relevant provisions of national law.	I Murder and massacres-systematic terrorism III Torture of civilians VIII Internment of civilians under inhuman conditions XIII Pillage Criminal Code /1932/ art.225, 230/2, 235/1 a,b, 246 and 248,257. War Crimes Responsibility Decree /1943/ art.2,3,4 and 10

SHORT STATEMENT OF FACTS.

In connection with the liquidation of the Jewish ghettos throughout Poland during the period 1942-1943 and in order to facilitate and speed up the mass-killing of Jews several special camps for the extermination of Jews were established by the Germans in Poland in which more than one and a half milion Polish Jews were murdered as well as a large number of foreign Jews were exterminated by means of mechanised methods i.e. electric current and gas.

Dr. J. Litawski
Officer in charge.

TRANSMITTED BY Polish War Crimes Office

*Insert serial number under which the case is registered in the files of the National Office of the accusing State.

(26752) Wt.P.1505 1120 500 1/44 A.& E.W.Ltd. Gp.685
(26924) Wt.P.1817 P.1139 5,000 3/44

Continuing page 1 **0836**

1/ Dr. FRANK, Hans,	Governor General of Central and South-Eastern Poland /the so called General Governement /
2/ Dr.FISCHER, Ludwig,	Governor of the Warsaw District
3/ ZORNER, Ernst,	Governor of the Lublin District
4/ Dr.WENDLER, Richard,	Governor of the Cracow District
5/ KUNDT, Ernst,	Governor of the Radom District
6/ Dr.WACHTER , /-/,	Governor of the Lwów /Galizien/ District
7/ GREISER, Arthur,	Reichsstatthalter und Gauleiter der NSDAP für Gau Wartheland
8/ BRACHT, Fritz,	Reichsstatthalter und Gauleiter der NSDAP für Gau Oberschlesien
9/ FORSTER, Albert,	Reichsstatthalter und Gauleiter der NSDAP für Gau Danzig- Westpreussen
10/KOCH, Erich,	Reichskommissar of the Białystok District
11/WOLFF ,/-/,	SS.Major, Commander of the concentration camp for Jews at Bełżec
12/BARTECZKO,/-/,	Deputy commander of the concentration camp for Jews at Bełżec
13/ N.N.,	Commander of the concentration camp for Jews at Majdanek, near Lublin
14/ N.N.,	Commander of the concentration camp for Jews at Sobibór
15/ N.N.,	Commander of the concentration camp for Jews at Kosów Podlaski
16/ N.N.,	Commander of the concentration camp for Jews at Chełmno /Kulmhof/
17/HOESS, /-/,	SS.Obersturmbannfuehrer, commander of the concentration camp at Oświęcim
18/SCHOPPE, /-/,	SS.Oberscharfuehrer, attached to the command of the concentration camp at Oświęcim
19/STIBITZ,/-/,	SS.Oberscharfuehrer, attached to the command of the concentration camp at Oświęcim
20/MULLER,/-/,	SS.Hauptsturmfuehrer, attached to the command of the concentration camp at Oświęcim
21/WILHAUS,/-/,	late commander of the concentration camp for Jews in Lwów , since 1942 attached to the officer in command of the concentration camp of Oświęcim.

Page 2

PARTICULARS OF ALLEGED CRIME **0835**

Aiming at a complete extermination of Polish Jews as well as Jews deported to Poland form other occupied countries the Germans either established in Poland several special camps for biological mass killing of Jews or adapted some of existing concentration camps for this purpose.

In these camps installations have been made for a quick mass extermination of the Jewish nation, and the climax of this action coincides with the liquidation of the ghettos which took place during the second half of 1942 and the whole year 1943.

With true German thoroughness the German were aiming to destroy the Jewish population all over the territory of Poland, the object being the radical clearance of all places of the Jewish element /"Judenfrei machen"/.

Some of these camps are operating till now though the intensity and efficiency of their "work" has been automatically reduced owing to the gradual exhaution of the Jewish people condemned to die. Among the most notorious of these camps the horrible memory of which will live for ever in the history of mankind the first place is held by the "death camp" of Treblinka, which has been the subject of a separate charge /No.15/. The other "death camps" were those of:

1/ Bełżec
2/ Majdanek
3/ Sobibór
4/ Kosów Podlaski
5/ Chełmno, and
6/ Oświęcim.

Four of these camps /1,3,4,5/ were established for the only purpose of the extermination of Jews and were originally not intended for any other use. The remaining two camps /2,6/ were meant to be concentration camps for Poles, but in course of time when the mass killing of Jews approched its climax the German authorities were compelled to make use of the steam chambers installed in these two camps, too, in order to speed up the work of destruction. For this purpose the camp at Oświęcim was especially suitable as its steam chambers were sufficient to kill thousands of victims daily.

Owing to the fact that the German authorities took all necessary precautions to prevent reports about these camps from spreading in the outside world, and owing to the small number of people who succeded in escaping from these camps, we are not yet in the possession of all details concerning the organisation of these camps and especially, the members of their staff. But we are able to reconstruct the events in each camp with the possible maximum of exactness out of the confidential reports from the Polish Government's Plenipotentiary who has his residence in occupied Poland, whilst gaps, especially those in the lists of the German hangmen, can be filled in future.

1. The first of the "death camps" has been erected in the district of Lublin, in Bełżec, north-west of Lwów, between Rawa Ruska and Tomaszów Lubelski, on the border of the territories occupied in 1939 by the German and Russians forces.

This camp founded late in 1940 was originally intended for the detention of deportees and used mainly for the confinement of deported Jews. But gradually the character of the camp changes into a place in which numerous executions are carried out whilst adverse conditions and diseases destroy large proportions of the detained Jews.

The camp of Bełżec was situated in the neighbourhood of the railway station and was linked with it by a special track on which the trains carrying arrested Jews were brought close to the barbed wire of the camp. In the beginning only smaller transports of Jews amounting to several hundreds of people were sent to this camp. But early in April 1941 a bigger group arrived, about 5.000 Jews picked up in a street chase in the ghetto of Warsaw.

Early in 1942 the first reports have leaked out that special electric installations were used in this camp for a quick mass killing of Jews. On the pretext of bathing, completely undressed Jews were brought to a special building called "baths", whose floor consists of slabs through which flows electric current of a high voltage.

Continuing page 2 /a/. 0837

In this way big masses of Jews were killed ; their corpses were cremated or buried in huge common graves.

In the course of 1942 numerous transports of Jews arrived in the camp of Bełżec ,who were picked up all over the territory of the General Government ,chiefly in the district of Lublin and in Galicja and especially in Lwów, where about 100.000 Jews were gathered.In autumn 1943 during the period of second phase of the ghetto liquidation a large number of Jews was executed in this camp who came from the district of Kraków /Tarnów, Bochnia, Rzeszów /.Several hundreds up to several thousands of Jews were killed there every day.But also Jews from abroad ,especially from the Reich, Austria, Czechoslowakia ,Belgium, the Netherlands,France and the Balkans were brought in huge masses to this camp.

The guard of this camp -as well as of the other camps- consisted of SS. men and Ukrainians ,and the commander in charge of the whole camp was an SS.Major named DOLFF who was previously commandant of the notorious concentration camp at Dachau.His chief assistant was BARTECZKO who used to torture the Jews crually before they were executed.

The staff of the camp as well as the guards were in the possession of big fortune as they plundered on a large scale the luggage and objects of value left behind by the killed Jews.In consequence they wasted money ,which may be illustrated by the fact that they used to pay up to 20 amer.dollars for a pint of whisky.

2.The second "death camp " was at Majdanek near Lublin.It was established in the middle of 1940 by the Gestapo in Lublin for their own purposes and was put under their direct supervision .It was originally for the detention of deported Poles from the district of Lublin and the city of Lwów.

The camp covers an area of about 25 ha. and was intended for the confinement of tens of thousands of pridoners.It resembles in fact a town of barracks within miles of barbed wire entanglements and hundreds of turrets for the warders and their machine-guns.

The barracks are made of wood and have no stores and no windows-panes ,which made numerous persons starve to death with cold .Appalling sanitary conditions ,lack of water and even of a hospital,caused the spreading of contagious diseases ,especially thyphus ,and an immense increase in the death-rate of the prisoners.

There are five fields with barracks in which the prisoners are confined.The so called "representative" field I.contains Jews from abroad, especially from Czechoslowakia ,and from Warsaw.The field II is occupied by Poles and Jews condemned to death -there is the highest number of prisoners here.In the field III live political prisoners,in field IV people picked up in street chases who are gradually released, and the field V is reserved for women.

The prisoners wear a special striped dress made of a wooden fabric.At the left breast and at the thigh a triangle and the prisoners number are attached,in different colours,that of Jews being yellow.

Apart from the German SS.men specially selected Ukrainian warders torture the prisoners by continuous whipping.

The first reports about large scale deportations of Jews into this camp coincide with the beginning of the liquidation of ghettos in the General Government and the liquidation of the Jewish concentration camp at Lublin /on November 22,1942 /.At that time the SS.Sturmbannfuehrer SCHMIT was in command of the Majdanek camp ,who later /in May 21.1943 / was killed after having been sentenced to death by the Polish Underground Movement.Early in 1943 the first of the numerous transports of Jews from Western Europe and France arrive in Majdanek.

Already in 1942 reports are spreading that in this camp old or sick people and children were murdered in gas chambers and that nearly all of the Jews brought in masses to this camp faced this fate.Thrice weekly such huge numbers of victims were murdered in the gas chambers that the cremation-stoves of the camp were altogether unable to fulfil their task, a fact which caused that many corpses had to be destroyed in open air.

0838

Continuing page 2 /b/.

3. The third torture place for Jews was the "death camp " of Sobibór near Włodawa on the river Bug /to the south of Brześć Litewski / in the district of Lublin.

This camp was used for the concentration of Jews during both the first and the second period of the liquidation of ghettos. In the first period /August 1942 /enormous masses of Jews from the General Government were brought to this camp to be destroyed in gas chambers. Besides Jews from foreign countires ,especially from Low Countries and France, were brought there, who are given the assurance of being send to factories in the Reich, but in fact share the fate of the Polish Jews in the gas chambers ,whilst their luggage and other movables become a booty of the warders. In summer 1943 large numbers of Jews from the district of Lublin and especially from the neighbourhood of Włodawa and Hrubieszów are brought to Sobibór. In the first half of 1943 a group of about 1.000 Jews were murdered in Sobibór who were employed in war factories and brought from the Warsaw ghetto. These people had been previously promised by the German authorities .their lives would be spared in recognition of their war effort. During the same period thouthands of Russian Jews were destroyed in Sobibór who had been deported in masses from the Mohilew ,Smoleńsk and Bobrujsk districts. In the second half of October 1943 a sedition broke in the camp of Sobibór among several hundred of surviving Jews ,who killed a number of hangmen, SS. men and Ukrainians, burned down the barracks and escaped.

4. Another extermination camp for Jews was erected ,during the first liquidation of Jewish ghettos ,in the village of Kosów Podlaski , /north-east of Warsaw /in the district of Warsaw.

There are only few reports about this camp but all of them agree with each other in one point viz., that in this camp too, Jews were subject to mass murders and treated in the same way as in the camps mentioned above. The victims came mainly from Warsaw.

5. Another camp belonging to the category of "death camps " was that of Chełmno /Kulmhof /near Kolo /Warthebrücke/ on the river Nev /north-east from Łódź /in the Reichsgau Wartheland.

It was mostly the provinces incorporated in the Reich- mainly the Gau Wartheland 'from where the Jews were deported to this camp. The first transport took place in December 1941 ,when the district of Kolo was cleared of the Jews :the Germans deported at that time about 2.000 Jews from Kolo and about 1.000 Jews from the neighbouring Dębie.

As from the middle of January 1943 also Jews from the ghetto of Łódź are being brought in tehs of thousands to the camp of Chełmno.

According to the reports from Poland the transports of Jews directed to Chełmno were first penned in the local church where their luggage was stored ,and then confined in the old castle of the town. The camp was under strict control of the Gestapo and completely surrounded by warders, members of the SS.. In the beginning the prisoners were assured they would be brought to Germany proper to work there whilst their wives would keep house for them. They were only to be asked to take a bath and have their clothes disinfected before continuing their jou,rney. Then all of them were ordered to undress and give their money and valuables into the warders custody. Afterwards all were conducted to the alleged baths, but ,in reality, through a subway ,to lorries which were already waiting for them. As soon as the victims reache the tunel the pretended correct behaviour of the warders changes thoroghly -the Jews are pushed and beaten to speed up their steps. The lorries into which resisting Jews are thrown forcibly have the shape of huge box covered hermetically with sheet - iron. Also the little entrance doors close hermetically whilst in the floor outlets of tubes are connected with a gas container hidden in the driver's box.

The lorries loaded with Jews were driven to a forest, several miles from town, in the direction of the town of Kolo. The travel took about 15 minutes. In the forest the lorries stopped at a small clearing where a deep ditch was already prepared. Then the driver /who was at the same time executioner / set the gas apparatus going and the lorries mobile gas chambers ,were at once filled with gas. After a few minutes the hangman looked through a small window into a lorry lit up by him for this purpose, and after having satisfied himself that all the victims are dead he drove the lorry nearer to the ditch where the

Continuing page 2 /c /.

corpses were unloaded to be buried by Jewish grave -diggers under the supervision of SS.men.These later often searched the dead bodies once more for valuables like rings hidden in the hands or golden teeth,and stole what they found.

Each common grave contained hundreds of corpses and the graves were gradually placed deeper in the woods as the transports of Jews increased. As from the middle of January 1943 the dead bodies were choked up with chloride of lime to kill the odours of putrifaction.In the period when these mass-murders reached their culminating point 6-till 9 lorry-loads of suffocated Jews were buried every day.

It happened many a time that the grave -diggers had to bury their nearest relatives.Some examples may by quoted : the grave-digger Ajzensztab of Kłodawa buried his wife and his 15 years old dauther,Chrząstkowski of the same village his 14 years old son,Wiener of Dębica Kujawska his parents and his brother ,Pochlebnik his parents,his wife and 2 children ,and Rosenthal his 60 years old father.The grave-diggers ,however used to share the fate of the victims they had buried: they were ,as a rule, murdered after they had finished their job.It was only owing to the successful escape of three of them that the Polish Government 's Plenipotentiary in occupied Poland has been informed about the above details.

6.Finally the notorious concentration camp of Oświęcim must be mentioned,a town called by the Germans "Auschwitz "and situated in the neighbourhood of Biała in Upper Silesia.Though details about this camp and its conditions will be dealt with in a separate charge ,particulars concerning the Jews confined in that camp should be mentioned here.

The concentration camp of Oświęcim was originally intended for Poles only ,but later on Jews from the liquidated ghettos were brought there, too.They were treated like the other prisoners and their number was at first. comparatively small.

From the beginning of 1942 ,however ,i.e. since the organized mass- extermination of Jews began,the number of Jews deported to the Oświęcim concentration camp was growing constantly ,probably owing to the fact that the gas chambers and crematoria of this camp were the best and had the highest capacity of those existing in other concentration camps.

Towards the middle of 1942 the number of Jews deported to Oświęcim reached 15.000 approximately and all of them perished in the Oświęcim gas chambers ,creeted as early as June 1941 ,or in the nerly creeted 5 chambers of Brzeziniec ,some miles away from the main camp.These later chambers were finished in April 1942 i.e. at a time when the fate of the Jews confined in ghettos was sealed.

Toward the end of August 1942 the first mass transports of Jews arrive in Oświęcim from the Polish provinces incorporated in the Reich, especially from the coal-basin of Dąbrowa /Sosnowiec,Będzin, Dąbrowa /.,but also from France,Holland and Belgium. Estimated from this period show that more than half a million Jews were killed in Oświęcim before the end of 1942 the main propartion of them being Jews from abroad.

In 1943 also Jews from remote parts of Poland were deported to Oświęcim :in January 10 trains arrived there packed with Jews from the Grodno and Białystok districts,in March several thouthands of Jews from the Kraków ghetto and the remainders from the coal-basin of Dąbrowa.In the middle of 1943 great numbers of Jews from Greece and Jugoslavia arrived in Oświęcim.

It was at this time that the German authorities decided to use the whole camp of Oświęcim for the purpose of extermination of Jews exclusively and so to speed up their ultimate annihilation .As far the Polish prisoners they were to be transferred to other concentration camps or to forced labour camps .How far this plan has been realized is not known yet ,but it is known, that in the authumn 1943 some 30.000 more Jews were murdered at Oświęcim.

Continuing page 2 /d/. **0840**

Here must be mentioned that toward the end of 1942 a department for medico-biological research was created in Oświęcim, in which experiments in artificial impregnation and sterilization were made upon Jewesses selected from among the camp prisoners according to their health conditions and physical fitness.A great many of these "human guinea - pigs " died in consequence of these experiments ,but those who survived were killed afterwards like all other Jews.This chapter of special tortures will be treated separately as soon as the names of the responsible will be available.

During the period of mass extermination of Jews in Oświęcim /1942-1943 / a certain Obersturmbannfuehrer HOESS was in command of the camp .His assistants were Oberscharfuehrer SCHOPPE,a certain STIBITZ and Hauptsturmfuehrer MULLER, who dealt with all questions concerning Jews and their extermination.These three men were the foremost tormentors of the Jewish prisoners who had to endure their sadistic treatment ,beating,and kicking for the slightest failure.

Toward the middle of 1943 the accused WILHAUS arrived in the camp of Oświęcim ,who was previously in command of the ghetto of Lwów and whose anti-Jewish atrocities were notorious there.His transfer to the Oświęcim camp was probably connected with the above mentioned plan of an ultimate extermination of Jews and of using the camp of Oświęcim for this purpose.He employed here fully the experience acquired in Lwów as well as the methods used in that ghetto.

7.The informations available at present allow neither an exhaustive description of what happened in the above "death camps"nor an exact statement of the number of Jews murdered there.

But statistic data show that there was a number of over 3 millions of Jews living in Poland in 1939 ,whilst only 10% i.e. 300.000 approximately were surviving at the end of 1943 according to official reports from Poland.That means that about 90 % of all Polish Jews have been exterminated.

This extermination was effected by an endless chain of persecutions inflicted on the Jewish population of Poland by the German invaders from the very beginning. of the occupation.A great number of Jews died as a result of the radical change of their living-conditions or of the impoverishment caused by mass confiscation of their property and by deportations.A great many ~~perished~~ perished during the period preceding the establishment of ghettos when reprisals of every description imposed on them usually ended with mass executions.A huge number of Jews died during the confinement in the ghettos owing to starvation and diseases ,but the largest number of Jews were murdered in the "death camps ".

It may be mentioned here the fact that from the March 1942 till April 1943 a million of Jews approximately were killed in two only of the "death camps ",those of Treblinka and Bełżec.Taking into consideration the Jews deported to Poland from other European countries i.e.the Reich,Austria, Czechoslowakia,Holland ,Belgium, France,Jugoslavia and Greece,we can assert without any exaggeration that in these camps several millions of Jews were slain and among them at least 1 and a half million Polish Jews.

8.The accused /1/as a chief of the General Government and the accused /2,3,4,5,6,7,8,9 and 10 /as chiefs of the districts in the General Government or as Reichsstatthalters of the provinces incorporated in the Reich,and as Reichskommissar of the Bialystok district respectively, participated in the mass - killing of Jews during the period 1942-1943 by ordering the deportation of Jews out of the respective provinces and districts to the extermination camps mentioned on page 1, in which at least one and a half million Polish Jews and a large ~~xxxxxx~~ number of foreign Jews were murdered either by electric current or by gas.

The accused /2,3,6,7,/ are responsible for establishing in the respective districts governed by them the extermination camps as follows:

Page 3

PARTICULARS OF EVIDENCE IN SUPPORT

0842

1/. Statement of above facts and other particulars were contained in the confidential reports from the Polish Government's Plenipotentiary residing in occupied Poland ,addressed to the Polish Government in London.

II/. The original communications from the said Plenipotentiary are in the possession of the Polish Ministry of the Interior in London.

III/ A large number of witnesses will be available later.

Page 4

NOTES ON THE CASE 0843

(Under this heading should be included the view taken as to (*a*) the degree of responsibility of the accused in view of his official position, e.g., was offence committed on the offender's own initiative, or in obedience to orders, or in carrying out a system approved by authority or a legal provision ; (*b*) the probable defence ; (*c*) whether the case appears to be reasonably complete.)

I.The above mentioned offences were committed by the accused /1,2,3,4,5,6,7,8,9 and 10 / partly on their own initiative and partly in carrying out the Reich's general policy of persecution of Jews aiming at their complete extermination.

The accused /11,12,13,14,15,16,17,18,19,20 and 21 /were acting on their own initiative so far as ill-treatment and beating of Jews are concerned,whilst the mass-killing of Jews in the gas - chambers and by means of electric current was committed by them in obedience to orders received from superior authorities.

II. The accused will propably defend themselves by stating that they were acting in accordance with the general policy of the Reich,as fixed by the supreme German authorities and in obedience to orders.

III.The case appears to be reasonably complete.

INDEX

Page numbers in italics signify figures.

The Abandonment of the Jews (Wyman), 69–70
Ackermann, Josef, 120
acquittals, 139–40
Adenauer, Konrad, 185, 188–89
African Union, 54, 201
aggression, crimes of. *See* crimes of aggression
Akuni, Yamaguchi, *105*
Allied Control Commission, 89, 180
Altemeyer, 39–40n86
America, Hitler, and the UN (Plesch), 197
Annan, Kofi, 162
antisemitism: in France, 79, 118; in Poland, 122–23, 127; today, 195. *See also* Jews
appeal, right to, 146
Arab League, 54
Armenian Genocide, 8, 54, 108, 160, 193
Army Lawyer, 95
al-Assad, Bashar, 199
Atrocities on Trial (Heberer and Matthäus), 69, 113
attempted rape, 23
Auschwitz-Birkenau concentration camp, 19, 116–17, 124
Auschwitz concentration camp, 123, 128, 129, 185, 196–97
Aus der Funten, Ferdinand, 121
Australia: war crimes cases filed by, *16,* 103–4; war crimes trials conducted by, 18, 21–22, 104, 142, 151
Badoglio, Pietro, 93
Baker, Leonard, 148
Baldwin, Raymond Earl, 187–88
Bankier, David, 113
Barteczco, SS deputy commander, 233, 235
al-Bashir, Omar, 162, 199
Bassiouni, Cherif, 93
Bassy, Giovanni, 200
Battle of the Bulge, 143, 165, 187
Beevor, Anthony, 143
Belgium, 182; Nazi crimes against Jews in, 79, 114, 116–17; Nazi prisoner release opposed by, 180; and war crimes prosecutions, *16,* 18–19, 56, *91, 92,* 114, 116–17
Belsen trials, 53, 96–97, 113, 145
Benes, Eduard, 55
Bergen-Belsen concentration camp, 129, 185
Bihler, Anja, 100
Blair, Tony, 162
Blind Eye to Murder (Bower), 186, 189
Bloxham, Donald, 113, 132
bombing of cities, 143
Bosnia and Herzegovina, 38n58, 44–45n146, 201
Bower, Tom, 186, 189
Bracht, Fritz, 233
Bracken, Brendan, 72
Brauckmann, Willy, 120
Breendonk concentration camp, 116, 133n10
British Royal Warrant, 58, 90

British War Crimes Executive, 58
British war crimes trials, 96–97, 185; in Belsen, 53, 96, 113, 145; in Essen and Wuppertal, 149; and fairness issue, 151–52; in Singapore, 5, *105–7,* 142. *See also* United Kingdom
Brownmiller, Susan, 30
Brundage, Howard, 95
Brunner, Alois, 26, 119
Burke-White, William, 200
Burkhaus, Obersturmbannführer, 18
Buscher, Frank, 186–87
Bush, George W., 162

Cambridge Commission, 143, 147, 211
Canada, *91,* 183
Canadian Commission of Inquiry on War Criminals of, 186
Cassin, René, 55–56, 119
Catholic Church, 186
Central Intelligence Agency (CIA), 194
Central Register of War Criminals and Security Suspects (CROWCASS), 58, 216
Charles I, 164
Chiang Kai-shek, 100
China: civil war in, 100, 103; on crime of aggression, 172; and Far Eastern Sub-Commission, 47, 101–2; leadership role in UNWCC of, 51–52, 53, 101; war crimes trials conducted by, 17, 19, 27, 102–3
Churchill, Winston S., 2–3, 165, 189; on Nazi war crimes, 70, 81–82; on UNWCC role, 88–89
Cline, Donna, 62, 149
Cold War, 3, 9, 48, 181, 188, 194
collective responsibility, 113, 186; concept of, 61–62. *See also* group responsibility
"comfort women," 17–18
command responsibility: concept of, 146–47; for rape, 19, 28
Commission on Responsibilities (1919), 33n15, 54, 144, 147
common design, 26, 41–42n117, 150, 156n39; as form of responsibility, 148, 149
complementarity: defined, 198; ICC and, 53, 198, 199, 200, 204; UNWCC and, 198–202
complementary justice, 53–59
Complete History of the United Nations War Crimes Commission and the Development of the Laws of War, 4, 61, 95, 130, 205–6; on crime of aggression, 59–60, 171, 172–73; statistics from, 90, *140–41*
complicity, concept, 149–50
Congo, Democratic Republic of the, 200
consent, sexual, 20–23
conspiracy, 148, 149, 156–57n39
Control Council Law No. 10, 16, 35n31, 95
Control Order 10, 114, 142
Copelon, Rhonda, 31n3
Cowles, Willard B., 174
Craigie, Sir Robert, 55, 181, 184
Cranbourne, Viscount, 82
crimes against humanity: as accepted international norm, 171; Nuremberg trials and, 8, 171; opposition to concept of, 54, 164–71; rape and sexual violence as, 15–17, 23; UNWCC and concept of, 160–64, 193; and war crimes, 17
crimes against peace, 52, 60–61, 149, 185, 212
crimes of aggression: Kampala Conference definition of, 67n54; Kellog-Briand Pact on, 172, 173; as legal concept, 59–61, 160, 171–72; UNWCC and, 59–60, 161, 162, 171, 172–73
Croatia, 128
Czechoslovakia: crimes against Jews in, 79, 117–18; reports on Nazi atrocities by, 70, 79; UNWCC closure protested by, 183–84; and war crimes prosecutions, *16, 91,* 99, 117–18

Dachau concentration camp, 72, 117, 121
Dachau trials, 53, 95, 96, 113, 129, 142
Darwin trials, 104, 142
David-Fox, Michael, 70
Davies, Joseph, 166
Davies, Stephan, 185–86
Deák, István, 113
death penalty, 51
de Baer, Marcel, 55, 114, 180, 182, 184
Declaration by the United Nations (1942), 2–3, 69, 78, 164, 205
de Gaulle, Charles, 71, 79, 118
Denmark, 99; and war crimes prosecutions, *16,* 19, *91,* 118
Deppner, SS officer, 121
Dibelius, Otto, 186
Dischner, SS officer, 121
Dolff, SS major, 233, 235
Dönitz, Karl, 162
"Double V" campaign, 158, 196
due process, 139, 152

Dulles, Allen and John Foster, 194
du Plessis, Max, 201
Dutt-Majumdar, Niharendu, 52–53

Ečer, Bohuslav, 55
Economic and Social Council (ECOSOC), 2, 56, 61, 90, 146, 173–74
Eden, Anthony, 71, 76–77
Edwards, Michael, 85n10
Einsatzgruppen, xii, 7, 186, 188
Eisenhower, Dwight D., 58, 189
Ellis, Mark, 141–42, 152, 198, 200; International Technical Assistance Office plans of, 202–3
El Zeidy, Mohamed M., 200
Essen trials, 149
Ethiopia, 92–94
"ethnic cleansing," 51
Etlinger, SS officer, 120
European Convention on Human Rights, 132, 141, 194–95
European Union, 194–95
execution of hostages, 150–51
Extraordinary Chambers in the Courts of Cambodia (ECCC), 15–16, 17, 50

fair trials, 151; fundamentals of, 141–43; Rome Statute on, 141, 153n7; UNWCC standards for, 7, 138–40, 152–53
Falstad concentration camp, 122
Farben, I.G., 96
Far Eastern Sub-Commission (FESC), 47, 52, 60, 99, 184, 194, 217; review of work by, 101–3
Fawthrop, Tom, 199
Ferencz, Benjamin B., xi–xiii, 172
Fischer, Ludwig, 223, 224, 233
Fite, Katherine, 165, 181, 194
Fitzpatrick, Georgina, 100, 151, 152
forced prostitution: coercion as element of, 23–25; by Germans, 5, 39–40n86, 40n106; by Japanese, 17–18, 19, 28–29; as war crime, 14, 32–33n12
Ford, Jolyon, 201
Ford, Stuart, 50
Form, Wolfgang, 7
Forster, Albert, 233
Four Freedoms, 3, 205
France: antisemitism in, 79, 118; on crime of aggression, 172; crimes against Jews in, 79, 118–19; Vichy regime in, 75, 118; war crimes prosecutions, *16,* 18, 19, 26, 36n40, 65n29, *91, 92,* 118–19, 142, 149, 150
Frank, Anne, 121
Frank, Hans, 123, 223, 225, 233
Frings, Cardinal Josef, 186
Frommer, Benjamin, 99
Fujie, Takeo, *107*
Fujita, Masao, *105*
Fyfe, David Maxwell, 59

Garner, F. F., 182
Gemmeker, SS officer, 121
Geneva Conventions, 34n22, 144, 195
genocide, 160, 199; Armenian, 8, 54, 108, 160, 193; concept of, 173; in Rwanda, 31n6; sexual violence as, 34–35n22
Genocide Convention, 48, 132, 192, 195–96
Global South, 193–94
Glueck, Sheldon, xi, 161, 168
Goda, Noboru, *106*
Goering, Herman, xii
Goeth, Amon, 126
Goldstone, Richard, 19–20
government leaders' responsibility, 161, 162–63
Graziani, Rodolfo, 93
The Great Escape, 9, 178
Greece: civil war in, 98, 182; and war crimes prosecutions, *16,* 18, 19, 26, 42–43nn121–22, 60, *91, 92,* 119–20
Greiser, Artur, 126, 233
Grew, Joseph, 161, 166–67, 181
Grini concentration camp, 122
Groening, Oskar, 113, 139, 150, 178, 195
Gros, André, 47, 55–56, 67n46, 172
Gross, Jan, 113
Gross, Leo, 206
group responsibility: concept of, 148–49; UNWCC and, 149, 150, 152. *See also* collective responsibility
Guam, 23–25, 29, 44n139
Guatemala, 201
Günther, Rolf, 118

Hackworth, Green, 161, 165, 168, 169–70, 194
Hague, William, 4
The Hague, 121, 201
Hague Conventions, 150–51; of 1899, 8, 16; of 1907, 16, 38n56, 143, 144; bombing of cities outlawed by, 143; and rape, 13, 16, 38n56
Hale, Kip, 62, 149

Hamasaki, Naoki, 28
Hampel, Walter, 185–86
hearsay, 65–66n34, 145
Heberer, Patricia, 69, 113
Hebersteidt, Horst, 149
Helleiner, Eric, 193
Heller, Kevin, 95, 129, 145, 152, 186
Henderson, J. N., 181
Hess, Rudolf, 75, *159,* 163
Heusinger, Adolf, 188–89
Heydrich, Reinhard, 117
Hilberg, Raul, 69
Hildebrandt, Lieutenant, 120
Himmler, Heinrich, 79, *159*
Hitler, Adolf, xi, 87–88, 108, 122, 189; assassination attempt against, 165, 188; extermination program of, 69, 76, 77–78; indictment of, xvi, 1, 4–5, 116, 124, *159,* 162–63, 174
Hitlerite forces, 70, 77, 81, 167
Hodgson, Joseph, 170–71
Hoess, Rudolf, 11–12, 125, 126, 238
Holocaust and Justice (Bankier and Michman), 113
Holocaust denial, 6, 69, 83, 127, 132, 195
The Holocaust in the East (David-Fox, Holquist, and Martin), 70
Holocaust Memorial Museum, 4, 127, 214, 215
Holquist, Peter, 70
hostages, 150–51
Hua-Cheng, Wang, 101
Hull, Cordell, 161
human rights: of the accused, 145–46, 147; British declaration on, 77; and Christianity, Jews, and Muslims, 8, 75; and crimes against humanity, 8, 160–64, 171; and crimes against peace, 52, 60–61, 149, 185, 212; and crimes of aggression, 59–61, 160, 171–72; Declaration by United Nations on, 2–3, 74–75, 78; European Convention on, 132, 141, 194–95; and international law, 124–25, 132, 192–93, 194, 196–97, 205; leading promotors of, 108, 194; legal activism and, 5, 58, 132, 181, 185, 193; and non- Western countries, 51–52, 64n10, 193-94; and responsibility question, 19, 26, 27–28, 47, 61–62, 113, 146, 147, 148–49, 161, 162–63, 186; and sexual violence, 15–17, 18, 23; Universal Declaration of, 2, 48, 58, 132, 195, 196; UNWCC and, 59–60, 161, 162, 171, 172–73; UNWCC legacy and, 132, 192, 195–202, 205–6; and "UNWCC 2.0," 4, 203–5
Hunt, Lynn, 192
Hurst, Sir Cecil, 55, 163, 165, 166, 169

India, 104, *105–7*; leadership role in UNWCC of, 52–53
Inter-Allied Information Committee, 78
International Commission for Penal Reconstruction and Development, 147
International Criminal Court (ICC), 4, 54, 93; and complementarity, 53, 198, 199, 200, 204; cost of, 50; on crime of aggression, 160; early proposals for creating, 58; on group and collective responsibility, 62, 148–49; on rape and sexual violence, 21, 23, 34–35n22, 40–41n107; Rome Statute of, 15, 31n5, 34n22, 35n25, 58, 60, 141, 153n7, 198
The International Criminal Court and Complementarity (Stahn and El Zeidy), 200
International Criminal Trial for (the Former) Yugoslavia (ICTY): acquittal rate at, 140; cost of, 50; on criminal responsibility, 41n110, 41n112, 42n117; Milošević trial by, 162; and Nuremberg trials, 48; rape and sexual violence prosecuted by, 5, 15, 19–21, 31n3, 31n6, 38n55, 38n58, 43–44n130; UNWCC precedents for, 218–21
International Criminal Tribunal for Rwanda (ICTR), 50, 203; on criminal responsibility, 26, 41n110; rape and sexual violence prosecuted by, 15, 20–21, 31–32n6, 34n20, 43–44n130
International Military Tribunal at Nuremberg (IMT), xii, 50–51; creation of, 48, 181; and crimes against humanity, 8, 171; and crimes of aggression, 160; criticisms of, 142, 146; impact on international criminal law, 59, 196, 204; London Charter of, 59, 60, 163, 173, 212; number of trials and cases, 46, 95–96; on rape and sexual violence, 16, 32n8; on responsibility issue, 62, 147, 148, 149; rights of accused in, 151. *See also* Nuremberg trials
International Military Tribunal in the Far East (IMTFE), 142, 151, 160, 204; China's role in, 100; Indian judge at, 53, 172; rape and sexual violence charges before, 16, 17, 32n8
International Technical Assistance Office (ITA), 202–3

Iraq War, 162
Ireland: murder of merchant seamen from, 97
Italy: and Ethiopia, 92–94; war crimes charges against citizens of, *90, 92*
Ito Takeo, 142

Jackson, Robert, xii, 88, 108, 194; on collective responsibility, 61–62; and crimes against humanity, 164, 171; and work of UNWCC, 59, 167
Japanese surrender, 143
Japanese war crimes, 7, 212–13; rape and sexual violence, 17–18, 21–25, 27–29; statistics on prosecution of, 99–100, 102–4, *105–7*; Tokyo Trials of, 16, 17, 32n8, 53, 100, 142, 151, 160, 172, 204
Jarvis, Helen, 199
Jefferson, Thomas, 125
Jewish Agency for Palestine, 130
Jews: Anglo-American abandonment of, 82–84; in Belgium, 79, 114, 116–17; in Czechoslovakia, 79, 117–18; in Denmark, 118; in France, 79, 118–19; in Greece, 119–20; in Luxembourg, 79–80; in Netherlands, 80, 120–21; in Poland, 73, 122–27; Roosevelt and, 74, 83; in Soviet Union, 70–71; UN Declaration on persecution of, 69, 75–82, 173, 212; in Yugoslavia, 79, 128
Jobst, Willy, 18–19
joint enterprise, 26, 42n117, 62; charges around, 155–56n39; concept of, 149–50
Judge Advocate General (JAG), 94, 95, 170, 181, 185; Military Commission of, 23–24
Judt, Tony, 113

Kajelijeli case, 26
Kaltcheff, Anton, 18, 19
Kampala Conference (2010), 60, 67n54
Karski, Jan, 74
Katanga and Ngudjolo case, 149
Katsarov, Ivan Georgi, 42n122
Katyn massacre, 5
Kellogg-Briand Pact (1928), 60, 172, 173
Kennan, George, 194
Kenya, 200
Kerno, Ivan, 3
Kharkov trials, 82
Khmer Rouge, 199
Kilpe, Max, 185–86
Kissinger, Henry, 96
Kleeman, Ulrich, 120
Kobayashi, Matsuo, *105*
Koch, Erich, 223, 233
Kochavi, Arieh, 82
Kolbert, Elizabeth, 113, 178
Koo, Wellington, 52
Kramer, Josef, 146
Krankenbau, Major, 128
Krupp, 96, 185
Kuala Lumpur tribunal, 104
Kuboki, Noboru, *107*
Kundt, Ernst, 223, 233
Kushner, Barak, 100, 101, 102

Lai, Wen-Wei, 100, 101
Langer, William, 186, 187–88
Lansing, Robert, 160
Lasco, Chante, 11
Lasik, Alexander, 123, 126
"The Last Trial" (Kolbert), 113, 178
Lauterpacht, Hersch, 58, 108, 132, 164, 192
Law Reports of Trials of War Criminals, 146, 205–6
Lazaridis, Eftymia, 43n122
League of Nations, 55, 58, 93, 108n7
Leipzig War Crimes Trials, 61
Lemkin, Raphael, 108, 132, 192
Lewis, Mark, 54, 160
Lidice, 117
Lie, Trygve, 71
Lieber Code of 1863, 16
Lienau, Paul, 168
Lingen, Kerstin von, 100
Linton, Suzannah, 100, 151, 152
London bombing, 47
London Charter (1945), 59, 60, 163, 173, 212
London International Assembly (LIA), 54–55, 58, 143, 147, 173, 211
Lutz, Bertha, 30
Luxembourg, 79–80, *91,* 120

MacArthur, Douglas, 95
Maisky, Ivan, 76
Mao Zedong, 100
Marseilles trials, 142, 149
Martin, Alexander M., 70
Matthäus, Jürgen, 69, 113
Matthews, H. Freeman, 181
Mayr Harting, Herbert, 55

McCarthy, Joseph, 187–88, 194
Meiser, Bishop Hans, 186
Michman, Dan, 113
Mikolajczk, Stanislaw, 72
Milch, Erhard, 146
Mildner, Rudolf, 118
Milošević, Slobodan, 162
Mitsev, Kosta, 42n122
Mizukani, Iwao, *107*
Molotov, Vyacheslav, 77
Monighan, John, 88
Morgenthau, Henry, 165, 171
Morris, Narelle, 100, 104
Moscow Declaration (1943), 128, 132, 163; text of, 80–82
Mouton, M. W., 99
Moyn, Samuel, 192
Mueller, Friedrich Wilhelm, 19
Muller, Hans, 18, 36n40
Muller, Hauptsturmfuehrer, 233, 238
multilateral cooperation, xiii, 87, 130, 142, 203–4
Mussolini, Benito, 92
Muszkat, Marian, 126

National Association for the Advancement of Colored People, 196
National Offices Conference (NOC), 56, 89, 99, 101, 212
Natzweiler concentration camp, 117, 129
Nazi nostalgia, 160, 195
Nazi war crimes: Allies' political responses to, 212–14; in Belgium, 79, 114, 116–17; Churchill on, 70, 81–82; and "common design" cases, 26, 41–42n117; curtailing prosecutions of, 9, 178–79, 188–89; in Czechoslovakia, 79, 117–18; Declaration by United Nations on, 2–3, 69, 78, 164, 205; Declaration on Persecution of Jews on, 69, 75–82, 173, 212; in Denmark, 118; early Allied condemnations of, 70–75, 112–13; in France, 79, 118–19; in Greece, 119–20; in Luxembourg, 79–80; Moscow Declaration on, 80–82, 128, 132, 163; in Netherlands, 80, 120–21; in Poland, 73, 122–27; rape and sexual violence, 11–12, 19, 26; release of perpetrators of, 9, 178, 180, 185–88; Roosevelt on, 51, 70, 74–75, 80, 81–82, 127; Soviet condemnation of, 70–71; St. James Declaration on, 52, 71–72, 97, 98, 132, 142, 145, 205, 211; supposed ignoring of, 69–70, 112; tables on prosecutions of, *90, 91, 115*; US State Department and, 75, 161, 164–65, 166–70, 179, 181–82, 194; Wannsee conference and, xi–xii, 6, 72; in Yugoslavia, 79, 128
"The Neglected Southern Sources of Global Norms" (Helleiner), 193
Netanyahu, Benjamin, 129–30
Netev, Petko Stefan, 43n122
Netherlands: and conspiracy charges, 149; extradition request by, 183; Nazi crimes against Jews in, 80, 120–21; role of in UNWCC, 121; UNWCC closure protested by, 182, 183; and war crimes prosecutions, *16,* 56, 65n29, *91,* 99, 120–21
Neuengamme concentration camp, 96–97, 129, 151
Neuhausler, Bishop Johannes, 186
New Guinea, 21, 103–4
New Yorker, 113, 178
New York Times, 77, 166, 180–81
Nolle, Wilhelm, 185–86
None Shall Escape, 2
North Atlantic Treaty Organization (NATO), 188, 189, 194–95
Norway: charges brought by, *16, 91,* 122; war crimes trials conducted by, 5, 142, 147
nullum crimen sine lege argument, 12, 15–18, 20, 35n25, 38n55
Nuremberg trials: achievements of, 8, 59, 171, 196, 204; cases heard, xii, 46, 95–96; and collective responsibility, 62, 148; Truman and, 181. *See also* International Military Tribunal at Nuremberg

Oette, Lutz, 7
Ogden, Harry, 6–7
Oslo trials, 5, 142
Oswald, Bruno, 19

Pal, Radhabinod, 53, 172
Paris Peace Conference (1919): Commission on Responsibilities of, 33n15, 54, 144, 147; list of war crimes adopted by, 30, 33n15, 37n54, 144–45
Pearson, Drew, 166–68
Pell, Herbert, 51, 52, 58, 127, 128; biographical background, 55; and bombing of cities, 47, 143; firing of, 8, 165–66; on group responsibility, 148; key role played by, 8,

164, 171, 194; memo to Truman by, 167–70; motivation of, 160; public campaign by, 8, 166–67; Roosevelt and, 8, 55, 160, 161, 165, 166, 169, 171; State Department confrontation with, 160, 161, 164–65, 167–70
Philippines, 27–28, 78, 95, 96, 100, 207n7
Pispas, Nicolaos, 42–43n122
Pohl, Oswald, 189
poison gas, 93; as method of execution, 73, 97, 120, 149–50
Poland: antisemitism in, 122–23, 127; condemnations of Nazi atrocities by, 6, 70, 72–73, 80, 85n10, 160, 231–40; government in exile of, 75, 122; UNWCC closure protested by, 182, 183; and war crimes prosecutions, *16,* 18, 19, *91,* 98, 122–27, 130–31
Politics of Retribution in Europe (Deák, Gross, and Judt), 113
population transfer, 51, 98
Power, Samantha, 48, 164
Prelude to Nuremberg (Kochavi), 82
presumption of innocence, 141, 153n7
Preuss, Lawrence, 168
prima facie cases, xiii, 6, 96, 180, 189; decisions in, 57; term, 6, 54, 114
prisoners of war, 59, 96, 119, 129; executions of, 17, 27, 143; Geneva Convention on, 144, 195
Protestant Church, 186
public trials, 141
"Punishment for War Crimes" (ILA report), 54–55. *See also* St. James Declaration

Quisling, Vidkun, 122

Ramcharan, Bertrand, 193
rape, 11–30; attempted, 23; and consent issue, 20–23; as crime against humanity, 15–17, 23; definitions of, 20–21, 38nn57–60; as form of torture, 19–20; Hague Conventions and, 13, 16, 38n56; mischaracterization of, 12–13, 31n3; responsibility question for, 12, 19, 27–28; UNWCC data about, 18–20; victims as witnesses to, 28–29, 43–44nn130–33, 44–45n146; as war crime, 5, 14, 32n11; as "weapon of war," 31n3. *See also* sexual and gender-based violence
rape shield laws, 43n130
Rauter, Hanns, 120
Ravalli, Giovanni, 18, 19
Ravensbruck concentration camp, 97
Rego Rangel, Luiz Felippe de, 55
religious persecution, 8, 125, 161, 168–69
reprisals, 150–51
responsibility: collective and group, 61–62, 113, 148–49, 186; commanders', 19, 28, 146; and common design liability, 26, 41–42n117, 148, 149; for "following orders," 27–28, 47, 61, 147; of government leaders, 161, 162–63
retributive justice, 97–98, 99, 185, 194–95
Riedel, Durwood, 95
Riegner Telegram, 78
rights of accused, 145–46
Robertson, Geoffrey, 164
Romany, 124, 195
Rome Statute, 58, 198; concept of aggression in, 60; on fair trial provisions, 141, 153n7; and *nullum crimen* principle, 35n25; on sexual violence, 15, 31n5, 34n22
Roosevelt, Eleanor, 108, 194
Roosevelt, Franklin D.: as advocate of war crimes trials, 51, 70, 74–75, 80, 127; and Declaration of United Nations, 2–3; and Jews, 74, 83; and Moscow Declaration, 81–82; and Pell, 8, 55, 160, 161, 165, 166, 169, 171
Russell Tribunals, 48
Rwanda courts, 203; *gacaca* trials by, 54, 64–65n22. *See also* International Criminal Tribunal for Rwanda

Sablan, Nicolas, 22, 26, 29, 44n139
SáCouto, Susana, 11
Sakai, Takashi, 17, 18, 19, 27, 60, 146–47
Sakamoto, Suefusa, *107*
Sandberger, Martin, 186
Sandifer, Durward, 168
Sargent, Orme, 183
Sasel concentration camp, 97, 129
Sauer, SS captain, 123, 223, 226
Schabas, William, 58
Schmitt, Philipp, 116
scholarship of war crimes trials, 4, 30, 84, 113–14, 129–30, 205–6
Schommer, George, 78
Schoppe, Oberscharführer, 233, 238
Schouten, Lisette, 121
Schween, Walter, 184
Schwelb, Egon, 55, 195

sexual and gender-based violence (SGBV): criminal responsibility theories about, 25–28, 41n110, 41n112; defined, 11–12, 20, 38n56; forced prostitution, 14, 17–18, 19, 23–25, 28–29, 32–33n12; key issues of prosecuting, 13–29; *nullum crimen* challenges to prosecuting, 15–18; rationalization and toleration of, 12–13, 31nn3–4; rediscovering UNWCC lessons for, 11, 29–30; sexual slavery, 25, 40–41n107; treatment of victims of, 28–29, 43n130; World War II case files involving, 14–15, *16*. *See also* rape
Shawcross, William, 108
Shinohara, Samuel, 23–25, 28–29, 44n133
Siegfried, Sternberg, 116
Sikorski, Władysław, 71, 161
Silvermann, Sidney, 76
Simana, Walter, 119
Simpson Chris, 179, 181, 182, 183
Singapore trials, 5, *105–7,* 142
Slatef, Stephan, 42n122
Solef, Gregory, 42n122
sovereignty, state, 160, 161
Soviet Union: crimes committed by, 5; invasion of Manchuria by, 143; Moscow Declaration signed by, 81–82; and St. James Declaration, 71; support for war crimes commission by, 75; UN declarations signed by, 70–71, 76, 77; and UNWCC, 5, 82; war crimes trials conducted by, 40n86, 82
Special Court for Sierra Leone (SCSL), 15, 21, 50
Special Panels for Serious Crimes in East Timor (SPET), 15
The Splendid Blond Beast (Simpson), 179, 181, 182, 183
Stadelhofer, Henri, 149
Stahn, Carsten, 4, 198, 200, 204–5
Stalag Luft III massacre, 9, 185
Stalin, Joseph, 5, 81–82, 84, 122
Stalingrad, Battle of, 75, 83
Steains, Cate, 31n5
Stettinius, Edward, 161
Stibitz, Oberscharführer, 233, 238
Stimson, Henry, 94, 165; as advocate of war crimes trials, 158, 160; on crime of aggression, 160, 173; on US human rights abuses, 158, 196
St. James Declaration ("Punishment for War Crimes"), 98, 132, 145, 205, 211; China and, 52; full text of, 71–72; and international public opinion, 97, 142
Stroop, Jürgen, 119
Student, Kurt, 146
Sudan, 162, 199
summary justice, 98, 194
superior orders, 27–28, 47, 61, 147
"swift and effective" justice, 66–67n46
Syria, 199, 203

Takayanani, Yoshinobu, *105*
Tanaka, Renji, *107*
Tanaka Chuichi, 18
Taylor, Telford, xii, 113, 170, 185, 189, 194; on attempted rape, 23; on execution of hostages, 150–51
Terboven, Josef, 122
terrorism, systematic, 19, 30, 116, 144
Theresienstadt concentration camp, 80, 117, 121
Theunis, Sjoerd, 120
Thompson, James G., 158
Thyssen, Major, 118
Tito, Josip Broz, 128
Tokyo Trials. *See* International Military Tribunal in the Far East
torture: by Japanese, 18, 19–20, 27; in list of war crimes, 30, *144*; by Nazis, 42n117, 70, 73, 117, 118, 119, 120, 122; US waterboarding as, 7, 194
Toshio, Itzuki, *106*
Totani, Yuma, 99–100
translation, courtroom, 141
Treanor, Patrick, 129–30
Treblinka concentration camp, 114, 123–24, 126, 222–30
Truman, Harry S., 9, 51, 88, 167, 180–81, 182
Truman Doctrine, 182
Tsernosemski, Boris, 18

Uganda, 200
Unable or Unwilling? Case Studies on Domestic Implementation of the ICC Statute in Selected African Countries (du Plessis and Ford, ed.), 201
Unger, Oberscharführer, 118
unilateralism, 142
United Kingdom, 55, 71, 93; abandonment of Jews by, 82, 83–84; British Royal Warrant issued by, 58; charges brought by, *91, 92*; declaration on crimes against Jews by, 76–77; and establishment of war crimes commission, 74–75; opposition to crimes against humanity concept in, 164–71; and

prosecution of anti-Jewish crimes, 128–29; and UNWCC, 55, 57, 96–97, 182, 183, 184; war crimes prosecutions halted by, 9, 178, 185–86. *See also* British war crimes trials
United Nations Charter, 2, 132, 192
United Nations Declaration on the Persecution of the Jews (1942), 69, 75–82, 173, 212; key points of, 77–79
United Nations Development Program (UNDP), 200, 201, 203
United Nations Information Organization (UNIO), 78, 85n21
United Nations Review, 79, 80
United Nations War Crimes Commission (UNWCC): archives of, 3, 132, 214–17; chairs of, 55; China's role in, 51–52, 53, 100–103; Churchill on, 88–89; closure of, 9, 179, 181–82; Committee 1 (Facts and Evidence), 56, 139, 184, 203; Committee 2 (Enforcement), 56, 58; Committee 3 (Legal Affairs), 56, 58, 203; committee structure of, 56–57; and complementarity, 198–202; *Complete History* of, 4, 61, 59–60, 90, 95, 130, *140–41,* 171, 172–73, 205–6; creation of, 1, 48–50, 80; and crimes against humanity, 160–64, 193; and crimes of aggression, 59–60, 161, 162, 171, 172–73; and European war crimes trials, 97–99; fairness standards of, 7, 138–40, 141–43, 152–53; Far Eastern Sub-Commission of, 47, 52, 60, 99, 101–3, 184, 194, 217; female commissioners in, 30; as forerunner of international justice system, 13, 47, 58, 195–98, 205, 218–21; funding of, 49–50, 57, 181; genocide considered by, 173; and group responsibility, 149, 150, 152; hostility and opposition to, 48, 180–82; India's role in, 52–53, 104; indictment of Hitler by, 116, *159,* 162–63; indictments by, 89, 90–92, 112–32; lack of scholarly attention to, 4, 30, 84, 113–14, 129–30, 205–6; legacy of, 192–206; list of member states, 54; member governments in, 13, 54; membership list of, 55–56; as multilateral body, xiii, 87, 142, 204; National Offices Conference of (1945), 87–88, 89; national offices of, 56–57; opposition to closure of, 182–84; organizational predecessors of, 54; reliance on military authorities by, 58–59, 66–67n46; report to ECOSOC by, 2, 56, 61, 90, 146, 173–74; role and powers of, 1, 53–54, 139, 142–43, 145; secrecy of, 1, 3, 48, 87–88; and sexual violence, 11–30; Soviet Union and, 5, 82; State Department efforts to undercut, 179, 181–82; statistics on cases of, 5–6, 46, *49,* 57–58, 89, 90–92, 139, *140–41,* 179; United Kingdom and, 55, 57, 96–97, 182, 183, 184; and universal jurisdiction, 173–74; and "UNWCC 2.0," 4, 203–5; war crimes list and categories of, 37n54, 143–45, 161–62; working conditions of, 47
United States, 71, 88, 93; abandonment of Jews by, 83–84; civil rights struggle in, 158, 196; Congress in, 77, 131, 181, 187–88; creation of war crimes office in, 94–95; debate over war crimes prosecution in, 129; Judge Advocate General of, 94, 95, 170, 181, 185; opposition to crimes against humanity concept in, 164–71; release of Nazi prisoners by, 186, 189; and UNWCC closure, 181, 182; UNWCC funding by, 57, 181; war crimes prosecutions halted by, 9, 181–82, 186; War Refugees Board in, 83, 128
United States State Department: efforts to undercut UNWCC by, 179, 181–82; opposition to war crimes prosecutions in, 166–67, 194; Pell confrontation with, 160, 161, 164–65, 167–70; report on Nazi war crimes by, 75
United States war crimes trials, 95–96; in Dachau, 53, 95, 96, 113, 129, 142; of Japanese for sexual violence, *16,* 19, 22, 23–24, 27–28, *91, 92*
Universal Declaration of Human Rights (UDHR), 2, 48, 58, 132, 195, 196
universal jurisdiction, concept, 173–74

van der Kroon, F. J., 120
Vernichtung Kommando, 79
Versailles Conference. *See* Paris Peace Conference
"Versailles List" of war crimes, 30, 33n15, 37n54, 143, *144*
Vichy regime, 75, 79, 83, 118
Victor Emmanuel, 93
"victor's justice," 1, 138, 142, 143, 152

Wächter, Dr., 223, 233
Waldheim, Kurt, 3, 130
Wang, C. T., 102
Wannsee conference (January 1942), xi–xii, 6, 72

war crimes: based on religion, 168–69; and crimes against humanity, 17; forced prostitution as, 14, 32–33n12; group and collective responsibility for, 61–62, 113, 148–49, 150, 152, 186; rape as, 5, 14, 32n11; UNWCC categorization of, 161–62; UNWCC list of, 37n54, 143–45; "Versailles List" of, 30, 33n15, 37n54, 143, *144*
war crimes prosecutions: attempts after 1919 for, 54, 160; Belgium and, *16,* 18–19, 56, *91, 92,* 114, 116–17; Cold War impact on, 3, 9, 48, 181, 188, 194; for crimes against humanity, 8, 15–17, 54, 160–71, 193; for crimes of aggression, 59–61, 160, 161, 162, 171, 172–73; Czechoslovakia and, *16, 91, 99,* 117–18; Declaration by United Nations on, 2–3, 69, 78, 164, 205; Declaration on Persecution of Jews on, 69, 75–82, 173, 212; Denmark and, *16,* 19, *91,* 118; ending of, 175–89; Ethiopia and, 92–94; fairness of, 7, 138–40, 141–43, 145–46, 152–53; France and, *16,* 18, 19, 26, 36n40, 65n29, *91, 92,* 118–19, 142, 149, 150; Greece and, *16,* 18, 19, 26, 42–43nn121–22, 60, *91, 92,* 119–20; of Italians, 18, 92–94; Luxembourg and, *91,* 120; Moscow Declaration on, 80–82, 128, 132, 163; Netherlands and, *16,* 56, 65n29, *91,* 99, 120–21; Norway and, 5, *16, 91,* 122, 142, 147; official resistance to, 50–51; Poland and, *16,* 18, 19, *91,* 98, 122–27, 130–31; for rape and sexual violence, 11–30; and responsibility issue, 19, 27–28, 47, 61–62, 113, 146–47, 186; scholarship on, 4, 30, 84, 113–14, 129–30, 205–6; St. James Declaration on, 52, 71–72, 97, 98, 132, 142, 145, 205, 211; United Kingdom and, 5, 9, 53, 54, 96–97, *105–7,* 113, 128–29, 142, 145, 149, 151–52, 178, 185–86; United States and, 9, *16,* 19, 22, 23–24, 27–28, 53, *91, 92,* 95, 96, 113, 129, 142, 181–82, 186; Yugoslavia and, *16,* 60, *91, 92,* 128. *See also* International Criminal Court; United Nations War Crimes Commission
War Refugees Board, 83, 128
Warren, Fletcher, 165
water boarding, 7, 194
Weinbacher, Karl, 97
Weiss, Thomas G., 197
Wells, H. G., 164
Wendler, Richard, 223, 233
Wenzler, Herbert, 185–86
Westerbork concentration camp, 120, 121
West Germany: and Nazi past, 178–79, 186–87; rearmament of, 188
Whitney, Dwight, 88
Wiener, Frederick Bernays, 173
Wiener Library, 127
Simon Wiesenthal Center, 127
Wiessliscennyi, SS officer, 120
Wilhelm, Dr. H., 40n106
Winant, John Gilbert, 74, 76, 161
Witt, Harold, 185–86
Wolfenbüttel execution center, 180
Wolff, John, 171
Woo, Betty, 18, 21
Wouters, Nico, 116
Wright, Lord, 3, 47, 55, 87, 89; on crime of aggression, 60, 171; on fairness of trials, 142, 145, 146; on superior orders, 61; and UNWCC closure, 181
Wuppertal trials, 149
Wurm, Theophil, 186
Wu Yi-fang, 30
Wyman, David, 69–70

Yad Vashem, 116, 127, 130, 189
Yamanie, Nikei, *105*
Yamashita, Tomoyuki, 27–28, 146
Yantzev, Nicola, 42n122
Yoshida, Susumi, *105*
Yoshio Yaki, 18, 19, 21–22
Yu, Kuan, 102
Yugoslavia (civil war): and Milošević trial, 162; rape and sexual violence in, 5, 15, 19–21, 31n3, 31n6, 38n55, 38n58, 43–44n130. *See also* International Criminal Trial for (the Former) Yugoslavia
Yugoslavia (World War II): Nazi crimes against Jews in, 79, 128; UNWCC closure protested by, 182; and war crimes prosecutions, *16,* 60, *91, 92,* 128

Zhang Tiangshu, 100
Zorner, Ernst, 223, 233
Zyklon B case, 149–50

ABOUT THE AUTHOR

Dan Plesch, PhD, is a reader (senior associate professor) and director of the Centre for International Studies and Diplomacy at SOAS University of London. He is the author of *America, Hitler, and the UN* and *The Beauty Queen's Guide to World Peace*; and he is the coeditor (with Thomas G. Weiss) of *Wartime Origins and the Future United Nations.* He has written and broadcast extensively for many years on problems of international peace and security, including, most recently, international criminal law. Plesch founded the British American Security Information Council (BASIC) in 1986 and directed it from Washington, DC, until 2001, when he became senior research fellow at the Royal United Services Institute for Defence and Security Studies in London. He has held fellowships at the Universities of Bradford, Keele, and Birkbeck London; he has worked as an analyst for the BBC and CNN International and in the City of London for Kroll Security. He has published opinion pieces in newspapers including the *New York Times*, the *Washington Post,* and the *Guardian* of London. He lives near Canterbury, England, with his family.